W9-DFH-869

Slavery in the American Mountain South

Wilma A. Dunaway

Virginia Polytechnic Institute and State University

MAISON DES SCIENCES DE L'HOMME

CAMBRIDGE UNIVERSITY PRESS

PUBLISHED BY THE PRESS SYNDICATE OF THE UNIVERSITY OF CAMBRIDGE
The Pitt Building, Trumpington Street, Cambridge, United Kingdom

CAMBRIDGE UNIVERSITY PRESS
The Edinburgh Building, Cambridge CB2 2RU, UK
40 West 20th Street, New York, NY 10011-4211, USA
477 Williamstown Road, Port Melbourne, VIC 3207, Australia
Ruiz de Alarcón 13, 28014 Madrid, Spain
Dock House, The Waterfront, Cape Town 8001, South Africa

http://www.cambridge.org

First published 2003

Printed in the United States of America

Typeface Plantin 10/12 pt. *System* LaTeX 2ε [TB]

A catalog record for this book is available from the British Library.

Library of Congress Cataloging in Publication Data

Dunaway, Wilma A.

Slavery in the American Mountain South / Wilma A. Dunaway.

p. cm. – (Studies in modern capitalism)

Includes bibliographical references and index.

ISBN 0-521-81275-5 – ISBN 0-521-01215-5 (pbk.)

1. Slavery – Social aspects – Appalachian Region, Southern – History.
2. Slaves – Appalachian Region, Southern – Social conditions.
3. Plantation life – Appalachian Region, Southern – History. 4. African Americans – Appalachian Region, Southern – Social conditions.
5. Appalachian Region, Southern – Race relations. 6. Appalachian Region, Southern – Social conditions. I. Title. II. Series.

E443 .D87 2002
306.3′62′0974 – dc21

2002071480

ISBN 0 521 81275 5 hardback
ISBN 0 521 01215 5 paperback

In memory of
Woodrow Z. Wilson, Jr.
(1939–1978)
Executive Director
Knoxville Area Urban League
Knoxville, Tennessee
(1968–1978)

The companion website for this book is located at
http://scholar.lib.vt.edu/vtpubs/mountain_slavery/index.htm

Contents

Maps

Introduction

This study breaks new ground by investigating enslavement in a subregion of the American South that has been ignored by scholars. I will explore the complexities of the Mountain South where slavery flourished amid a nonslaveholding majority and a large surplus of poor white landless laborers. In geographic and geological terms, the Mountain South (also known as Southern Appalachia) includes that part of the U.S. Southeast that rose from the floor of the ocean to form the Appalachian Mountain chain ten thousand years ago (see Map 1). In a previous book, I documented the historical integration of this region into the capitalist world system. The incorporation of Southern Appalachia entailed nearly one hundred fifty years of ecological, politico-economic, and cultural change. Beginning in the early 1700s, Southern Appalachia was incorporated as a peripheral fringe of the European colonies located along the southeastern coasts of North America. During the early eighteenth century, the peripheries of the world economy included eastern and southern Europe, Hispanic America, and "the extended Caribbean," which stretched from the Atlantic colonies of North America to northeast Brazil. As the geographical space for several wars, the Mountain South became one of the major frontier arenas in which England, France, and Spain played out their imperialistic rivalry. Within two decades, the region's indigenous people were integrated into the commodity chains of the world economy to supply slaves to New World plantations and to produce deerskins to fuel western Europe's emergent leather manufacturing. After the American Revolution, Southern Appalachia formed the first western frontier of the new nation, so it was quickly resettled by Euroamericans.[1]

Incorporation of the Mountain South into the World Economy

On a world scale, Southern Appalachia's role was not greatly different from that of many other such peripheral fringes at the time, including

Map 1. Where is the Mountain South?

inland mountain sections of several Caribbean islands, Brazil, the West Indies, and central Europe. Incorporation into the capitalist world economy triggered within Southern Appalachia agricultural, livestock, and extractive ventures that were adapted to the region's terrain and ecological peculiarities. Yet those new production regimes paralleled activities that were occurring in other sectors of the New World that had been colonized by western Europe. Some Appalachian counties specialized in the cultivation of tobacco or cotton for export. Fundamentally, however, Southern Appalachia was a "provisioning zone" that supplied raw materials to other agricultural or industrial regions of the world economy.[2]

On the one hand, this inland region exported foodstuffs to other peripheries and semiperipheries of the western hemisphere, those areas that specialized in cash crops for consumption by the core. Appalachian agriculture was neither irrational nor precapitalist; crops were planned and cultivated in response to distant market prices. The demand for flour, meal, and grain liquors was high in plantation economies (like the North American South and most of Latin America) where labor was budgeted toward the production of exotic staples, not foods. So it was not accidental that the region's surplus producers concentrated their land and labor resources into the generation of wheat and corn – often in terrain where such production was ecologically unsound. Nor was it a chance occurrence that Southern Appalachians specialized in the production of livestock, as did inland mountainous sections of other zones of the New World. There was high demand for meat, work animals, animal by-products, and leather in those peripheries and semiperipheries that did not allocate land to less-profitable livestock production.

On the other hand, Southern Appalachia was also a production regime that supplied raw materials to the emergent industrial cores of the American Northeast and western Europe. The appetite for Appalachian minerals, timber, cotton, and wool was great in those industrial arenas. In addition, regional exports of manufactured tobacco, grain liquors, and foodstuffs provisioned those sectors of the world economy where industry and towns had displaced farms. Much of the Appalachian surplus received in Southern ports was reexported to the urban-industrial centers of the American Northeast and to foreign plantation zones of the world economy. By the 1840s, the northeastern United States was specializing in manufacturing and international shipping, and that region's growing trade/production centers were experiencing food deficits. Consequently, by 1860, three-fourths of the Upper South grain received at Southern seaports was being reexported to the Northeast. In return for raw ores and agricultural products, Southern markets – including the mountain counties – consumed nearly one-quarter of the transportable manufacturing output of the North and received a sizable segment of the redistributed international imports (e.g., coffee, tea) handled by Northeastern capitalists.

Beginning in the 1820s, Great Britain lowered tariff rates and eliminated trade barriers to foreign grains. Subsequently, European and colonial markets were opened to North American commodities. Little wonder, then, that flour and processed meats constituted the country's major nineteenth-century exports, or that more than two-thirds of those exports went to England and France. Outside the country, then, Appalachian commodities flowed to the manufacturing centers of Europe, to the West Indies, to the Caribbean, and to South America.

Through far-reaching commodity flows, Appalachian raw materials – in the form of agricultural, livestock, or extractive resources – were exchanged for core manufactures and tropical imports.[3]

Peripheral capitalism unfolded in Southern Appalachia as a mode of production that combined several forms of land tenure and labor. Because control over land, the primary factor of production, was denied to them, the unpropertied majority of the free population was transformed into an impoverished *semiproletariat*. However, articulation with the world economy did not trigger only the appearance of free wage labor or white tenancy. Capitalist dynamics in antebellum Southern Appalachia also generated a variety of unfree labor mechanisms. "The process of incorporation . . . involved the subordination of the labor force to the dictates of export-oriented commodity production, and thus occasioned increased coercion of the labor force as commodity production became generalized." As a result, the region's landholders agglomerated an ethnically and sexually diverse labor force that combined *free* laborers from the ranks of the landless tenants, croppers, poor women, and wage laborers with *unfree* workers from four sources. Legally restricted from free movement in the marketplace, the region's free blacks, Cherokee households, and indentured paupers contributed coerced labor to the region's farms. However, Southern Appalachia's largest group of unfree laborers were slaves who supplied long-term labor to one of every three farm owners and who accounted for one of every five agricultural laborer households.[4]

Why Study Slavery in the Mountain South?

Consisting of 215 mountainous and hilly counties in nine states, this large land area was characterized in the antebellum period by nonslaveholding farms and enterprises, a large landless white labor force, small plantations, mixed farming, and extractive industry. Because the Lower South was such a sharp contrast to these traits, Mountain South slavery has been historically misrepresented. Scholars have idealized the region's yeomen farmers as egalitarian people whose lifestyle was alien to that of slaveholding Southerners. Consequently, the region's economy is believed to have "generated no need or desire for slaves." The conventional wisdom has long been that Appalachian agriculture "rested not on the labor of slaves but rather on small land-owning cultivators." Poor soil, rugged terrain, and a cooler climate are offered as the causes for the failure of the Appalachian "enclave of plain folk farmers" to cultivate the labor-intensive staple crops that typified the Lower South. Beyond these economic and environmental factors, Southern Appalachians are portrayed as culturally "loath to follow the fortunes of the ardent pro-slavery element." Southern mountaineers have been lauded for their political opposition to slavery, and the birth of the abolition movement is inaccurately credited by some to the Mountain South.[5]

The prevailing scholarly view is that slavery was largely absent from the Mountain South and that the region's few slaveholders were more kindly than their Lower South peers. In the words of Trouillot, "slavery here is a ghost, both the past and a living process." As a result, Mountain slaves have remained a *people without history* because too many researchers have claimed that "the 'peculiar institution' never influenced Appalachian culture and society." Over the last two decades, a few scholars have begun to cast doubt on the notion that Appalachians "hated slavery," as Woodson claimed in the early 1900s. Indeed, writers like Inscoe have argued that slavery played an energetic role in some local economies, including the significant contributions of unfree laborers to the region's antebellum railroad, salt, iron, and gold industries. The extent of slavery among the region's Cherokees has even been documented. However, there are four weaknesses in these existing analyses. First, empirical evidence about Appalachian slavery has not been region-wide. Even revisionists have claimed to be talking about "Appalachian" slavery, even though they target only a single county or a handful of counties, failing thereby to depict subregional differentiation. Second, these writers have used very little quantitative analysis from census manuscripts, tax lists, or slaveholder records. Third, these studies do not explore the narratives of Mountain slaves, even when they ground their generalizations in the biased manuscript collections of slaveholders. Finally, these studies remain provincial in that they offer no comparative analysis between the Mountain South and other slaveholding regions. Consequently, the tendency has been to idealize this region as less racist and to overstate the degree to which its white residents were opposed to slavery.[6]

Unearthing historical silences and misperceptions is not the only reason we should be intrigued by the Mountain South. Analysis of Appalachian enslavement offers unusual opportunities to explore several areas of omission and debate within international slavery studies. First, the prevailing scholarly view is that enslavement of indigenous peoples ended abruptly with the import of Africans into the New World. However, there must have been an undocumented historical overlap between the two forms of slavery, as evidenced by the genealogy of mountain slaves. Indeed, one of every eight black Appalachians was a descendant of a Native American. Second, there is very little research about slave life on small plantations, like those that typified Appalachia. Fogel stresses that "failure to take adequate account of the differences between slave experiences and culture on large and small plantations" has been a fundamental blunder by slavery specialists. Despite Crawford's ground-breaking finding that plantation size was the most significant determinant of quality of slave life, there has never been a study of a slaveholding region that was characterized by small plantations. On the one hand, the Mountain South was part of the Upper South where the median slaveholding was 15.3 black laborers, and more than one-third of all slaves were held in units smaller than ten. On the other hand, the Mountain South also contained some Lower South counties, thereby permitting internal comparisons between differently sized slaveholdings, between crop specializations, and between agricultural and nonagricultural producers.[7]

As a model for understanding the changes that occurred during different historical eras and geographical regions, Berlin drew an historical distinction between *societies with slaves* and *slave societies*.

> Slaveholdings in societies with slaves were generally small, and the line between slave and free could be remarkably fluid, with manumission often possible and sometimes encouraged. But neither mildness nor openness defined societies with slaves. Slaveholders in such societies could act with extraordinary brutality precisely because their slaves were extraneous to their main business. . . . What distinguished societies with slaves was the fact that slaves were marginal to the central productive processes; slavery was just one form of labor among many. . . . In societies with slaves, no one presumed the master-slave relationship to be the social exemplar.
>
> In slave societies, by contrast, slavery stood at the center of economic production, and the master-slave relationship provided the model for all social relations. . . . Whereas slaveholders were just one portion of a propertied elite in societies with slaves, they were the ruling class in slave societies. . . . Historians have outlined the process by which societies with slaves in the Americas became slave societies. The transformation generally turned upon the discovery of some commodity . . . that could command an international market. With that, slaveholders capitalized production and monopolized resources, muscled other classes to the periphery, and consolidated their political power. . . . Other forms of labor – whether family labor, indentured servants, or wage labor – declined, as slaveholders drove small farmers and wage workers to the margins.

An export for the world economy was not enough, according to Berlin, to transform a society with slaves into a slave society. More important than the discovery of an export commodity was "the presence of a planter class able to command the region's resources, mobilize the power of the state, and vanquish competitors. . . . The slaveholders' seizure of power was the critical element in transforming societies with slaves into slave societies."[8]

Using that model, Berlin delineated four slave societies in eighteenth-century North America: the North, the tobacco-producing Chesapeake, the Southern coastal rice-growing low country, and the sugar and cotton plantations of the lower Mississippi Valley. Even though the Mountain

South formed the western frontiers of two of his identified societies, Berlin ignored this massive land area. There has been a scholarly presumption that slavery did not capture a region unless there were large numbers of plantations and/or large numbers of slaveholders and slaves. Such a generalization leaves unexplored several variables other than size. On the one hand, a Lower South farm owner was twelve times more likely to run a large plantation than his Appalachian counterpart. On the other hand, Mountain slaveholders monopolized a much higher proportion of their communities' land and wealth than did Lower South planters. This region was linked by rivers and roads to the coastal trade centers of the Tidewater and the Lower South, and it lay at the geographical heart of antebellum trade routes that connected the South to the North and the Upper South to the Lower South. Consequently, two major slave-trading networks cut directly through the region and became major conduits for overland and river transport of slave coffles. Moreover, this region was more politically divided over slavery than any other section of the South. Black and poor white Appalachians were disproportionately represented among the soldiers and military laborers for the Union Army. The Civil War tore apart Appalachian communities, so that the Southern Mountains were probably more damaged by army and guerilla activity than any other part of the country. Thus, the Mountain South was characterized by trends that Berlin associates with both his ideal types, most noticeably lacking only *largeness of scale* in its slaveholding operations. If his theoretical model is historically correct, where should we put a region like the Mountain South that fits neither of these ideal types neatly?[9]

Methods and Definitions

As in my previous work, this study avoids the socially constructed regional definitions that emerged in the 1960s around the War on Poverty. Instead, I define the Mountain South in terms of *terrain* and *geological formation*, resulting in a target area that stretches through nine states from western Maryland to northern Alabama. The vast majority of the Mountain South is not mountainous at all. Hill-plateaus and valleys adjacent to long ridges make up more than 80 percent of the acreage. Most of the highest, longest ridges of the mountain chain lie in the Appalachian counties of Virginia, a zone that some scholars would exclude because it was characterized by such a high incidence of slaveholding. Geologically, these counties are part of the Appalachian Mountain chain, so it requires some artificial, non-terrain construct to justify their ejection from the regional definition. Indeed, it is crucial to include Appalachian Virginia. The prevailing view has been that terrain like Virginia's ridges prevented the expansion of slavery in North America. Thus, one could reasonably ask why slavery was so entrenched in Appalachian Virginia if rough terrain precluded the use of slave labor. Obviously, it is important to include all the subsections of the Mountain South in order to draw comparisons between zones characterized by diverse terrain, differently sized slaveholdings, and varied economic specializations. Even though it did not achieve statehood until 1863, the reader will find discussions of West Virginia throughout the book, and those references are not an historical error on my part. Because that area had the lowest incidence of enslavement in the American South, it is crucial to set it apart from the rest of Virginia. To ensure that my statistical analysis would not be corrupted by either an overestimation of slavery in Virginia's most western counties or an understatement of the extent of plantations in Blue Ridge and southwestern Virginia, I have separated out quantitative data and slave narratives for those counties that became West Virginia during the Civil War.[10]

Sources and Term Definitions

To research this complex topic, I have triangulated quantitative, archival, primary, and secondary documents. I derived my statistical analysis from a database of nearly 26,000 households drawn from nineteenth-century county tax lists and census manuscripts. In addition to those samples, I relied on archived records from farms, plantations, commercial sites, and industries. A majority of the slaveholder collections utilized for this research derived from small and middling plantations. However, I did not ignore rich Appalachian planters, like Thomas Jefferson or John Calhoun. Never to quote or cite an Appalachian planter is to deny that they existed and to ignore that they were the richest, most politically powerful families in Appalachian counties. Indeed, I present information about them to demonstrate that they are similar to their Lower South counterparts and, therefore, very different from the typical farmers in their communities. It is also necessary to draw upon planter documents to show that the larger plantations implemented different crop choices, surveillance strategies, and labor management practices than did smallholdings. Still, those rich planters account for less than 1 percent of all the citations and details provided in this study.[11]

Throughout this book, I have used the term *plantation* consistently to refer to a slaveholding enterprise. I have purposely done this to distinguish such economic operations from the nonslaveholding farms that characterized the Mountain South. Far too many scholars confront me at meetings with the mythological construct that the "typical Appalachian slaveholder" was a benign small farmer who kept only a couple of slaves to help his wife out in the kitchen. By using the term *plantation* to distinguish all slaveholding farms, I seek to erode the stereotype that small plantations might be the social, political, and economic equivalent of small nonslaveholding farms in their communities. On the one hand, small slaveholders could not have owned black laborers if they or their families had not accumulated surplus wealth far in excess of the household assets averaged by the majority of nonslaveholding Appalachians. On the other hand, planters and smallholders alike controlled far more than their equitable share of the political power and economic resources in their communities. Because small slaveholders aspired to be planters, they did not often align themselves with the political and economic interests of nonslaveholders. According to Berlin, "what distinguished the slave plantation from other forms of production was neither the particularities of the crop that was cultivated nor the scale of its cultivation.... The plantation's distinguishing mark was its peculiar social order, which conceded nearly everything to the slaveowner and nothing to the slave." That social order was grounded in a racial ideology in which chattel bondage and white supremacy became entwined. For that reason, it is crucial to distinguish a nonslaveholding farm from a slaveholder. In the Mountain South, a slaveholder did not have to reach planter status to be set apart from neighbors whose antagonism to enslavement would cause them to align themselves with the Union in greater numbers than in any other region of the American South. In order to distinguish plantations by size, I utilize the definitions that are typically applied by U.S. slavery specialists. A *planter* or *large plantation* held fifty or more slaves while a *middling plantation* or slaveholder owned twenty to forty-nine slaves. Thus, a *small plantation* was one on which there were nineteen or fewer slaves.[12]

Capturing Diversity Through State Subregions

In addition to contrasting county groups according to terrain types, this study analyzes intraregional variation by comparing the nine state subregions. Are state subregions the best method to analyze subregional economic variation? On the one hand, I previously published the only region-wide economic history of antebellum Southern Appalachia that exists to date.[13] No other scholar has collected or analyzed an antebellum Appalachian statistical data set as massive or as chronologically extensive as mine – a data set, with which I have lived, eaten, slept, and traveled for twelve years, reevaluating data analysis methods numerous times with quantitative experts, cliometricians, and agricultural economists at six universities. Bottom line, I have not found any better analytical tools than state subregions. When county economic indicators are grouped without regard to their state jurisdictions, the findings mask subregional diversity and obscure causative factors associated with political boundaries. Neither terrain nor an artificially constructed set of economic ideal types provide more effective mechanisms for analyzing subregional diversity. While state-level analysis permits ten levels of comparison across this vast geographical space, other possible approaches provide only two to four comparative categories. Simply put, there is no other economic or terrain variable that will generate more economic subregions than state-level analysis. On the other hand, no unified economic subregions clearly emerge from that regional data set. It is certainly not sound methodology for me to apply conceptual constructs that were derived from studies grounded in one or a few counties or that are grounded in economic trends that emerged after the antebellum period.

There is a second significant reason that I organized my statistical analysis by states. Because alternate economic subregions (e.g., terrain types) combine counties that are scattered all over the region, the findings would be suspect. First, antebellum residents of these areas did not identify themselves as "Appalachians" who coalesced politically, culturally, or economically across multistate boundaries. Nor is there any evidence that there were economic subregions of Appalachia that acted in a unified manner. Second, Appalachian counties have never been autonomous from their state governments. Antebellum states were strong determinants of subregional variation because they shaped the political economies of the counties within their jurisdictions, particularly through laws regulating land, labor, debt, taxation, and slavery. Moreover, the nine states that controlled Southern Appalachia enacted different laws and implemented disparate levels of funding for transportation networks, poor relief, schools, and economic development projects. Quite often, differences in those public policies accounted for or exacerbated economic trends. Furthermore, there are significant terrain differences within each of the state subregions, and each of them is characterized by the presence or absence of river systems, the most crucial conduits for distant travel and external trade in this historical era. Such terrain similarities among adjacent counties would disappear if those units were regrouped into economic subregions rather than states.

Slave Narratives from the Mountain South

History does not belong just to those who are reified in government and archival documents. The past is also owned by survivors of inequality and by those who live through injustice at the hands of powerful elites.

As Trouillot has recognized, "survivors carry history on themselves," and care must be exercised in the construction of knowledge from their indigenous transcripts. "Silences enter the process of historical production at four crucial moments: the moment of fact creation (the making of *sources*); the moment of fact assembly (the making of *archives*); the moment of fact retrieval (the making of *narratives*); and the moment of retrospective significance (the making of *history* in the final instance)." To be as inclusive as possible in the final moment of history production, I have grounded this study in analysis of narratives of nearly 300 slaves and more than 400 white Civil War veterans. I spent many months locating Appalachian slave narratives within the Federal Writers Project, at regional archives, and among published personal histories. Beginning with Rawick's forty-one published volumes of the WPA slave narratives, I scrutinized every page for county of origin, for interregional sales or relocations that shifted slaves into or out of the mountains, and for occurrences during the Civil War that displaced slaves. After that process, I identified other archival and published accounts, finding several narratives in unusual locations, including archives at Fisk University and the University of Kentucky. In this way, I did not ignore the life histories of slaves who were born outside the Mountain South and then migrated there or those who were removed to other regions. Ultimately, I aggregated the first comprehensive list of Mountain South slave narratives.[14]

How representative of the Mountain South are these narratives? In comparison to the entire WPA collection, Appalachian slave narratives are exceptional in the degree to which they depict small plantations. By checking the slave narratives against census manuscripts and slave schedules, I established that the vast majority of the Appalachian narratives were collected from individuals who had been enslaved on plantations that held fewer than twenty slaves. Consequently, Blue Ridge Virginia is underrepresented while the Appalachian counties of Kentucky, North Carolina, and West Virginia are overrepresented. Thus, those areas that held the smallest number of slaves in this region are more than adequately covered by narratives from slaves who resided there. Appalachian slave narratives are not handicapped by the kinds of shortcomings that plague the national WPA collection. Large plantations, males, and house servants are overrepresented among the entire universe of respondents. In addition, two-fifths of the ex-slaves had experienced fewer than ten years of enslavement. The most serious distortions derived from the class and racial biases of whites who conducted the vast majority of the interviews. Most of the Appalachian respondents had been field hands, and very few were employed full time as artisans or domestic servants. In terms of gender differentiation, the Appalachian sample is almost evenly divided. In contrast to the entire WPA collection, three-quarters of the Appalachian ex-slaves were older than ten when freed. Indeed, when emancipated, one-third of the Southern Mountain respondents were sixteen or older, and 12 percent were twenty-five or older. Thus, nearly half the Appalachian ex-slaves had endured fifteen years or more of enslavement, and they were old enough to form and to retain oral histories. Perhaps the greatest strength of the Appalachian collection has to do with the ethnicity of interviewers. More than two-fifths of the Mountain narratives were written by the ex-slaves themselves or collected by black field workers, including many Tennessee and Georgia interviews that were conducted under the auspices of Fisk University and the Atlanta Urban League. The Southern Mountain narratives were collected over a vast land area in nine states. This collection offers another advantage. The geographical distances between respondents offer opportunities for comparison and for testing the widespread transmission of African-American culture.[15]

I have come away from this effort with a deep respect for the quality and the reliability of these indigenous narratives. When I tested ex-slave claims against public records, I found them to be more accurate than most of the slaveholder manuscripts that I scrutinized, and quite often they were much less ideologically blinded than many of the scholarly works I have consulted. Therefore, I made the conscious intellectual decision to engage in "the making of *history* in the final instance" by respecting the indigenous knowledge of the ex-slaves whose transcripts I analyzed. That means that I did not dismiss and refuse to explore every slave voice that disagreed with intellectual fad or convention. In most instances, I triangulated the indigenous view against public records and found the slave's knowledge to be more reliable than some recent scholarly representations. In other instances, I perceived that Appalachian slaves are a *people without written history* and that it is important to document the oral myths in which they grounded their community building. Because Mountain slave narratives present a view of enslavement that attacks the conventional wisdom, I recognized that they and I were engaging in a process that Trouillot calls "the production of alternative narratives." When contacted by a Fisk University researcher in 1937, one Chattanooga ex-slave comprehended that he possessed a knowledge about slavery that was different from the social constructions of the African-American interviewer. "I don't care about telling about it [slavery] sometime," he commented cynically, "because there is always somebody on the outside that knows more about it than I do, and I was right in it." Clearly, this poorly educated man understood that historical facts are not created equal and that knowledge construction is biased by differential control of the means of historical production. On the one hand, I set myself the difficult goal of avoiding the kind of intellectual elitism the ex-slave feared while at the same time trying to avoid the pitfall of informant misrepresentation. On the other hand, I heeded the advice of C. Vann Woodward and did not view the use of slave narratives as any more treacherous or unreliable than other sources or research methods.[16]

Organization of This Research Project

As we shall see in the following chapters, slaves made a much greater economic contribution to the Mountain South than scholars have previously acknowledged, especially to its antebellum development of town commerce, transportation networks, travel capitalism, manufacturing, and extractive industries. This book documents subregional variations in economic activities, the multifaceted occupations of slaves, the diverse business portfolios of slaveholders, the differences between small and large plantations, and the economic ties between slavery, agriculture, commerce, and industrial development. Moreover, the study offers numerous comparisons between mountainous, hill-plateau, and ridge-valley subregions. This study seeks to answer these important questions.

- To what degree did African and Native American enslavement overlap?
- Was a region buffered from the worst political, economic, and social impacts of enslavement so long as it was characterized by small slaveholdings, as Berlin's conceptualization contends?
- In this region characterized by small plantations and mixed farming, how were slaves utilized economically?
- How did labor management differ on small, middling, and large plantations?
- To what degree did slaves engage in resistance and community building?
- To what degree did slaves share the African-American culture that has been attributed to large plantations?
- Was Mountain South slavery exceptional, as some scholars have claimed?

Chapter 1 documents slavery's political and economic grip on the Mountain South, beginning with the colonial era of indigenous enslavement. Chapter 2 focuses on the agricultural labor management strategies of Mountain masters, drawing contrasts between differently sized plantations and between different slaveholding regions. Chapters 3 and 4 investigate the extent to which Mountain slaves were employed at nonagricultural occupations. Chapter 5 examines the ways in which Mountain masters captured the labor of poor whites, pinpointing the functional relationship between white tenancy and slavery. Chapters 6 and 7 examine resistance and community building by Mountain slaves, calling into question many scholarly presumptions about the absence of such counter-hegemonic activism on small plantations. In the conclusion, I have recast the most significant findings about the Mountain South within the context of ongoing debates in the field of slavery studies and against the backdrop of earlier assumptions about small plantations. This research project does not end with this monograph, however. A second book will explore the living conditions and household risks faced by black Appalachians during enslavement and early emancipation, calling into question the conventional paradigm of the African-American slave family.[17]

Online Archive of Source Materials

To publish all the information from sources, methods, and quantitative evidence would require publication of a third volume. To make those materials available to other researchers as quickly as possible, I have created a permanent electronic library archive. That site provides the tables that support the findings throughout this study, as well as a detailed discussion of methodological issues. A comprehensive list and a descriptive analysis of the collection of Mountain South slave narratives can also be found there. In addition, antebellum photographs and drawings have been put online for use by other researchers. Throughout the notes, you will see references to sources that can be accessed at this website: **http://scholar.lib.vt.edu/vtpubs/mountain_slavery/index.htm.**

1 Slavery's Grip on the Mountain South

> The good prices the English Traders give them for slaves Encourage the Cherokees to this trade Extreamly and some men think it both serves to lessen their number before the French can arm them and it is a more Effectuall way of Civilising and Instructing them.
>
> – A British colonial official, 1680

Slavery has a long history in the American Southern Mountains. Enslaved indigenous laborers were the first valuable commodities to be exported from this region to the world economy. In the sixteenth century, the Spanish tramped into the Southern Appalachians to capture slaves and to search for an overland route that would link Florida to their gold mines in Mexico. Ironically, the Spanish labeled the inland Southern Mountains the Appalachees, after a northern Florida people they had extinguished through slave exports to West Indies plantations. A century and a half later, the region's indigenous peoples were once again attractive to European invaders. Because of the demands for labor in the West Indies and in the emergent North American colonies, Indian slaves were the first profitable commodity exported by British settlers from the southeastern coast of North America. The colonial governors of South Carolina, Georgia, North Carolina, and Virginia "gave permission to sell in the West Indies the Indians captured by the colonists." By 1681, the capture and selling of Cherokee slaves had begun, and the Cherokees' first diplomatic mission to Charleston in 1693 was aimed at seeking relief from slavery raids. By 1700, guns had been introduced so that the Cherokees could protect themselves against the slave raids of neighboring Indians, and by 1703, the Cherokees were marketing indigenous slaves. During the early 1700s, Indians represented one-quarter of the total slave population in South Carolina. By 1710, perhaps as many as twelve thousand Indians had been exported from South Carolina to the northern colonies and the Caribbean. Throughout the period, emphasis was placed primarily upon Cherokee women and children as slaves; captured males were generally killed.[1]

The house of Cherokee slaveholder John Ross was typical of small Mountain South plantations. *Source: Scribner's*, 1874.

Indigenous Slavery in the Mountain South

Prior to their incorporation into the capitalist world economy, the indigenous peoples of the Southern Appalachians enslaved prisoners of war, but slaves certainly were not central to indigenous economic activities. Until the development of a European market for war captives, Cherokee clans frequently adopted prisoners of war to replace kinsmen who had died, or captives could be ransomed by their enemies. Once traders began exchanging goods for war captives, "the value of the captives as saleable items meant that the frequency and extent of warfare increased." By the early seventeenth century, Cherokees had begun to engage in warfare for the sole purpose of obtaining prisoners to sell to the whites as slaves. After they had engineered Cherokee dependence upon foreign manufactured goods, European traders "began to incite intertribal warfare in order to profit from the sale of captives." The British even organized slave raids in which white traders led warriors to attack the settlements of Indians allied with their European rivals.[2]

Cherokee participation in the international slave trade was an outgrowth of the global conflict between France, Spain, and England to colonize and control the New World. Indian enslavement was not just lucrative business; it also offered military advantages. Through enslavement and the warfare it stimulated, the European rivals depopulated the frontiers of their colonies. When the French began to feel the disadvantage from these frequent wars, they outlawed slave raids. "It is not an evil that the Indian nations should be at war with each other," wrote a Louisiana official. However, he recognized that the English were "seeking to have [Indians] destroyed among themselves in order to be masters of their country." In short, the French strategized that "when they see that we do not wish any slaves and that we forbid the trade in them they will be easily persuaded that we are better friends of theirs than the other European nations."[3]

Almost simultaneously on the other side of the world, Europeans implemented similar enslavement strategies in the capture and export of black laborers. When African enslavement was predominant in the world economy, the trade in Southeastern Indians diminished dramatically. In place of intertribal warfare, the Cherokees took on another economic activity to benefit their European allies. In most of their early treaties with the British, the Cherokees contracted to return runaways to slaveholders on the coast. In the 1730 treaty, for example, Chief Ketagustah vowed:

> In War we shall always be as one with you, the Great King George's Enemies shall be our Enemies, his People and ours shall be always one, and shall die together. We came hither naked and poor as the Worm of the Earth; but you have every Thing, and we that have Nothing must love you, and can never break the Chain of Friendship which is between us. . . . If we catch your Slaves, we shall bind them as well as we can, and deliver them to our Friends again.

By the mid-eighteenth century, Cherokee youth could earn warrior status by trading in slaves or by retrieving runaway slaves. In fact, a "certain Number" of captives were "required from the Hands of a young Indian before he c[ould] be honoured with the first military Title, which [wa]s a Slave-Catcher." Antebellum trade in Indian slaves never disappeared completely from Appalachia, for speculators continued to kidnap Cherokees and to sell them into bondage. In addition, the wealthiest Cherokees owned black slaves. Consequently, enslaved Appalachians were ethnically mixed with Indians to a greater extent than their counterparts in the rest of the United States. For those reasons, we cannot historically isolate the enslavement of indigenous Appalachians from the import of slaves of African heritage.[4]

Slave Population Trends Between 1800 and 1860

From the opening of regional frontiers to Euroamerican settlers, black slaves played a key role in the political economy of Southern Appalachia. In 1810, 17 percent of the region's population was enslaved, a level that was about half the Southern average. In the Appalachian counties of Alabama, Georgia, and South Carolina, the enslaved population increased dramatically between the frontier years and 1860. In Tennessee, the percentage of enslaved Appalachians remained relatively stable, with small population increases between 1820 and 1860. Between 1820 and 1860, western Maryland and western North Carolina experienced steady declines in the percentage of enslaved Appalachians. In eastern Kentucky, the percentage of enslaved Appalachians declined between 1820 and 1860, with one growth spurt between 1820 and 1840. In West Virginia, the percentage of enslaved Appalachians doubled between 1810 and 1820 and then declined dramatically between 1820 and 1860. The Appalachian counties of Virginia exhibited the most erratic pattern, with a 7 percent decline between 1810 and 1820, a 7 percent increase between 1820 and 1840, and another small decline between 1840 and 1860.[5]

One explanation for these population trends lies in the overall national picture. The U.S. free population expanded more than the enslaved population between 1820 and 1860. After 1807, the United States prohibited the import of blacks through the international slave trade; and the British aggressively curtailed African slave imports to New World colonies after 1838. During this same time period, the immigration of white Europeans to the United States steadily increased. These national population trends were reflected in the trend for Southern Appalachia as a whole; but that average disguises significant differences among the zones. Because whites were not repeopling most of the Mountain South as rapidly as they were moving into other sections of North America, we must unscramble the riddle by following other directions of inquiry.[6]

The first explanation for Appalachia's erratic population trends lies in the late opening of the region's southernmost frontier. Public land opened in northern Alabama after an 1819 treaty with the Creeks and Cherokees. After the forced removal of the Cherokee in 1838, northern Georgia, parts of western North Carolina, and southeastern Tennessee were opened to resettlement by Euroamericans. Planters initiated intense land speculation, and tobacco and cotton production quickly became entrenched. In the Appalachian counties of Alabama, Georgia, and South Carolina, the enslaved population expanded 2.5 times more than the free population, spurred by the shift to cotton cultivation. In Appalachian Tennessee, the enslaved population increased nearly 40 percent more than the free population, perhaps reflecting the trend toward tobacco and cotton production in those southeastern counties that had previously been part of the Cherokee Nation.[7]

Agricultural specialization does not explain all the long-term changes in population, for slavery increased most dramatically in the worst terrain. Between 1810 and 1860, the enslaved population of the region's

Mountain masters held diverse economic portfolios, so they invested in pursuits such as railroad construction. Most of the antebellum railroad construction in the Mountain South depended heavily on slaves and immigrant laborers. *Source:* Colyer, *Brief Report*.

mountainous counties expanded three times more rapidly than the enslaved populations of the hill-plateau or ridge-valley counties. Moreover, slaves were being imported into those mountain counties at a level that exceeded by nearly 20 percent the increase in the free population. We must seek the second explanation for Appalachia's forty-year trend in other economic activities. By 1860, extractive industries had emerged in two-thirds of the region's counties. As we shall see in Chapter 3, slaves were crucial to iron production, gold mining, salt manufacture, and coal mining – industries that were concentrated in mountainous counties.[8]

However, there is a third explanation for the fifty-year demographic trends. By 1820, the northern and middle sections of Southern Appalachia were losing black population. Western Maryland lost nearly half its slave population between 1820 and 1860. West Virginia's free population expanded eight times more than its enslaved population over this forty-year period. Similarly, Appalachian Virginia's free population expanded nearly twice as much as its slave population. Immigration into the United States cannot explain why these trends were occurring, for Appalachian free populations did not expand at levels anywhere near the national average. Moreover, the slow growth of the slave population cannot be explained by a regional shift toward a widespread antislavery ideology, for the proportion of Appalachian slaveholders increased between 1800 and 1860. Another national trend caused the slow growth of black population in this region. As part of the interregional transfer of slaves from the Upper South to the Lower South, Southern Appalachia exported surplus laborers.[9]

Appalachia's Unfree Laborers on the Eve of the Civil War

In 1860, nearly three of every ten adults (aged fifteen to fifty-nine) in the region's labor force were enslaved (see Map 2). Nearly three hundred thousand black Appalachians accounted for about 15 percent of the region's 1860 population. In the Appalachian zones of Alabama, Georgia, South Carolina, and Virginia, enslaved and free blacks made up one-fifth to one-quarter of the population. In the Appalachian zones of Maryland, North Carolina, and Tennessee, blacks accounted for only slightly more than one-tenth of the population. West Virginia and east Kentucky had the smallest percentage of blacks in their communities. The lowest incidence of slavery occurred in the mountainous Appalachian counties where 1 of every 6.4 laborers was enslaved. At the other end of the spectrum, the ridge-valley counties utilized unfree laborers more than twice as often as they were used in the zones of the most rugged terrain.[10]

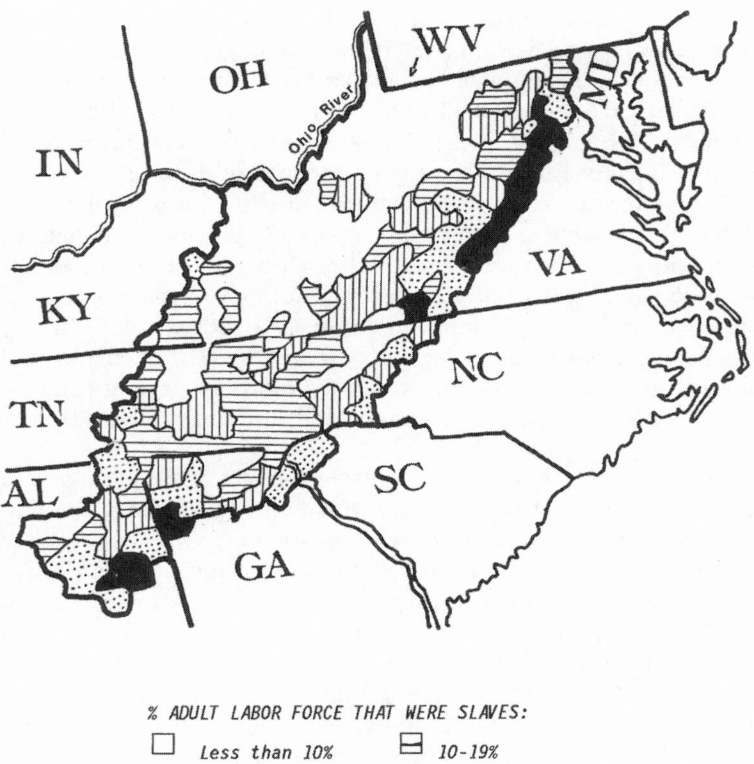

Map 2. Slaves in the Appalachian labor force, 1860. *Source:* Aggregated from NA, 1860 Census of Population.

Slaves were not the only unfree laborers in Southern Appalachia, for laws regulated free blacks in ways that kept them structurally and economically immobile. By implementing discriminatory laws, Southern Appalachian employers could, by the mid-nineteenth century, exploit free blacks as oppressively as they did slaves. In Appalachian counties, free blacks were among the poorest of the poor; that is probably why they were underrepresented in the region's population. In 1860, 7 percent of the U.S. population resided in Southern Appalachia, but only slightly more than 2 percent of the country's free blacks could be found in the Mountain South. Two-fifths of them reported no stable means of income and were unemployed three or more months every year. For those reasons, free blacks probably endured more precarious day-to-day circumstances than enslaved Appalachians. Free black adults averaged only 8 percent of the accumulated assets reported by white Appalachians in 1860. More than one-half of all white Appalachian households owned land, but less than one-fifth of free black Appalachian families had access to farm land. As a result, less than one-tenth of these emancipated families lived above the national poverty line of $300 annually. The typical free black Appalachian family had acquired less than $85 in land or personal wealth, and they were earning less than $30 per year. Three-fifths of these emancipated families carried the same surnames as local whites, indicating their dependence upon previous masters. Most likely, they remained in Appalachian counties only so long as they maintained positive relations with their previous owners and only so long as those white families assisted them in their annual registration with local county courts.[11]

After 1830, every Southern state regulated free blacks, requiring them to register and to place a financial bond with county governments and to remain stably employed. Unemployment, unpaid debts, vagrancy, public drunkenness, or violations of local statutes were sufficient legal justifications for the indenturement or reenslavement of emancipated blacks. By the mid-nineteenth century, Southern poor relief programs had been shaped by public hostility toward the growing population of free blacks. According to the philosophy of the times, unconditional assistance to the poor failed to check their demoralization and encouraged "habitual indolence." The laboring poor were characterized in the press as "virtually a different, permanently degraded species of mankind." It was believed that nothing should be done to mitigate the near-starvation of the "vagrants and offals of society," for only those who were responsive to hunger – the most elemental of labor incentives – could be induced "to fulfil the most servile, the most sordid, the most ignoble offices in the community." Consequently, *compulsory labor by paupers* was touted as the only effective act of public benevolence. Southern poor relief was structured to provide temporary relief to the elderly or to the disabled destitute; the able-bodied poor were required to work. By 1860, about two-thirds of the Southern Appalachian counties operated poorhouses, but the only inmates residing in these facilities were elderly, physically or mentally handicapped, or insane whites. Free blacks were institutionalized only long enough to auction or indenture them to long-term labor with local employers.[12]

Archival records reflect three placement strategies that were followed by Appalachian poor houses to "solve the pauper problem" in their local communities: (a) vagrancy laws, (b) county court indenturement of debtors, abandoned or indigent children, unemployed free blacks, or black offspring of whites, and (c) the indenturement of children by black parents. First, vagrancy laws authorized poorhouses to "auction off" to community employers adults with no visible means of support. Most counties merely sold the pauper to the person with the highest bid for a work contract. Second, the county sheriff could arrest and auction off the labor and possessions of persons against whom the courts had made legal judgment for unpaid debts. Third, able-bodied paupers were contracted to work for a local farmer or merchant in exchange for their subsistence.

In every Southern Appalachian state, trouble-making or illegitimate children, the offspring of adults assigned to poorhouses, or orphans were apprenticed to farmers or artisans until they reached the age of eighteen or twenty-one. For instance, the West Virginia Humane Society "placed" homeless children through such long-term labor contracts. Similarly, in 1828 and 1846, the Winchester, Virginia, Poor House apprenticed orphans for fourteen years to a local shoemaker. Homeless street children were indentured for as long as fourteen years by the western Maryland "orphans court." Even in the early stages of local government formation, Appalachian county courts set up procedures for handling destitute children. Even before Tennessee was formed as a separate state, for instance, the Washington County Court was indenturing orphans. Similarly, indigent or illegitimate children of the Carolinas were never permitted to become paupers dependent upon the public; rather they were apprenticed until the age of twenty-one. From 1831 to 1835, the Poor Wardens of Rutherford County, North Carolina, indentured more than one hundred orphans annually. Western North Carolina children were even bound out by the sheriff when the mother was caught "abusing & beating her children in a barbarous & inhuman manner."[13]

Discriminatory procedures were invoked when the pauper was a free black. Local courts criminalized behaviors of free blacks that were tolerated among whites. County judges often ordered the poorhouses to auction, to apprentice, or to place at compulsory labor some indigent, unemployed, "troublesome," or unwanted free black who had already been warned to "stay out of the county." Any free resident black found spending time "in idleness and dissipation, or having no regular or honest employment" was typically arrested and bound out for three to ten years. After 1826, the Southern states placed severe restrictions upon migration by free blacks. In Tennessee and North Carolina, Appalachian counties led the political push for severe restrictions on migration by free blacks, a prohibition that quickly was adopted by most of the Southern legislatures. In their 1824 petition for a new law, Buncombe Countians complained that free blacks were "a public nuisance" because "there ha[d] been a constant influx of free negroes of every character and description into the western part of the state." Subsequently, any nonresident black who remained longer than twenty days in North Carolina was subject to arrest and long-term indenturement. Abandoned, orphaned, or impoverished black children were taken from their free parents and assigned to the poorhouse "to be bound out." Free black Appalachians led a precarious existence, for the courts placed the burden upon them to prove their emancipation. Even when they could do so, their freedom was often denied. For example, one Augusta, Virginia, slave was emancipated by her master. After his death, however, the master's sons sold her along with other slaves. When she declared her freedom and "manifested some unwillingness to go," she was "put in irons and taken by force."[14]

Even more significant were the Southern state ordinances that criminalized a "socially embarrassing" category that encompassed a great number of slaves. Black children who were "free issue" descendants of whites were assigned to the poorhouse for apprenticeship to a distant farmer or artisan until their manumission at the age of twenty-one. Of the 701 free blacks registered by Augusta County and Staunton, Virginia between 1801 and 1864, more than one-fifth were ordered by public officials to be "bound out by the Overseers of the Poor" to long-term labor arrangements that provided them nothing except their subsistence. Similarly, the Monroe County, West Virginia, courts disposed of nearly two-thirds of its registered free blacks in this manner.[15]

However, there is one other method of indenturement that is not reflected in public records. Locked into an economically marginal position, poor free black Appalachians were often forced into a most extreme form of the *contractualization of kinship*. In a desperate attempt to sustain their households, impoverished free black parents "bound out" their own offspring or kin. Unmarried women with several children often apprenticed their sons for seven years or longer "to learn a trade" from some artisan or farmer. As early as the 1820s, upcountry South Carolina parents indentured their children to work on annual contracts in the cotton mills. Virtually slaves, two Appalachian free children were bound out by their grandmother to work for their "vittils and clothes and schoolin'." Several black Civil War veterans also reported that they were indentured on annual contracts as farm laborers. For example, one McMinn County, Tennessee, son of a tenant farmer was bound out "from the time [he] was nine yeares of age every year until the [Civil] war as a hired hand on other men's farmes." A Coffee County, Tennessee, veteran reported that, from the age of eight, he "plowed every day" because his unmarried mother bound him out "for two dollars a month."[16]

As a result of these discriminatory policies, two-fifths of all free black Appalachian children younger than fifteen lived in households headed by whites. Of those children employed away from their families, about one-fifth were the sons and daughters of local free blacks, and they were either earning wages, auctioned off by the poorhouse, or indentured voluntarily by their parents. Less than one-tenth of them appeared to be living with former masters with whom they shared the same surname. The majority appear to have been orphans or abandoned children whose surnames did not match those of local free blacks or local slaveholders. It is clear, then, that they were indentured because they were either "free issue" offspring of white Appalachians, the children of poor white mothers, or the children of deceased or absent black parents.[17]

How Many Appalachian Families Owned Slaves?

On the Appalachian frontiers, about 8 percent of Cherokee households and more than one-quarter of the white families owned slaves of African or of mixed African-Indian heritage. In 1800, nearly half of Appalachian Virginia's households were slave masters. In the Appalachian counties of Alabama, Georgia, Kentucky, and South Carolina, one-third of the families held slaves. One-quarter of the Appalachian families of Maryland and Tennessee and one-fifth of western North Carolina's households owned slaves in the early 1800s. There were fewest slave owners in West Virginia, but even in that zone there were enslaved blacks in 18 percent of the households. In fact, slaveholding reached a level during the frontier years of eastern Kentucky and West Virginia that those two zones would never exhibit in subsequent decades.[18]

In 1860, the vast majority of Appalachians still did not own slaves. Nearly half the region's families were landless and impoverished; roughly another two-fifths were land-owning nonslaveholders. Nearly 29 percent of all Southern families were slaveholders, while only 18 percent of Appalachian households owned slaves. Mountain slaveholding developed in an uneven pattern. Coming near the Southern average, one-fifth to one-quarter of the Appalachian households of Alabama, Georgia, South Carolina, and Virginia owned slaves. Nearly one-fifth of the Appalachian households of Maryland and Tennessee were slaveholders, but only about one-tenth of eastern Kentucky and western North Carolina families were masters. There were fewest owners in West Virginia where only one of every sixteen households held slaves. In fact, there were 4.5 Southern masters to every West Virginia slaveholder.[19]

To have the clearest picture of where the 40,370 Appalachian masters resided, it is necessary to aggregate county information from the published census. In 103 Appalachian counties that made up about half the regional land area, fewer than 10 percent of the families held slaves. Forty-one of those low-slavery counties were located in eastern Kentucky and West Virginia. In fifty-one counties, about one-tenth of the families held slaves while 15 to 24 percent of the households owned slaves in another forty-five counties. In seventeen counties of Georgia, North Carolina, Tennessee, and Virginia, one-fifth to one-quarter of the families owned slaves. However, twenty-two Appalachian counties exceeded or came near the Southern slaveholding average, and there are some striking contrasts. Fewer than 15 percent of families owned slaves in forty West Virginia counties, but one-third of Jefferson County's households were slaveholders. In twenty-seven eastern Kentucky counties, less than 15 percent of families owned slaves, but more than two-fifths of Madison County's households were slaveholders. In 90 percent of Appalachian Tennessee counties, fewer than 15 percent of families owned slaves, but more than one-third of Franklin County's households were slaveholders.[20]

The extent of slaveholding also varied by terrain. Less than 8 percent of the residents of Appalachian mountain counties held slaves. However, slavery occurred twice that often in the other two terrain types. About 16 percent of hill-plateau households and 18 percent of ridge-valley families owned slaves. Even though the Appalachian slave population narrowed between 1800 and 1860, regional slaveholding actually increased during this period. Over the long term, slaveholding declined dramatically in eastern Kentucky and dropped slightly in West Virginia. In the remainder of the region, however, the percentage of households owning slaves rose between 1800 and 1860.[21]

Statistics give the impression that slavery had little presence in about half the land area of Southern Appalachia, had a weak hold on about one-quarter of the counties, and reached Lower South proportions in only about one-quarter of the land area. However, we really know very little about the true impact of slavery upon the Mountain South if we leave our assessment at this superficial level. Below the Mason-Dixon Line, Appalachia existed within Southern states where legislatures protected the institution of slavery and represented the economic interests of planters. Moreover, the Mountain South was locked into an economic and political symbiosis with the plantation economies of the U.S. South, Latin America, the Caribbean, and the West Indies. Acting as a periphery of the world economy that provisioned staple-producing zones, the Mountain South exported work animals, grains, hogs, cattle, wool, textiles, minerals, and timber, in addition to surplus laborers. In turn, those distant plantation economies cultivated the staple crops that were in highest demand in the capitalist world economy. Consequently, we must examine the impacts of slavery on other levels than just "head counts" of the numbers of slaves and slaveholders in Appalachian counties. In the sections that follow, I will explore the extent to which plantation economics shaped Appalachian agriculture, and I will examine the degree to which nonslaveholders controlled regional resources and shaped community political decisions.[22]

Impact of Slavery on Appalachian Agriculture

The structural integration of Southern Appalachia into the capitalist world economy tended to stimulate "the establishment of larger units of economic decision-making" and "the increased coercion of the labor force." Thus, nearly one-third of the region's farm owners held slaves in 1860. The greatest dependence on these unfree laborers occurred in Appalachian Virginia where nearly three of every five farm owners were slaveholders. Because cotton cultivation was entrenched in the Appalachian counties of Alabama, Georgia, and South Carolina, two of every five farm owners held slaves. Tobacco production pushed the proportion of slaveholders to one of every three farm owners in the Appalachian counties of Maryland and Tennessee while one of every four western North Carolina farm owners held slaves. Reliance on slave labor was least characteristic of West Virginia and eastern Kentucky where fewer than one in every eight farm owners held slaves.[23]

In its reliance upon slave laborers, Southern Appalachia fell behind the rest of the South, but not nearly as far as previously portrayed. Empirically, one-half of all Southern farm owners held slaves, in comparison to one-third of Southern Appalachia's farm owners. In their lack of opposition to slavery, two Appalachian zones were barely distinguishable from the rest of the South. Indeed, farm owners in the Appalachian counties of Virginia held slaves at a level that exceeded the Southern average. In their proportion of farm owners holding slaves, the Appalachian counties of Alabama and Virginia fell only slightly behind the planter-dominated counties of these states. Farm owners in the non-Appalachian sections of Georgia, Maryland, South Carolina, and Tennessee held slaves only 1.5 times more often than Appalachian farm owners in those states. In North Carolina, Tidewater farm owners held slaves nearly twice as often as western farm owners. Similarly, there was only one eastern Kentucky slaveholding farm owner to every three located in the Bluegrass and western sections of that state. However, the sharpest contrast existed between the farm owners of West Virginia and those of Tidewater Virginia. Eastern Virginia farm owners were five times more likely to hold slaves than were the farm owners of West Virginia.[24]

Incidence of Plantations

The popular view has been that there were no plantations in Southern Appalachia because it was a region dominated by small-scale agriculture. Most scholars have ignored the contributions of black Appalachians and have argued instead that the regional mode of production "rested not on the labor of slaves but rather on small land-owning cultivators." Moreover, the traditional claim has been that plantations simply did not exist in the Mountain South because this type of economics was alien to Appalachian yeomen farmers. Some empirical evidence supports such a narrow judgment. We can arrive at a rough indicator of the presence of plantations by using county totals in the published census to determine the ratio of slaveholders to farm owners. When we make that calculation, we discover that there were no large slaveholdings in more than one-quarter of the region's counties. On the eve of the Civil War, fifty-seven counties did not have a single farm that owned twenty or more slaves, and forty-eight of these counties lay in eastern Kentucky and West Virginia. Large plantations accounted for less than 4 percent of the farms in twenty-seven of the eastern Kentucky counties and forty-seven West Virginia counties, so large slaveholders were scattered through only three counties in these two zones. However, the lowest per capita incidence of large plantations occurred in western Maryland. In fact, a farm owner in eastern Kentucky or West Virginia was twice as likely to be a large slaveholder as a western Maryland farm owner.[25]

On the one hand, there was only one large Mountain South plantation for every five large Southern plantations. On the other hand, one of every fifty-six farm owners held more than twenty slaves (see Map 3). Large plantations were concentrated in nine cotton-producing counties of northern Alabama, in northern Georgia, in Pickens County, South Carolina, and in seventeen tobacco-wheat producing counties of Blue Ridge Virginia. Only 1 of every 143 farms in mountainous counties was a large plantation, but large plantations occurred three times more often than that in the counties of hill-plateau or ridge-valley terrain. Terrain did not prevent the spread of large slaveholdings, however. In mountainous Jackson County, Alabama, cotton was king, so one of every twenty-six farms was a large plantation. Indeed, fourteen Appalachian counties exceeded the Southern average for the incidence of large plantations. In the Appalachian counties of Alabama, Georgia, South Carolina, and Virginia, one of every thirty-one farm owners operated a large plantation. Talladega County, Alabama, and the Georgia counties of Cass, Catoosa, Floyd, and Polk were specializing in cotton cultivation; so agriculture in these areas was much more like the Lower South

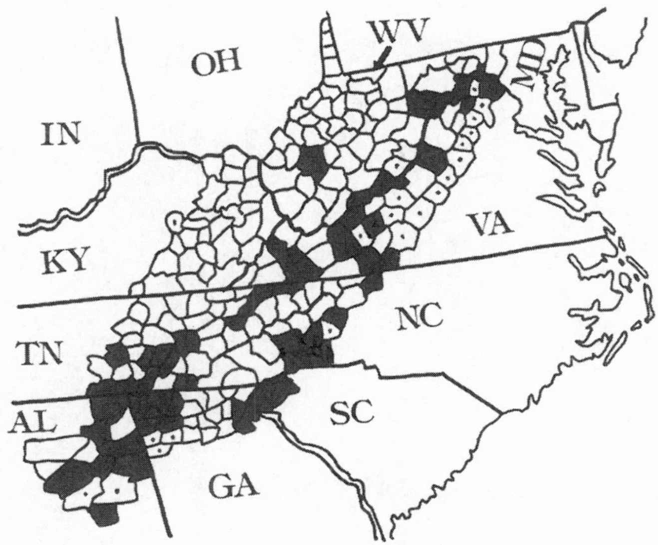

Map 3. Large plantations in the Mountain South, 1860. *Source:* Ratio of owners of more than fifty slaves to number of farms, NA, 1860 Census of Agriculture.

in their reliance on slaves. Similarly, Virginia's counties of Albermarle, Bedford, Clarke, Fauquier, Madison, Nelson, Rappahannock, Roanoke, and Amherst were cultivating large quantities of wheat and tobacco for export; so large plantations in those areas exploited slave laborers to an extent that exceeded Southern averages.[26]

Who were the large Appalachian planters? These large slaveholders were the wealthiest, most powerful elites of the region, as we can see from a list of twenty-five masters who owned more than one hundred slaves. Large Appalachian plantations were multifunctional "capitalist creations par excellence" that blended crop cultivation and livestock raising with the manufacture of agricultural commodities, commercial enterprises, or extractive industries. Indeed, Appalachia's large plantations may have

A slave chambermaid in an Abingdon, Virginia, hotel. More than one-third of all Appalachian slaveholders and at least one-fifth to one-quarter of all Mountain slaves were engaged in such nonagricultural pursuits. *Source: Harper's*, 1857.

been more diversified than their counterparts in the Lower South. These regional planters used slaves to produce most of the subsistence needs of their labor forces while Lower South plantations purchased items like clothing, shoes, small tools, and household items. Mountain masters generated wealth from several economic activities, including commercial mills, blacksmith shops, tanneries, distilleries, and cotton gins. Often these planters operated ferries or collected tolls for adjacent roads or bridges. The largest slaveholder among the pre-Removal Cherokees was George Waters, who applied the labor of 100 slaves to 464 river-bottom acres to grow corn, wheat, and cotton. As a waystation for itinerant livestock drives, the Waters farm encompassed eighteen corn cribs, five smokehouses, twelve stables, a mill, a ferry, and sixteen outbuildings for laborers. At Monticello, Jefferson's mill, distillery, and nail factory were more profitable than crops. In addition to their cultivation of 1,000 pounds tobacco, 450 bushels wheat, 1,000 bushels corn, and 114 livestock, 88 slaves on the Hale plantation of Franklin County, Virginia, carded wool, wove clothing, milled and distilled grains, and manufactured tobacco into plugs and cigars for export.[27]

Appalachia's large planters often used part of their land for nonagricultural activities. On a thousand-acre Lumpkin County, Georgia, plantation, Tom Singleton's master blended farming with gold mining and copper smelting. Farming was only a sideline for Kanawha County, West Virginia's, richest planter, William Dickerson, who utilized 104 slaves to manufacture salt. Dickerson's only white employees were two clerks, a furnace manager, and one skilled laborer. His farm produced only 2,500 bushels of corn and 117 livestock because laborers bought most of their essentials at the company store. As we will see in Chapter 3, this pattern was not uncommon in Appalachian counties.[28]

Large plantations may have been more scarce in the Mountain South than in the rest of the South, but we discover a different pattern when we examine the degree to which Appalachian agriculture was organized around small plantations that owned one to nineteen slaves. Small slaveholders operated more than 10 percent of the farms in nearly three-quarters of the Appalachian counties (see Map 4). Nearly one of every three Appalachian farms was a small plantation. In counties of ridge-valley terrain, two of every five farm owners was a small slaveholder. Small plantations accounted for less than 5 percent of the farms in only twenty-nine of the region's counties, and twenty-five of these counties were located in eastern Kentucky and West Virginia. In the region's mountainous counties, only one of every seven farms was a small plantation. For eastern Kentucky and West Virginia, then, we can surmise that there were few plantations of any size. For the rest of the region, however, the picture

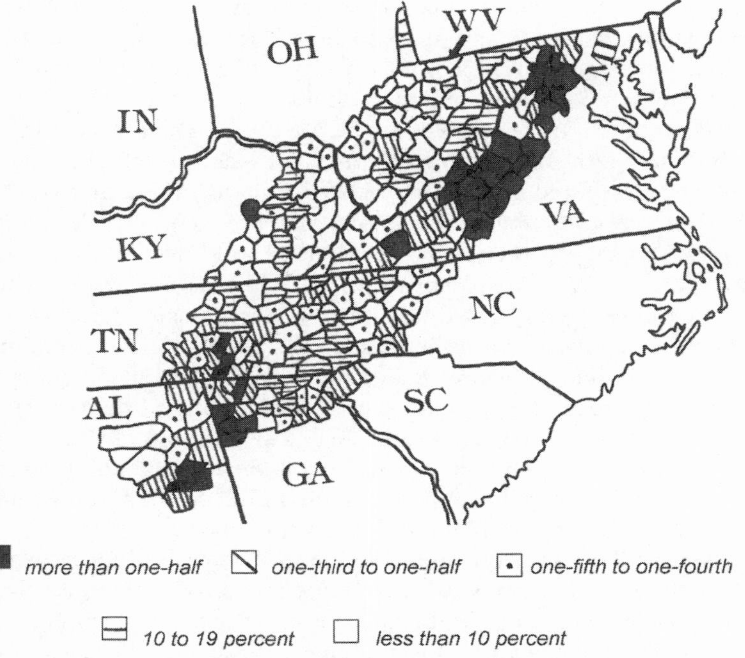

Map 4. How many farms were small plantations, 1860? *Source:* Ratio of owners of fewer than twenty slaves to number of farms, NA, 1860 Census of Agriculture.

is much more complicated. In forty-five counties, the level of small plantations exceeded or came near the Southern average. Thus, two-fifths to one-half of the farms in 21 percent of the Appalachian counties were small plantations. In another third of the region's counties, one-fifth to more than one-third of the farms were using small numbers of slaves. In eighty-one counties, 5 percent to 19 percent of the farms were small plantations.[29]

In contrast to the rest of the South, Southern Appalachia was a region characterized by nonslaveholding farms and small plantations. In 1860, about one-third of the Appalachian farm owners in Alabama, Georgia, Maryland, and South Carolina operated small plantations. One-fifth of the western North Carolina farm owners and one-quarter of Appalachian Tennessee farm owners were small slaveholders. While nearly half of the Appalachian farm owners in Virginia operated small plantations, fewer than 15 percent of the farm owners of eastern Kentucky and West Virginia were small slaveholders. These farm owners were very diverse in their household characteristics and in their crop cultivation. The poorest of them would have been like one Dunbar, West Virginia, master who had recently married and begun to construct a new house. Even though they had inherited two hundred acres and two slaves, this couple lived in "a 2 room house built of rocks and covered with boards split of logs by hand. Cowhides were hung over the doors to keep out the rain and cold." Most of the region's small plantations were prosperous, however, and about one-fifth of them combined professional careers, retail shops, government service, manufacturing, or extractive industry with their crop cultivation.[30]

In its spatial organization, Southern Appalachia exhibited a key characteristic of capitalist agrarian peripheries. The "creation of large-scale economic units" accompanies incorporation into the capitalist world economy, and the pressure toward larger units of production was evident in the Southern Mountains. Local economies replicated the spatial organization common to societies impacted by the expansion of agrarian capitalism. In its uneven and erratic development, the emergence of agrarian capitalism in Southern Appalachia mirrored global patterns. Throughout the region, capitalist farms were operated to meet three interdependent functions: (1) production of the subsistence requirements for local households, (2) growth of surplus grains and meat that were reinvested to feed the laborers and livestock required to generate more profitable market crops, and (3) cultivation of cash crops and livestock for export. Consequently, regional agriculture was not just a single homogeneous type of production. About one-tenth of the region's farm owners were small, subsistence producers who eked out a minimal survival, but a majority were nonslaveholding farmers who produced agricultural surpluses for distant markets. These two groups existed alongside the region's slaveholding farm owners, a few of whom were planters who "employed a large labour-force made up of those who had no option but to work for others."[31]

Land Concentration

The popular view has been that "slavery was of little concern to most of the mountainous counties" because "they lacked the large bodies of fertile land of other parts of the South." That notion is not supported in empirical history, for the region's plantations engrossed much more than their equitable share of the best farm acreage. In reality, antebellum landholding patterns discouraged subsistence agriculture by concentrating farm acreage under the control of the largest surplus producers and by relegating poorer households to the worst terrain. In the region as a

Monticello, the Blue Ridge plantation of Thomas Jefferson, typified the wealthiest slaveholding elites of the Mountain South. *Source: Harper's New Monthly,* vol. 7, no. 38.

whole, the bottom half of the population controlled less than 12 percent of the land. There were so many landless households because the region's farm acreage was heavily concentrated into the hands of slaveholders in every Appalachian geographical zone.[32]

Even though they represented less than one-fifth of Appalachian households, slaveholders controlled more than half of the region's agricultural land. On average, Appalachian slaveholders operated farms that were five to ten times larger than those owned by nonslaveholders. In the Appalachian counties of Alabama, Georgia, South Carolina, Tennessee, and Virginia, slaveholders owned three-fifths or more of the farm acreage. In the Appalachian counties of Maryland and North Carolina, slaveholders engrossed more than two-fifths of the farm acreage, leaving only one-seventh of the resources available to the poorer bottom half of the farm households. Even though there were few plantations in eastern Kentucky or West Virginia, the slaveholding elites engrossed one-third to two-fifths of the farm acreage.

Such resource concentration occurred all over the region. For instance, farm lands in twelve counties of Appalachian Virginia were cut up into immense estates that were "held by a few individuals who derive[d] large incomes from them, whilst the generality of the people [we]re but in a state of mediocrity." In similar fashion, a little more than one-tenth of the parental households of 474 Appalachian Civil War veterans were wealthy planters. Still, those large plantations monopolized nearly two-thirds of the farm land in their counties. Landholding patterns in Cherokee communities paralleled the elite concentration typical of white Appalachians; the wealthiest minority of slaveholders monopolized nearly half the improved acreage.[33]

The extent of farm land concentration becomes evident when the actual holdings of poorer farmers are examined. Even though holders of fewer than 100 acres constituted nearly one-fifth of the region's farm owners, they controlled less than 4 percent of the agricultural land. Thus, the region's poorest farm owners held fewer than one of every twenty-five acres. In Appalachian Tennessee and Appalachian Virginia, the bottom decile of farm owners held land at relatively negligible levels, controlling less than 2 percent of the total acreage. Conditions were even worse in northern Alabama where subsistence producers owned little more than one-half an acre out of every one hundred. In western North Carolina and West Virginia, subsistence producers made up nearly one-fifth of the owner households, but they owned only 4 to 8 percent of the farm land. In antebellum Southern Appalachia, farm land was concentrated into the hands of those farmers who were producing large surpluses for distant markets. Nearly three-fifths of the agricultural acreage was monopolized by slaveholders, and one-fifth of the farm land was monopolized by a tiny plantation elite.[34]

Moreover, farm land ownership was most concentrated in those sections of Southern Appalachia where agricultural production was made most difficult by mountainous terrain. In the region's most mountainous counties, two-thirds of the agricultural acreage was monopolized by slaveholders. In three southeastern Kentucky counties, twelve families owned 48 percent of the slaves and nearly 10 percent of the farm land. In those mountainous counties, nearly one-third of the farm operators were landless while the slaveholding elites ran plantations that averaged 4,921 acres. In rugged Monroe County, Tennessee, less than 8 percent of the farms were smaller than 100 acres; and they encompassed less than 2 percent of the total farm land. In contrast, the few Monroe County slaveholders monopolized more than one-third of all the farm acreage. Similarly, the wealthiest decile of slaveholding farm owners controlled more than three-fifths of the agricultural acreage in counties characterized by ridge-valley terrain. For the region as a whole, slaveholders averaged about 800 acres; however, slaveholders farming in ridge-valley terrain averaged more than 3,400 acres.[35]

Incorporation into the capitalist world system stimulated structural distortions of local Southern Appalachian economies. First, landed propertyholders progressively strengthened their dominant position because land and the means of production were heavily concentrated into the hands of a few local elites. During the late 1700s, nearly three-fifths of this region's resident households were unpropertied. Strikingly, Southern Appalachians were 1.7 times more likely to be landless than their counterparts who resided in the northern sector of the Appalachian Mountains. In comparison to New England during this era, resident households were twice as likely to be unpropertied on the Southern Appalachian frontier.[36]

The small minority of Appalachian slaveholders accumulated wealth by leasing or selling tracts to settlers, by acting as agents for absentee engrossers, or by holding natural features that were attractive as resorts. Land was the basis for the capital accumulation required for the development of local industry and commerce. Local elites utilized their landed estates to profit from legally mandated towns, toll roads, ferries, railroads, canals, mills, and iron foundries that were operated as publicly subsidized monopolies. Yet land also provided the economic basis for the structuring of polarized local economies in which the wealthy landed gentry amassed a majority of the acreage while more than half the white households remained landless.[37]

Monopolization of Wealth and Economic Power by Slaveholders

Nonslaveholders accounted for more than 80 percent of all Southern Appalachian households, but less than half of those nonslaveholders owned land. Even though they made up a large majority of the population, these nonslaveholding families controlled less than one-quarter of the region's wealth. In sharp contrast, slaveholders represented less than 18 percent of Appalachian households. These families, however, averaged $19,388 in accumulated wealth. The typical slaveholding household held nine times more wealth than its nonslaveholding neighbors. Even small slaveholders had lifestyles that set them apart from nonslaveholders. Small masters averaged $13,051 in assets – six times more wealth than the typical landed nonslaveholder and seventy-five times more wealth than a

Mountain masters invested in commercial stage and wagon lines, and they allocated slave laborers to such ventures much more frequently than Lower South large plantations. *Source: Harper's*, 1855.

landless family. However, wealth was concentrated into even fewer hands. Less than 2 percent of the region's households held twenty or more slaves, but this tiny elite owned 29 percent of regional wealth. These planters averaged $108,110 in household assets, and they held forty-six times more wealth than the typical nonslaveholding family. A slaveholding household in the top echelon controlled 618 times more wealth than a typical family in the entire bottom half of the population.[38]

Like other agrarian peripheries of the nineteenth-century capitalist world economy, Southern Appalachia was heavily impacted by "gentlemanly capitalism" based on "landed wealth." Slaveholders monopolized land and held the dominant economic and sociopolitical positions in the region's local economies, and the wealthiest planter-merchant elites stood at the pinnacle of local status. Because of their land speculation, slaveholders had acquired a disproportionate share of the region's land, mineral resources, and timber. Moreover, they overwhelmingly controlled the region's town development, transportation infrastructure, factories, and extractive industries. Appalachian slaveholders also owned part interest in most of the hotels, inns, and mineral spas that attracted external tourism to the region. Acting as representatives of distant speculators and investors, the region's slaveholders played central roles in syndicating absentee ownership of a high percentage of Appalachian industries, banks, towns, railroads, and canals.[39]

In the half century between 1810 and 1860, inequality in the ownership of wealth remained relatively constant throughout the rest of the

United States. In sharp contrast, there was growing internal polarization between Southern Appalachian slaveholders and the rest of the region's residents. In the early nineteenth century, the top decile of the region's slaveholding households controlled a little less than three-fifths of the total wealth reported in county tax lists. By 1860, the top slaveholding decile was monopolizing nearly three-quarters of the total regional wealth. This pattern of growing inequality characterized every geographical zone of Southern Appalachia, western Maryland, and eastern Tennessee, exhibiting the greatest increases in the proportion of resources held by elites. While the small minority of Appalachian slaveholders grew wealthier, half the region's households struggled in poverty, living on annual incomes of about $100 and unemployed three or more months each year. As wealth was increasingly concentrated into the hands of the region's slaveholding elite, Appalachian communities were sharply polarized. While the region's slaveholding minority engrossed resources and lived a lifestyle out of the reach of most families, Southern Appalachia was becoming the poorest geographical section of the United States. By 1860, Southern Appalachian households were nearly twice as likely to be poor as families in the country as a whole, but the region's slaveholders were comparable in wealth, power, and lifestyle to their counterparts in the Lower South.[40]

Slavery and Regional Economic Investments

Local Appalachian economies were structurally distorted because the region's slaveholders guided development toward economic activities and public infrastructure improvements that would bolster their profits from exports. Consequently, there derived an asymmetric manufacturing sector propelled by "boom-to-bust cycles" in the processing of raw materials that were in demand at distant markets. It was no accident that low-level processing of agricultural surpluses and mineral ores received such priority, for the manufacturing sector was dominated by the region's agrarian and commercial elites. This slaveholding comprador bourgeoisie invested their own wealth and channeled absentee capital into enterprises that strengthened their profits from external trade. Consequently, Southern Appalachia's antebellum regional economy was characterized by a structural distortion toward tertiary activities that were controlled by slaveholders. Retail trade, town shops, and travel capitalism grew much more rapidly than did the industrial base.[41]

Before the Civil War, the region's slaveholding elites kept the region's manufacturing closely linked to the processing of the raw agricultural commodities they cultivated for export. Firms involved in agriculturally linked manufacturing accounted for nearly three-fifths of the gross annual value of all Appalachian industrial commodities. Thus, Southern Appalachia specialized in manufacturing agricultural tools, milling flour and cornmeal, distilling grains into liquors, packing beef and pork, finishing livestock hides into leather products, manufacturing tobacco plugs and twists, and producing textiles from cotton and wool. As a result of slaveholder dominance, manufacturing was concentrated in small and middle-sized firms to a much greater extent than was true of the rest of the United States. The typical Appalachian firm produced less than one-half of the national average in annual gross output because the region's manufacturing enterprises were established with only seven-tenths of the average fixed-capital investment that occurred in the rest of the country. The region's manufacturing firms averaged only about four laborers, while the national average was more than nine workers per manufacturing enterprise. As in other peripheral areas of the world economy, Southern Appalachia's industries developed in an uneven and inequitable pattern that concentrated industry in a few counties, sprinkled most of the counties, and left a few counties only minimally industrialized. Fifty-six of the region's counties were industrialized at levels equivalent to Midwestern averages or higher, but three-quarters of the Appalachian counties lagged behind Midwestern and national averages.[42]

The explanation for this pattern of development lay in the *disarticulation* between economic sectors. In the core regions of the world system, capital was allocated to all branches of production, resulting in sectors that were economically "articulated." In 1860, the American Northeast invested $1.00 in manufacturing for every 84 cents put into farms. In sharp contrast, investments in peripheral areas of the world system were concentrated in land and in areas of export activity; the Mountain South was following this path of development. In Southern Appalachia, local and absentee capital were overwhelmingly sunk into export agriculture, slaves, and extractive enclaves – those sectors stimulated by the region's integration into the world market and those economic activities into which local slaveholders were placing their investments.[43]

Because available capital was invested in land and slaves, too little surplus remained for investment in diversified manufacturing. For every 1860 dollar allocated to regional industry, $14.11 was invested in agriculture. As a result, capital was invested in Appalachian farms at a level that was more than twice the national trend. Comparisons with the Northeastern core are even more startling. While agricultural and manufacturing investments per capita were relatively equal in the Northeast, per capita investments were made in Appalachian agriculture twelve times more often than they were made in industry. For every dollar invested in Northeastern farms, $16.80 was sunk into Southern Appalachia's agricultural

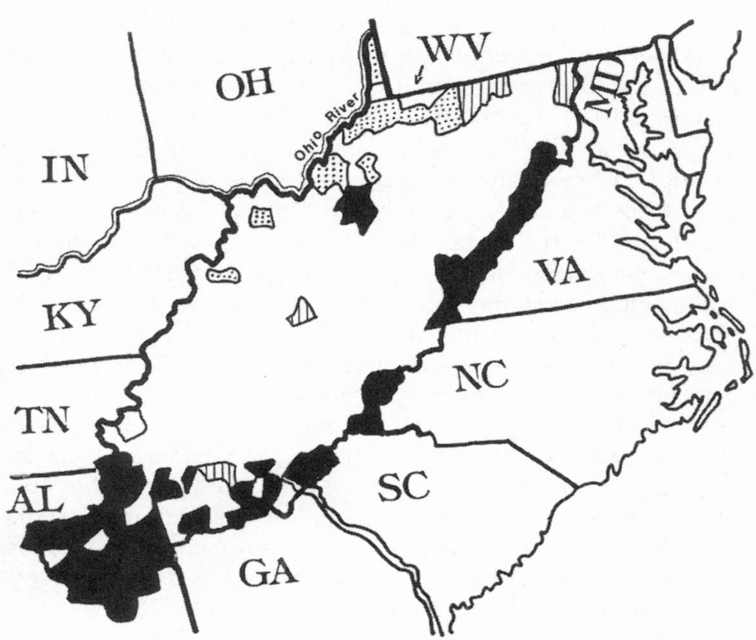

■ *Highest investments in slaves, with farms second*

□ *Highest investments in farms, but slave investments exceeded industrial capital*

▥ *Highest investments in extractive industries, with slaves second*

⊡ *Slaves were least significant investment sector*

Map 5. Mountain South investments by economic sector, 1860. *Source: The First American Frontier: Transition to Capitalism in Southern Appalachia, 1700–1860*, by Wilma A. Dunaway. Copyright © 1996 by The University of North Carolina Press. Used by permission of the publisher.

sector. Three-quarters of the Appalachian counties exhibited the highest concentration of fixed capital in farms; however, regional investments in slaves far surpassed capital allocations to manufacturing and extractive industries (see Map 5).[44]

In contrast to Northeastern sectors that were growing at a relatively even pace, Southern Appalachia was dominated by agrarian capitalism;

and less than 5 percent of regional investments fostered the growth of manufacturing and extractive enterprises. Appalachian elites were made wealthy by a comprador trade with western Europe, the Lower South, and the U.S. Northeast that exchanged low-priced primary exports for expensive manufactured imports. Locally, those economic elites reinvested their profits, not in industry, but in the purchase of land and slaves. These investment patterns meant "a loss for the economy comparable to the hoarding of gold," for agrarian capitalism did not generate sustainable growth. Thus, Appalachian slavery "present[ed] an obstacle" to industrial development. Even though the Mountain South had a much lower incidence of slavery than the rest of the South, investments in unfree laborers had a significant impact upon the development of regional manufacturing. In reality, nearly two-fifths of the region's combined fixed assets were tied up in slaves. In the region as a whole, 65 cents was sunk into slaves for every dollar invested in farms. Moreover, Southern Appalachians sunk $9.15 in slaves to every dollar allocated to the development of manufacturing or extractive firms. Consequently, slaves were the most important investment sector in nearly one-fifth of the region's counties. In fact, slaves were the least significant investment sector in only eleven Appalachian counties. As a result of the predominance of agriculture and slavery, extractive investments exceeded or equaled resource allocations to agriculture and surpassed the capital sunk in slaves in only four Appalachian counties.

The astonishing reality is that antebellum Southern Appalachia had the wealth and mineral resources to parallel Northeastern investments in industry! Yet local elites reinforced the peripheral development trajectory of the region by allocating their capital into slaves rather than diversified manufacturing. Because of the concentration of regional investments into slaves, Southern Appalachia's manufacturing position in the national economy spiraled downward between 1810 and 1860. In 1810, Southern Appalachia was producing manufactured commodities at a per capita level nearly twice the national average. By 1860, U.S. manufacturing output per capita had nearly tripled, while Appalachian manufacturing was marginalized. By 1860, the region's manufacturing gross per capita had declined to a level that was just slightly more than one-third of its 1810 output.[45]

Class Struggle Between Slaveholders and the Appalachian Majority

Capitalism "gives birth to a cultural sphere predominantly divided along class lines." In the nineteenth-century capitalist world system, the attainment of land and wealth were the social indicators of "high culture." The aspiration of all rising groups was to gain enough wealth to become part of the leisured, landed upper class. Articulation with the world system created in Southern Appalachia a peripheral comprador bourgeoisie who were tied by kinship to elites in other parts of the South and who remained loyal to external political and economic agendas. Because those regional elites embraced the capitalist values dominant in the core, they aspired to rise to the economic level of Southern merchant-planters. Since wealth, land, and political power were heavily concentrated into their hands, this Appalachian minority could utilize their local positions to sustain within their communities an exploitative division of labor.[46]

Little wonder, then, that their views of respectability, thrift, and cultural refinement dominated local society. Appalachian elites "were in separate and distinct classes," according to the son of an eastern Tennessee large slaveholder. Supposedly, those "Southern gentlemen always recognized *worth* and *merit* under all circumstances, and mingled freely with those who were *respectable* and *honourable*." The acknowledgment of those positive cultural characteristics hinged, of course, upon the extent to which the persons of lower status "were of equal intelligence, refinement and education," thereby making such equality an impossible achievement in Southern Appalachia. Culturally, the working classes were stigmatized because "the larger land, and slave-owners did not regard manual labor as respectable for a gentleman." A Charleston, West Virginia, minister showed the extent to which elite stereotypes were dominant in the local society when he wrote: "To work with our hands is contrary to the pride of this life and to the customs." Similarly, the wife of a Frederick County, Virginia, small slaveholder lamented that "it almost broke [her] heart" to see her sons "work as hired labourers for other people."[47]

"Respectable" Appalachians reflected the cultural and class biases that typified attitudes of wealthy elites throughout the nineteenth-century Western core. In that dominant ideology, people had "low culture" only because they had a faulty genetic endowment or had failed to acquire "cultural capital" (i.e., education, attire, speech, social connections, and pursuit of materialist goals). This philosophy shifted blame for poverty upon the victims and away from the structural inequalities of the capitalist system. The poorest three-fifths of the region's households averaged less than $100 in accumulated wealth, and their precarious lifestyle was the economic and cultural antithesis of Appalachian slaveholders. Although they made up a majority of the region's resident households, the most culturally degraded group were these landless workers. These families were seven times more likely than slaveholders to be lacking in the "cultural capital" that was reflected in literacy and education. In sharp contrast to the dominant cultural ideology, nine-tenths of the laborers believed there was "no chanc for a poor man" because "the big land owners controlled everything and kept the poor man down."[48]

On the one hand, slavery was rationalized by Appalachian owners as a system that saved these unfree laborers from the destitution and savagery of the African wilds and "civilized" them away from their biological weaknesses. Furthermore, all "respectable" white Appalachians abhorred "the disreputable rabble," that tiny community segment of free blacks, ethnically mixed persons, Indians, and white paupers. On the other hand, there was a cultural "contempt on the part of thriving non-slaveowners and thrifty slave-owners for the thriftless known as 'poor white trash.'" Wage differentials were justified by Appalachian industrialists on the basis of *ethnic* indicators of innate skills levels and worker malleability, and company-town operators did not hesitate to use force to quell laborer resistance to such cultural derogation. Unskilled and very often illiterate, poor rural laborers were socially stigmatized as "a distinct and rather despicable class," with whom "respectable" Appalachians "wanted to have as little to do as possible." In short, the idealization of wealth and the derogation of "working for a living" unfolded as cultural expressions of peripheral capitalism in Southern Appalachia. Attributions of status served as cultural legitimations of the inequitable division of labor. Moreover, "respectable" Appalachians idealized the *cultural distance* between those who engrossed the region's resources and those who were impoverished.[49]

By directing attention away from "dominant structural realities, such as those associated with ... resource exploitation or class-based inequalities," Appalachian slaveholders and middling land owners embraced a local community culture that threw "a warm glow upon the cold realities of social dislocation." The causes for the inequities were located in the weaknesses of those at the bottom, not in the exploitation of those who held the resources at the top. Southern Appalachia's slaveholders, those households that controlled much more than their equitable share of the region's resources, believed that anyone could be economically mobile – even from the worst of circumstances, simply "by applying himself." Even though they did not lead comparable lifestyles, most landed non-slaveholders tended to agree with the ideology of planters about local economic opportunities and about work habits of the poor. Three-quarters of the landed Appalachians were convinced that ordinary laborers experienced few difficulties in buying a farm or business. In their denials of any class distinction except that between "hard-working people" and the "shiftless poor," middling nonslaveholders embraced the Southern planters' myth that laborers could rise from poverty with relative ease and frequency. The hegemonic philosophy of the day was that "discredit must attach itself to those who are unfortunate and poor. A Man, in America, is not despised for being poor in the outset . . . but every year which passes, without adding to his prosperity, is a reproach to his understanding or industry." By affirming the cultural code of help only for the "respectable" and the "deserving," Southern Appalachia's middling nonslaveholders blamed the "poor white trash" for their own impoverishment.[50]

Despite such class stereotypes, the chances of a nineteenth-century Southern Appalachian rising from the bottom of the social ladder were empirically delimited by three harsh realities. First, land was heavily concentrated, and in antebellum America, economic wealth did not trickle down to those households on the bottom rungs. "Monthly wage rates appear to have collapsed during the early 1840s" because there was a relative labor abundance. During this period, "there emerged an agricultural proletariat larger than at any previous time." Land was increasingly concentrated into a few hands, and "inheritance practices were more inegalitarian." By the middle of the nineteenth century, opportunities to purchase and to own land "were more constricted than ever." Between 1810 and 1860, only a small minority of propertyless households moved into the ranks of landholders; so at least one-quarter of Southern Appalachia's agricultural families experienced intergenerational landlessness.[51]

Second, there were few employment and entrepreneurial opportunities in the region, and wages for agricultural labor were seasonal and low. Consequently, nearly one-half of the veterans were poor, defined as those who described their parents as landless with very limited assets or as struggling owners of small farms. Averaging 23.4 years of age at the beginning of the Civil War, these young men at the bottom of the Appalachian social scale had few jobs available to them, except unstable agricultural labor at wages averaging $6.00 per month. For these households, "money was mighty scarce . . . money jobs were hard to be had." In contrast to the slaveholder's myth of an easy rise to prosperity, nearly nine-tenths of the impoverished Appalachian veterans were convinced that poor men never accumulated enough wealth to buy land.[52]

Food and land prices rose across the country, while agricultural wage rates became stagnant. Between 1840 and 1855, the differential between unskilled farm wages and those for skilled workers widened dramatically. At best, the antebellum economy promised the laborer a living, but little more. Poorer households barely earned enough to meet subsistence needs; so there were no assets left over to accumulate toward the future. Conditions were so bad that great numbers of Southern Appalachia's landless families were emigrating further westward in search of affordable land, as one Civil War veteran recalled. "Most of [the] emigrants to

[the] northwest were of [the] lower classes. North Carolina and E. Tenn. supplied thousands of these. 'Twas a standing saying that poor whites moving in covered wagons from North Carolina or E. Tenn. [when] asked 'whence and where to' always replied 'Come fun Nawth Caliner; gwyne ter the Ielinoy.'" Because "it took all that a family could make to live," Appalachian veterans with limited antebellum means experienced work histories in which there was little possibility of acquiring land – either through purchase or inheritance. In their estimation, it took considerable "time and toil for a young man to save enough to buy a farm for some of them had to take trade for their labor." Consequently, very few of the poorer veterans ever "saved enough to buy a farm." In some counties, even the opportunities to become a tenant farmer were seriously limited because the largest slaveholders would rather "allow their lands to grow up in sprouts" than rent parcels to poor men. Consequently, the region's nineteenth-century farm laborers were a distinctively underprivileged group who were sharply differentiated from the slaveholders who employed them.[53]

Finally, those antebellum workers who improved their lot were those who acquired a professional or specialized skill to supplement their agricultural pursuits. In Southern Appalachia, however, education was accessible only to those who could afford to pay subscription fees or to send their children to distant academies. In Appalachian Tennessee, for example, the school term ran only four months, and fewer than a quarter of the school-age children were enrolled. As a result, more than one-quarter of the whites older than twenty were illiterate. Of western North Carolina, the state school superintendent reported that even in "the most enlightened country neighborhoods, the leading heads of families could not succeed oftener than once in two years in getting up a subscription school for the three winter months."[54]

Class polarization between nonslaveholders and slaveholding Appalachians played out in local and state politics. On the one hand, planter interests became dominant within the eight state governments where Appalachian counties were located. With support from Appalachian legislators, planters were relatively secure and resistant to challenges from the contradictory needs of those aspects of community life that were not oriented toward export to the world market. Throughout the latter two decades of the antebellum period, nonslaveholding Appalachians were polarized within their state governments. On the other hand, slaveholders were grossly overrepresented as state legislators for the Appalachian counties. Except for West Virginia, western Maryland, and eastern Kentucky, Appalachian counties exceeded the Upper South and the Lower South in their tendency to elect slaveholders to represent local interests in state legislatures. Only 14 percent of eastern Kentucky landholders owned slaves, but three-fifths of that zone's legislators were slaveholders – meaning that this nonslaveholding area elected slaveholding legislators almost as often as citizens of the Lower South. Similarly, West Virginia's tiny slaveholding elite was three times more likely to serve in the Virginia State Legislature than their presence in the population warranted.[55]

Antebellum newspapers lamented, for example, that western North Carolina had "been borne down by the unequal influence of the East." Appalachian counties populated primarily by nonslaveholding families were politically subordinated to the political and economic interests of the Southern planters who produced cotton and tobacco for international markets. Free public primary schooling was one of the major issues over which Appalachians battled planter adversaries throughout the antebellum period. With the exception of western Maryland, none of the Appalachian zones provided free public education. In their resistance to higher taxation, the planter-controlled legislatures repeatedly voted down bills to create funding for public schools. Since slaveholders paid for their children to be educated at exclusive academies, they refused to be taxed to benefit those great numbers who made up the middling and lower classes. The result of this sectionalism was growing illiteracy in the Appalachian counties. In 1840, white Appalachian adults were 1.2 times more likely to be illiterate than other Americans; and 1.5 times more likely than other Southerners to be unable to read and write.[56]

Despite the lack of education for the majority, universities and academies received public support from Appalachian elites who aligned themselves more closely with the interests of distant planters than with the needs of their neighbors. The class conflict between Appalachian Virginians and eastern Virginians was typical of the controversy throughout the region. West Virginia's tiny slaveholding minority opposed support of public primary schools on the grounds that outsider-teachers would corrupt the youth. Mirroring the interests of Tidewater planters, one Appalachian newspaper editorial warned that no person should "be employed to teach and instruct Virginia youths unless he be of the 'Manor born.'... [T]he influence exerted in the trans-Alleghany by Yankee teachers is entirely too great, and it behooves every true Virginian to correct this evil. No education is better than bad education." While opposing public funding of primary schooling for the majority of West Virginians, Appalachian elites sang the praises of the University of Virginia because it was educating Southern students "with similar thoughts, with like principles, who are united by a common devotion to Southern rights, to Southern institutions, to Southern manners and Southern chivalry. . . . [I]t is uniting the young men of the South together and making them more and more attached to her peculiar institutions."[57]

Ironically, the primary sources of state funds for education were the sales of tax-delinquent lands, most of which lay within the Appalachian counties! Even though a majority of the state educational budget was allocated to support the University of Virginia, less than 10 percent of that school's students came from counties west of the Blue Ridge. An 1841 West Virginia educational conference criticized that "a splendid university ha[d] been endowed accessible only to the sons of the wealthy planters of the eastern part of the state and to the southern states." According to these Appalachians, scarce public school funds were "frittered away in the endowment of an institution whose tendencies [we]re essentially aristocratic and beneficial only to the very rich" while "men of small farms [we]re left to their own means for the education of their children. They c[ould] not send them to the University, and they [we]re prohibited, if they would, from joining in the scramble for the annual donation to the poor."[58]

The sectional split over state funding of internal improvements was just as rancorous. Consistently, the state legislatures funded transportation projects in those counties dominated by the planters while the Appalachian counties paid a higher proportion of taxes than their share of internal improvements. For instance, Tidewater politicians defeated western North Carolina bids for improved roads from the 1830s onward. "Nature has supplied us with the means of reaching a good market," planters objected to the western representatives, "and we will not be taxed for your benefit." Similarly, eastern Tennesseans saw themselves as "mere supplicants at the gate of the Nashville temple" where the legislature was under the control of the "Middle Tennessee aristocracy." By the late 1830s, the state had subscribed $277,000 for turnpike construction, all in the planter-dominated counties of middle and western Tennessee. In every Appalachian state, the sectional rivalry over internal improvements resulted in the funding of roads, canals, river channeling, and railroads that benefited staple-producing counties. By 1860, there were ten miles of railroad for every ten thousand residents in the United States, but railroads were only developing half that fast in Southern Appalachia. While railroad construction in the non-Appalachian counties of their home states *surpassed* national averages, Appalachian counties received less than one-half mile of track for every mile laid in the planter-dominated areas.[59]

2 Labor Management on Mountain Plantations

> De overseer got 'em up by 4:00 o'clock and de mens had to be in de fields by sunrise. De 'omans went out 'bout 8:00 o'clock. Dey stopped wuk at sundown and by de time dey et and done de chores for de day it was 10:00 o'clock 'for de hit de bed.
>
> – Callie Elder, northern Georgia slave

Antebellum Southern Appalachia was not a "subsistence refuge region" characterized by precapitalist farming. Most of the region's farm owners *exceeded* national averages in per-capita production of wheat, corn, and hogs and were equivalent to national averages in their per-capita output of tobacco and cattle. Moreover, they fell only slightly below national averages in per-capita production of cotton. For all crops except cotton, Southern Appalachia's farm owners cultivated at a level that far exceeded output by Southern farms. Per capita, Appalachians generated seven times the wheat, four times the corn, twice the tobacco, two-and-one-half times the cattle, and three times the swine of all Southern farms. Most surprisingly, Southern Appalachia fell only a fraction below Southern per-capita production of cotton, the crop believed to have been absent due to the region's more rugged terrain and shorter growing season.[1]

Except for seven counties, Southern Appalachian farmers exported grains and livestock at levels well above the global average in 1860 (see Map 6). Thirteen counties exported more than two-fifths of their total grains and livestock, but they cultivated no tobacco or cotton. More than half of the region's counties specialized in the export of grains and livestock, averaging fewer than two hundred pounds of staples per farm. On average, these counties exported a little more than two-fifths of their food crops, supplemented by small amounts of cotton or tobacco. A fourth tier of counties exported high levels of grains and livestock, but they also produced moderate levels of staple crops. These thirty counties generated enough food crops to export one-third of their total production, but they also averaged 425 pounds of staples per farm. The market orientation of a fifth tier of Appalachian counties is very clear. These counties specialized

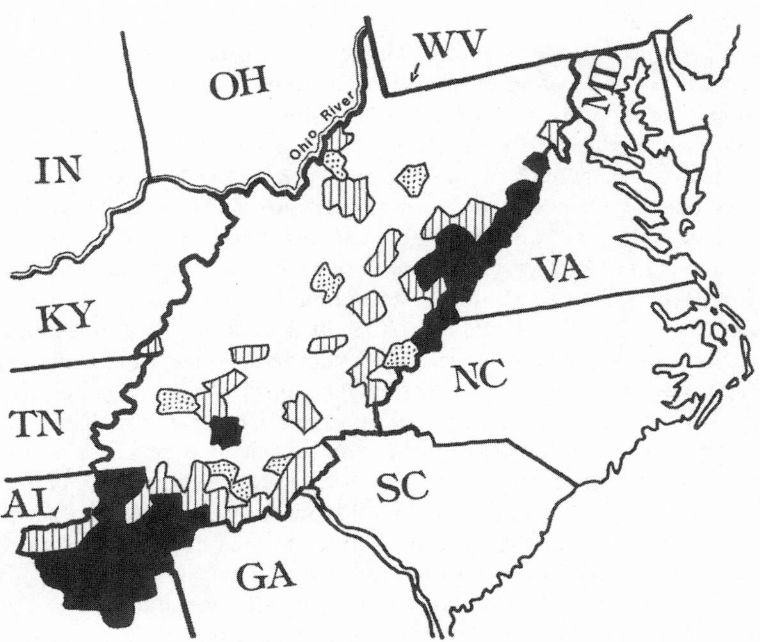

Exporting grains and livestock below global average, with very little staples production

Exporting grains and livestock above global average, with very little staples production

Exporting high levels of grains and livestock, with moderate levels (425 pounds) of staples per farm

Exporting high levels of staples (average 2,826 pounds per farm), with low to moderate surpluses of grains and livestock

Map 6. Agricultural exports from the Mountain South, 1860. *Source: The First American Frontier: Transition to Capitalism in Southern Appalachia, 1700–1860*, by Wilma A. Dunaway. Copyright © 1996 by The University of North Carolina Press. Used by permission of the publisher.

in the production of staples, with grains and livestock playing a secondary role. Eight of these counties produced only enough grains and livestock to export about one-fifth of their total corn equivalencies; however, they utilized their farm land to cultivate 2,613 pounds of staples per farm. Another nineteen counties exported nearly one-third of their food crops, but they also generated nearly three thousand pounds of staples per farm.[2]

Overwhelmingly, the farmers of this region were producing for the market and were striving to become ever larger and wealthier in their holdings. In reality, nine-tenths of the Appalachian farm owners produced agricultural surpluses, and the average farm consumed less than one-quarter of its total annual grain and livestock production for subsistence. The region's typical farm owner generated three times more wheat, corn, cattle, and hogs than were necessary to meet minimal survival needs. On average, then, the region's farm owners consumed less than one-quarter of their total annual grain and livestock production. In the Appalachian counties of Alabama, Georgia, South Carolina, and Tennessee, farm owners consumed, on average, less than one-fifth of their food crop production. Similarly, Appalachian farm owners of Maryland and Virginia utilized less than one-quarter of their food crops for household subsistence. After meeting subsistence and crop reproduction requirements, east Kentucky farm owners cultivated two-thirds to seven-tenths of their crops as surpluses. West Virginia's farm owners absorbed a greater proportion of their crops for subsistence than did households in other Appalachian zones. Even these Appalachians, however, produced twice as much grain and livestock as they needed for minimal survival needs.[3]

Two-thirds of the region's farm owners were nonslaveholders who operated small to middling farms. However, nearly nine-tenths of the region's farm owners (a) consumed less than one-fifth of their total food crop production and/or grew staple crops, (b) used laborers other than family members, (c) had assets well above minimal survival needs, and (d) often drew on income from nonagricultural endeavors. However, the region's crop and livestock production was disproportionately produced by the farms owned by slaveholders. That one-third of farm owners who held slaves produced about one-half the region's corn, wheat, and cattle and two-fifths of its hogs and sheep. Slaveholding farms also dominated the region's antebellum staple crop production. Two-fifths of Appalachian tobacco and nearly 70 percent of the region's cotton was grown on farms where unfree laborers were utilized.[4]

Agrarian capitalism in Southern Appalachia was grounded in the systematic reproduction of low-wage and non-wage forms of labor. Thus, three-fifths of the region's farm owners maximized several free and coerced labor mechanisms. From the large population of free landless households, farm owners captured the labor of eight types of wage and non-wage workers, including tenant farmers, sharecroppers, farm managers, cottage tenants, squatters, indentured persons, annual contract laborers, and day laborers. In addition, nearly three-fifths of the region's slaves worked in agriculture full time, and another 12 percent worked as part-time farm laborers. In fact, slaves accounted for more than one-third of the agricultural labor force in the Appalachian counties of Alabama, Georgia, South Carolina, and Virginia. In western North Carolina, one-fifth of the agricultural labor force was slaves, while one of every six farm laborers in eastern and middle Tennessee was a slave. In eastern Kentucky and West Virginia, about one of every ten farm laborers was enslaved. Slaves were least significant to western Maryland agriculture where only one of every fifteen farm workers was enslaved. In that zone, however, free blacks made up more than one-tenth of the agricultural labor force. In addition, Appalachian farm owners exploited two other categories of coerced laborers whose freedom was legally tenuous: emancipated and indentured blacks. As a result, one of every four of the region's agricultural laborers was an African-American.[5]

Free Black Agricultural Laborers

Free blacks accounted for 1 of every 333 Appalachian households that were engaged in farming. Nearly one-half of all free black household heads were engaged in agriculture; however, three-quarters of them worked as farm laborers or as sharecroppers who averaged less than $30 in 1860 assets and were dependent upon their employers for their subsistence. Overwhelmingly, these agricultural laborers appear to have been emancipated slaves who continued to work for their former masters; two-thirds of them resided near white slaveholders who bore the same last name.[6]

Less than 10 percent of free black Appalachian families operated farms, and less than 0.1 percent of the region's farm owners were African-Americans. More than two-thirds of the free blacks living in agricultural households were day laborers, most of whom *resided off farms* – often in adjacent towns. Most of these free wage laborers were engaged to complete specific short-term tasks or to assist with planting and harvesting. In Cumberland County, Virginia, for example, the Hubards hired free blacks to construct irrigation ditches. The other third of the free black agrarians worked either as sharecroppers or as indentured laborers.[7]

By 1860, one of every seven Appalachian farms was cultivated by a sharecropper, and 1.5 percent of these landless agrarian households was headed by an emancipated African-American. Antebellum Southern laws drew sharp distinctions between "cash renters" and "croppers." Declaring that "the case of the cropper is rather a mode of paying wages than a tenancy," antebellum laws clearly specified that payment for labor could take the form of shares of the goods produced. Throughout the antebellum South, the cropper was considered to be an employee of the landlord, with no property rights in the crop. Southern legal custom recognized an implication of cropping whenever the arrangement was on shares and the landlord furnished provisions. A major portion of the laborer's household subsistence was to be advanced by the landlord. Since none of the sharecroppers owned work stock, landlords typically supplied seed, mules, and farm tools. In return, the cropper gave the owner "first call" on all production, agreed to clear land and build fences, and indentured personal assets and labor time for the entire year as collateral against any indebtedness. As remuneration, the sharecropper was entitled to receive a fixed share of the crop production (ranging from one-tenth to one-third), minus indebtedness to the landlord.[8]

What set the antebellum sharecropper apart from other landless farm operators was the extent to which subsistence provisions were advanced by the landlord. More than four-fifths of the free black Appalachian cropper households were food-deficient; that is, they failed to produce enough food crops to supply their household consumption needs. To maintain greatest control over labor time, landlords characteristically agreed to "find provisions" for the laborer households, including a garden lot, food, housing, and often cash advances. In return, the cropper was often obligated to produce a set amount of tobacco or cotton. Antebellum farm account books from all over the region show clear evidence of landlords advancing provisions and housing to croppers. At annual settling up, the landlord credited the cropper's proceeds from the crop sale against the laborer's accumulated indebtedness. More often than not, the cropper signed a note for outstanding debts.[9]

The Nancy Young household of Greene County, Tennessee, was typical of free black sharecroppers. In 1860, Nancy headed a household that included her adult sister and six children younger than nine. She reported only $5 in accumulated assets, and she owned neither farm implements nor work animals. However, she farmed a twenty-acre parcel adjacent to a white slaveholder of the same last name. Her entire crop production for the year included one milk cow, one beef, ten hogs, fifty-four bushels of wheat, and fifty bushels of corn. To meet its subsistence needs and feed its livestock, Nancy's household required 391 corn equivalencies, but it produced only 173. Despite the food deficiency, however, the Young household cultivated thirty pounds of tobacco, no doubt to meet contractual obligations set by its landlord.[10]

About 15 percent of the agricultural laborers residing on the region's farms and plantations were adults and children who had been bound out by county poorhouses, and free blacks were disproportionately represented among those indentured workers. Free blacks represented about 1 percent of the total regional population, but they accounted for more than 6 percent of the indentured farm laborers. Local courts routinely placed at compulsory labor free blacks who were in the county without legal permission. After 1826, the Southern states placed severe restrictions upon migration by free blacks. When nonresident blacks remained longer than twenty days, they were subject to arrest and long-term indenturement. Any free resident black found spending time "in idleness and dissipation, or having no regular or honest employment" was typically arrested and bound out for three to ten years. Moreover, Appalachian poorhouses regularly bound out the free children of impoverished single black women. As a result, free black Appalachians routinely worked alongside slaves.[11]

Finally, Southern ordinances mandated special public treatment for "free issue" slaves who were the offspring of whites. State laws prescribed the manner in which such offspring were to be handled by public officials. In all the Appalachian states, they were assigned to the poorhouses for apprenticeship until their manumission at the age of twenty-one. As required by state law, the courts of Augusta County and Staunton, Virginia, registered 701 free blacks between 1801 and 1864. Of this group, 123 were ordered by public officials to be "bound out by the Overseers of the Poor." The Monroe County, West Virginia, court disposed of nearly two-thirds of its registered free blacks in this manner. In 1860, seventeen western North Carolina counties indentured 160 free blacks to long-term apprenticeships.[12]

As the result of such policies, one small Calhoun, Alabama, slaveholder reported among his workforce three poorhouse inmates who had been "bound out as farm laborers." In Wayne and Magoffin Counties, Kentucky, slaveholders included among their labor force eight-year-old and twelve-year-old children who had been "bound out by the poor house to work." In Rockbridge County, Virginia, one planter enumerated twenty-one free black workers on his farm – ten of them having been "auctioned off by the Poor house." Elderly free blacks were regularly sold into service by poorhouses. When free blacks became indebted to whites and could not repay them, they sometimes indentured themselves until they worked off their unpaid debts. In western Maryland, free blacks outnumbered slaves. Consequently, "NEGROES FOR SALE – by virtue of an order from the orphans' Court" was a frequent newspaper advertisement. Orphans could be bound to service from the time they were infants until they were twenty-one. In such circumstances, no attention was paid to keeping families intact. In three counties of eastern Tennessee, for instance, twenty-eight free black children were bound out so that none of them resided with the same employer as their siblings or parents.[13]

Empirical analysis of a sample of free black households provides a revealing view of the treatment of these emancipated slaves. One-fifth of the region's free African-Americans lived away from their families in the households of employers, a sizeable segment of them indentured by local poorhouses to farmers. Moreover, almost one-fifth of free black children worked separately from parents in employer households. Nearly three-fifths of these youngsters had been indentured by local poorhouses. Nor was indenturement limited to older offspring; three-quarters of the bound children were younger than fifteen. For example, Catherine Slim's free mother died during childbirth, so the infant was bound out by the poorhouse to a small slaveholder. By the age of ten, she was working alongside adults in the fields. Impoverished and ill, freedwoman Phebe Grinten of Wilkes County, North Carolina, indentured her five young children until they were twenty.[14]

Appalachian Slaves Doing Field Work

We can glean from the Appalachian slave narratives extensive detail about the ways in which masters organized and distributed the work assignments of their unfree laborers. Three-quarters of adult Appalachian slaves worked in the fields at some point during the work schedule. Less than one-quarter of the adult slaves were assigned to duties that kept them out of the fields. For instance, one of every eight adult slaves was employed as a servant in the master's household or combined domestic service with artisan crafts. Still, only about one-fifth of the adult slaves worked exclusively at field work. The vast majority of the adult slave labor force was assigned to a complex blending of field tasks with other chores. Masters freed younger mothers for field work by assigning about 5 percent of the laborers (mostly elderly) to care for slave children. About one of every six adults was a slave driver who supervised teams of laborers. A few of these drivers advanced to become overseers. For instance, "Great George" rose from labor foreman to overseer of Monticello in 1797, and Mollie Kirkland's master turned over plantation supervision to his "lead slave."[15]

Women as Field Laborers

About one-half of adult Appalachian slave women worked in the fields full time, more than one-third of them completing artisan tasks in the evenings. If we exclude elderly child care workers, less than one of every seven able-bodied females worked outside the fields on a permanent basis. About 15 percent of the household servants were reassigned periodically to field chores, especially during harvests. For instance, Henry Williams's mother "cooked, ironed, and worked in the field in time of push." One

Warren County, Tennessee, mother "worked everywhere, out in the field and in the house." On small plantations, "all the women worked in the fields," except one or two house servants. During harvests on small farms, all able-bodied women were assigned to field tasks. In the summers, Sarah Gudger "had t' wok outdoo's," but her Asheville, North Carolina, master shifted her to house duties and wood cutting during the winter. Sarah did all kinds of "men's work," except split rails. "She "jes wok all de time f'om mawnin' till late at night" doing "ebbathin' dey wah t' do on de outside. Wok in de field, chop wood, hoe cawn, till sometime [she] feels lak [her] back sholy break."[16]

On larger Appalachian plantations, assigned tasks were gender-specific, and field women worked primarily in the company of other women. Typically, men plowed and women hoed, supervised by a woman leader. The diary of James Hervey Greenlee provides a detailed look at how Appalachian plantations segregated workers by gender. On his Burke and McDowell County, North Carolina, plantations, this middling slaveholder organized slave women into separate crews to cut briars, plant pumpkin seed, pull flax, gather clover seed, dig sweet potatoes, sprout new ground, and hoe corn. Women harvested corn and fodder and stacked it at the ends of rows, while males hauled it from the fields. Later women shucked and shelled the corn and packed the fodder into the barn. Men cut firewood and timber, while women carried it to the road and stacked it. While men tanned leather, women collected the tanning bark from trees in Greenlee's woods.[17]

On small Appalachian plantations, however, there were not enough workers to permit a strict gender division of labor. On such farms, 3 percent of the slave women acted as drivers and overseers over all the other laborers. On one White County, Tennessee, farm, "the women would plow, hoe corn, just like the men would." A Dunbar, West Virginia, master "worked men or women slaves just alike, and women done all kinds of work, such as hoe tobacco, pull and dry it, then [they] cut rails for fences." Delia Garlic "was a reg'lar fiel' han'" on a large plantation; her duties included "plowin' an' hoein' an' choppin' cotton." In their productivity levels, some of these women competed with males. Aunt Clussey of Etowah County, Alabama, "could plow as well" as any male field hand. Liza Tanner's mother "was a fast hand in the field" who could still outwork her husband when "she was getting old." Anna Lee's master operated a small mountain plantation with only a few slaves, so he "made [her] plow just like the men slaves," and her production quotas matched those of males. The overseer awoke them every morning about 4:30 "with a great large bell" so they "could be in the field waiting for daylight to come." Anna, all the other women, and several men "would be in the field

This small plantation acquired a large centralized workforce by pooling laborers with neighbors through a cotton ginning party. Notice the hilly terrain in the background. The child acted as "water toter" for the adults. *Source: Harper's Weekly*, 1873.

sitting on the end of the row when it got light enough for [them] to work and [they] worked then until dark run [them] in." Lula Walker "hadda work powerful hard," just "like a man." She "hoed, plowed, ditched, split rails an' anything else dat needed to be did."[18]

During planting and harvest on mid-size and large plantations, women frequently worked alongside men. Western Maryland's Ferry Hill Plantation integrated men and women into task teams. Budgeting one hand for every five acres, Thomas Jefferson organized crop cultivation by dividing his slaves into "gangs of half men and half women" under drivers. Subsequently, he redistributed the same laborers for harvest duties. For example, Jefferson allocated five female gatherers for every two male wheat cradlers, led by a male driver. On two western North Carolina plantations, males usually plowed, the women following behind to lay out hills for corn, potatoes, or tobacco. Males plowed wheat fields and sowed the seed; women brushed the sown wheat to cover hills. Males plowed, followed by women "plastering." Because they did not employ huge labor forces, few Appalachian masters maintained a finely honed gender division of labor. The smaller the plantation, the more varied and gender-integrated was field work. When tasks required great numbers of laborers, even large Appalachian plantations dropped gender conventions. Poor white Appalachian women worked alongside males at field work; and these women often hired out to work in plantings and harvests of slaveholders.[19]

Slave Children in the Fields

By 1820, agricultural guides and journals advocated early field training for slave children. One typical manual recommended that

> Negro children, after they pass five or six years of age . . . should be taken from the nurse in the negro houses, and put under the tuition of the driveress, who has the conducting of the weeding gang. It is best to send them with those of their own age, to associate together in industrious habits . . . by degrees to conform them to minor field work. . . . When any of the children becomes 12 years old, and are healthy, they are fit subjects to be drafted into the second gang, going on thus progressively from one gang to the other, till they are incorporated with the great gang, or most effective veteran corps of the estate.

By age seven, more than two-fifths of U.S. slave boys and half the girls had entered the field labor force, and the training process was completed before they were teenagers. In the United States, slave girls entered the fields at a younger age than boys for two reasons. First, girls matured at an earlier age and were better physically coordinated. Second, masters

As in this scene, slave women were overrepresented among field laborers. Women were considered by northern Alabama masters to be especially efficient at cotton harvesting. *Source:* Library of Congress.

discovered that females younger than sixteen had higher cotton-picking rates than boys of the same ages.[20]

Appalachian masters followed the labor customs of the day with respect to the field duties of slave children. As they matured and work loads demanded, children were shifted from childhood to adult jobs. Thomas Cole describes in some detail the manner in which small Appalachian plantations structured the training and socialization of young laborers.

> As I gits older dey just gradually puts more work and heavy work on me. Marster Cole started us out workin' by totin' in wood and kindlin' and totin' water and jest sech odd jobs, den later on as we got older we had ter feed de hogs . . . and de cows, horses, and goats and chickens. All dis kind of work was work fer boys too young fer heavy work.

By the time they were eight or ten, Appalachian slave children were assigned to field chores. About half the Appalachian ex-slaves remembered that they worked most of their childhood at field duties. Perhaps the earliest field task assigned to young boys and girls was that of water carrier. Ann Ladly's master "load[ed] up a barrel full of water, and haul[ed] it out to de field whar de hands [were] working, and [she] fill[ed] [her] bucket from it" to distribute drinks throughout the rows. Young children also seeded cotton after adults harvested the crop. Alex Montgomery and "a drove of black chilluns" gathered potatoes "piling dem in rows"; then adult men "wid a wagon wud come an' haul dem to de big barn whar dey stored dem."[21]

Slave children contributed significant labor during planting. The least-skilled young boys were taught to plow on new ground where "a lack of skill in making straight furrows did not matter." Beginning in April, Appalachian slaves transferred tobacco seedlings from covered beds to the fields. The seedlings were dropped into "every hill by the negro children; the most skillful slaves then . . . planting them." Children dropped corn while adults followed behind to cover the hills. To increase children's efficiency, they "made a cross" to allow them "to put the corn right." One Warren County, Tennessee, slave girl was assigned this task before she was physically mature enough to drop the seeds into the hills. She recalled that she "got a whipping" for being clumsy until she "learned to drap" the corn correctly. Children "would have to drap it fast" because adults "would be behind [them] to cover it up."[22]

By the time they were twelve, Appalachian slave children were hoeing, clearing new ground, thinning corn, and harvesting. Like adults, they "worked as long as [they] could see a stalk of cotton or a hill of corn." Masters also started early to train their sons to supervise black laborers. Samuel Sutton reported that his master "take us boys out to learn us to work, me and Baby Marse. I was to he'p him and do what he told me to do." The first work Sutton remembered was "learning to hoe the clods." Some Appalachian masters constructed short hoes to be used by children and short women. When children "wah too small to hoe, dey pull weeds." Henry Williams "was put to work at six years old." As he became more physically coordinated, "they started [him] to clearing new ground," and he "thinned corn on [his] knees" after the seeds sprouted in the hills. As a young boy, William Brown picked worms off tobacco leaves.[23]

During harvests, Appalachia's cotton producers exploited child labor to a greater extent than Lower South plantations. Fanney Sellers recalled that children on her cotton plantation "never had no time to play" because they were always in the fields or doing night chores. Andrew Goodman's owner "put his little [slaves] in the field" as soon as "they's big enough to work." To learn to harvest crops, children worked alongside adults, putting their "pickin's in some growed slave's basket." As soon as northern Alabama children "got big enough ter pick and puts de cotton in baskets," they joined the fall harvest crews. Each day, every field hand was assigned a number of rows to pick into a large bag fastened by straps around the neck. As they moved down the rows, workers deposited cotton into the long bags. Children either worked with their parents or alongside another hand. Sally Brown "wuz put to work in the fields when [she] wuz five years ole, pickin' cotton," adding it to the bag of the older woman who was teaching her. At the end of each row, the picker emptied the bag's contents into a large basket. According to a Jackson County, Alabama, slave, "dese baskets would hold about seventy five ter one hunderd pounds. De little chillen would pick and puts in a basket wid some older person so de older person could move de basket long."[24]

Field Labor Management on Mountain Plantations

Unlike the Tidewater and the Lower South, the Mountain South was characterized by mixed farming. In the region as a whole, staple crop production consumed many fewer laborer-hours than the cultivation of grains and food crops. Even those plantations that specialized in the production of tobacco and cotton also cultivated grains and livestock. To generate their variety of market surpluses, Appalachian plantations aggregated labor from family, wage laborers, tenants or croppers, squatters, and slaves. How, then, did Southern Appalachia's slaveholders organize and manage their racially and ethnically mixed crews of free and unfree laborers? Archival sources make it clear that the region's plantations were very creative in structuring labor management strategies to match the scale of their particular farm operations. The recollections of Civil War veterans and Appalachian slaves offer fruitful insights into the labor management styles of plantations of diverse sizes.[25]

Small Plantation Labor Management

On small plantations, four-fifths of the owners organized and supervised field labor personally. Most small slaveholders stayed in the field with laborers to lay off the work, issue instructions, and make reprimands. Most of these masters "went to the field, same as the Negroes." The extent these small slaveholders engaged in manual labor varied from farm to farm. Even when their own sons worked, at least half of the owners went to the fields with their laborers only to supervise and instruct. It was not unusual for a small slaveholder to see "to all de work heself" or to do "most of his overseeing with his horse and buggy." Consider this comment from a Rhea County, Tennessee, veteran about labor management customs among the small slaveholders in his community. "All the boys in our neighborhood worked on the farm when not in school. Idleness was not tolerated. Most all land owners lived on their farms and cultivated them. If they had slaves they worked them, but their sons, if they had any also worked." Not only was the division of labor less clear-cut on these smaller farms, but laborers were also much less likely to be assigned tasks on a permanent basis. When the greatest number of laborers were required, for example, "all of the slaves were required to go to the field," even those who usually worked in the house.[26]

At least 15 percent of the region's small slaveholders supervised more loosely from the house. In these cases, free and unfree laborers were given daily task assignments to be completed without direct supervision. On some small farms, "everybody am 'signed to dey main duties" and allowed to work with minimal oversight. An Alleghany, Virginia, slave reported that "we all had task work to do.... We began work on Monday and worked until Saturday." Slaves "wuz give so much work to do in a day"; and "jus' so de wo'k am done lak [the master] sez [slaves] could do lak [they] please." One Kanawha County, West Virginia, owner managed by delegating tasks and checking work, but he also left much discretion to the individual laborers. After being called to work by the master at 4:00 A.M., the slave husband "tended the stock while [the slave wife] cooked breakfast then [they] would be in the field or tobacco shed by daylight." The slaves "would work every day just long as [they] could see how.... [Their] masser he never was so strict on [them] just long as [they] stayed on the farm."[27]

At least one-tenth of the small plantations relied upon black drivers or foremen to organize and supervise the work. In these cases, the slave foreman assumed the duties of an overseer to control the other laborers. Elderly owners often relied upon trusted slaves to direct and monitor outdoor work. In one instance, a slave artisan "was the one in charge, and he took his orders from Marse Fred, then he went out to the farm, where he seed that the [other slaves] carried them out." In another case, "warn't no overseer" because the master "allus had confidence" in an older male slave "who uster look after de fiel' hands." Females occasionally functioned as labor managers, as was the case on one small farm operated by a widow. A trusted slave woman "was kinda the overseer of things. She hired hands and would see about food and everything." On a Washington County, Tennessee, farm of 180 acres, the owner assigned his five slaves to act as the "lead farm hands" in charge of hired white workers. A McMinn County, Tennessee, slave reported that "they always had a man in the field to teach the small boys to work." In other circumstances, small owners simply relied on an informal system in which the "oldah men guided de young ones in deir labors."[28]

Labor Management on Medium-Sized Plantations

As Appalachian plantations increased in size, more labor time was demanded; and supervision over laborers tightened. On medium to large plantations, only 2 percent to 5 percent of the owners assigned daily tasks to be performed by unsupervised laborers. On medium-sized slaveholdings, more than half of the owners "bossed all de hands" directly, usually by riding through the fields to observe and to lay off the expected work; however, none of them actually worked in the fields with their hands. Even when they relied on slave drivers, medium-sized slaveholders maintained tighter controls than did small owners. James Hooff cultivated his Jefferson County, West Virginia, farm by organizing his small force of slaves around task systems. On about one-quarter of the medium-sized farms, slave foremen organized the farm work under the scrutiny of their owners, as in this situation. "I uster dribe ol' marster 'roun' so's he could see de fiel's and de han's. He mek me git out and count de rows off for de han's to do dey wuk. . . . Dey uster figger dat twenty rows to hoe for a growed up man was a good task." Only one of every seven medium-sized plantations employed overseers to organize and supervise the laborers; and the work day was closely regulated.[29]

Labor Management on Large Plantations

Agricultural labor was most closely planned and controlled on the region's larger plantations. More than one-half of all large Southern plantations were managed by overseers. In similar fashion, less than one-third of the largest Appalachian slaveholders supervised personally, and none of them actually worked alongside their laborers. Pickens County, South Carolina, planter John Calhoun described "every plantation" as a "little community" that must be kept "perfectly harmonized." Northern Georgian Devereaux Jarrett addressed "his people" from the second-story porch of his plantation home every morning, setting the work goals for the day. Many small Appalachian plantations allowed their slaves great latitude when assigned tasks were completed, but large plantations tried to maintain control over a greater proportion of the slave's day. Even the nighttime hours of slaves were structured by the larger plantations. One mountain master "had a gin run by horsepower and after sundown, when [slaves] left the fields, [males] used to gin a bale of cotton every night." Because of the large surpluses produced, harvests demanded extended work hours on larger farms, as in this instance. "If Marse Billy got behind in his crops, he just sent us back to de fields at night when de moon was bright and sometimes us picked cotton all night long."[30]

On these plantations, thirty to three hundred free and unfree workers were utilized; thus, the owners structured work environments in which there were strict divisions of labor and lines of authority. Slaves on these farms were assigned to task specializations, and two-thirds of the larger Appalachian plantations relied upon overseers to tell their workers "what to do an' to see dat hit wuz done." On the larger slaveholdings, the work day spanned the daylight hours. "De overseer got 'em up by 4:00 o'clock and de mens had to be in de fields by sunrise. De 'omans went out 'bout 8:00 o'clock. Dey stopped wuk at sundown and by de time dey et and done de chores for de day it was 10:00 o'clock 'for de hit de bed." The overseer was given a clear line of authority to organize work, to dismiss free laborers, and to set the pace by using physical punishment. In the Shenandoah Valley, overseers almost always "participated in the labors of the field." It was not unusual for an Appalachian overseer to

> ride up and down de rows in de field behind his slaves wid his bull whip across his saddle or in his hand, and iffen one of de slaves gits on a bad row, he'd ride along behind him and holler at him ter ketch up, and iffen he didn't pretty soon he would hit him wid his bull whip a couple of times.[31]

Throughout the United States, one-third to one-half of all slaves worked in gang systems of production. Similarly, at least one-third of Southern Appalachia's larger plantations utilized this labor management tactic. These larger slaveholders preferred gangs or crews of laborers working under the supervision of overseers. On these farms, a division of labor was drawn between the overseer and several slave or tenant drivers. One Warren County, Virginia, plantation "was divided into many fields each of which was used to cultivate a particular produce. Each field had its special crew and overseer." A Floyd County, Georgia, slave reported that "in all [his] working life [he] ha[d] always worked with gangs of men." By maximizing slave crews, James Mallory averaged four bales of cotton per hand on his Talladega, Alabama, plantation. One Roane County, Tennessee, farm owner utilized twenty-two slaves and numerous white tenants and laborers to cultivate his large 5,000-acre plantation. To do so, he organized his laborers into racially mixed gangs, under black drivers who answered to the overseer. On that farm, a sawmill and a grist mill also were operated by labor gangs.[32]

Thomas Cole described in some detail the manner in which slave gang labor was organized by his Jackson County, Alabama, master.

> De slaves was woke up every mornin at four thirty by a slave blowin a horn. . . . All de slaves gits up at four thirty, breakfast is eat and de men folks goes on ter fiels and as soon as de women finished up de house work and takes care of de babies, dey comes ter work. All de slaves carried der dinnah ter de fiel wid dem. . . . We

all works til noon den we eats our dinnah in de shade and res bout an hour and half iffen it is very hot and iffen it is cold we res bout an hour, den we goes back ter work and stays up wid de lead man all evenin' jest lak we did in de mornin, and den 'tween sun down and night[fall] we takes out, goes ter de quarters and eats supper.

The gang labor system was particularly popular among those Southern Appalachian owners who held large, dispersed, and disconnected landholdings. One such owner, for instance, operated three separate small plantations under one overseer who rode from one section to another to inspect the work of organized gangs supervised by slave drivers. These drivers set the pace in their gangs, and the rest of the laborers had "ter work and stay up wid de lead man." On one farm, each gang member was required to pick an assigned amount of cotton daily.[33]

Other Slave Labor Assignments

The production schedule was guided so that bad weather or seasonal changes would not be an excuse for lost work time. In bad weather, laborers were shifted from outdoor work to other significant tasks. For example, slaves were organized into crews to cut wood, mend fences, repair roads, or assist with hog killing during off seasons. Similarly, "after de crops was caught up good in de summah all de slaves would start cuttin' wood and gittin' it ter de houses for de wintah." In the fall, fence rails were cut in gangs, the slave driver demanding the production of 100 rails each per day. On tobacco plantations, slaves prepared tobacco for market during the winter. Cured leaves were stripped from stalks, "prized" or graded by quality, and then packed into hogsheads. Women could "break and dress flax" during winter. On those days, the owner "give [the laborers] something to do, in out of the weather, like shellin' corn and the women could spin and knit." In Buncombe County, North Carolina, Sarah Gudger's master was less considerate. "Ole Boss he send us . . . out in any kine ob weathah, rain o' snow, it nebbah mattah," she recalled. "We had t' go t' de mountains, cut wood an' drag it down t' de house" during bad weather.[34]

Some plantations even organized a strategy to alert slaves that they would be reassigned to bad weather chores. Fleming Clark's overseer "would ring a bell in de yard" when workers were expected to undertake their normal field duties. "If it wuz too cold," the overseer "would cum and knock on de doors" in the quarters to assign alternate tasks and work teams for the day. James Hervey Greenlee managed his own work schedule, so his diary provides good detail about such reassignments during inclement weather. When Greenlee sent "4 hands to work the

About 10 percent of all Appalachian slaves were livestock specialists. This southwest Virginia drover is exporting his owner's cattle to Richmond. *Source: Harper's*, 1855.

road" on the coldest day of January, "the ground [was] so hard frozen the overseer dismissed them" from that task and sent them to the fields. When "the cold caused the ground to refuse the plow admitance," workers were shifted again to clearing underbrush, repairing tools, salting the livestock, and tanning bark. During the winter months, Greenlee routinely assigned male slaves to haul firewood, split rails, work his coal pit, kiln lime, repair buildings and fences, and tan leather. Women spent much of the winter in textiles production, clearing underbrush, gathering bark for the tannery, building irrigation ditches, shucking corn, and threshing grains. On a rainy day in February, Greenlee had his male slaves "working in the smith shop, making mule shoes – some shoe making"; later they "halled some manure" and split trees into fence rails. Women plaited corn shucks to produce horse collars, cleaned out stables, picked up fallen branches from the yards and fields, and "brought the cattle from the Lower field" to a pasture nearer the house.[35]

Appalachian slaveholders engaged in an activity that did not characterize most U.S. plantations; they produced large surpluses of cattle, hogs, sheep, horses, mules, geese, and turkeys for export. In many years, livestock production and marketing of animal by-products were more profitable for small Appalachian plantations than crop cultivation. Although not as labor-intensive as crop cultivation, livestock raising required Appalachian masters to employ slaves who were specialists in this type of agricultural production. Nearly 10 percent of the adult male slaves identified themselves in the Appalachian narratives as artisans and specialists who worked full time tending or training livestock. In addition, about one-fifth of the slave children were assigned to feed, milk, pasture, and tend livestock before they were old enough to work in the fields. Appalachian slaves also supplied labor to the livestock transhumance that characterized Southern Appalachia's production of large export surpluses. During warmer weather, cattle, hogs, and sheep were turned loose to forage in the forests, and higher mountain balds and meadows were used for seasonal pasturage. As weather conditions changed or grass and mast were depleted, livestock were shifted between higher and lower grazing areas. Meat processing was one of the most important work regimens on Appalachian plantations. Slaveholders prepared meat for their own use, but they also marketed surplus pork, beef, mutton, bacon, and lard. To transport herds to distant markets, mountain plantations organized massive annual livestock drives, and they often utilized slaves as drovers.[36]

Meat processing was one of the most important work regimens on Appalachian plantations. Slaveholders prepared meat for their own use, but they also marketed surplus pork, beef, mutton, bacon, and lard. Benjamin Johnson sold more than eleven thousand pounds of his Blue

Ridge pork every year to Tidewater planters. For forty years, West Virginia's McNeill family barreled beef and pork to ship to Baltimore butchers. Sometimes, skilled slave drivers organized and managed the slaughtering and preservation of meats. On the Cole Plantation of Jackson County, Alabama, slaves killed and processed three hundred to four hundred hogs every winter. They would "have two killings, de first in November and de last one in January.... Bout two or three weeks fore killin time, [the slaves] would all gits out and round up what [they] wanted ter kill and puts dem in a big rail pen and feeds nuff corn ter dem ter sorter harden de flesh and den go ter killin."[37]

The slaughtering and salting stages had to be completed within two days, so every slave "had a job till hit was ovah." Preparations were made the day before slaughtering, and laborers were assigned to work teams. "Big iron pots and heavy tables were moved out doors; [slaves] were everywhere. Some scrubbed wooden tables and the hand sausage mill, some were put to crushing rock salt." All the slaves "took a hand in the hog killing time," even the children who "trotted to and from the rock furnace with a basket of chips and arm loads of wood." The hog was killed, then dipped in hot water repeatedly to loosen hair. On a small Blue Ridge, Virginia, plantation, the slaves "built a big fi[re] an put on stones an' when dey git hot [they] throw 'em in a hogshead dat has watah in it. Den moah hot stones till de watah is just right for takin' de hair off de hogs." On a western North Carolina farm, they "would take the hog, plunge it head first into the scalding water of a big iron pot, quickly swing it over, catch the front legs, drop the other end, throw it over on a low platform. Others with a long knife or old blades from the scythe held in both hands quickly scraped off all the steaming bristles."[38]

Slaughtering became an assembly line in which "some would be killin and stickin, some would be scalding and scrapin' and some would be dressing dem, some cuttin em up." After scalding and scraping, the hog was hung, cut, gutted, and washed down. "One would split the hind leg of each hog and slip a seasoned hickory stick under the strong sinews to hold the legs apart. Then up went the hog, to hang from a strong bar, fastened between two trees." Males cut the meat into sections while the women processed lard and prepared the head and intestines. "De women folks would be fixin de meat fer lard and renderin de lard. And some de women would be fixin chitlins, hog head sauce, sausage." Women also boiled the heads to prepare "souse meat," cleaned and prepared pigs feet, ground and packed sausages.[39]

After cooling, the meat was salted, packed in wooden boxes or on shelves, and stored in the smokehouse. This final preparation was critical, so slave artisans were often assigned to oversee salting and smoking. On

This was hog slaughtering day on an Augusta County, Virginia, small plantation. Mountain slaves raised, herded, slaughtered, and processed the pork and lard consumed on small plantations, plus the surplus meat products exported by their owners. *Source: Harper's*, 1867.

one small plantation in Warren County, Tennessee, a male slave single-handedly "had charge" of "fixin' de meat," especially "ham an' bacon." Women also directed this crucial process, like Ursula Jefferson, who supervised meat preservation at Monticello. Pork required four months to cure in salt; then it was "smoked wid hick'ry wood." During this process, "the chillun would have to pick up chips to smoke the meat." When it was time to begin the final stage of preservation, slaves "would haul in plenty of hickory wood ter smoke de meat." In a "big log smokehouse," they would "hangs hit full of meat and den builds a smoke fire in de middle of hit and den de men folks would work in shifts ter keep dis wood fire goin fer several days, den dis meat was ready ter hang up in another building made specially fer meat." Other plantations utilized underground storage. On one eastern Tennessee farm, "the fresh meat would be placed in the upper cave and covered with walnut leaves." The hillside cavern maintained such a cool temperature that the meat "would keep there just as though it were a refrigerator."[40]

3 Slaves in Commerce and Travel Capitalism

> A black man was growed fo' he knowed that the whole world didn't belong ter his ole Marster. – Oliver Bell, northern Alabama slave

Well before the Civil War, the Mountain South was integrated into national and world markets. The region was incorporated into the world economy as a peripheral fringe that produced raw materials and foodstuffs to provender the plantation economies of the U.S. South, Latin America, and the West Indies. In addition, Appalachian raw agricultural produce, light manufactures, and extractive commodities were exported to the U.S. Northeast and to western Europe to be exchanged for manufactured goods and tropical imports. Rivers, canals, turnpikes, roads, and railroads provided the vast majority of the land area of Southern Appalachia direct access to distant markets. The region's export systems were highly rationalized around wagoning, boating, and overland livestock drives. Because of the natural beauty and the cooler climate, travel capitalism was entrenched in Southern Appalachia to serve Americans and Europeans who sought to escape the unhealthy conditions of humid coasts and crowded cities.

Support services for external trade and for travel were concentrated in the region's towns and villages. External trade triggered a network of commodity chains in which urbanizing centers subsumed nearby smaller towns, villages, and hamlets. In this way, the region's fragile town economies were integrated into the spatial organization of the capitalist world system. For it was through these towns and villages that the region's trade goods and travelers moved. Public inspection stations, banks, merchants, manufacturers, canals, railroads, and shipping wharves were centralized in these towns. Smaller villages and towns moved commodities to regional bulking centers that had better access to transportation or were more commercialized. For example, many small river villages temporarily warehoused goods to be forwarded to larger towns. Reeds' Landing located in Greenup County,

Kentucky, was such "a public trading place and shipping place. In bad weather they kep' the grain an' things they was going to ship in the warehouse."[1]

From these smaller towns, trade goods moved to larger regional trading hubs, which provided "export linkages" for the distant transport of bulky or perishable produce and "import linkages" for the wholesale distribution of foreign commodities. For example, Tidewater Virginia grain brokers received regular consignments from farmers in several Blue Ridge counties through Lexington, Milton, and Warren, three Appalachian towns with access to the James River and Kanawha Canal. Such small towns were intermediate distribution points for large volumes of trade goods moving out of and into the Appalachian hinterlands. Consider, for example, three tiny eastern Tennessee towns. In the 1840s, the little community of Jonesboro exported vast amounts of agricultural produce and imported merchandise "direct from Baltimore through the Lynchburg market, and cotton and sugar and other heavy articles [were] imported from Charleston, Hamburg and Augusta." Further southeast, merchants in the towns of Kingston and Athens expended nearly $170,000 annually to import goods from Eastern markets and to transport agricultural produce down river via Chattanooga to Alabama and Mississippi markets.[2]

Situated at major transportation crossroads, the region's larger towns functioned as "bulking centers" for adjacent smaller villages, agricultural hinterlands, and extractive enclaves. Cumberland and Hagerstown, Maryland; Staunton and Winchester, Virginia; Wheeling, Morgantown, and Charleston, West Virginia; Knoxville and Chattanooga in Tennessee; and Rome, Georgia, were regional distribution centers for the export of Appalachian commodities and for the import of foreign goods back into the countryside. In a sense, then, these centralized towns served as first-level "distribution zones" for large adjacent agricultural, manufacturing, and extractive "production zones." From these Appalachian bulking centers, exports were shipped to several intermediate, inland distribution centers, including Cincinnati, Pittsburgh, Memphis, St. Louis, Louisville, Williamsburg, Petersburg, Richmond, Lexington, Nashville, Montgomery, Augusta, Columbus, and Greenville. From these inland transshipment points, Appalachian exports finally arrived at one of several southern or northeastern seacoast trade centers, from which these goods were redistributed inland to nearby consumers or were shipped by ocean to distant domestic or foreign markets. Philadelphia, Baltimore, Charleston, and New Orleans processed and reexported Appalachian grains, cotton, tobacco, hogs, cattle, or livestock by-products.[3]

This slave woman operated her owner's small inn that served rafts and boats on the Tennessee River outside Chattanooga. *Source: Harper's*, 1858.

Nonagricultural Occupations of Mountain Slaves

Town commerce, transport systems, travel capitalism, and industrial enterprises generated a demand for laborers, including slaves and free blacks. We can determine one rough estimate of the nonagricultural occupations of Mountain South slaves by examining the occupations of their masters. Nearly one-quarter of Appalachia's slaveholders identified themselves as being employed full time in retail trades, transportation, tourism, manufacturing, or extractive industry. Another 11 percent described themselves as "gentleman farmers" who mixed farming with nonagricultural enterprises. When we allocate slaves to their masters' occupations, we discover that nearly one-third of the region's slaves may have been employed full time in commerce and industry, and another 12 percent were shifted between agricultural and nonagricultural tasks. Clearly, Appalachian slaveholders invested their unfree laborers in nonagricultural enterprises to a much greater degree than did Lower South planters. Only about one-quarter of all Southern slaves worked outside agriculture. In comparison, Appalachian slaveholders were applying less than three-fifths of their unfree laborers exclusively to agricultural production. In addition, 55 percent of Appalachian free blacks were employed in town commerce, manufacturing, and extractive industry. In reality, slaves and free black Appalachians were probably more critical to regional manufacturing, commerce, and extractive industry than they were to agriculture.[4]

Nearly ninety thousand black Appalachians comprised more than two-fifths of the region's nonagricultural labor force, and 88 percent of them were enslaved workers. In the Appalachian counties of Alabama, Kentucky, South Carolina, Tennessee, and Virginia, slaves and free blacks accounted for more than half of all the nonagricultural workers. More than two-fifths of the nonagricultural occupations in western North Carolina and northern Georgia were held by black Appalachians. Slaves and free blacks made up only about 15 percent of the population, but they accounted for more than two-fifths of the nonagricultural labor force. Surprisingly, slaves and free blacks had a dramatic presence in those parts of Southern Appalachia where there were fewest slaves. In eastern Kentucky, black Appalachians represented less than 8 percent of the population, but they made up more than half the nonagricultural labor force. Similarly, that 6 percent of West Virginians who were black held nearly one-fifth of the nonagricultural occupations.[5]

Even though they constitute 85 percent of the region's population, white Appalachians were underrepresented in occupations outside agriculture. In fact, there were only 1.3 white laborers to every black worker outside agriculture. In the Appalachian counties of Kentucky, North Carolina, South Carolina, Tennessee, and Virginia, there was more than one black worker for every white laborer in nonagricultural enterprises. Slaves offered a dramatic presence in eastern Kentucky's nonagricultural enterprises. Only one of every thirteen eastern Kentuckians was black, but that tiny fraction of the population filled more than half of the nonagricultural jobs. Even in West Virginia, blacks appeared in the nonagricultural labor force nearly three times more often than their presence in the population would cause us to predict.

Dramatic as these statistics are, they are probably undercounts of the black Appalachian presence in nonagricultural sectors. The two earlier estimates offer no picture (a) of those slaves hired out by agricultural masters to nonagricultural employers or (b) of those slave artisans who worked in commerce or industry on plantations that commingled farming with commercial or industrial enterprises. To investigate these two categories more closely, we must incorporate evidence from the slaves themselves. Probably one-quarter of all Appalachian slaves were hired out each year. Almost 87 percent of slave hires were made to nonagricultural occupations, for these were the economic activities that offered highest annual wages to owners. As a result, more than one-fifth of all Appalachian slaves were probably hired out to work in nonagricultural occupations.[6]

To arrive at the most accurate portrayal, however, we must also incorporate those slave artisans and laborers who were employed by their own masters in occupations other than agriculture. No matter the size of their farms, Mountain South slaveholders were multifunctional in the range of their economic activities. For example, Steve Connally described his master's plantation in Murray County, Georgia, as "a whopper" on which they "made everything an' fixed [thei]r cotton, tanned hides an' made shoes and all jes like all de big places did. De big house, de weavin' house, de tannin' yard an' sugarmill an' slave quarters made a little town itself." Because of that diversity, nearly one-third of the work time of Appalachian slaves was divided among tasks other than crop cultivation and livestock tending. Moreover, one of every nine Appalachian slaveholders mixed farming with nonagricultural enterprises. Medium to large plantations integrated stores, inns, hotels, and toll gates for roads, bridges, and ferries. In addition, slaveholders operated most of the region's commercial mills, distilleries, and blacksmitheries. Cotton ginning and tobacco manufacturing were common commercial activities on the medium to large plantations.

Elite occupations were those that released slaves from field labor and permitted slaves more time to work with minimal white supervision. In addition, elite occupations were those skills associated with the master's production of market commodities or those skills prized in the operation of the masters' households. While all slaves were assigned some nonagricultural tasks, a sizable minority were highly skilled and specialized. In the United States, about one-third of all male slaves and about one-quarter of all female slaves were employed in occupations other than common field labor. Among male slaves, 3.2 percent were drivers; 3 percent were domestics; and another 26 percent were skilled and semiskilled artisans and livestock specialists. Slave women had fewer opportunities for acquiring skills, so 18.4 percent were domestics, and 8 percent were textile artisans or semiskilled specialists. Mountain South plantations structured opportunities for the emergence of elite artisan occupations more often than these national trends. Appalachian slaves were skilled industrial artisans and commercial laborers 1.3 times more often than other U.S. slaves, but they were three times more likely to rise to "driver," the top management position to which a slave could aspire. Appalachian slaves were allocated to full-time domestic occupations 1.4 times more often than other U.S. slaves. Moreover, more than 3 percent of Appalachia's slaves were employed full time as literate toll collectors and as commercial and industrial laborers in nonagricultural enterprises that operated on plantations.[7]

When information is aggregated from the Appalachian slave narratives about slave hires and about nonagricultural specialists, the estimate of nonagricultural occupations of Appalachian slaves is considerably higher than the previous rough estimate. In reality, Appalachian slaveholders allocated less than half their slave labor to full-time agricultural production. Nearly three-fifths of the region's slaves probably worked full time or part time in nonagricultural occupations. About one-fifth of Appalachian slaves were employed as full-time drivers or as domestic servants, and another 9 percent were part-time skilled artisans who produced market commodities for their masters. However, more than one-quarter of the region's slaves were employed full time as artisans, specialists, and laborers in commercial and industrial activities.

Black Appalachians in Town Commerce

By 1860, nearly one-quarter of the Appalachian population was concentrated in towns, villages, and hamlets, and black Appalachians formed a significant component of the commercial labor force that resided in those small urban areas. About 6 percent of the region's slaves were employed full time in commerce and trade. More than 10 percent of the slave hires were contracted with commercial enterprises, like stores, shops, inns, hotels, and travel resorts. Between 1850 and 1860, Appalachian masters were probably hiring out nearly six thousand slaves per year to work as laborers and artisans in commerce and trade. In addition, more than one-half of free black Appalachians resided in the region's towns, and one-quarter of them were employed in commerce, trade, or transportation. Moreover, one of every three free blacks bound out by the region's poorhouses was indentured to a town-dweller who was engaged in some commercial pursuit. Throughout the region, black Appalachians supplied labor for public works, for retail enterprises, for inns and hotels, and for artisan shops; were servants in town households; and were highly visible in the informal economy. In larger towns, like Knoxville or Winchester, one-third to two-fifths of the residents were slaves and free blacks. In middle-size towns, like Hagerstown, black Appalachians could constitute as much as one-quarter or more of the population. In towns located in the Appalachian counties of Alabama and Georgia, slaves and free blacks accounted for nearly half the population. Even in the region's smaller villages – like Richmond, Kentucky, or Martinsburg, West Virginia, or Franklin, North Carolina – one-quarter to one-third of the residents were black Appalachians.[8]

Free blacks formed small communities within Appalachian towns, and they tended to be concentrated into small houses in a few alleyways. Black Appalachians were such a significant part of local commerce that their contributions were acknowledged – both positively and negatively – in public documents. Because free blacks were a "valuable labor supply," several Loudoun County, Virginia, merchants and shop owners petitioned the state legislature for relief from the law requiring emancipated slaves to leave the state. In contrast, a Knoxville newspaper editor complained about the large numbers of "poor, raggedy" free black males who were "seen every day of the week, lounging on the street corners," seeking day labor. When the First Baptist Church of Knoxville opened its doors in 1850, the local newspaper commented that twenty of its forty-six members were black. Because of the frequent presence of slaves and freedmen, Appalachian municipalities developed "black codes" to regulate their behavior and employment. Town sergeants attempted to prevent free blacks and slaves from purchasing liquor and from attending public assemblies. Blacks were forbidden to stand, smoke, or spit on sidewalks, to empty kitchen slops in public areas, to dance or run in the streets, to utter profanity publicly, to collect on street corners, to ride in licensed hacks, or to be abroad after the 7:30 P.M. "black curfew." Moreover, town ordinances specified the circumstances under which free blacks and slaves could engage in trade. To justify the reenslavement of free blacks, state and local laws "criminalized" poverty and vagrancy and prohibited

In addition to agriculture, many mountain slaveholders invested in town enterprises to which they allocated slave laborers, like this hotel valet and hostler. *Source: Harper's*, 1855.

numerous forms of conduct that were usually tolerated when committed by whites. Unemployed free blacks were subject to arrest and indenturement by the county poorhouses that operated in Appalachian towns.[9]

Throughout the South, public works were constructed by blacks; thus, slaves graded, paved, and cleaned streets, built bridges, maintained canals and sewers, and collected garbage. Like other urban centers, Appalachian towns also employed slaves on public works and in public services. Slaves provided most of the labor to construct courthouses in McDowell, Cherokee, Watauga, Macon, and Henderson Counties and university buildings in Blue Ridge Virginia. After one Virginia slave burned his master's barn "containing about 1500 lbs Tobacco, Straw & Shucks Corn & Oats," the court sentenced him to lifetime labor on public works in the towns and villages of Nelson County. In all eight Southern states where Appalachian counties were located, laws permitted county sheriffs to hire to towns for public service the runaway slaves in their custody. For example, the towns of Roanoke and Charlottesville in Virginia and McMinnville and Knoxville in Tennessee used black convicts or hired slaves for all kinds of public services. Knoxville hired slaves at $10 monthly to fight fires, collect garbage, and handle other public services. Slaves manned the "volunteer" fire company at Lexington, Virginia. Charleston, West Virginia, and other river towns paid free blacks to light lanterns around the landings. "Men who live[d] in nearby houses [were paid] for lighting them every night and putting them out every morning." In Blue Ridge Virginia, slaves and free blacks worked as "mailboys" to deliver mail between towns and outlying rural areas.[10]

About 8 percent of the region's free blacks and more than 7 percent of the region's slaves were hired as domestic servants in towns. Slaves could be hired at regular courthouse auctions for town domestic service. On "hiring day" in January 1858, for example, "at least 500 servants were for hire" at the Warrenton courthouse. Throughout the year, rural masters frequently hired surplus slaves to work in the households of nearby town families; even middling families used the services of slave nurses for infants and young children. A tiny minority of free blacks were employed in service occupations, most often as teachers or clergy. In Knoxville, Philip Fields worked as a schoolmaster, and Alf Anderson was a Methodist preacher. In Calhoun, Alabama, "a popular negro preacher" officiated at "nearly all the dark weddings." In some Blue Ridge Virginia towns, white congregations assisted the formation of separate black churches. For instance, Winchester Methodists trained four "colored preachers" and two "colored exhorters."[11]

Slaves and free blacks also worked in retail stores and shops. Isaac McNeel used slave laborers in the family store at Mill Point, West Virginia. Calvin Cowles, a western North Carolina merchant, specialized in roots and herbs that he exported to the U.S. Northeast and to England. He paid $8 monthly, plus clothing for slaves who worked in his Wilkesboro store. Cowles also hired and purchased slaves and then sublet them to other commercial or industrial enterprises. At his Murphy, North Carolina, store, William Holland Thomas utilized part of his slave labor force to organize and shelve merchandise and to pack commodities for shipment. The store at Traveler's Rest, Georgia, assigned slaves to load and unload, to wagon goods to distant towns and to make deliveries in the countryside. Even in tiny villages in places like Lee County, Virginia, or Fentress County, Tennessee, slaves worked as laborers in general stores and retail shops.[12]

Another 8 percent of the region's slaves were employed part-time or full time in artisan shops that flourished in towns. Appalachian owners increased the lifetime value of their laborers by contracting out idle children to learn trades. When they were adults, these new artisans could be hired at much higher rates. One Floyd County, Georgia, master regularly hired out young male slaves to a nearby town carpenter. One Washington County, Maryland, master "often hire[d] the children of [his] slaves out to nonslaveholders." In this way, James Pennington and his brother learned several trades through their successive hires to a pump-maker, a stonemason, a blacksmith, and a carpenter. About 5 percent of the region's slaveholders were artisans who employed their slaves full time in those enterprises. For example, Darst and Jordan, a Rockbridge County construction company, built large homes for slaveholders and undertook public works projects. Because they relied solely on a large slave labor force, the company regularly published newspaper advertisements warning townspeople not to distract them from their gruelling construction labor by hiring them for evening or weekend chores. In Hagerstown, Maryland, a "shrewd, active, enterprising, and faithful" slave helped publish the local newspaper for several years.[13]

Along two narrow alleys in Winchester, Virginia, nineteen free blacks operated shops, including a baker, a druggist, four blacksmiths, three coopers, two potters, five shoemakers, and three wagonmakers. In 1860 western North Carolina, there were forty free black artisans, including blacksmiths, shoemakers, carpenters, bakers, harness makers, tailors, barbers, mattress makers, hatters, saddlers, and stonemasons. In the tiny village of Blountville, Tennessee, Stephen Hopkins lived in a ramshackle shed adjacent to the blacksmith shop in which he labored for a white artisan. At Charleston, West Virginia, a free black undertaker buried poor whites and slaves. Numerous bricklayers, stonemasons, and stone fencers capitalized on the quarries in the vicinity of Warrenton, Virginia. The brooms of one western Maryland free black were so prized in the countryside that the owner of the Ferry Hill Plantation noted his name in his daily journal.[14]

Nearly one-fifth of the region's free blacks worked as artisans in manufactories, mills, or independent shops; and these town enterprises offered them the best avenues to wealth accumulation. Less than 8 percent of free black Appalachians owned land or their own town lots. In fact, they were seven times less likely to own land than their white counterparts. Still, a lucky few free blacks owned their own shops, and about 5 percent of free black Appalachians operated boarding houses or were small merchants. In Knoxville, there were several tiny shops owned by such artisans, situated along an alley off one of the main streets. Off that alley, John Dogan owned a blacksmith shop valued at $3,000; in his household also resided a hired blacksmith apprentice. Alfred Anderson ran a saloon and ice cream parlor. Henri Franklin, a brickmason, and James Brown, a shoemaker, also owned their own small businesses. Next door, other black households lived more precarious existences. George Boylett maintained his five-person household working as a landless blacksmith. Also nearby were a shoemaker, a barber, a basketmaker, and a cooper who were landless and poor. Several blocks away, Nathan Wright operated a boarding house on a town lot he did not own. William Lewis made a much more spectacular showing in Chattanooga. Lewis had been a slave who, "being an expert blacksmith, had purchased his time for $350 a year. He was soon able to buy his wife and himself at $1,000 each." He set up a shop, hired other hands, and expanded into the production of wagons. Subsequently, he accumulated enough wealth to build a house and to purchase the freedom of his six-year-old son, his mother, his aunt, his two brothers, and his sister. Lewis's artisanry was so respected in the 1830s that the aldermen hired him to forge Chattanooga's town emblem. Despite his reputation, however, Lewis "was not able to do business in his own name, under the black laws, and was obliged to pay a white man largely to legalize his transactions."[15]

Black Appalachians in Travel Capitalism

Nearly one-half of the region's counties were heavily dependent upon travel capitalism (see Map 7), including sixty-six local economies that attracted tourists to 134 mineral spas: four in northern Alabama, thirteen in northern Georgia, nineteen in east Kentucky, six in western Maryland, six in western North Carolina, twenty-three in Appalachian Tennessee, forty-nine in Blue Ridge Virginia, and thirteen in West Virginia. Several horse-racing centers also attracted travelers. The region's inns, hotels, and tourist resorts drew their profits almost exclusively from those passing through Appalachian counties, while the region's stage lines, toll roads, canals, and railroads drew a significant segment of their livelihood from tourists and drovers.[16]

Black Appalachians in Regional Tourism

Periodicals like *DeBow's Review* chastised well-to-do Southerners to "cease their annual migrations to the North" where they "squander[ed] millions." Trade journals claimed that the South had "watering places

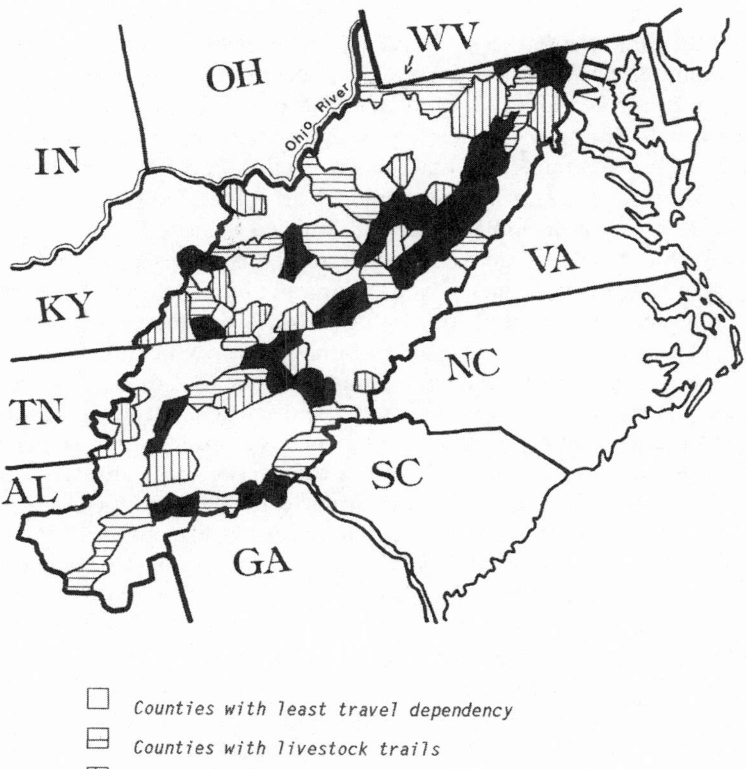

Map 7. Significance of travel capitalism in the Mountain South, 1860. *Source: The First American Frontier: Transition to Capitalism in Southern Appalachia, 1700–1860*, by Wilma A. Dunaway. Copyright © 1996 by The University of North Carolina Press. Used by permission of the publisher.

that need but fashion to make them equal, if not superior to Saratoga or Cape May." Rather than traveling to the politically alien North, Southern tourists could find in their own inland mountains "health, pleasure, intellectual pastime, and fashion, when it was vainly imagined they existed only afar off." Southerners were stoutly informed that the highlands of the Southern states contained "some of the wildest and most beautiful scenery that ever inspired a poet; spots sequestered from the busy routine of commercial life, where the spirit m[ight] find repose and revel in a satisfied sense of the grandeur and loveliness of Nature." Besides, reminded the *Southern Literary Messenger*, "the very difficulties of getting there have had the effect of rendering the society more exclusive."[17]

To support the sectional "stay-at-home" campaign, planter families trekked annually into the Southern mountains to avoid the humid conditions that bred epidemics of cholera and yellow fever in their home climates. The social season at the Appalachian mineral springs catered to Tidewater and Lower South elites who traveled the same circuit every year, many of whom constructed elaborate absentee homes in the vicinity of their favorite watering spots. Since "taking the cure" required at least three weeks, spa-goers visited four or five resorts during "the season." Visits to the mineral springs also offered important political opportunities for powerful planters who were separated by distance during the rest of the year. At Appalachian summer resorts, wealthy planters and merchants commingled with powerful politicians, "communicating to each other the information they br[ought] from their respective countries."[18]

Widely promoted by European and American medical journals and travel books, several Appalachian springs emerged as "celebrated resorts of fashion and abodes of health." By the late 1840s, tourists could combine road, railroad, steamboat, canal, and stage connections to reach the mountains "with far greater ease, safety and expedition." Northeastern and southern newspapers regularly advertised travel routes, the medicinal applications for the waters, and the schedule of entertainment at major Appalachian spas. By the 1830s, a Richmond newspaper foresaw that the "high prices of cotton and tobacco in the South and the superabundant capital in the North, w[ould] bring multitudes to the mountains who have never before experienced the incalculable value of these fountains of health." The prediction was accurate, for by 1835, the Appalachian resorts were being annually patronized by ten thousand to fifteen thousand tourists. By 1840, these summer resorts were among the wealthiest commercial enterprises in the Mountain South.[19]

Census manuscripts and company records document the extensive employment of slaves at mineral resorts. All the larger mountain spas owned slaves and advertised to lease slaves during their busy seasons. Appalachian slaveholders hired out surplus laborers to service baths, provide music, clean, and cook. Richmond slave exchanges recruited laborers for the mineral spas of Virginia, West Virginia, and North Carolina. In 1853, one such agent advertised "Fifty servants wanted for the Springs, viz. Dining Room Servants, Chambermaids." Another advertised a Nelson County "celebrated musician and fiddler" for hire. A few examples will demonstrate the pervasive presence of slave laborers at these exclusive resorts. West Virginia's White Sulphur Springs, the queen of the

Slave musicians at a Chattanooga hotel. *Source: Harper's*, 1858.

Appalachian resorts, boasted $100,000 worth of real estate and $56,000 in slaves. An 1848 European visitor to "the White" reported that three slave musicians played for their nightly jigs, using a fiddle, a tambourine, and "the third the skull of an ass, played upon by a collar bone of the same animal." Because he "play[ed] well on the fiddle," a slave named Ochrey was hired every summer to Shannondale Springs. In western North Carolina, James R. Love used part of his labor force of eighty-five slaves to operate a fashionable mineral spa. James and John Patton distributed seventy-eight slaves between their Asheville hotel and their resort at Warm Springs.[20]

In 1854, slave trader John Armfield purchased Beersheba Springs in Grundy County, Tennessee. The four-hundred-guest hotel and adjacent springs were staffed by numerous slave coachmen, guides, musicians, and servants. Every year, nine hundred tourists visited east Kentucky's Estill Springs where the peak attractions were several masquerade balls at which slaves supplied the "Superior Band of Music." At eastern Tennessee's Montvale Springs, slaves serviced the one-hundred-room hotel, ballroom, ten-pin alley, shooting gallery, billiard parlor, bar, and croquet grounds and guided tourists on hunting, fishing, or hiking expeditions. One western Carolina master hired a slave blacksmith to the Fauquier County hot springs. Subsequently, the slave hired his time from his owner to open his own artisan shop there. Working for his own master, William Davis did "a little bit of everything 'round de hotel" and resort at Warm Springs in Scott County, Virginia. As a youngster, he "helped folks off the stage" while his parents did the cooking, and several other slaves worked as waiters, maids, and valets. During the off-season, Lower South planters were invited to send their work-worn slaves to Tennessee's Rhea Springs "to rejuvenate them and increase their value" prior to being sold or hired.[21]

As early as 1774, Thomas Jefferson built an inn to attract visitors to the Natural Bridge in Rockbridge County. A slave named Patrick Henry was Jefferson's unsupervised caretaker. By 1806, a lodge staffed by slaves made Weyer's Cave of Augusta County accessible to travelers. Slaves guided tours and played music for dances in one of its largest caverns. Eastern Kentucky slaves acted as cave guides for visitors and led hunting trips into the mountains. By the 1840s, Charleston speculators were developing the Black Mountains as tourist attractions. From Asheville, slaves drove travelers by hacks to the Stapp Inn at the foot of the mountains. Over three days, slaves guided guests on trout fishing, hunting, and sight-seeing excursions. As guests made the trek up the mountains, they stopped at the "Mountain House" to be served champagne and cold salmon by slaves. By the 1850s, slaves guided tourists to shelters on Mt. Mitchell and on Clingman's Dome, the highest points in the Smokies. Slaves staffed the fashionable hotel atop Lookout Mountain, and they led regular expeditions to mountain sites nearby, like Tallulah Falls in northern Georgia.[22]

Itinerant livestock drives, transport of trade goods, and visitations to the mineral spas spurred the proliferation of inns and hotels along major travel routes, on plantations, and in towns. These enterprises relied heavily upon slave labor, as a few examples will illustrate. For instance, "the business" of an Asheville inn was "left mostly to the black servants." In Sevier County, Tennessee, where there were very few slaves,

John McMahan owned five adults to staff his hotel. Similarly, G. G. Mitchell owned ten adult slaves to work in his McMinnville hotel. Even in tiny villages, stage waystations used slaves, as was the case for the Netherland Inn near Blountville. At more luxurious enterprises like those in Asheville, hotels drew on fifty or more slaves. James McConnel Smith, for instance, employed seventy-five slaves at the Buck Hotel. Plantations that offered public accommodations, like Traveler's Rest, assigned slaves to service their inns. Appalachian masters routinely hired surplus laborers to hotels and inns located in major Tidewater cities; in addition, about 1 percent of free blacks worked in hotels and inns.[23]

Black Appalachians in Livestock Driving

In addition to tourism, more than one-third of the Appalachian counties relied on grain sales and inns for itinerant livestock drives (see Map 7). By the 1820s, several major drover trails crisscrossed Southern Appalachia. The Wilderness Road and Cumberland Gap linked Kentucky to routes leading to the eastern seaboard and to southern routes through North Carolina. The Cumberland Road, western Virginia's Northwestern Turnpike, the Great Kanawha Turnpike, and the connector between Wheeling and Pennsylvania provided Midwestern access to eastern cities. By 1808, regular cattle drives were passing from Ohio over the Kanawha route to eastern markets. By 1826, more than sixty thousand hogs a year passed from Ohio across the Kanawha route to eastern markets. Livestock also moved south to the Atlantic Coast down the Tennessee River valley or across the French Broad trail in western North Carolina. Following these routes, drovers from outside the region moved 1,355,000 hogs, 100,600 cattle, and 86,870 horses and mules annually across Appalachian counties. In addition, Southern Appalachians exported more than one million hogs, nearly 450,000 cattle, and more than 90,000 horses and mules across these trails in the late 1850s. Highly rationalized for maximum efficiency, herds averaged 120 to 200 livestock, which traveled ten to twenty miles daily. Wealthier graziers and masters regularly utilized skilled slaves to move their large herds to market, as is evidenced by one journalist's sketch of a Blue Ridge slave drover. Because he "assisted frequently . . . in driving hogs," one West Virginia slave escaped after a livestock delivery to Alexandria.[24]

At one-day intervals along the trails, commercial "livestock stands" provided stables, pens, pastures, and feed for the herds and lodging for the drovers. Itinerant drives consumed nearly six million bushels of Appalachian corn every year, and each Appalachian farm owner could dispose of thirty-two bushels of surplus corn in this manner.

Consequently, more than one-fifth of the region's corn exports left the region "on the hoof." By the early 1800s, the Cherokees were operating "stock stands" and taverns to cater to the itinerant livestock droves headed south. For example, Cherokee slaveholder Joseph Vann used slaves to operate his large livestock stand on the Federal Road through northern Georgia. Some small Appalachian towns, like Bean Station, Benton, or Crossville in Tennessee, offered numerous large livestock stands to serve the itinerant drover trade. Smaller stands emerged at ferries, at turnpike crossroads, and near mountain gaps. Between eastern Tennessee and Asheville, herds were fed at fifteen livestock stands that were frequently manned by slaves. Each stand provisioned thirty to one hundred drives per year, feeding three thousand to ten thousand livestock. At the peak of the season of one western Maryland drover inn, "there would be thirty six-horse teams on the wagon yard, one hundred Kentucky mules, in an adjacent lot, one thousand hogs in other enclosures, and as many fat cattle." Several western Carolina masters utilized slaves at the livestock stands they operated to feed Blue Ridge Virginia mule drives and the horse and hog drives moving from east Tennessee and east Kentucky into South Carolina.[25]

Black Appalachians in Horse Racing

Horse racing was a common sport throughout the antebellum South, so it is not surprising that travel capitalism developed around this industry in Southern Appalachia. As part of their gala season for planter families, the region's mineral spas often sponsored thoroughbred races. In addition, several mountain towns were renowned for horse racing and stud farms. Racing, horse trading, and gambling were routine in Knoxville, Tennessee; Gainesville, Georgia; Morganton, North Carolina; Richmond, Kentucky; Warrenton, Virginia, and numerous other towns of Blue Ridge Virginia. In Shenandoah County, the town of New Market "was 'bout de head place . . . fur horse racin', an' all de gen'lemen fum far and near" competed and gambled on "de second Tuesdays in May an' October." Slaveholders organized a statewide association called the New Market Jockey Club, and the town was a center for breeding and training prime racing stock.[26]

Horse-racing masters purchased slaves who were expert jockeys, grooms, and livestock doctors. Cherokee planter Joseph Vann owned several skilled artisans to breed, train, and race his thoroughbreds throughout North Carolina, southeastern Tennessee, and northern Georgia. Charles Stewart worked all his life as a jockey and trainer for his master. During his teenage years, Stewart was a jockey who regularly "rid [sweep]stakes" and shorter races. Stewart was so skilled that his owner assigned him to supervise "studding" for other wealthy Virginia planters and frequently hired him out to train the horses of other Virginia, North Carolina, and Kentucky slaveholders. By the time he was twenty, Stewart had gained too much weight to continue as a jockey. However, he was promoted to the rank of stable boss so he could "take everything into [his] own keer" at his master's New Market stud farm and regional horse training center. At the commercial stable, Stewart "was de 'boss' ober nine little [slaves] an' four big ones, 'sides two white trash dey called 'helpers.'" In comparison to the typical Appalachian slave, this horse artisan led a privileged existence. Unlike the vast majority of Appalachian slaves, Stewart "had plenty o' money," and he worked without white supervision, "nobody to say nothin'" to him. In addition to serving townspeople and travelers, Stewart managed "a nice stable full of nags," and he "train[ed] an' exercise[d] horses, an' sen[t] 'em up" to seasonal races at Warrenton "when dey was wanted." There was always "a big force of [slave] boys an' men at wuk" on the animals, "two boys to each horse." His duties expanded to every facet of running the renowned stable and stud farm, so the slave driver always "had [his] helpers an' jockeys, grooms an' stablemen, under [him]." In the spring and fall every year, Stewart "would take de horses 'bout fum place to place, en 'cordance wid [his] marster's orders." When he moved horses to distant races in Kentucky, Virginia, or North Carolina, Stewart supervised several other slaves for long periods of time. "At such a distance from his master, and unable even to read his letters of instruction himself," Stewart was astute at "keeping long accounts in his head, and handling the large sums of money which were constantly passing through his hands." When he needed to read or write his master's correspondence, "de squire or de jedge was always somewhar 'bout to read [the] marster's letters" to him.[27]

Black Appalachians in Transportation

Southern Appalachians exported commodities to distant markets through interconnected rivers, canals, and overland routes. By 1860, more than 8 percent of Appalachian slaves were employed in the transportation systems that moved trade goods into and out of the region. More than one-fifth of the region's slave hires were contracted with companies that operated, maintained, or constructed transportation systems. Between 1850 and 1860, Appalachian masters were probably hiring out more than eleven thousand slaves per year to water and overland transportation companies. At least 4 percent of the region's slaveholders operated their own transport enterprises as part of multifunctional plantations,

Slave roustabouts provided most of the labor for steamboats. Such long-term hireouts kept black Appalachian husbands away from their families most of the year. *Source: Harper's*, 1855.

thereby employing another seventy-five hundred slaves to operate ferries, toll roads or bridges, wagons, stages, or boats. In 1856, one of southwest Virginia's large iron manufacturers complained that the building of canals and turnpikes was draining slaves away from industry and that this competition had raised the prices for annual hires. An 1859 Virginia newspaper commented that "contractors on public works are hiring men at $150 which affects all other classes."[28]

Black Appalachians in Water Travel

Rivers were the dominant transportation mechanism for accomplishing interregional trade throughout the antebellum United States. Contrary to popular stereotypes, Southern Appalachia was not land-locked in mountainous isolation. Fourteen navigable river systems and three canals linked the region to the broader system of waterways that fed ultimately to the Atlantic or Gulf seacoasts (see Map 8). Until the 1850s, the region's external trade was effected through interconnected networks of major rivers, secondary tributaries, state turnpikes, and county roads. Seven of the region's counties were connected directly to the Atlantic Ocean, either

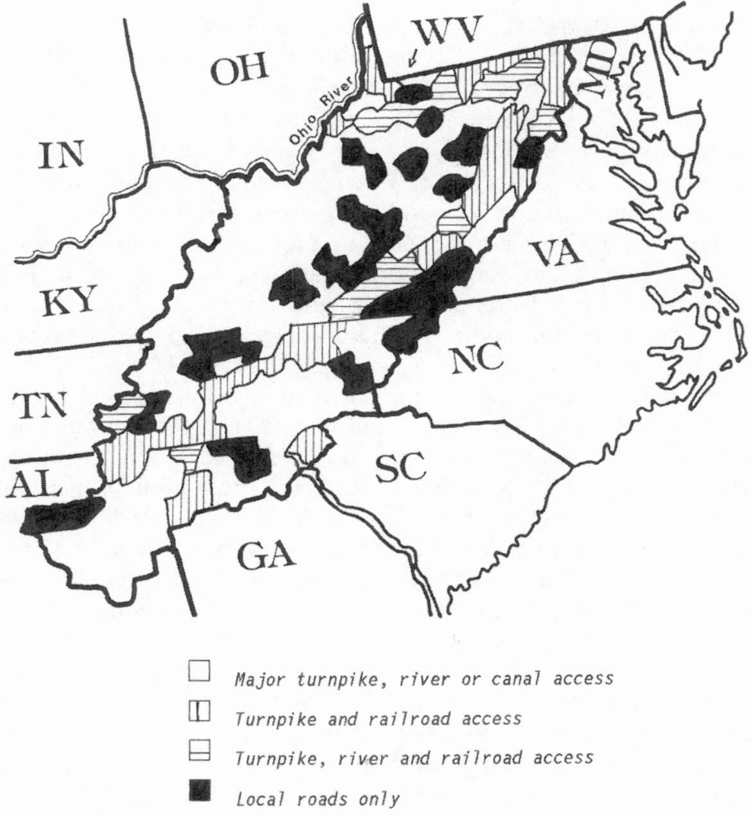

Map 8. Mountain South transportation networks. *Source: The First American Frontier: Transition to Capitalism in Southeren Appalachia, 1700–1860*, by Wilma A. Dunaway. Copyright © 1996 by The University of North Carolina Press. Used by permission of the publisher.

through river systems or canals. In the northern tier, the Chesapeake and Ohio Canal connected western Maryland directly to the coast. At the southeastern extreme, the Tugaloo-Savannah River system linked four Appalachian counties of Georgia and South Carolina directly into the Atlantic Ocean. One-third of the Appalachian counties were situated within the Ohio River Basin and linked to the Gulf of Mexico. Twelve West Virginia counties and three eastern Kentucky counties lay immediately upon the Ohio. Another thirty-three West Virginia, eastern Kentucky, and eastern Tennessee counties enjoyed secondary access to the Ohio River because they were transversed by the Monongahela, the Kanawha, the Guyandote, the Tug, the Kentucky, the Big Sandy, and the Cumberland Rivers, which fed into the Ohio. To the south, the Tennessee River system meandered through the valleys and mountains of thirty-three Tennessee, Georgia, and Alabama counties, ultimately to connect with the Ohio River. At the southern extreme, twenty-three Georgia and Alabama counties were served by the Coosa River, which fed into the Alabama River at Montgomery to link this zone of Southern Appalachia to Mobile and the Gulf of Mexico. State legislatures created as public monopolies numerous navigation companies that were authorized to make river improvements, construct boats, operate landings for tolls, and accept payment to transport passengers and commodities. These navigation companies relied heavily upon slave laborers.[29]

Along the region's major waterways, more than five hundred small communities became landings for commercial activity and boat construction. Even natural sites like large caves were transformed into boat landings and warehouses where slaves loaded and unloaded commodities. Most of the river systems were improved with canals, locks, sluices, or dams to bypass shoals and falls. Probably the most famous was the Muscle Shoals of the Tennessee River, where the federal government funded the development of a canal. Because of the interruption in the flow of commodities, merchandise was transferred to canal boats or barges for transshipment to steamboats. The Muscle Shoals canal contractor advertised to hire five hundred slaves annually, and the company drew most of those laborers from the Appalachian counties of northern Alabama. The canal was so desperate for workers that it offered day wages to entice temporary hires, in addition to the customary annual contracts. In the 1830s, the canal company was paying $15 monthly for slave hires. The canal also assured slaveholders that it would take medical responsibility "for any injury or damage" that occurred to slaves "in the progress of blasting of rock or the caving in of banks."[30]

Seven Appalachian counties of Virginia were connected to Richmond and to the Atlantic coast by way of the Roanoke River and the James River and Kanawha Canal. Virginia's James River and Kanawha Canal purchased slaves and exploited black convicts. The Canal Company also regularly advertised to hire slaves from Appalachian counties. In April 1838, for instance, the canal was "in immediate want of SEVERAL HUNDRED good laborers." John Jordan and John Irvine contracted to construct the canal extension from Lynchburg to Buchanan, relying on forty-eight owned and six hundred hired slaves. In addition, a Rockbridge County contractor used slaves to build the extension between Lexington and the main canal. After construction, slaves were used to repair locks

Slaves regularly transported trade goods on rafts and batteaux on the three major canal systems that connected the Mountain South to major rivers. *Source: Harper's*, 1852.

and to do regular maintenance. When the canal began to experience labor shortages in the 1850s, the superintendent "urge[d] on the board the propriety of purchasing a sufficient number of young men and boys" to keep the canal "in repair." The company found it cheaper to purchase slaves than to endure the "difficulty, trouble, and expense" of hiring laborers "at exorbitant rates." Moreover, the canal considered slaves "an economical measure" because of "the great savings" over the cost of hiring white laborers. In the northern tier of Appalachian counties, the Shenandoah and Potomac Rivers and the Chesapeake and Ohio Canal linked together into a network that drew eighteen Appalachian counties of Virginia, West Virginia, and Maryland into the wider system of national commerce. The Maryland canal relied on slaves just as heavily as the Virginia and Alabama canals. By the 1850s, *DeBow's Review* was claiming that "in ditching, particularly in canals" a female slave could "do nearly as much work as a man." The periodical had arrived at this conclusion because slave women had been employed extensively to do canal ditching during construction of the Chesapeake and Ohio Canal.[31]

Export by river was highly rationalized, for this mode of transportation required skilled specialists. Because professionals were needed to construct boats and freight goods to market, some large farmers and merchants owned skilled boatmen. A large flatboat required four laborers and a pilot to make three or four round trips yearly from Appalachian rivers to distant markets. Large plantations and merchants often managed their own keelboats, canal boats, or packet boats to transport goods to market for commissions. River wharves, landings, and warehouses were owned and operated by companies that accepted goods on consignment for transport to distant markets. On all the Appalachian rivers, boatyards developed as points for accumulating commodities for export or for wholesale distribution. Slaves built and repaired boats, worked as laborers, oarsmen, or pilots, and loaded commodities at Appalachian river sites like McNair's Boatyard in northwestern Georgia, Hildebrand's Boatyard on the Ocoee River, the wharf at Jordan's Point in Rockbridge County, Virginia, or the boatyard at Kingsport, Tennessee.[32]

Several types of river craft linked together the region's major waterways, canals, and ferries. For unidirectional transport down river, local companies constructed flatboats, tobacco canoes, broad horns, Kentucky boats, and bateaux. To permit round-trip travel, exporters relied on larger keelboats or packet boats and, after 1840, more versatile steamboats. The flow of Appalachian commodities often involved the use of all three types of craft. Smaller craft carried commodities to transshipment sites for transfer to larger packets or steamboats, forming an interdependent network of shipping methodologies that used different parts of the rivers. Flatboats and arks carried goods out of tributaries where larger boats could not float safely. Special barges and tows were used on canals, while stationary, horse-propelled boats were operated at ferries.[33]

Skilled slave boatmen were common sights on Appalachian rivers, and many of them transported goods without white supervision. By the early 1800s, Blue Ridge Virginia and upper West Virginia masters were already dependent upon water transport and upon income from the lease of slaves to Richmond companies, as evidenced by the frequency with which black boatmen escaped from their masters. In 1809, an Amherst County master offered a reward for the return of his "noted Water-man" who had been hired out on annual contract and had "been accustomed to run the river from Lynchburg to Richmond for many years." Owned by Sears Ferry, Ned Henderson had "been engaged in running the river for several years" when he ran away in 1816. Some Blue Ridge Virginia and western Maryland masters had annual contracts with the U.S. Navy and with the Merchant Marine, which employed slaves as waiters, cooks, and general servants. One Staunton slave had "been frequently at sea" and had "made trips to the West Indies and other places" because his master had hired him frequently to the U.S. Navy before 1815. By 1860, Virginia free black Appalachians reported "boatmen" as the second most frequent category of employment. Several times a year, West Virginia enterprises shipped salt, coal, manufactures, and farm produce from Charleston, West Virginia, to Cincinnati and New Orleans on fleets of twenty flatboats manned by ten hands each, many of them slaves. Trained slaves also operated canal and river boats to inland regional markets, like Richmond, Lynchburg, Augusta, Savannah, or Columbia. Blue Ridge Virginia plantations used slaves to boat produce to Richmond and Lynchburg, and they routinely hired out young slave boys to work on James River and Kanawha Canal boats. The Oxford Iron Works assigned slaves to man canal barges from southwest Virginia to Richmond. Unsupervised slaves regularly operated locks and boats along the Chesapeake and Ohio Canal. While traveling along the canal between Cumberland, Maryland, and Harper's Ferry, West Virginia, one passenger observed: "the black boy who drove the horses that was attached to the Boat fell into the lock and was drowned."[34]

On all the rivers in Appalachian Virginia, slaves regularly transported commodities on boats that were seventy-five to one hundred feet long, each manned by five artisans. Slave crews usually traveled in fleets that used eighteen-feet-long tin horns to signal to one another and to alert river wharves they were about to land. On the Shenandoah River, forty- to eighty-feet-long gundalows hauled vast quantities of iron and lumber to Harper's Ferry. Each of these large flatboats was operated by two slave boatmen standing on platforms at the bow and stern. In northern Georgia, Traveler's Rest slaves boated produce down the Tugaloo River to Augusta. Slaves even traversed the two Appalachian rivers that contemporary historians have believed were unnavigable. The New River fed into the Ohio River indirectly through its linkage to the Kanawha, but it received no state funding to alleviate blockages at several shoals. Consequently, the New was believed to have been of little utility to the seven West Virginia, Virginia, and North Carolina counties it bisected. In contrast to those contemporary notions, antebellum travelers and journalists documented slave boatmen "shooting the rapids" on the New River in West Virginia. Jutting out of the Smoky Mountains, the French Broad River is the second Appalachian waterway that has been described as too shallow and rugged to permit river traffic. The narrative of a Spartanburg, South Carolina, slave casts doubt on the inaccessibility of the French Broad, as well. Dick Lookup was owned by a Spartanburg plantation that used boats to export cotton via Columbia. The master also operated an absentee plantation in Polk County, North Carolina, and he ran batteaux between the two locations. Five slaves used long poles and paddles to steer the boat. A "steerman" gave orders, two "privates" used paddles, and two "seconds" used poles. According to Lookup:

> Dey made de poles to suit de job. Some of de poles was longer dan others was. Some of dem was broad and flat at de end; others was blunt and others was made sharp. When de Broad River rose, sometimes de waves got higher dan [his] house. Den it was a real job to handle one of Marse's boats. Fact is, it was five men's jobs. Wid water a-roaring and a-foaming and a-gwine round like a mad tiger a-blowing his breath . . . you had to be up and a-doing something real fast. Sometimes dat river take your boat round and round like a merry-go-round. . . . Den it swing from dat whirl into a swift stream dat take you a mile a minute. . . . Den you see a tree a-coming right straight at you. . . . You had to git your poles and somebody had to let a pole hit dat tree ahead of de boat. Of course dat change de boat's course.

On one spring trip into western North Carolina, "Broad River was real narrow when [they] went up and she look like a lamb." When the slaves started back down river, however, "it had done tuck and rained and dem banks was vanished." The boatman recalled that "de rocks up dar" in North Carolina "was mo' scary looking" than the shoals in South Carolina. The crew managed to keep the boat afloat during the day, but that night they "run into a nine-mile shoal" that "throwed [their] boat in shallow water." After several hours work the next morning, the crew maneuvered the boat back into the main channel. The water was so deep and swift that they could not control it, so they "lay over a day and a half" to wait for the water to "recede back some." The water "was still so high dat [they] run over de shoals widout a tremor" and traveled nearly thirty miles in one day.[35]

By 1840, steam towboats, packet boats, and larger steamboats regularly served all the major navigable Appalachian rivers and many of the secondary tributaries of the Mountain South. As the primary vehicle for antebellum export trade, Appalachian steamboats relied heavily upon slave labor to make twelve round trips annually, many losing only ninety days per year due to unnavigable waters. In 1835, the down-river steamboat trade on the Ohio River totaled nearly $15 million, at least half that amount deriving from the Appalachian counties of the Ohio Basin. Several mountain masters operated steamboats as part of their portfolio of economic activities. In the 1830s, Cherokee master Joseph Vann manned a steamboat with slaves in order to act as a commission merchant to export and import between Chattanooga and New Orleans. Using slave pilots, engineers, and laborers, James King and Company plied the Tennessee with keelboats and steamers, averaging one trip monthly. Northern Alabama planter-merchant Robert Kyle invested in steamboats that hauled freight to New Orleans; except for the captains, his steamers were run by all-black crews. In the 1840s, Gabriel and Joseph Hughes purchased all the land from the foot of Lookout Mountain to the Coosa River to monopolize the river trade. To maximize profits, they owned and leased slaves, including pilots.[36]

Beginning in the 1830s, Ohio River steamboats hired slaves from eastern Kentucky, West Virginia, and Blue Ridge Virginia. An antebellum journalist described the bustle of activity on the Charleston, West Virginia, wharf where 125 slaves loaded and unloaded the steamboats that landed.

> They would jog along rolling barrels aboard with little spiked sticks, next they appeared each with a bundle of brooms on his shoulder, and in another two minutes the long, zigzagging, shambling lines was metamorphosed into a wriggling sinuosity formed of soap-boxes, or an unsteady line of flour-bags, each with ragged legs beneath it, or a procession of baskets or of bundles of laths. As each one picked up an article of freight, an overseer told him its destination. The negro repeated this, and kept on repeating it, in a singsong tone, as he shambled along, until one of the mates on the boat heard him and told him where to put it down, the duty of the mate being to distribute the cargo evenly, and to see that all packages sent to any given landing were kept together.[37]

Licensed by county courts as public monopolies, hundreds of local ferries played a crucial part in the flow of commodities from inland areas to the river systems. Since they were transshipment points between wagon and water transport, ferry sites stimulated the emergence of adjacent inns, warehouses, stores, and manufactories. As the "staging areas" for down-river flatboat movements, ferries were often collection points for agricultural or extractive exports and for the redistribution of imported goods. For example, ninety such communities developed around trade functions on the Tennessee River tributaries. Slave ferrymen were common throughout Southern Appalachia. One Fauquier County slave effected a successful escape because he had worked "several years as a ferryman." Numerous ferries operated throughout the Cherokee Nation. Since these ferries were situated in the flow of commerce southward, they were profitable enterprises. For instance, the small Downing Ferry in Forsyth County, Georgia, collected $550 annually in tolls in the 1830s. Little wonder, then, that most of these key transport points were owned by the Nation's elites. Eighteen wealthy Cherokees utilized slaves to operate boats and make repairs at their twenty-three ferries in southeast Tennessee, northern Georgia, and northern Alabama. At most of these ferries, slaves also worked in the supply depots and warehouses. In the panhandle of West Virginia, the Potomac Bridge Company's ferry was manned by Obed, a slave, and another bondsman piloted the Blue Ridge

Ferry of the James River and Kanawha Canal. West Virginia's Ansell Ferry Company used slave ferriers and toll collectors. At Traveler's Rest, slaves operated the ferry and the toll bridge across the Tugaloo River.[38]

Western Maryland's Ferry Hill Plantation has left us the clearest picture of how Appalachian masters employed slaves to operate ferries. John Blackford held a state franchise to operate a ferry across the Potomac River adjacent to his western Maryland plantation. Because it cut across the Chesapeake and Ohio Canal, the ferry was a profitable investment that returned more than $500 annually in the late 1830s. Two slaves were appointed as "Foremen of the Ferry," and they worked without supervision in a stone cottage near the ferry landing. One of the slaves was literate, so he daily recorded all ferriage tolls and delivered the cash to his master. Blackford afforded these slaves relative independence, as is evidenced from his daily reports of ferry management. He makes an entry, for example, that one of the slaves had been "in the Boat and has been during my absence." He comments several times in his journal that he has received no ferry report that day; however, he never expresses any particular concern about this, nor does he indicate that he punished the foremen. On one such occasion, he noted without anger or further comment: "Ned in the Boat. He has made no return of the ferriages since Saturday last, four days."[39]

Black Appalachians in Overland Transportation

In addition to river access, more than one-half the region's counties depended upon turnpike connections to move livestock and trade goods to distant markets (see Map 8). Two major national highways crisscrossed Southern Appalachia. Running east to west, the National Turnpike linked Baltimore to the Ohio River at Wheeling. From Philadelphia via Hagerstown, Maryland, the Great Philadelphia Wagon Road proceeded down the Valley of Virginia to link with eastern Kentucky's Wilderness Road and routes into eastern Tennessee. Interlinked with these national turnpikes were several major Appalachian livestock and wagon routes that connected the region to Philadelphia, Baltimore, Richmond, Louisville, and Lower South cities. With more than three-quarters of its land area linked by major trade routes to interstate thoroughfares, pre-1850 Southern Appalachia was no more isolated from the national economy than were most rural areas of New England or the Midwest.[40]

Most large and small towns routinely hired slaves to maintain roads and turnpikes. Hired slaves are listed in the Census manuscripts for the villages of Jacksonville, West Virginia, and Athens, Tennessee. The Massie family regularly hired slaves to maintain roads and bridges in Bath and Alleghany Counties. Private companies owned and hired slaves who were used to construct and repair these turnpikes in Virginia and West Virginia: Junction Valley, Swift Run Gap, Rockymount, Martinsburg and Potomac, Sinking Creek, and Craig's Creek. The Western Plank Road Company of North Carolina hired Appalachian slaves on monthly and annual contracts. The James River and Kanawha Turnpike Company and the Giles, Fayette, and Kanawha Turnpike used slaves for road construction and repairs. The Guyandotte Turnpike, the Beverly-Fairmont Turnpike, and the Frederick and Valley Turnpike Companies employed mixed labor forces of whites, slaves, and free blacks to construct and repair roads. Slaves were used to build, repair, and collect tolls for the Rockbridge County bridge across North River. Because roads were developed by private companies, they frequently crossed plantations where one of every three hundred Appalachian slaves was employed as a tollgate keeper. Plantations, like Traveler's Rest in northern Georgia or Brabson's Ferry in eastern Tennessee, kept slaves on duty full-time to collect tolls and to operate their bridges and ferries. The Ellerslie plantation of eastern Kentucky housed a slave family in a small cottage beside the Richmond Turnpike to collect tolls, make nearby repairs, and control the tollgates.[41]

Throughout most of the antebellum period, Southern Appalachians relied on five techniques of direct transport: packhorses, stages, wagons, boats, and overland drives. During the frontier years, residents of the most rugged terrain exported iron bars, salt, ginseng, furs, whiskey, and a variety of produce by packhorses. Stage coaches also hauled commodities to and from farms, merchants and towns along their routes. People who lived along major roads sent their goods to market by passing wagoners or stages that brought imports on their return trips. Some Appalachian slaves operated stages as their full-time employment. For instance, one western North Carolina master leased slaves annually to "a daily line of Stages running from Guntersville [Alabama] to Rome [Georgia]." Another Blue Ridge Virginia master employed a slave to drive the stage between Charlottesville and Richmond. To operate his stage line and mail contract from Augusta, Georgia, via Greenville, South Carolina, to Greeneville, Tennessee, Valentine Ripley of Henderson County, North Carolina, owned and hired slave artisans. Ripley's drivers averaged sixty miles per day because the company maintained contracts with inns along the route. The slave stage drivers sounded blasts on their long tin horns to notify innkeepers about the number of arriving guests and to alert them to ready a fresh team of horses for the next leg of the trip.[42]

As roads and turnpike connections improved, however, the more typical method of overland trading was transport by wagons. The region's major thoroughfares were busy places, filled with "jostling processions of freight wagons." Along the Appalachian turnpikes and roads of Maryland, Virginia, and West Virginia, "wagons were so numerous that the leaders of one team had their noses in the box at the end of the next wagon." In order to specialize in long-distance hauling, plantations or merchants often used slaves to operate their "line teams." For example, the Fotheringay Plantation of Montgomery County, Virginia, used slaves to operate the Alleghany Turnpike and to wagon long-distance freighters. Larger merchants who made monthly or bimonthly trading trips kept slave wagoners in their regular employ. In addition, a few free black Appalachians regularly hauled freight. Thomas Hewett and John Lipscomb owned their own small teamster businesses in Knoxville and in Botetourt County, Virginia, and two free black wagoners worked on contracts with Winchester merchants.[43]

Appalachian manufacturers and farmers often disposed of their products by sending their own trade wagons to market their commodities in distant communities. By the early 1800s, Blue Ridge Virginia masters prized their "good waggoners" who were "fond of the business" of making repeated trips to transport agricultural commodities to commission merchants in Alexandria, Richmond, and Lynchburg. The Oxford Iron Works used six slaves to wagon iron to Richmond and to return goods to the company store. At the Washington Iron Works in Franklin County, Virginia, slaves "drove wagons full of iron to landings on the Pigg and Staunton rivers for transportation by shallow-draft flatboat to distant markets." One small western North Carolina slaveholder regularly reported in his letters that slave wagoners were "hauling off iron" to Athens, Georgia. William Holland Thomas regularly employed a slave named Wagoner Dick to travel to South Carolina and Georgia to sell commodities and to purchase items for his stores. Similarly, the Traveler's Rest Plantation employed full-time slave wagoners to export commodities to Columbia and to Athens. A traveling journalist provides a description of the typical freight wagon managed by Appalachian slaves. On the turnpike in Fauquier County, a slave was seen driving a wagon that was twenty feet long, "higher at both ends than at the middle," and covered with a sailcloth. Drawn by six horses, the wagoner's skillful maneuvering kept the two-ton load moving up and down hills.[44]

James Hervey Greenlee provides a close look at the manner in which Appalachian masters entrusted much of their exporting business to skilled slave wagoners. Greenlee regularly sent freight teams from his western North Carolina plantation to market his surpluses to a Columbia commission merchant, and he utilized two skilled slaves to handle those transactions. Rarely did he accompany the wagons, and never did he note that he had hired some white to supervise the ventures. In March 1847, Greenlee prepared to send "a team of 6 mules & waggon to market" at Columbia, South Carolina. On that trip, his two slave wagoners hauled "2000 lb bacon & 270 lb Lard" in the large wagon, and "in the small waggon 1000 lb bacon 64 lbs Lard & some food." Two months later, Greenlee "had some corn shelled & started the waggon to Columbia with 33 bush Corn to sell 16 bushels to feed [the wagon mules] on & 43 lb feathers." Greenlee reported wagon trips to Columbia almost every month when the weather was suitable, so the wagoners were almost continuously on the road. They must have begun a new trip almost as soon as they returned from the previous load. In November of that year, Greenlee's slaves wagoned thirty bushels of corn, some fodder, thirty-five pounds of bacon, with thirteen pounds of dried beef for the slaves to eat on the road. Nearly a month later, the master noted in his diary that "Peter & Jerry got back with the wagon about dark from Columbia after being gone 26 days – all well could not sell the team brought our necessaries." During January and February, his slaves wagoned corn, meal, and flour to the nearby town where it was sold to merchants and at the public market. Since the two slave wagoners averaged three weeks or longer on Columbia trips and also hauled during the winter, these two artisans were clearly employed full time at commercial transport.[45]

Southern railroad construction surpassed national averages after 1845. As a result, annual hires to railroads became one of the most profitable economic enterprises of Appalachian slaveholders. By 1859, railroad construction companies solicited laborers from slaveholders at $150 annually plus insurance. By 1860, Appalachian masters were making one-fifth of their annual slave hires to transportation companies, and most of those contracts were with railroads. Between 1854 and 1862, the Baltimore and Ohio Railroad Company hired and purchased western Maryland and West Virginia slaves to work in construction gangs and to provide services to passengers. After 1850, railroad advertisements to purchase and to hire one hundred to four hundred slaves for construction projects appeared regularly in Virginia newspapers. In the 1840s, the Randolph Family hired slaves to work in construction gangs on the Louisa Railroad. After 1850, railroad advertisements also began to appear regularly in western North Carolina newspapers, usually recruiting large slave forces for construction. A railroad agent assured one western Carolina master that he could hire his male and female slaves "to advantage" prior to his harvest and that "the men especially w[ould] command high prices." Northern Alabama masters hired their slaves to railroad construction projects in central and southern Alabama at $20 monthly, with the proviso that slaves return temporarily for cotton harvests. One Alabama

Hired mountain slaves provided the labor to operate this steamboat that is being maneuvered through "the sucks" at Chattanooga. *Source:* Bryant, *Picturesque America.*

contractor advertised to hire 600 slaves for railroad construction and repair.[46]

By 1855, however, railroad development had occurred in fifty-three of the region's counties, linking the region even more firmly to Baltimore, Philadelphia, Richmond, Louisville, Nashville, St. Louis, and Charleston. Several regional railroads were constructed, repaired, and operated by slave laborers, including the Virginia-Tennessee Railroad, the Virginia Central, the Blue Ridge Railroad, the East Tennessee and Virginia Railroad, the Nashville and Chattanooga, the East Tennessee and Georgia Railroad, the Macon and Western of Georgia, and the Greensville and Roanoke Railroad. In the late 1830s, western Carolina masters began to hire slaves for railroad development in Georgia. Hamilton Brown was advised that "the state [wa]s building a Rail Road through the heart of Cherokee Country" and that "there [wa]s a great demand for labourers." Georgia companies were willing to hire slaves "for $30 per month payable every month," rates that were twice the average annual contract. To recruit the large labor force needed for railroad construction, several of western North Carolina's large slaveholders bought and hired slaves. Buncombe Countian James W. Patton, advertised to buy one hundred such laborers for his company's independent railroad spur through Asheville. By 1860, nearly six hundred slaves were engaged in railroad construction in western North Carolina. Male slave gangs dug track beds and laid rails while female slaves cooked and washed for the construction crews. By 1860, railroad construction was under way in a few Appalachian Alabama counties, so thirty-five slaves were enumerated in that year's census as "hired railroad laborers," supervised by a white foreman.[47]

Working eight-hour shifts for the Virginia Central Railroad, sixty slaves dug from each end of the Blue Ridge Tunnel. Two sets of hands regularly spelled each other on another Virginia line. The Blue Ridge Railroad relied on an integrated labor force made up of recent Irish immigrants and slaves. Georgia's Western and Atlantic Railroad and the Nashville and Chattanooga hired hundreds of slaves. The Virginia and Tennessee Railroad employed a year-round agent who traveled the countryside recruiting slave hires. When the company sent agents into Albermarle, Nelson, and Bedford Counties in 1851, they met little success, complaining to the owners "the great competition for hands will.... Keep prices up." After the railroad was constructed, the Virginia and Tennessee advertised for three hundred slaves each year to make repairs. By 1856, two-thirds of the 643 workers on the Virginia and Tennessee were hired slaves. Even at $200 per year, the company was convinced that hired slaves cost half as much in wages as white laborers. To overcome their labor shortages, Appalachian railroads implemented several strategies. The Virginia and Tennessee began to permit hired slaves to return temporarily to their masters during tobacco harvests. The East Tennessee and Virginia Railroad awarded grading contracts in two-mile stretches to nearby slaveholders who utilized their own laborers. "The grading of the line was all done with pick and shovel, mule and cart." Appalachian railroads also purchased and leased convict labor. When the state sold free blacks who had been convicted of crimes, railroads often purchased the re-enslaved laborers. The Tennessee Railroad Company and the Nashville and Chattanooga lobbied for preferential treatment so that they could hire and purchase large blocks of black convicts for long periods.[48]

4 Slaves in Industry and Manufacturing

> Christmas was a season of great rejoicing on account of the home-coming of a large number of coloured people who had been at work in different industries in different parts of the state. Some of them had been hired out to work on the farms, some were employed on the railroads, and others were mechanics.
>
> – Booker T. Washington, Appalachian slave

The transition to industrial capitalism was under way in Southern Appalachia by the early nineteenth century. Rather than being isolated or autonomous from the international economy, this region replicated many of the patterns of development that had characterized other peripheries of the capitalist world economy. Because the region's manufacturing remained closely linked to agriculture, the processing of farm crops and animal by-products generated more than four-fifths of the annual gross value of the region's manufactured commodities. For export, Southern Appalachia specialized in the production of consumable goods (particularly grain by-products, leather goods, textiles) and in the low-level processing of tobacco and cotton. Consequently, the region's light manufacturing was labor-intensive and required low-level mechanization. For that reason, medium to large plantations integrated with agriculture the region's two predominant manufacturing processes: *artisan shops*, which depended on small manual labor forces (e.g., blacksmith, tanner), and *small manufactories and mills*, which combined manual labor with mechanization (e.g., flour mill). By 1860, however, centralized factory production of grains, meats, tools, glass, textiles, tobacco, machinery, and railroad cars had also developed unevenly in about one-quarter of the region's counties, and company towns emerged to centralize and control the labor forces needed by those enterprises.

However, extensive diversification of the region's industrial sector was deterred because local elites and absentee speculators allocated most of their investment capital, labor, and infrastructure into production of agricultural and extractive materials for export to world markets. Speculation in Appalachian mineral lands and hoarding of the region's natural resources by absentee investors spanned the entire antebellum period. In sharp contrast to the rest of the United States, Southern Appalachia's antebellum industrial investments were much more heavily concentrated into low-wage mining, quarrying, smelting, intermediate ore processing, and timbering than into manufacturing. As a result, extractive industries made up the region's predominant employer of nonagricultural laborers and accounted for the second most important industrial category in terms of annual gross. By 1860, Southern Appalachia had already experienced a series of boom-to-bust cycles triggered by the dependence of local economies upon the availability of profitable distant markets for their raw materials. The expansion and heavy capitalization of the region's extractive industries was neither accidental nor autonomous. Local elites "cashed the industrial potential of their territories" by gambling their own wealth accumulation and by syndicating absentee investments into Appalachian minerals for which there was a demand in national and international markets. Since iron production was the leading industry of the nineteenth-century world economy, Appalachians maximized their large iron deposits. Bloomeries, forges, furnaces, rolling mills, naileries, machine shops, and tool factories proliferated. While the region's iron, lead, manganese, and saltpeter were greedily sought by the growing industrial cities of the American Northeast, western Europe voraciously devoured Appalachian gold and copper. The Lower South demanded steady supplies of Appalachian iron, stone, marble, and timber. After 1840, Southern Appalachia's deposits of coal, oil, and natural gas were tapped as ancillary fuel resources to make possible increased output of salt, one of the region's primary exports.[1]

Allocation of slaves to industrial production distinguished Appalachian masters from the rest of the U.S. South. Nearly 16 percent of the region's slaves were employed full time in their masters' manufacturing enterprises, and another one of every twelve Appalachian slaves worked part-time as artisans or laborers in manufacturing on plantations. Appalachian masters allocated more than 8 percent of their skilled slave artisans and another small segment of semiskilled laborers to run mills, distilleries, tanneries, and several other types of artisan shops. About 7 percent of all Appalachian slaves worked full time as extractive laborers, and one of every fifteen regional slaves was engaged in mining, smelting, ore processing, or timbering. In addition to those slaves who worked for their own masters, more than two-fifths of all hired Appalachian slaves were employed in manufacturing and extractive industries. As a result, Appalachian masters utilized slaves in industry three to four times more often than slaveholders in the rest of the United States. Free black Appalachians were just about as concentrated in industry as slaves, for nearly one-quarter of them worked in manufactories, mills, and extractive industries.[2]

Black Appalachians in Manufacturing

Dominant in their local economies, the region's agrarian capitalists sunk local monies and absentee investments into enterprises that were complementary to those agricultural activities stimulated by integration into the world market. As a result, the region's manufacturing remained closely linked to the processing of raw agricultural commodities for export. About one-third of the region's surplus corn, wheat, and wool and one-fifth of its tobacco was manufactured prior to export. Agriculturally linked manufacturing accounted for nearly three-fifths of the gross annual output of all Appalachian industries, and it took six forms: milling flour and corn meal, distilling grains into liquor, packing beef and pork, finishing livestock hides into leather products, manufacturing tobacco plugs or twists, and producing textiles from cotton and wool. Using two-fifths of the region's manufacturing labor force, these industries were quite often situated on plantations.

On average, each Appalachian farm owner could supply enough surplus grain to permit local mills and distilleries to process for export 1,058 pounds (5.4 barrels) of flour. East Tennessee was shipping nearly 70,000 barrels of flour to New Orleans and Charleston; the Appalachian counties of Alabama, North Carolina, and Georgia were sending nearly 30,500 barrels to the same markets. Likewise nearly 4,700 barrels of flour were exported from eastern Kentucky via the Ohio River to New Orleans. In addition to flour exports, the average Appalachian farm owner could supply enough surplus grain to permit local mills and distilleries to process for export 1,588 pounds (8.1 barrels) of meal and twenty-six gallons of whiskey or malt liquor. In 1860, the region's manufacturers also utilized local grains to process for export more than 1,600,000 barrels of meal, a staple food for the laborers on plantations in the Lower South, the West Indies, and South America. By 1819, New Orleans was already receiving two million gallons of Appalachian whiskey yearly, most of it arriving by flatboat down river. In 1860, Southern Appalachia was exporting more than four million gallons of whiskey, malt liquors, and rectified liquors.

Appalachian manufactories also processed livestock into export commodities. Two large meatpacking plants in eastern Kentucky and eastern Tennessee exported more than eighteen thousand barrels of pork and nearly seven thousand barrels of processed beef to New Orleans. Another important derivative commodity produced by the Appalachian meatpacking hubs was lard. After export to New Orleans, Charleston, or Baltimore, Appalachian lard was re-stamped in its barrels as "whale sperm oil"; then these barrels were shipped to European markets for consumption as fuel. In addition, nearly one-half of the region's output of leather products ended up in regional and distant markets. In addition to foodstuffs, Appalachian manufacturers exported commodities derived from the region's staple crops. Eighty-five firms in the Appalachian counties of Georgia, Maryland, North Carolina, Tennessee, Virginia, and West Virginia manufactured nearly seven million pounds of tobacco twists and plugs for export to Northeastern and European markets. In addition, several Appalachian counties were utilizing nearly 2.5 million pounds of cotton and more than one million pounds of wool to manufacture cloth, about one-half of which was exported to regional and distant markets. Eastern Tennessee's "Chilhowee cloth" and South Carolina's "Pendleton cotton-wool blend" were popular with Lower South planters who needed cheap, durable fabrics for slave clothing. By 1860, there were a few large wool manufactories in West Virginia and Virginia, which absorbed much of the local wool production to produce textiles for export to Tidewater cities. Two Appalachian counties were also famous for their export of jeans.

In fact, the regional manufacture of agricultural raw materials was heavily oriented to external trade. The total gross value of the region's output of flour, meal, whiskey, meat provisions, and manufactured tobacco accrued from exports to distant markets. In addition, nearly one-half of the output of Appalachian leather products, agricultural implements, small tools, and textiles was sent to markets outside the counties in which those goods were produced. All told, then, more than four-fifths of the gross value of the region's agriculturally linked manufactures derived from exports to non-Appalachian regional markets or to distant coastal trade centers. Only about one-quarter of the gross value of the region's total output accrued from sales in the county of production or at adjacent regional markets. Instead, three-quarters of that gross value derived from exporting to distant Southern or Midwestern markets. About one-half of the region's output of household goods, tools, and hardware and about one-quarter of the region's output of building materials, paper, and textiles were exported to distant markets. Northern Alabama and western North Carolina sent sashes, doors, and blinds to Lower South consumers, while eastern Kentucky and two Virginia counties produced bricks and cement for export. To fill the special orders of distant planters, northern Georgia and northern Alabama constructed fancy carriages, while western North Carolina and northern Georgia produced furniture. Out of eastern Tennessee and West Virginia, the Lower South and

Midwest received large quantities of nails and spikes. Cotton and woolen cloth, iron household goods and tools, pottery, and an array of patented drug products were also exported to distant markets by Appalachian manufacturers.[3]

Slave Labor in Plantation Manufacturing

In order to generate market commodities and services, to manufacture the equipment and work tools required for export production, and to produce their subsistence needs, Appalachian plantations engaged in a wide variety of nonagricultural activities. For example, most of the slaves at Traveler's Rest, a Habersham County, Georgia, plantation, were employed either full time or part time in their master's cotton gin, blacksmith shop, tanyard, sawmill, and cotton mill. One Henderson County, North Carolina, plantation kept many of its slaves busy in "his own mills and tanyards." In mountainous Sevier County, Tennessee, Brabson Ferry utilized slaves to operate a tannery, blacksmith shop, sawmills, flour mill, and grist mill. James Hervey Greenlee, a middling western North Carolina slaveholder, kept 60 percent of his slave laborers engaged in a wide variety of nonagricultural tasks. The Baumgardner Distillery of Augusta County, Virginia, owned and hired slave brewers and distillers. Appalachian masters valued skilled artisans, as evidenced by numerous advertisements that offer high rewards for the capture of slave specialists. For instance, an 1813 newspaper offered a $100 reward for the return of Anthony Page, "a slave of great capacity and considerable ingenuity." The Frederick County, Virginia, master noted that the bondsman was literate, "possesse[ed] a great mechanical turn," and could "do rough carpenter's work and make combs."[4]

To a much greater extent than Lower South plantations, Appalachian masters were engaged in the production of textiles for market production. To supply the consumption needs of black laborers and masters' families, most small to medium plantations produced leather and cloth. However, a few Appalachian slaveholders marketed these artisan crafts. Two-thirds of the region's textile manufacturers were small artisan shops located on plantations, such as the weaving room at Brabson Ferry where slaves carded wool and spun thread. Appalachian slaves carded wool, spun thread, and wove small cloth surpluses that were sold by their masters. In the 1830s, Cherokee masters used slaves to produce large textile surpluses that were marketed in New Orleans. Families adjacent to plantations, like that owned by the Egglestons of Floyd County, Georgia, "could buy leather from the tan shop" operated by Appalachian slaves.[5]

Grain milling and distilling were highly profitable enterprises for Appalachian slaveholders. The typical plantation flour mill required only 1.4 slave laborers to generate an annual gross of $8,747, like the merchant mill operated by William Noland's slaves on the Aldie Plantation of Loudoun County, Virginia. One of every 167 Appalachian slaves was a full-time millwright or miller who built and maintained buildings and equipment or processed grains. For example, Tommy Angel and John Van Hook were talented slave artisans who could design, construct, repair, and oversee mills for their Macon County, North Carolina, master. Because of the community demand for cornmeal, Appalachian plantations frequently assigned slave artisans to operate grist mills. One of every seventy-seven Appalachian slaves manufactured barrels, constructed the distillery, or operated the complex equipment. Some larger slaveholders operated several types of distilleries and cider mills. The region's typical distillery employed three slave laborers, but it produced an annual output just under $7,300. There was "a distillery in every neighborhood," usually on a plantation, and these facilities processed cider, vinegar, brandy, and liquors for their communities. Isaac Sayer was "an excellent distiller" on a Shenandoah County plantation.[6]

The processing of staples was also significant to regional manufacturing. Cotton ginning occurred only in northern Alabama and northwestern Georgia, where a gin run by eighteen slaves could process $16,500 worth of cotton annually. On one Talladega plantation, "de gins were run by a horse or oxen pullin' de lever an' going in a circle." Tobacco, however, was manufactured in every Appalachian zone except northern Alabama and eastern Kentucky, and the production of tobacco plugs and cigars was heavily dependent upon slave labor. One Patrick County, Virginia, plantation was the forerunner of the contemporary R. J. Reynolds corporation when he established a tobacco factory that relied on more than one hundred slaves to cultivate and to cure tobacco on three small plantations. In the fall and winter months, one-third to one-half of the slaves were shifted to tobacco manufacturing. In Burke County, North Carolina, Richard Michaux's slaves divided their labor between cultivating tobacco and manufacturing it into plugs and twists.[7]

Even the region's output of small tools and hardware was linked to plantation agriculture. About 7 percent of the region's slaves were skilled artisans who manufactured tools, hardware, wheels, buckets, barrels, household equipment, wagons, and carts in blacksmith shops and small facilities located on plantations. During the early 1800s, plantation slaves produced all kinds of small tools and household utensils that their masters marketed. For instance, a Fauquier County, Virginia, slave invented a machine in 1818 that would cut corn and prepare the land for the subsequent crop. John Finnely recalled that his northern Alabama master employed slave artisans part-time to manufacture "all de harness for de mules and de hosses" and all "de carts for haulin'." Oliver Bell's grandfather manufactured wooden plows that his Jefferson County, Alabama, master used in his own fields and marketed locally. Bell "made cudder stock plows" for which he devised an attachment "ter sweep cotton" and a "corey plow whut had er wooden wall board." A western North Carolina merchant used slaves to produce the carriages and furniture that he marketed. On a small plantation in Rhea County, Tennessee, Alfred Day worked full time as "a first-class blacksmith" to manufacture "axes, mattocks, hoes, plow shares, knives and even jew's harps." Appalachian slaves routinely engaged in specialized production of commodities in high demand. Supervised by a black foreman, twelve trained slaves manufactured one-and-one-half tons of nails monthly in the blacksmith shop and nailery at Monticello. To market them extensively, Thomas Jefferson paid general grocers a 5 percent commission to retail his nails. William Holland Thomas assigned several of his western North Carolina slaves to make bricks regularly, and slaves on the Barbour plantation produced fifty thousand bricks yearly. Other mountain plantations owned slaves who specialized in cabinetmaking or in skilled carpentry and woodwork. Some middling plantations routinely operated commercial sawmills that produced lumber and rails for local consumers and for export. Appalachian slaves even built flatboats, canal boats, and keelboats.[8]

Black Appalachians in Centralized Factory Production

In addition to the farming and nonagricultural tasks regularly performed on plantations, Appalachian slaves were purchased or hired for every type of centralized factory job. Many manufacturers integrated slave and white workers "indiscriminately together." The region's merchant mills were heavily dependent upon slave artisans and laborers. More than one-third of the commercial mills were centralized in giant industrial complexes made up of grist, flour, and saw mills; an iron forge; a distillery; and sometimes a paper mill. Typical of these commercial ventures was the four-story flour mill in Cass County, Georgia, which generated 250 barrels of flour daily. These large mills grossed nearly $16,000 annually and stimulated the growth of distribution towns, like Wellsburg and Wheeling, West Virginia. Similarly, Hagerstown, Maryland; Knoxville, Tennessee; Staunton, Virginia; and a commercial belt of four towns in Frederick County, Virginia, emerged as wheat processing centers for adjacent rural areas. The region's most highly commercialized mills were the 177 large firms in western Maryland and fifty-eight merchant mills in Page and

Mountain slaves were frequently hired out on annual contracts to industries, such as this tobacco manufactory at Lynchburg, Virginia. *Source: Scribner's,* 1874.

Shenandoah Counties, Virginia. Merchant mills regularly advertised to hire slave artisans and unskilled laborers, even teenage boys who could handle light lifting and deliveries. For instance, one Madison County slave had learned to be a "cooper by trade" during his "apprenticeship at the Occoquan Mills."[9]

Fifteen percent of the region's distilleries were larger commercial enterprises grossing an average $37,017 per year. One of the ten largest firms in eastern Kentucky was a Greenup County distillery with a work force of twenty-five free and slave laborers. Three large commercial firms packed beef and pork, including one in Madison County, Kentucky, that employed eighty free and enslaved laborers to gross $216,000 and one in Hamilton County, Tennessee, that applied fifty-four free and enslaved workers to generate an output of $130,000. Eighty-five tobacco manufactories employed some of the region's largest industrial labor forces. In Appalachian Virginia, twenty-eight firms each employed more than twenty-two free and slave laborers and grossed $11,865; another twenty-five firms used similar large labor forces to generate an output of nearly $19,000 annually. As much as 5 to 6 percent of Blue Ridge Virginia slaves were hired annually to Appalachian tobacco factories and to larger firms at Lynchburg and Richmond. Large firms also operated in northern Georgia and western North Carolina. In Burke County, for instance, plug tobacco factories employed thirty-seven slaves. Western Maryland and middle Tennessee firms averaged twelve to fifteen slaves to gross about $4,300 annually. Slaves were organized into assembly-line manufacturing in tobacco factories. At the beginning of the process, younger males unpacked the bales from hogsheads and carried them to older slaves who "separat[ed] leaf from leaf." Women then stripped stems and extraneous debris from the leaves. Farther along, "others were arranging the leaves in layers and sprinkling each layer with the extract of licorice." In another room, a large number of women and children "rolled the [leaves] into long, even rolls" and placed them in presses. The final step was to "cut them into plugs of about four inches in length."[10]

By capitalizing upon regional production of wool and cotton, textile producers represented the fourth most important category of Southern Appalachian industry. Absorbing 8 percent of the region's manufacturing labor force and 5 percent of the total annual gross, textile industries encompassed cloth manufacturing, calico printing, and wool carding, as well as the manufacture of staves, shooks, and headings for women's undergarments and the production of finished clothing, mittens, hats, and caps. By national standards, the 299 Appalachian textile manufacturers were medium-sized operations that averaged six laborers and an annual gross of $5,433. To "render many of [their] slaves who [we]re generally idle in youth profitable at an early age," Appalachian slaveholders hired out children to attend looms and spindles in cotton mills. Skilled women artisans were regularly hired to cotton mills, like the eastern Tennessee firm at which fourteen slaves operated three hundred spindles. Newspapers regularly advertised to hire slave artisans and common laborers for textiles mills, like those of northern Alabama or Albermarle County's Union Cotton Factory and Thadwell Cotton Mill. Seven slaves produced clothing for an Ashe County firm, while nine slaves turned out cotton and wool at a small Pickens County, South Carolina, factory. Situated on a plantation at the edge of the Great Smoky Mountains, Abram's Creek Manufactory produced the well-known "Chilhowee cotton" that was popular with slaveholders. On his Pickens County, South Carolina, plantation, Senator John Calhoun allocated slaves to the full-time manufacture of "Pendleton blankets and saddle cloths," an unusual blend of cotton and wool, in demand in the Lower South. One White County, Tennessee, plantation employed twenty-one slaves to produce export textiles from the cotton he cultivated on his fifteen-hundred-acre plantation.[11]

One-third of the region's textile mills were larger operations that required fourteen or more laborers and generated outputs of at least $12,475 yearly. Located in only eleven of the region's counties, twenty-two cotton mills averaged thirty-one slave and free laborers and an annual gross of $32,000 each. Two of the region's largest cotton mills in Coosa County, Alabama, and in Chatooga County, Georgia, averaged seventy-one slave and free laborers and marketed $42,842 worth of goods each year. Concentrated in only five counties, thirty-one clothing factories averaged fifteen workers and a yearly gross of $8,000. Some Appalachian factories were famous throughout the South for their manufacture of jeans, like the Warren County, Tennessee, slaveholding company, which perfected "Faulkner's Jeans" or the Habersham County, Georgia, plant whose female slaves were "remarkably skilful in weaving jeans." Small factories, like western North Carolina's Henderson Weavers or Blue Ridge Virginia's Elkin Manufactory, commingled white and slave laborers, assigning the most complex artisan tasks to slaves. In Franklin County, Tennessee, five slaves and six whites lived in small shacks adjacent to the Butterworth cotton spinning mill where they worked twelve hours per day.[12]

Forty-three medium-sized firms, two-thirds of them concentrated in western Maryland and Appalachian Virginia, hired slaves to manufacture agricultural implements. By far the most famous antebellum manufacturer of farm tools was Cyrus McCormick. With the assistance of his slave, Joe Anderson, McCormick invented the wheat reaper.

Subsequently, slaves were building six thousand wheat reapers yearly. Eastern Kentucky slaveholders hired their surplus laborers to hemp producers and ropewalks in Lexington. Slaves manufactured hats at small shops throughout the region, such as two locations in Asheville, North Carolina. Averaging an annual gross of $22,033 were thirteen large regional leather manufacturers that used slave and free laborers in Whitfield County, Georgia; in Hamilton and Warren Counties, Tennessee; and in Roanoke and Rockbridge Counties, Virginia.[13]

Black Appalachians in Regional Extractive Industries

By 1860, extractive industries had emerged in two-thirds of the Southern Appalachian counties (see Map 9). Nearly one-half of the region's antebellum extractive output was generated for out-of-county markets, and eighty of the region's counties shipped raw materials to distant markets before the Civil War. Wythe County, Virginia, began exporting lead in the eighteenth century. During the 1830s and 1840s, gold was exported from fifteen Appalachian counties of Georgia, Tennessee, Virginia, and Alabama. By far the largest and most tightly controlled antebellum company towns were associated with Southern Appalachia's production of iron, coal, salt, coal, and copper. Forty-three counties exported one-third or more of their total iron production from large year-round forges, furnaces, bloomeries, and rolling mills. Four West Virginia, eastern Kentucky, and southwest Virginia counties supplied salt to the Lower South and to the Midwest. Thirteen Appalachian counties of Tennessee, Virginia, North Carolina, and Georgia produced much of the nation's copper. Two Appalachian counties supplied the nation's entire production of manganese. From another twenty-five Appalachian counties of Alabama, Georgia, Kentucky, Maryland, Virginia, and West Virginia, coal was exported to fuel distant industries and to supply urban households. Integrated workforces of slaves, free residents, and immigrant laborers were common in the region's extractive industries.[14]

Another fifty-one Appalachian counties were secondary extractive exporters that supplied regional markets, usually within a one-hundred-mile radius of the production sites. These smaller industries generated iron, salt, coal, lumber, marble, stone, and petroleum products for adjacent markets. Thirty-six counties produced iron in small amounts, part of which was exported across county lines to supply nearby markets. For example, the iron manufacturers of western North Carolina predominantly served a narrow target area of less than one hundred miles, exporting only a small segment of their production to urban centers in South Carolina and to Augusta or Athens, Georgia. Small salt operations in Washington

In a Rockbridge County, Virginia, workshop, Cyrus McCormick used slave artisans to design and construct his famous wheat reaper. *Source:* Truman, *History of World's Fair*, Appendix.

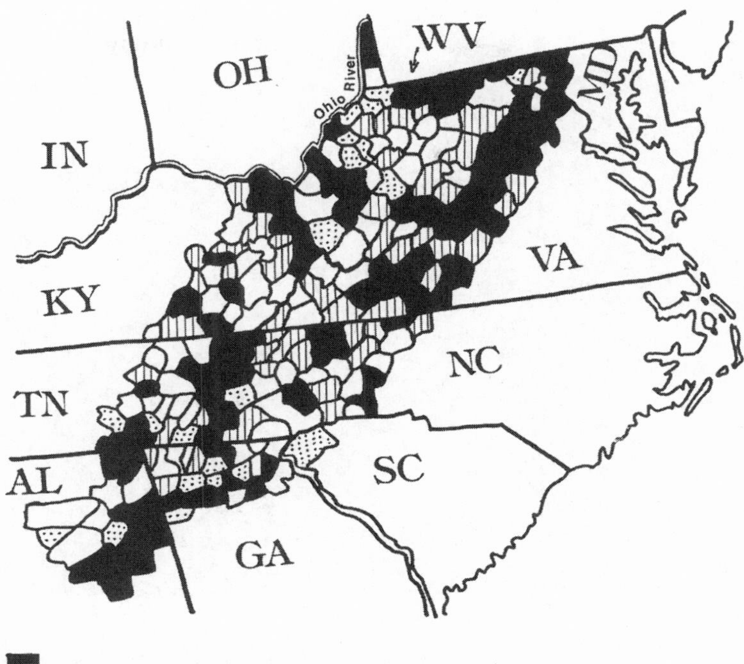

Map 9. Extractive exports from the Mountain South, 1860. *Source: The First American Frontier: Transition to Capitalism in Southern Appalachia, 1700–1860*, by Wilma A. Dunaway. Copyright © 1996 by The University of North Carolina Press. Used by permission of the publisher.

County, Virginia, and Mercer County, West Virginia, supplied adjacent areas. In some instances, extractive resources were exported to fuel other intraregional industries. For example, coal and lumber were floated by river from several West Virginia counties to the salt furnaces located on the Ohio River.[15]

Black Appalachians in the Salt Industry

One of the first Appalachian resources to be exported was salt derived from several wells in West Virginia, southwestern Virginia, and eastern

Slaves supplied most of the labor to produce Appalachian salt, one of the region's most important exports. At this salt manufactory in southwestern Virginia, slaves did most of the skilled labor, such as kettle tending (right) and boiler tending (left). *Source: Harper's*, 1857.

Kentucky. By the late eighteenth century, salt was being manufactured in Clay County, Kentucky, and in the Kanawha Valley, Braxton County, and the Clarksburg area of West Virginia. By 1810, Southern Appalachia led the nation in salt production. With its twenty commercial salt works averaging twenty-six laborers and grossing $22,594 each, the region was second only to New York in this industry in 1860. By the early nineteenth century, Abingdon, Virginia, had been transformed into a manufacturing and commercial center "in consequence of the salt works." As a result, southwestern Virginia had become "a place of considerable resort of, and importance to, all the western country." That zone's salt works sent spring shipments by flat boats down the Holston River, and Knoxville merchants regularly advertised for wagoners to haul the commodity from that works. From Knoxville, Virginia, salt was reexported to southeastern Tennessee, Alabama, and New Orleans. By the 1840s, one southwestern Virginia operation had expanded to five furnaces of eighty-four kettles each. There were only two salt works in production in that zone by 1860: a small furnace in Washington County employing five laborers to gross $20,000 and a large firm in Smythe County that utilized fifty workers to gross $52,000 annually.[16]

In eastern Kentucky, salt manufacturing began in Clay, Floyd, Greenup, Lewis, and Pulaski Counties. Even on the frontier, eastern Kentucky salt was exported by river via Nashville to planter markets, was sent overland by wagon to the Blue Grass Basin, or was carried out by packhorse through the Cumberland Gap to Virginia, Tennessee, and North Carolina. In the early 1800s, Greenup County maximized its Ohio River location to export 89,200 bushels of its salt to Louisville and Cincinnati, much of which was absorbed by meatpackers preparing provisions for the New Orleans market. By 1840, however, the fifteen wells of Clay County had become the most important production area. Initiated from two small 1802 establishments, the Clay County salt industry grew to fifteen wells in 1845, producing 250,000 bushels, and the boom town of Manchester was promoted as the "Athens of the West." In 1846, fifteen Clay County furnaces were producing 200,000 bushels – much of which was transported great distances overland by ox-drawn wagons or packhorses or by river southward. By 1850, salt manufacturing had all but died out in Lewis, Floyd, and Greenup Counties. Still there remained, in 1860, eight eastern Kentucky salt furnaces, averaging twelve laborers and an annual gross of $6,865 each.[17]

However, Southern Appalachia's largest salt exporters were situated in Kanawha and Mason Counties, West Virginia. Southern grocers could not "do better than to send to the salt mines of Virginia for pure table salt," *DeBow's Review* proclaimed. In 1810, West Virginia furnaces were already producing 540,000 bushels annually, much of which was sent on log rafts down the Ohio River. By 1817, thirty wells and twenty furnaces extracted nearly 700,000 bushels per year. By 1828, salt was big business in West Virginia, and there were sixty-five wells sunk along ten miles of the Kanawha River. With a labor force of 471, these manufacturers produced a total of 787,000 bushels of salt each year. By 1835, the industry had grown to nearly three thousand laborers (mostly slaves). Charleston emerged as the center of this industry, sporting the fine homes of the salt barons along its Front Street. Kanawha salt production expanded to three million bushels by 1846.[18]

As a result, this economic sector stimulated ancillary development of adjacent lumber, coal, and natural gas resources and triggered the expansion of cooperage, blacksmithing, boatbuilding, and shipping. In addition, the West Virginia salines "used $47,600 worth of agricultural produce each year; 1,695,000 bushels of coal; 142 tons of iron; and 130,000 salt barrels worth $32,000" and "paid $8,000 a year to blacksmiths, $7,950 to mechanics." By 1852, four hundred flatboats per year carried three million Kanawha Valley bushels to be marketed in Ohio, Illinois, Indiana, Iowa, Missouri, Tennessee, and Kentucky. To export salt from Mason County, West Virginia, tram roads were constructed from the salt furnaces to the boat landings. Slaves rolled barrels down the trams and loaded them onto packet boats and barges for transport down the Ohio River. However, West Virginia's salt industry had declined, by 1860, to only fourteen manufacturers in Kanawha, Marion, Mercer, and Mason Counties, averaging thirty-three laborers and an annual gross of $28,224 each. Even though salt manufacturing was not established there until 1849, Mason County quickly outstripped the production of its predecessors, and the Kanawha Salines were in decline by the mid nineteenth century.[19]

Between 1835 and 1845, one Clay County, Kentucky, manufacturer used slaves to produce 250,000 barrels of salt. The Abingdon saltworks used slave artisans continuously between 1807 and 1838. In Virginia and West Virginia, salt manufacturers "advertised at almost every store and tavern door . . . that from 12 to 15 Dollars a Month hire w[ould] be given for any Number of Labourers." In 1854, James Cowey used fifty-eight slaves and six whites to operate two furnaces in Mason County, West Virginia. Kanawha salt producers leased more than half their slave labor force of nearly fifteen hundred. In 1850, salt manufacturers were employing 63 percent of all male slaves and 29 percent of all female slaves in Kanawha County. The West Virginia salt companies were convinced that "slave labor [wa]s usually cheaper than free" and that, "for the business in which [they] were engaged," enslaved workers were "the best."

Throughout the 1850s, saltworks could hire slaves for less than half the annual wages for free workers, so whites held only a few managerial, supervisory, and distribution positions. One salt manufacturer reported that his few white laborers required more supervision than all the slaves used.[20]

By 1818 around the Kanawha Valley salines, a town of slum shanties housed eight hundred to one thousand slaves and transient white laborers. By 1830, there were twenty dwellings, three stores, two churches, a hotel, a post office, a cooper shop, a barber shop, and a tailor shop. County courts frequently indentured young free blacks to learn to be coopers and blacksmiths at the saltworks. Charleston attorneys also arranged to purchase slaves for the Kanawha Salines. Salt companies sent representatives to eastern Virginia to lease slaves, and Blue Ridge plantations frequently hired slave artisans and apprentices to the Kanawha Salines. Appalachian masters could earn annual leasing fees from the Kanawha Salines that were 30 percent higher than the wages their slaves could earn from other types of employers. In 1838, slaves hiring for $90 per year in Tidewater Virginia could be leased to Kanawha salt producers for $150.[21]

Salt furnaces assigned slaves specific tasks per day, and a few held supervisory positions. Salt companies "operate[d] a furnace by task work, a coal digger ha[d] a prescribed quantity of coal to dig, a hauler, a salt packer a prescribed quantity to pack, and engineer and kettle tender a certain time to be on watch." Coopers were required to construct six to seven barrels per day. In addition to three white managerial positions at one Mason County saltworks, slaves held positions as boss kettle-tender, coal bank manager, and salt well tender. In 1853, the slave labor force for one company included: one "negro man sort of manager," fourteen coal diggers, five wheelers of coal to the mine mouth, four haulers of coal from the mine to the furnace, three kettle-tenders, two "cat-hole" cleaners who removed coal ash, six engineers who operated steam engines to pump brine from the salt wells, two "salt lifters" who wheeled salt to the packing shed, seven "jim-arounds" who packed and loaded salt, two blacksmiths, and one cook.[22]

Black Appalachians in the First U.S. Gold Rush

The country's first gold rush occurred in Southern Appalachia, triggering the hasty development of a series of company boom towns. In fact, the Mountain South led the country in gold production until the California boom of the 1840s; and the first U.S. government mint was established at Dahlonega, Georgia. Between 1830 and 1855, there were nearly ten thousand free and slave laborers in the gold fields of seventeen Appalachian counties of Alabama, Georgia, North Carolina, South Carolina, Tennessee, and Virginia. Even as late as 1850, there were still forty-seven active gold mines in Southern Appalachia – requiring eight to sixty laborers each – and at least half these gold prospectors were slaves.[23]

Some Appalachian slaveholders engaged in gold mining as an adjunct to agriculture. Western North Carolina masters were prospecting in the early nineteenth century, even though Appalachian production of gold did not reach its peak until the era of 1828 to 1845. In 1807, Burke County masters were already sending their slaves to pan gold "whenever the corn [wa]s hoed, the cotton [wa]s weeded, and agricultural duties which engage[d] them w[ould] permit." Western North Carolina's gold rush began in the 1820s when two wealthy local planters (Isaac T. Avery and William Davidson) and several absentee eastern speculators began to hire slaves to prospect. Between 1828 and 1833, boom towns emerged, and slaves were hired in great numbers to work deposits in Burke and Rutherford Counties. By 1833, there were five thousand slaves employed in gold mining in Burke County, and local citizens worried that "the great number of Slaves employed about the mines" required "vigilance among Managers and Patrollers," if insurrections were to be prevented. When an eastern Kentucky farmer drove a herd of hogs to the Burke County mines in 1833, he was shocked by the exploitation of slaves. Wayne Countian Francis Goddard wrote in his diary that he "staid at the mines untill [he] was convinced that Money was the Root of all Evil, and that slavery would prove a curse to our Nation if nott its Ruin." With alarm, he added, "thousands of Slaves was engaged in these Mines under Cruel Masters who had a Great thirst for filthy Lucre."[24]

An 1836 newspaper observed that slaveholders shifted their slaves from farming to mining, as world market prices fluctuated. When the price of cotton was high, farmers abandoned the gold fields and then returned to the mines when cotton prices fell. "Farming and gold digging went, in many cases, hand in hand. When the crops were laid by, the slaves and farm hands were turned into the creek-bottoms, thus utilizing their time during the dull season. Where mining proved more profitable than planting, the former superseded the latter entirely." Planters like Calvin Cowles worked small gold deposits using their own slaves. Small slaveholders, like James Hervey Greenlee, used slaves to mine deposits on family lands and also regularly hired out several slaves each year to work for other mine owners in Burke, Wilkes, and Ashe Counties. On one stream in McDowell County, there were three thousand slave and free miners in 1848. In Rutherford County, numerous slaves washed ore under white supervisors who "watched closely to prevent their secreting any pieces of gold."[25]

Slaves, like these shaft borers, made up a significant part of the ethnically mixed labor force for the country's first gold rush in the Mountain South. *Source: Harper's*, 1857.

Many observers saw gold mining as a beneficial auxiliary enterprise for small western Carolina plantations because it allowed profitable returns on surplus slave laborers who could not generate equal returns through their agricultural production. For instance, Isaac T. Avery praised his "more intelligent, wealthy and enterprising" peers who "after personal examination, [we]re withdrawing their slaves entirely from the cultivation of cotton and tobacco, and removing them to the deposit mines." A State Legislative report touted the advantages of gold mining to the agricultural sector of the western counties. Many slave mechanics "of all descriptions," whose investment value could not be recovered from farming, could "receive high wages and constant employ" in the gold mines. For $3,000, Avery and Company hired slaves from sixteen owners to mine gold, and, until the 1850s, William F. McKesson employed forty-five of his own slaves, half of them women.[26]

In 1851, an Albermarle County, Virginia, planter sent his son to western North Carolina to explore the feasibility of shifting the family's slaves from agriculture to gold mining. The son wrote to his father: "The mining region of N. Carolina is greatly richer than that of Georgia. . . . [M]illion on millions of gold are hidden in the bowels of the Earth here." At one mine in Haywood County, he observed that the operations were "conducted almost entirely by the negroes, without supervision." From his conversations with the laborers, he learned that hired slaves "were greatly pleased with the mining life & would not willingly revert to the labour of tillage." It was the visitor's feeling that slaves "become much attached to the occupation" because "Labour close[d] at dusk & they ha[d] no tax on their time or exertions for the night." The son advised "the employment of the force [the family] propose[d] to [divert] from agriculture, in mining." The "slave boss" over one gold mining crew had told him that "20 hands w[ould] give $1,000 profit per month." He suggested that the family consider two possible approaches to make best use of their surplus laborers. They could mine on shares by paying one-quarter of all gold to the landholder, the "lessee paying all the expenses of fixtures & working." Or the family might arrange annual labor contracts with area mining companies who were hiring slaves "at $100 for men – $60 to $70 for women – $40 to $50 for boys from 12 to 15 yrs." In addition to the financial advantages, the son felt that the family would be "placing [its] people in a situation more pleasant to others." To "remove any reluctance" his parents might still feel, he added: "I was pleased with the songs of gladness to which [the slaves] measured their steps, as they . . . return[ed] to their homes at night."[27]

As early as 1829, the attention of Blue Ridge Virginia slaveholders was "being more and more drawn to the gold region." Contemporaries disagreed about whether Appalachian slaveholders should give greater priority to agriculture or to gold production. An English geologist advised Blue Ridge masters that they could work or hire surplus slaves more profitably in gold mining than in farming. However, the *American Farmer* warned that the reallocation of slaves would "prove injurious" because Virginia's "hidden treasures" of Appalachian gold would never be "adequate compensation for the abandonment of agriculture." In Amherst, Fauquier, Franklin, and Madison Counties, plantations shifted slaves to small gold deposits where free and enslaved laborers worked side by side. However, slaves were cheaper because they could be hired at $100 yearly, compared to white wages and board of $15 monthly. Between 1829 and 1860, slaves regularly dug gold part-time in Fauquier, Greene, and Amherst Counties. "With a small pan," Blue Ridge slaves "wash[ed] the earth in a tub, or in some brook or branch of water." By 1831, the price of slave hires had dramatically increased as a consequence of the demand in gold mining, and the region's iron manufacturers were having a hard time competing for laborers. As late as the mid 1840s, slaveholders were still forming partnerships, like the Jonesader Mining Company, to exploit limited gold deposits in the Virginia Blue Ridge.[28]

The mania for the yellow Appalachian mineral went into full swing after a lucrative 1829 gold discovery in the Cherokee Nation. By 1830, between six thousand and seven thousand workers were "engaged in gold-washing" in northern Georgia mines, and more than half of them were slaves. In northern Alabama, three thousand slaves and whites in shacks and tents produced $183,500 worth of gold from placer mines in Clay, Coosa, and Talladega Counties. Another forty-eight hundred slaves and free laborers populated two boom towns in Cleburne County, Alabama. In the Talladega Mountains, each slave averaged $1.50 to $3.00 per day in gold dust. Supervised by white overseers, slaves exploited gold deposits at five sites in Monroe County, Tennessee, and Pickens County, South Carolina.[29]

Regional newspapers advertised "liberal prices" for slaves that exceeded the hire-rates masters could earn from other employers. Strong male slaves were "in demand at the Mines, at $10 per month." One northern company offered to hire fifteen to twenty-five slaves to mine a deep shaft, and a group of Habersham County mine owners advertised that blacksmiths, miners, and other slave artisans would "meet with ready and profitable employment." In just four months, Thomas Lumsden's slaves claimed $30,000 in gold from his Nacoochee Valley site. When western North Carolina cotton was "all eat up with the rust" in 1832, Hamilton Brown decided that "where a man own[ed] the hands he could not do better than employ them in the gold Business." By leasing Lumpkin County,

Georgia, lots for periods of thirty to forty-five days, Brown expected to make a profit of $173 per slave, and he was convinced that "1 ounce pr. Day pr. Hand" would "be a better Pursuit than farming." Every summer, U.S. Senator John C. Calhoun reassigned twenty of his Pickens County, South Carolina, slaves to work his Dahlonega mine until cotton harvests. His slaves collected nearly $1,000 worth of gold every day, at the rate of $500 per hand annually, claiming nearly 1 million dollars in ore before the vein gave out. In addition to placer and water-pressure surface mining, slaves worked on huge barges that were used to dredge gold from northern Georgia river bottoms. One large company constructed "a boat with a diving bell attached to it for the purpose of... collecting gold from the bed of water courses."[30]

A few plantations, like Traveler's Rest of Habersham County, kept a few slaves busy in gold mines on their farm land. Cherokee masters shifted their slaves to gold mining during the winter months. In the Walhalla district, Ernest Cochran profitably mined the surface ore of an abandoned gold mine on his farm. Near Dahlonega, one poor farmer found a deposit on his land, so he "went to leasing small sections" to slaveholders who worked "a good many" slaves, providing the landholder "a decent living." A few Appalachian free blacks also attempted to work gold mines. In northern Georgia, slaveholders feared free blacks, and they often drove them from the mines. After buying their freedom from their master, Dan and Lucinda Riley panned for gold on shares with Cherokee County, Georgia, landholders. James Boisclair was the first free black gold mine owner in Lumpkin County, Georgia; he also earned wealth as a merchant. At first, Boisclair operated a small cake and fruit shop; then he bought a gold lot that he registered in the name of the U.S. Mint Superintendent. He named his mine the "Free Jim" and began to pan for gold. With the dust, he opened the largest dry goods and general merchandise store in Dahlonega, followed by an ice house, and a saloon.[31]

Although it is impossible to place a precise value on these exports, archival sources offer some insight into the extent of the extraction of surplus out of the region. Between January and October 1830, northern Georgia mines exported $230,000 worth of gold to Augusta, while the private mint at Gainesville manufactured 50,000 gold coins in a short period. By 1843, the Lumpkin County mint was annually processing more than $3 million worth of gold for export to the national mint at Philadelphia. From the Nacoochee Valley of northeast Georgia, one merchant purchased and exported $1.5 million worth of gold in a thirty-year period. Between 1834 and 1839, thirty-four companies operated by investors from Great Britain, New York, and New England exported to Europe $6,000,000 worth of Appalachian Virginia gold for use in art works and jewelry. Between 1829 and 1860, the Philadelphia mint coined $3,000,000 worth of gold harvested from Fauquier, Greene, and Amherst Counties.[32]

Black Appalachians in Iron Production

Some of the largest extractive complexes in antebellum Southern Appalachia were engaged in iron production. Established in eighty-four of the region's counties, Appalachian bloomeries, furnaces, forges, and rolling mills produced nearly one-fifth of the country's total iron in 1840. Employing 6,216 slave and free laborers, the region's 250 iron manufacturers turned out pig iron, blooms, castings, bar iron, and railroad iron. These firms averaged an annual gross of $19,154 with twenty-five workers. More than two-fifths of the region's iron manufacturers were "iron plantations," industrial enclaves that operated year-round by using slave laborers supervised by white managers. The blast furnaces, especially those linked with a forge or rolling mill, were among the region's largest industrial establishments with respect to capital investment, employment, and size of landholding. By 1860, at least fifty-one Virginia, forty-three Tennessee, and sixteen West Virginia furnaces and forges were systematized as industrial plantations. Because these facilities required a steady supply of iron ore, charcoal, and limestone, iron plantations often monopolized one-third to one-quarter of the total land area in the counties where they were located.[33]

From the late 1700s, Virginia furnaces advertised for "Sundry Hier'd Negroes for Extra Labour." The Oxford Iron Works of Bedford County employed 220 slaves in 1811; the Clifton Forge and the Lucy Selina Furnace of Alleghany County used ninety slaves in 1827; and the Bath Iron Works employed seventy. Slaves were even utilized regularly at smaller operations in Botetourt, Page, and Wythe Counties in Virginia and at the Monongalia Iron Forge in West Virginia. Appalachian Virginia and West Virginia furnaces averaged fourteen free laborers and seventy slaves, with unfree laborers making up three-fourths of the workforce on iron plantations. Slave women and children were utilized to feed ore into crushers and furnaces. In Virginia and West Virginia, Appalachian iron plantations averaged 12,146 acres, and some were so extensive that, like the Glenwood Iron Works, they spilled over into adjacent counties. Typically, these enclaves were large merchant mill complexes (like the Marlboro Iron Works or the Monongalia Iron Works) that engaged in iron and other manufacturing functions, integrated with agriculture. In addition, such plantations often operated a rolling mill, foundry, sawmill, flour mill, grist mill, lime kiln, barrel factory, or distillery. Some ironmasters also processed cloth, leather, or salt, and cut cordwood for resale. Besides the industrial facilities, these plantations encompassed warehouses, company stores, laborer housing, and the ironmaster's mansion. In addition, toll roads were often integrated into the spatial organization of the complex. Within the large landholding, there would be several farms, at least one that was operated for the furnace by a landless farm manager. Secondary to industry in economic importance, agriculture "provided all or part of the furnace community's food and provender, with the degree of involvement in farming depending upon the ironmaster's objectives."[34]

We can get a glimpse of one of these extractive enclaves by looking more closely at Buffalo Forge, a Rockbridge County enterprise that employed 114 slaves in 1840. According to Dew, "the hub of this varied agricultural and industrial enterprise was the forge itself, a solid stone building located on the banks of Buffalo Creek." Surrounding the forge were a harness and shoe shop, a sawmill, a mule stable, a horse stable, and a large blacksmith, all staffed by slave workers. The ironmaster's mansion and guest cottage, a large smokehouse, two corn cribs, a large granary, two ice houses, and two stores completed the enclave. Nine log slave cabins were scattered randomly about the property, and a road led to a slave cemetery behind the complex. Buffalo Forge specialized in the production of export iron, but the plantation also produced other market surpluses. The ironmaster's fields "yielded large crops of wheat, corn, oats, buckwheat, and rye, all grown and harvested by slave labor. The slaves also raised more than enough hay, clover, and timothy grass to maintain the numerous draft animals needed for farm and forge work." At two large, water-powered mills, slaves ground the cornmeal and flour that fed the labor force and supplied the owner with surpluses to be sold in the Richmond market. "Each winter, the slaves would slaughter enough hogs and cattle to fill the big smokehouse and provide a full year's rations for the entire population at Buffalo Forge." The company store supplemented that agricultural produce with items like tobacco, sugar, cloth, and clothing.[35]

The largest of these industrial enclaves was the Ice's Ferry Iron Works in Monongalia County, West Virginia, which employed seventeen hundred slave and free laborers at its peak between 1838 and 1848. Monongalia integrated five furnaces, a forge, a refinery, a rolling mill, a nailery, a powder works, blacksmith shops, a tavern, a hotel, a large store, a cooper shop, a firebrick kiln, a flour mill, and wagon shops. Monongalia developed one of the most complex transportation networks utilized by antebellum industries. A system of tramways ran back through the mountains, linking mining sites to processing plants. Across rails affixed to wooden cross-ties, slaves used horse-drawn trucks to move iron ore, coal and timber to the blast furnaces. Situated on twelve thousand acres in four counties, the Etowah Mining and Manufacturing (Cass County, Georgia) was probably the second largest iron plantation in Southern Appalachia. Consisting of furnace, forge, foundry, rolling mill, flour mill, grist mill, sawmill, Etowah employed five hundred to six hundred laborers (one-third of them slaves). The company also owned an ancillary coal mine in adjacent Dade County and a railroad spur line connecting the enclave to the coast. In contrast to Virginia enclaves which averaged only seventy-five to two hundred fifty inhabitants, Etowah was populated by two thousand to four thousand at its peak. More like an industrial town than a rural plantation, the complex housed laborers in company-owned boarding dormitories and small tenements. Also available on company premises were a school/church, a post office, a brewery, and a bordello staffed by enslaved women. Even though farms augmented the food supply and laborers were supplied with garden spots, agriculture played a minor role on this plantation. Instead, this facility placed greater emphasis on retailing imported goods; Etowah's $90,000 annual payroll was disbursed as vouchers credited to laborer accounts at the company store or bank.[36]

In 1851, there were 2,812 slaves employed in the iron facilities of Botetourt County, Virginia, and hundreds more were scattered at forges, furnaces, foundries, and rolling mills throughout the Appalachian counties of Virginia and West Virginia. Around Christmas each year, ironmasters or their agents traveled into adjacent Appalachian counties, attending auctions at courthouses and responding to newspaper advertisements. When iron manufacturing was at its peak in the 1850s, ironmasters had difficulty recruiting slave laborers. One fall, Botetourt furnaces advertised to hire "500 able-bodied Negro Men." For their iron furnace near Staunton, Virginia, the Davises hired twelve slaves on annual contracts by making a circuit of auctions on court days. By traveling the countryside, the Estill County, Kentucky, iron furnace hired twenty slaves yearly. The Empire State Iron and Coal Mining Company of Dade County, Georgia, advertised "to hire or buy 100 able-bodied hands," and they were desperate enough to accept women. The Gibraltar Furnace had difficulty hiring slaves because of "the high price of the produce of farms & the consequent demand for their labor in that direction." Another manufacturer complained that "none of the ironmen obtained more than a half force" in 1859 because "the Tobacco Factories & rail road contractors monopolized the market." The Buffalo Forge ironmaster often experienced years when "the prospect [wa]s very gloomy" because slaveholders were "asking $135 to $150 for good hands." On one occasion, he feared that he would not "be able to hire more than thirty or forty hands" because "there [wa]s all sorts of trickery" on the part of agents and owners.

When the ironmaster could not locate enough skilled artisans, Etowah Rolling Mill hired at $300 yearly from a Richmond furnace an experienced Virginia slave who would train unskilled Georgia, North Carolina, and Tennessee recruits.[37]

Iron plantations in Appalachian Tennessee were the smallest in scope, usually employing an average sixteen free laborers and eight slaves. Smaller size and less dependence upon slave labor were not the only characteristics that distinguished Tennessee iron plantations from those in Virginia or Georgia. A few operations, like the Embree Iron Works of Sullivan County, integrated as many economic activities as Etowah or Virginia enclaves. However, most Tennessee enterprises engaged in fewer activities ancillary to the furnace, usually only two other functions from among a forge, rolling mill, farm, or grist mill. In this zone, iron manufacturing and agriculture were probably of equal economic significance because the plantations coordinated work activities and land use to ensure seasonal compatibility. "The ironmaster-planter operated the furnace so that (1) iron making would not interfere with [farming] seasons, (2) labor could be shifted to the industry when free from agriculture, (3) ironware was manufactured in time to meet the spring and fall needs of the farmer and planter." Because iron furnaces depended on steady and reliable supplies of labor, numerous Southern Appalachian furnaces and forges "colonized slaves in cabins erected in rows about the furnace." Northern Georgia's Habersham Iron Works and Nobles Iron Foundry rented boarding-house rooms or small log cabins to laborers and sold them supplies at company stores.[38]

Western Maryland iron facilities depended heavily on slave labor in the eighteenth century and early nineteenth century. In 1796, the Cumberland Forge utilized forty-four slaves. However, these ironmasters increasingly shifted to cheap immigrant labor in the 1830s. Eastern Kentucky iron producers commingled immigrants and enslaved workers in industrial enclaves averaging populations of 386. In the Hanging Rock Iron District of eastern Kentucky, iron furnaces established company villages that typically consisted of fifty to seventy-five cabins, a boarding house, a general store, a school, and a church. Laborers were housed in one-story, one-room cabins with rear appendages in which they kept chickens and cows. Paid in vouchers, furnace workers exchanged their labor for company store commodities, never seeing cash unless they were due a balance when their employment was terminated. Consequently, Hanging Rock company stores retailed over $1,290,500 in goods each year, earning a markup profit of 75 to 100 percent.[39]

At Appalachian iron plantations, "slaves tended fires, worked the metal, and in fact did everything but manage the establishments." In addition to metal processing, slaves "planted and harvested crops, cut and charcoaled wood, mined iron ore, drove wagons and manned boats, made shoes, ground flour, and worked as carpenters and blacksmiths." Typically, "when the furnace was in blast, the slaves worked two twelve-hour shifts, dumping ore, flux, and charcoal into the furnace, opening the taphole so the iron could flow into the casting bed, hammering out bar iron, tending the charcoal heaps, and hauling ore." A puddler was expected to produce one ton of iron per day. When the weather was bad or agricultural tasks were needed, slaves hauled cinders, cut logs, repaired buildings and roads, made fence rails, chopped wood, planted corn, and threshed wheat. Unskilled laborers cut one-and-a-half cords of wood each day, while boys and girls worked as "leaf rakers" in the charcoal pits. Most iron laborers had "double trades." At Oxford Furnace, for instance, "blacksmiths [we]re also potters, and part of them [went] into the pot houses when the furnace [wa]s in blast."[40]

The elite among the iron slaves were the refiners, molders, and blacksmiths. An Appalachian slave narrative provides a close look at the skilled craftsmanship of a molder who worked at a Staunton, Virginia, foundry. Emanuel Elmore's father "moulded everything from knives and forks to skillets and wash pots." To shape items artistically, Elmore used a water-powered forge hammer that he affectionately called "Big Henry" because "it was so big that it jarred the whole earth when it struck a lick." At the Staunton foundry, slaves

> made everything by hand that was used in a hardware store, like nails, horse shoes and rims for all kinds of wheels. . . . There were moulds for everything no matter how large or small the thing to be made was. . . . The patterns for the pots and kettles of different sizes were all in a row, each row being a different size. . . . Now molten iron from the vats was dipped with spoons which were handled by two men. Both spoons had long handles, with a man at each handle. The spoons would hold from four to five gallons of hot iron. . . . As quick as the men poured the hot iron in the mould, another man came along behind them and closed the mould. The large moulds had doors and the small moulds had lids. They had small pans and small spoons for little things, like nails, knives and forks. When the mould had set until cold, the piece was prized out. [Elmore's father] had a turn for making covered skillets and fire dogs. He made them so pretty that white ladies would come and give an order for a 'pair of dogs,' and tell him how they wanted them to look. He would take his hammer and beat them to look just that way.[41]

Black Appalachians in Coal Mining

Appalachian coal deposits were discovered and mapped as early as the 1700s. In 1820, the United States was sixth in the world in coal production, and three-quarters of the country's exports were supplied by the mines, banks, and pits of southwest Virginia, western Maryland, and West Virginia. Commercially significant by 1820, western Maryland's coal companies relied heavily on slave labor during the eighteenth and early nineteenth centuries, but they had shifted to cheaper immigrant workers by the 1830s. By 1860, seventeen coal-mining operations in Virginia and West Virginia were using 2,012 slaves. Another seventeen firms in eastern Kentucky, four in northern Alabama (such as Shelby County's Montevallo Mining), and three in northern Georgia employed 319 slaves. Of the 3,579 coal miners in 1860 Appalachian enterprises, two-thirds were enslaved workers. Only the coal enterprises of Appalachian Tennessee depended upon free labor. Throughout the region, Appalachian masters employed slaves part-time to dig in coal pits located on their plantations.[42]

Developed initially to fuel salt manufacturing in the Kanawha Valley, twenty-five companies were incorporated in West Virginia by 1860, one of the largest being the British-financed Winifrede Mining and Manufacturing Company. In one year's time, thirty-three salt manufacturers consumed nearly six million bushels of coal. Because of that high demand, the region's largest antebellum coal producers were located in nine counties of West Virginia. By 1836, nearly one thousand slaves were employed in the coal pits that produced the 200,000 tons of coal consumed by Kanawha saltworks each year. By 1850, a large percentage of the 3,140 slaves employed by Kanawha saltworks were mining coal for those companies so that there were probably two thousand slave coal miners in West Virginia alone. To maximize external trade linkages, West Virginia firms used slides, wagons, wooden tramways, and narrow-gauge railroads to get their commodity to the Ohio River. At the river, steam-powered tugboats moved the barges that transported coal to Louisville and Cincinnati for consumption and reexport. West Virginia firms also exported cannel coal to be consumed in Midwestern and Lower South homes for heating fuel.[43]

Virginia and West Virginia coal mine companies advertised frequently to hire slaves for $120 to $200 per year, and Appalachian masters could also hire surplus laborers to the eastern Virginia coal companies. While male slaves made up most of the labor force in iron production, coal mines recruited women and children. At the Oxford Iron Works, for example, thirty-five women and girls worked the coal pits. In order to attract slave and immigrant "Mechanics, Miners, Boatmen," coopers, blacksmiths, and other workers to isolated rural areas, West Virginia coal operators constructed small mining villages made up of coal chutes, railroad spurs, sawmills, mechanical shops, laborer housing, and a company store adjacent to the mine openings. The Winifrede Mining and Manufacturing

Company in West Virginia invested $3,208 for laborer houses, but collected back one-third of that amount within a few months. With minimal investment in buildings and inventory, the Winifrede company store retailed $57,632 in less than a year, while the Western Mining and Manufacturing Company's store transacted nearly $15,000 annually in retail sales to workers. Even though the Board of Directors lamented that agriculture "should not be the object of a Coal Company," Coal River Cannel Coal used slaves to farm 150 acres, mostly to provide hay and grains for livestock.[44]

During early stages of development, eastern Kentuckians dug coal from outcrops and wagoned the commodity to waterways. At river landings, the coal could be sold to dealers who operated fleets of flatboats. Thus, early nineteenth-century speculators bought up Appalachian lands adjacent to rivers or major creeks when they were rumored to contain "A Coal Bank that appear[ed] valuable." To exploit their investments, frontier landholders opened crude coal pits to permit "digging by the bushel." The earliest coal exports from eastern Kentucky were generated by small producers at open pits. Some Blue Grass planters utilized slaves to mine coal at absentee-owned eastern Kentucky pits, shipping the ore by flatboats to Frankfort. In 1822, for instance, an Owsley County land agent managed "pits" and "banks" for absentee speculator Robert Wickliffe. He marketed coal "sometime at 50 cents per hundred bushels when anyone want[ed] to raise a load." In addition, he rented two coal banks on half-shares "by the year generaly on the creeks of the river." In the fall and winter, Wickliffe's slaves mined coal. Around March, the slaves hauled the coal to the river and loaded it on boats for export to Frankfort. One flatboat operator wrote to Wickliffe: "I can't build and load a Boat and Bring her down till toward Spring but agreeable to your Negroes I will Bring the Boat Down as soon as possible."[45]

There was very little local use of eastern Kentucky coal. Instead, producers maximized their profits by sending their commodity to distant markets. In the late 1830s, eastern Kentucky coal was selling for less than 3 cents per bushel at the pit, but bringing five times that price in the Blue Grass towns. Even in the early 1800s, Lexington and Frankfort consumed eighteen thousand bushels of eastern Kentucky coal annually, hauled in wagons or shipped on special canoes or flatboats. By 1840, an estimated one million bushels of coal moved annually across the Cumberland, Kentucky, and Big Sandy Rivers. Hazard emerged as the head of navigation on the Kentucky River, which carried most shipments to the Blue Grass Basin and a minority to steamboats on the Ohio for reexport to Mississippi and Louisiana. Eastern Kentucky coal was also exported to fuel the Nashville foundries and rolling mills. It was not unusual for the Nashville industries to order 100,000 to 150,000 bushels at a time. Such annual Nashville shipments averaged 2,100 tons in the 1830s, but Kentucky coal was also exported via the Big Sandy River for reexport from Maysville to Cincinnati. One Appalachian entrepreneur arranged annual fleets of boats to carry his coal via the Cumberland River. After the slave miners transported the coal to creek edges, white and black flatboaters hauled 3,500 bushels of coal each to steamboat landings on the Cumberland River for reexport to New Orleans and Nashville.[46]

Black Appalachians in Other Types of Mining and Timbering

In addition to their widespread employment in the regional production of gold, salt, iron, and coal, Appalachian slaves were utilized to some extent in practically every other type of antebellum extractive enterprise. In the eighteenth century, speculation was flamed by the search for lead and silver in some of the most rugged terrain of present-day West Virginia and southwest Virginia. By attracting British capital and equipment in the 1750s, Virginia's Governor and three other powerful planters syndicated a one-thousand-acre mine in present-day Wythe County. After the Continental Congress appointed a 1775 committee "to enquire in all colonies after virgin lead, leaden ore, and the best methods of collecting, smelting, and refining it," new mining operations emerged in Rockingham, Montgomery, and Botetourt Counties. In 1790, the secretary of the treasury reported that "A prolific mine of it has long been open in the southwestern parts of Virginia. . . . This is now in the hands of individuals, who not only carry it on with spirit, but have established manufactories of it at Richmond."[47]

Throughout the eighteenth and nineteenth centuries, the region's lead mining, transport, and smelting depended almost entirely upon slave laborers. Laboriously by wagon and river, slaves transported lead from the southwest Virginia mountains to Richmond and Philadelphia. From the furnace, slaves wagoned the lead ore "one hundred and thirty miles along a good road, leading through the peaks of Ottie and Lunch's ferry, whence it [wa]s carried by water about the same distance to [the foundry at] Westham," where slaves smelted the ore and then manned the boats to carry it "by James River and the Potowmac to the markets of the Eastern States." Although smaller mines were exhausted by 1820, two large industrial descendants of the eighteenth-century mines had expanded, by 1860, to require 165 slave laborers, in order to generate 480 tons of lead and 100 tons of lead shot exports valued at $61,000.[48]

Appalachian copper was extracted entirely for distant markets, for there were no secondary processing facilities in the region. By 1860, four Appalachian counties exported nearly $600,000 worth of copper, primarily to Northeastern and European ports. Between 1844 and 1848, the Front Royal Mining and Copper Company, the Shenandoah Copper Mining Company, and the South Shenandoah Copper Company mapped and began to exploit veins of Warren, Rappahannock, Page, Shenandoah, Madison, Greene, and Rockingham Counties in Virginia. At the "spur of the Blue Ridge . . . called Stony Man" in Page County, northern adventurers used engines and slaves to exploit a mine and run a smelting mill. Bethany Veney, a young enslaved woman, was hired to cook for the workers at the Page County copper facility. In the 1850s, a small copper-mining operation was initiated in Cherokee County, Georgia. By 1860, there were also copper mining and smelting firms in Fannin County, Georgia; in Alleghany County, North Carolina; and in Carroll and Fauquier Counties of Virginia. Even small operations, like western North Carolina's Peach Bottom Mine, owned and leased slaves. All large firms, these extractive industries averaged twenty-three enslaved and free laborers and an annual gross of $11,689 each. The "Copper Mining Mania" in Carroll County triggered a dramatic expansion of slave labor in the 1850s.[49]

However, the country's largest antebellum copper exports came from two adjacent mountainous counties in southeastern Tennessee and northwestern Georgia. A new Appalachian copper strike occurred in the 1830s as a by-product of the gold rush when a prospector panned a Polk County, Tennessee, tributary. News of the discovery attracted national and international attention, particularly in Baltimore and London. Prospecting boomed in 1851, and land speculation intensified in "the Switzerland of America," as *DeBow's Review* tagged the mineral-rich eastern Tennessee. By 1855, international attention was "fast being directed to the copper interests" of eastern Tennessee. In one mountainous county, "capitalists and miners [we]re investing in lands and bringing forth the heretofore hidden mineral to so surprising a degree as almost to be declared fabulous." With $2,700,000 invested in land and facilities, Union Consolidated Mining and Isabella Mining were two of the country's most heavily capitalized industries. From several mine locations, ore was hauled forty-five miles by mule trains or floated on the river to the railroad for export. In 1850, ore valued at more than $1 million was shipped, most of it destined for Liverpool via Savannah. Between 1850 and 1854, thirteen major copper sites were opened; and two firms employed 405 free and enslaved laborers by 1860. Julius E. Raht, mine owner, enumerated thirty male slaves housed in company barracks in the 1860 census. These copper facilities recruited slave hires aggressively in eastern Tennessee, northern Georgia, and western North Carolina, and some masters regularly hired artisans to the companies year after year.[50]

Perhaps the most extensive antebellum extractive industry was timbering and lumber manufacture. The leather, coal, iron, and salt industries spurred ancillary forest exploitation. In the Kanawha Valley, the antebellum salt manufacturers used slave artisans on thousands of leased acres to produce their barrels, wooden pipelines, and plank tramways. Throughout the region, slaves produced the charcoal that fired iron furnaces, collected and prepared bark for leather tanning, and timbered beams for shoring up coal mines. Slaves also operated the sawmills that were found in merchant mill complexes. For example, Gap Mills of Monroe County, West Virginia, frequently advertised to hire slave artisans to operate its tannery and sawmill.[51]

Plantations regularly allocated slave laborers to cut timber, cordwood, shingles, and fence rails that would be sold locally and exported. As early as the 1760s, northern Blue Ridge plantations were using slaves to produce barrel staves, clapboards, and shingles for export to the West Indies and to England. Western Maryland's Ferry Hill Plantation used white tenants and slaves to timber its western Maryland woodlands in order to market fuelwood, lumber, and fence railings to nearby townspeople and to itinerant canal barges. Between 1853 and 1856, the slaves of one western North Carolina plantation produced large lumber surpluses and wagoned them South. Appalachian slaves also spent a great deal of time producing tanbark and charcoal from the region's forests. To produce one ton of pig iron, the manufacturer needed 180 bushels charcoal, and every blast furnace consumed eight thousand acres of forest. Tanneries also consumed great quantities of tree bark, and slaves collected massive quantities to be sold by their masters.[52]

By 1860, the Census of Manufacturing identified 991 lumber operations in 150 of the region's counties; however, it is likely that there were sawmills in every county. A profitable business venture requiring only $60 to $500 in mechanical parts, Appalachia's early water-powered sawmills averaged two laborers and an annual gross of $2,007 each. However, larger operations characterized counties adjacent to iron, coal, or salt production, as was the case in Polk County, Georgia; Owsley County, Kentucky; Allegany County, Maryland; and Roane County, Tennessee. By 1835, the largest Appalachian lumber companies relied on circular saws powered by steam, and there were fifteen West Virginia firms applying this technological advance. In Pickens County, South Carolina, the largest manufacturing activity was such a progressive lumber mill. Utilizing fifteen slaves, this firm grossed $12,000 per year by marketing its production to Savannah for reexport to England. The most extensive

During fall and winter, Appalachian slaves produced lumber, cordwood, and other forest products. These workers are carting shingles and picket fence railings to market at Hagerstown, Maryland. *Source: Harper's*, 1856.

operations paralleled the sawmill located in Kanawha County. Powered by a twenty-two-foot-high waterfall, it produced thirty thousand to forty thousand board feet daily, using slave logging-crews organized into swampers (road makers), choppers (clearing limbs and brush), sawyers, loaders, and teamsters.[53]

Appalachian lumber was exported from the production sites in three ways: overland wagons, river rafts, or railroads. Within a one-hundred-mile radius, counties with river access sent timber, charcoal, and tanning bark to supply regional salt, iron, leather, cooperage, and furniture manufactories. In addition, cordwood was supplied to adjacent towns, and timber was transported to boatbuilding facilities. River towns also sent shingles, scantling, and finished lumber to distant trade centers on the Mississippi and Ohio Rivers, which were the major national conduits for

In lumber camps like this one, hired slaves lived in temporary lean-tos, ate a diet of fat pork and wild game, and were exposed to numerous injuries and waterborne diseases. *Source: Harper's*, 1851.

antebellum timber movement. The treeless Midwest absorbed part of the surpluses from eastern Kentucky and West Virginia; however, once at seaports, Appalachian exports were redistributed to Northeastern cities or to western Europe.[54]

Beginning in the early 1800s, timber was being exported from several Appalachian Virginia counties to the Tidewater, to the Northeast, and to Baltimore for reexport to the West Indies. To augment the output of river counties, inland West Virginia companies floated logs to Ohio River boatyards, sawmills, or manufactories. On a single rise of the Little Kanawha River, four hundred rafts of timber were floated to the Ohio. Much of this aggregated production was finished for reexport to Southern and Midwestern markets. In fact, some West Virginia sawmills specialized in the processing of pine for Southern markets. From northern counties, logs were rafted to Pittsburgh. From eastern Kentucky, timber rafts followed the Big Sandy River to be marketed at Louisville. Tanning bark, railroad cross-ties, cords of wood, shingles, staves, barrels, and semifinished wood also moved from the Appalachian counties into the Blue Grass Basin. In addition, lumber was shipped on Kentucky River flatboats to Ohio River landings for reexport. Even in land-locked western North Carolina, the Secretary of the Navy invited masters with surplus slaves to produce lumber for the shipyards at New York and Philadelphia. Out of eastern Tennessee counties along the Tennessee River, annual lumber rafts were shipped to Chattanooga for reexport by steamboat to Alabama and Mississippi Valley destinations. From the Clinch Valley of upper eastern Tennessee and southwestern Virginia, one thousand rafts per year headed south for reexport out of Knoxville and Chattanooga. By 1834, a Maine Company was using numerous slaves in its massive lumbering on the northwestern edge of Appalachian Georgia. As a result, Savannah emerged as a major national timber hub, which reexported surpluses to England.[55]

Even the most mountainous areas did not escape extractive exploitation. Appalachian saltpeter fueled the production of gunpowder in Southern and Northeastern manufactories. On ten acres adjacent to the railroad, one Talladega, Alabama, master operated a "saltpeter plantation" on which eight slaves processed nitre in 9,600 square feet of sheds. In a rugged section of Hamilton County, Tennessee, one small slaveholder used four adult slaves, several slave children, and several whites to operate a dangerous powder mill on his small plantation. Alum Cave, located on the highest peak in the Smoky Mountains, attracted the attention of the Epsom Salts Manufacturing Company, which bought up 10,050 acres and established ethnically mixed labor camps to mine the sheer bluffs. From a location "pent up amidst Cloud Caped Mountains," slaves packed alum and hauled it down steep, rough grades to a crude turnpike leading to Knoxville where it was reexported by rail or river to Northeastern canneries. In the western North Carolina mountains, slaves slaked and burned lime in kilns for their masters to market. For use in Northeastern steel manufacturing, Appalachian slaves mined and transported the country's only antebellum manganese. From the region's numerous mineral spas, slaves even bottled water for export to distant markets.[56]

5 Slavery and Poor Whites in the Mountain South

> The pore white folks mostly had a harder time than the colored folks under slavery, because the other white folks did not want them around. Many poor white folks would have starved if it had not been for slaves who stole food from their masters to feed the white folks.
>
> – Rachel Cruze, eastern Tennessee slave

In 1860, nearly one-half of Southern Appalachia's white households were landless nonslaveholders who fell below the national poverty line. The bottom half of the region's population owned less than 3 percent of all regional wealth. Nearly one-third of the white Appalachian households were desperately poor by national standards because they owned less than $100 in accumulated assets and were earning only about $30 per year. Throughout the antebellum period, Southern Mountain land was heavily concentrated into the hands of absentee speculators and a few local elites. Land provided the economic basis for the structuring of polarized local economies in which slaveholders amassed a majority of the acreage, while more than half the white households remained landless. Consequently, Southern Appalachians were 1.7 times more likely to be landless than their counterparts in other sections of the United States. In comparison to New England, residents were twice as likely to be unpropertied. The concentration of regional land resources into a few hands meant that Mountain farm operators were more likely to be tenants than were their counterparts in the United States as a whole and in the rest of the South. In 1860 Tennessee, for instance, farm operators in the Appalachian counties were 2.1 times more likely to be landless than their counterparts in the western counties of the state. By comparison, there were 1.4 Appalachian tenant farmers to every landless Midwestern farm operator and 5.4 mountain tenants to every landless Northeastern farmer. By 1860, nearly two-fifths of the farms in Southern Appalachia were cultivated by operators who did not own the land. These landless farm laborers lived a precarious existence, and they were constantly on the move in search of employment. One-third of these landless agrarians were tenant farmers; one-half were sharecroppers; and the rest were farm managers, cottage tenants, and squatters.[1]

The Functional Relationship Between Tenancy and Slavery

The Southern Mountain countryside was organized in a pattern that exhibited spatially the functional relationship between tenancy and slavery. The antebellum census enumeration order documents the proximity of slaveholders and poor landless farm operators. Indeed, white tenants and sharecroppers operated farms next to three-quarters of the region's slaveholders. The McMinn County, Tennessee, manuscripts offer an unusual verification of this pattern. In that county, enumerators identified tenants immediately after the owners from whom they leased, specifying the linkages between them. In this east Tennessee county, two-thirds of the slaveholders leased parcels to one or more tenants.[2]

The close spatial coexistence of slavery and tenancy resulted from the efforts of Appalachian slaveholders to maximize land and labor resources. In northern Alabama, Frederick Olmsted reported that the hilly country was "well-populated" by tenants, "living in log huts, while every mile or two, on the more level and fertile land, there [wa]s a larger farm, with ten or twenty negroes at work. A few whites [we]re usually working near them, in the same field." Adjacent to the small plantations of the Lytles and Steps of the Swannanoa district of Buncombe County, North Carolina, there were thirteen landless farm operators – identified by the enumerator as two blacksmiths, one renter, eight farm laborers, one cooper, and one weaver. In Albermarle County, Virginia, three small plantations captured the labor of eleven tenants and sharecroppers, described by the enumerator as five overseers, one bricklayer, three carpenters, one farm laborer, and one blacksmith. In similar fashion, two-thirds of the region's slaveholding farmers leased land to poor whites.[3]

What is striking about the census enumeration order is the extent to which slaveholders engaged the services of landless whites to supply specialized services that augmented their slave labor forces. For a share of crop production, overseers and farm managers worked under annual tenancy contracts. During planting and harvest, nearby landless families were hired to supplement slaves. For example, there were eight tenant households adjacent to a Loudoun County, Virginia, plantation, including a "toll gatherer" and a "hotel keeper" who managed the slaveholder's subscription road and inn. Slaveholders routinely employed millwrights, blacksmiths, and building artisans from among adjacent landless whites. Moreover, it was from this pool of landless whites that slaveholders drew the men to operate their community slave patrols.[4]

Poor white Appalachians lived in houses like this middle Tennessee tenant cabin, a dwelling very similar to the one-room cabins occupied by the region's slaves. *Source: Harper's*, 1857.

Slavery and white landlessness were also functionally related through the spatial organization of farms. In order to produce surpluses for the world economy, the region's agrarian capitalists centralized, rationalized, and restricted the mobility of an ethnically diverse labor force by organizing their land into multiple uses. In eighteenth-century eastern Kentucky, for example, land owners opened the new country by combining slaves and tenants. Utilizing "a few negroes and perhaps 40 Tennants," one small slaveholder produced "ten thousand bushels of corn & 3,000 bushls of wheat." To expand their capture of the labor of poor whites, many mountain slaveholders partitioned their farms, with leased parcels bordering their own fields. By 1815, the five thousand acres of Jefferson's Monticello were "divided into numerous leased farms that [were] well taken care of." In western North Carolina, one middling slaveholder maintained his thousand-acre farm by keeping two tenant parcels next to his own fields: one "with a house upon it, rented for one-third the produce, and another smaller farm, similarly rented." Other "gentleman-farmers" engaged overseers to manage slaves; then much of the remainder of their acreage was split into multiple crop-share farms. In Haywood County, North Carolina, Thomas Lenoir employed numerous slaves and tenants, all managed by an overseer. Similarly, the Ferry Hill Plantation of western Maryland was subdivided into quarters and garden patches for twenty-five slaves, tracts for three tenant farmers, a cottage tenant's parcel, the landholder's buildings and fields, and a ferry. In addition, the slaveholder housed many of his numerous white farm laborers in his nearby town houses.[5]

An 1839 travel account provides an unusual glimpse at land utilization on a family group of small Appalachian plantations. After spending the night at Traveler's Rest on the Tugaloo River, James Buckingham strolled over the grounds. He commented that the land was subdivided into several uses, including several tenant parcels, an observation that can be validated in census manuscripts. Buckingham reported that one of those poor white tenants

> had made up his mind to emigrate next year, to the valley of the Mississippi: and when [Buckingham] asked him what could induce him . . . to move so far from his home, he replied, that there was too much aristocracy here for him! [Buckingham] asked him who or what constituted the aristocracy of which he spoke. He said they were the rich men of these parts, who bought up all the land at extravagant prices, and left none for the poorer citizens to purchase. . . . [Buckingham] asked him whether he could not rent land from these proprietors, and live by farming in this way. He said yes; but added, that the rent demanded was extravagant also, amounting to ten barrels of corn for a small farm of twenty acres.

In order to comprehend the land rental cost, we must convert the ten barrels rent into their equivalents in the field. The slaveholder's crop share of ten barrels shelled corn required 158 bushels of unshucked corn on the cob, in other words four acres of crop cultivation. Since the average Appalachian farm household required 185 bushels corn for its subsistence needs and lost about 12 percent of stored grain to spoilage or rodents, this tenant would have needed to cultivate ten acres of corn (half his available parcel) to avoid indebtedness to the slaveholder and to prevent family hunger.[6]

In similar fashion, one absentee slaveholder subdivided the 1,000 acres of Ellerslie, an eastern Kentucky plantation, into eighteen tracts. With its direct access to the turnpike and the railroad, the farm exported grains, livestock, and tobacco. Adjacent to the owner's mansion were three slave dwellings, a woodlands tract, and the centrally located parcel upon which the farm manager resided. The owner also collected turnpike fees; so the parcel nearest the tollgate was utilized by a poor white tollgate-keeper who also grew grains on shares. Further away from the owner's house were four small tenant houses and a one-hundred-acre cash renter parcel with a house and two slave dwellings. In most instances, the owner specified the crops to be cultivated on each parcel; and he permitted none of the tenants, except the cash-renter, to produce tobacco. Even though there were no houses on them, five other parcels ranging in size from 16 to 115 acres were leased to sharecroppers and annual-contract laborers who boarded with tenants. Two tiny parcels were made available to cottage tenants who boarded with the farm manager, supplying their labor in exchange for subsistence and use of the garden plots. Two parcels were reserved to pasture and meadow and leased on shares to tenants raising cattle. In fact, a tract near the farm manager consisted of a pasture with an area for loading livestock on trains, evidence of the extent to which this plantation was exporting cattle and hogs.[7]

In addition to subdividing landholdings, slaveholders structured the spatial organization of their plantations to keep tight controls over their laborers. Usually, slave quarters were situated behind the owner's house in rows or a circle to make it easier for the owner or overseer to make "de rounds evvy night." A Murray County, Georgia, slave commented that the owner's home, weaving shed, kitchen facilities, slave quarters, farm buildings, mill, and tanning yard "made a little town itself." Considerable detail is available about the four adjoining small plantations of the Jarrett family of northeastern Georgia. Because their land was connected to the coast by the Tugaloo River, the Jarretts operated a covered toll bridge, an inn, and a prosperous store/tavern. A few miles away in Habersham County, Georgia, they mined gold. In addition, the family generated profits from its commercial mills, blacksmithery, cotton gin, and tanyard. When they were not preoccupied with these nonagricultural activities, the Jarretts utilized slaves, tenants, and hired laborers to produce yearly 13,500 bushels of corn, 1,920 bushels of wheat, 300 pounds of tobacco, 16 bales of cotton, 340 hogs, 45 cattle, and 202 sheep. Enslaved women and tenants' wives produced textiles in a large "loomhouse." To deter stealing and to allow close supervision over the slave rationing process, smokehouses and the master's garden were situated in view of the owner's house. The slave quarters were built near the heart of the estate, situated so as to be within easy walking distance of the fields and the various enterprises.[8]

The labor of tenants and croppers was monitored and supervised as closely as that of the slaves. It was common for Appalachian slaves, hired hands, and tenants to work the fields together, either under the supervision of the owner or of an overseer. At Ferry Hill, for example, one slave squad gathered and hauled wheat from the field, while a squad of white laborers loaded the grain into the barn. "Bad planned and poorly managed Negroe dictation," the master commented in his journal at the end of the work day – indicating that the white workers had been under the supervision of a black slave driver.[9] Poor whites, including women, also worked alongside slaves at community work parties, like corn huskings or log rollings. In one eastern Tennessee community, slaves, tenants, and croppers worked in the same field each day, under the supervision of the owner or overseer. In practice, the tenant or cropper "swapped his labor for the right to use a little of the owner's farm land." Typically, "the tenant's or cropper's share" amounted to no more than what the laborer's family could produce on an assigned field. In return for their labor, the slaveholder "set aside a large field" for the poor white. After the tenant worked for "the man," he could tend his own parcel, and "they'd loan him the horses to work with.... That corn was [the tenant's] to put in his crib."[10]

There was another form of white tenancy that was crucial to slaveholders in the Mountain South. About 5 percent of the region's farm operators were *farm managers* who managed the holdings of absentee slaveholders. Throughout the antebellum period, at least half the region's land was engrossed by nonresident speculators, and Tidewater and Lower South planters owned about one-third of those absentee holdings. For instance, John Norton subdivided his eighteenth-century Fauquier, Virginia, holdings into three overseer-managed plantations that were later inherited by his sons. One of the Fauquier farm managers negotiated an additional sharecropping arrangement for his sons. "Sir, I should be willing to serve you another year," he wrote, "if you would rent me the place ... for to put my stock at and boys." However, he specified, it would be essential for the slaveholder to advance provisions to the new sharecroppers. "As I have a large family," he continued, "I should wish for them to be agiting something as well as I for their maintenance." On the eve of the Revolutionary War, Tidewater planters were opening satellite plantations in the northern Shenandoah Valley. Each "quarter" was worked by an overseer and ten slaves. Robert Carter operated six such quarters in Frederick County, each managed by an overseer who earned crop shares. In similar fashion, Benjamin Yancey of South Carolina utilized overseers to manage absentee plantations in Cherokee County, Alabama, and in Floyd County, Georgia. By relying on farm managers who worked for crop shares, wealthy Milledgeville and Savannah planters Farish Carter and John Berrien operated summer estates in northern Georgia. Similarly, a nonresident planter used a white overseer and three slave drivers to manage his Coffee County, Tennessee, farm lands.[11]

In a second form of absentee ownership, owners of multiple estates in adjacent counties employed overseers to manage their far-flung holdings. Thomas Jefferson paid crop shares to farm managers that ranged from sixteen barrels of corn (for management of a small farm) to one-fifth of the tobacco (for management of a middling plantation with slaves). The Cunninghams of Sevier County, Tennessee, "owned several farms at different places." In Botetourt County, Virginia, one small slaveholder "had three plantations, had five slaves on one and four on another." James McDowell of Rockbridge County, Virginia, and Edmund Jones of Wilkes County, North Carolina, "absentee farmed" holdings in several adjacent counties by relying on farm managers who were paid crop shares. A sister wrote her wealthy Wilkes County, North Carolina, brother, hoping that he would "rent a place" in Gordon Springs, Georgia, "place his negroes on it," and allow her impoverished husband to manage the small absentee plantation. In order to "engage on any terms not involving the payment of money," Appalachian Tennessee and Virginia slaveholders hired sons of poor farmers "to work with the [slaves] for a term of a year for good wages or a share of crops and stock grown on the farm." A Haywood, North Carolina, overseer contracted for one-seventh of the grains, a share of blacksmithing receipts, all the butter churned, all goose feathers plucked, and one-tenth of the wool.[12]

Usually, the slaveholder supplied work stock, farm implements, seed, and early provisions, part of which was charged against the manager's annual wages. A typical agreement allowed the landless farmer to "take a support for himself and family out of what the farm grows. But whatever else he needs he is to pay for. . . . [The owner] has full right and privilege to take a proportion of all things of which the said [manager] shall charge [others] for." The farm manager agreed to keep no personal livestock and retained no right to any share of the production beyond his annual wages and subsistence. Determination of this subsistence level was at the discretion of the owner who charged extra provisions against the household's annual wage. In most instances, the farm manager agreed to purchase all food items, "foreign articles," and even furniture from the slaveholder. Lost work time was also debited against the manager's annual wage, as in one eastern Kentucky contract that deducted "$1 a day for personal time attending [church] meeting or handling family affairs."[13]

Agricultural Labor Pooling Strategies

In order to centralize a large labor force, mountain slaveholders pooled workers with neighbors in order to capture the labor of slaves and landless whites they did not control. Once a year, the aggregated labor forces of cooperating slaveholders "come fust to one place, den to de udder, 'til dey makes dr 'roun's." Situated on the Tugaloo River, the four Jarrett plantations shucked 13,500 bushels of corn in 1850, using the labor of nearly 150 slaves and numerous white tenant households aggregated from the neighborhood. Community activities like log rollings, corn shuckings, and barn raisings were closely structured to speed task completion. An eastern Kentucky slaveholder described how small plantations "had but few hands. They generally raised large crops of corn and could with their limited force do all their work in due season," except the harvest and the shucking. Locating a large workforce in a timely fashion was critical. "Unless corn [wa]s gathered promptly after it [wa]s dry enough to crib, there [wa]s likely to be considerable loss – in fact, the longer the corn remains in the shock the greater the loss."[14]

Mountain masters sent letters by horseback to their neighbors "to ask them to allow their slaves to come and help with the corn shuckings." Eastern Kentucky slaveholder Cabell Cheanult reported in his diary: "I understand that tomorrow night they will set a night to shuck out Colby McKinney's crop, and on that night they will arrange for another crop, and so on until every man who is short of hands will have his corn shucked." Chenault presents in some detail the manner in which the work was organized. Prior to the arrival of the workers, the corn was gathered into shocks in the fields. After the men were divided into ethnically segregated work pairs and gathered in the field, the overseer gave the word for the slaves to "start your song." Working to the rhythm of field chants, the men finished the shucking by 9 P.M. While they worked, the master and his white neighbors dined in the "big house." At the end of their work night, the slaveholder instructed the laborers to "file around to the rear of the house" where they were served food and whiskey by teams of slave women; the white workers were seated at separate tables.[15]

In middle Tennessee, "they would call up the crowd and line the men up and give them a drink." A *corn general* "would stand out high above everybody, giving out corn songs and throwing down corn to them. There would be two sides of them, one side trying to outshuck the other." One western Carolina ex-slave recalled:

> The man designated to act as the general would stick a peacock tail feather in his hat and call all the men together and give his orders. He would stand in the center of the corn pile, start the singing, and keep things lively for them. Now and then he would pass around the jug. . . . Great excitement was expressed whenever a man found a red ear of corn, for that counted 20 points, a speckled ear was 10 points and a blue ear 5 points, toward a special extra big swig of liquor whenever a person had as many as 100 points. After the work was finished they had a big feast spread on long tables in the yard, and dram flowed plentiful.

Sevier County, Tennessee, slaveholders also pooled free and unfree labor for flax pullings. Laborers "would meet at some house or plantation and pull flax until they had finished, then give a big party. There'd be the same thing at the next plantation and so on until they'd all in that neighborhood got their crops gathered."[16]

Slaveholders in eastern Tennessee, western Maryland, and Appalachian Virginia harvested wheat by pooling slave and free laborers. Even though tenants and croppers rarely cultivated wheat, they worked alongside slaves during harvest, as this oral history illustrates.

> All the owners up and down Hardin Valley, they'd check the wheat fields. Whichever one was ripest that's the one they'd start. They'd go from one farm to the other. The tenant wives and slave women would gather at the "big house" of the land owner and cook the midday meal for the work hands. There would be an enormous crowd of men – at least forty, two eating tables of twenty each. Sometimes it would take several days to get the crop of one farm in. Then they'd move to another until they got all the crops of wheat in.... They came in later after wheat harvest with the same big crews and baled the straw left behind by the wheat thresher.[17]

Mountain slaveholders aggregated slaves and poor whites to harvest wheat, corn, tobacco, and cotton; to husk and shell corn; to construct barns; and to kill and process hogs. "Wid plenty to eat and good liquor to drink on hand," the ethnically mixed workforce was organized to "shuck corn or pick cotton all night." Before a cornshucking, "dey hauled corn and put it in great piles." Laborers "sung all de time us was shuckin' corn." As the work progressed, the laborers were given "coffee and whiskey all night." Cotton pickings were held in a similar fashion, the masters giving "a day off" to the slave or tenant who picked the most cotton.[18]

Poor White Complicity in Slavery

Through their employment by slaveholders, poor whites benefited from and sustained slavery in their communities. Appalachian slaves encountered their first level of poor white racism in their day-to-day interaction with overseers. Maugan Sheppard expressed the common sentiment of regional slave narratives when she described her overseer as "po' white and mean," so the slaves "wouldn't Mister him." Silas Jackson added that hired poor whites drove slaves "at top speed and whipped at the snap of a finger." However, conflict with patrollers was mentioned by Appalachian ex-slaves much more frequently than brutality from overseers, probably because owners of small plantations typically supervised fieldwork themselves. Appalachian ex-slaves expressed great hostility toward patrollers. "Dey was de devil turned a-loose," recalled Callie Elder. According to

Jim Threat, "dat was one of the things dat the [slaves] dreaded most was a patroller. . . . Woe to the [slave] that didn't have [a pass]. . . . [D]own in the neighborhood just below us we was all the time hearing about the paterollers beating some [slave]." Patrollers often overstepped their legal role to harass slaves. Henry Freeman reported the common practice of administering "a paddlin'" to selected slaves on the roads. A middle Tennessee woman recalled that "slaves would be in the river washing sometimes, and the paddie rollers would . . . throw their clothes up in the trees," or steal them. When slaves were absent without leave or they ran away, patrollers would "git after them and bring them in with the hounds." From the perspective of poor whites, service on community patrols was not voluntary. In some Appalachian communities, there was rancorous class disagreement about whether the taxes of nonslaveholders should be allocated to pay for patrols. White males who refused to serve as patrollers were fined, and towns sued poor whites "for refusing to serve as patrol." Even the Cherokee Nation mandated that each of its settlements "organize a patroling company" to exert control over slaves. The compensation for patrolling included release from road work, jury duty, and part or all of the household's taxes. In addition, many tenants and croppers were required to man the slave patrols on roads adjacent to the slaveholder's land. For example, Glover Moore managed three small absentee-owned plantations in Calhoun County, Alabama. As a farm manager, Glover's social status was only slightly above that of a poor white tenant. Like other Appalachian overseers, Glover walked or rode through the fields to "push [the] work" of the slaves. In addition, he worked on nightly patrols "to regulate the comings and going of the Negroes" and to make sudden raids "on suspected Negro quarters to catch persistent offenders and runaways."[19]

The structural linkage between overseers and patrols caused a great deal of racial animosity between poor whites and black Appalachians. On William Irving's plantation, "de overseer lived between de cabins," in order to monitor slave movements closely. An overseer could be dismissed if slaves complained to their owners about abusive treatment, but the manager could shift that onerous disciplining to the patrollers. If any of Irving's peers "didn't work," the overseer "had de patty-rollers" provide the whipping, thereby avoiding any disfavor from his employer. To intimidate the slaves, Silas Jackson explained, "the overseers were connected with the patrollers, not only to watch our slaves, but sometimes for the rewards for other slaves who had run away from another plantation." In such an arrangement between overseer and patrollers, Zek Brown's uncle was whipped "so hard dat him am layed up fo' a week." Enraged "'bout dat whuppin'," Brown's owner "tried to find out who 'twas dat whupped uncle but never could."[20]

Poor white patrollers regulated the movements of mountain slaves. More often than they punished any other offense, patrollers whipped black males for being away without passes to visit abroad families. *Source: Frank Leslie's Illustrated Newspaper*, 11 July 1863.

The slave term *paddyroller* provides a linguistic hint of the deep racial hostility between landless Irish immigrants and slaves. An antebellum journalist visiting Appalachian counties captured the ethnic antagonism when he observed that "the Irish population, with very few exceptions, are the devoted supporters of Southern slavery. They have acquired the reputation of being the most merciless of negro task-maskers." It is also clear in the regional slave narratives that most black Appalachians identified patrollers as a class of people far beneath the status and the morality of their owners. Rachel Cruze's reaction is illustrative. "Paddyrollers were poor white trash," she said. "Nobody who amounted to anything would go about the country like they did – just like dogs hunting rabbits." In this regard, mountain slaveholders were highly successful at shifting hostility away from themselves, for Rachel and other Appalachian ex-slaves verbalized the very ethnic stereotypes they had been taught by masters. Within this context, the owner could deny any responsibility for the "uncontrollable" brutality or harassment of poor white patrollers, even though this form of policing was legally forced upon nonslaveholders by county courts and state legislatures that were politically shaped by the slaveholder agenda.[21]

Mountain slaves had another reason to fear poor whites. Nearly half of the Appalachians who identified themselves to census enumerators as slave traders or speculators were men of very limited assets. One-third of those who engaged in the human traffic were farm owners or retail operators who averaged $244 or less in total wealth. Another 15 percent of them owned neither land nor any other personal assets. How, then, could these poor Appalachians be actively involved in slave trading? First, such a person may have had dreams of future fortunes, like two "Negro traders" from Franklin County, Virginia, and Tyler County, West Virginia, who invested in cheap slave children in order to earn significant profits when they reached prime marketable age. However, most of these poor whites were involved in slave trading through activities that directed a great deal of violence toward black Appalachians. For instance, a landless laborer may have thought of himself as a slave trader because he worked for a commercial speculator, helping to transport coffles or acting as intermediary to buy up local slaves for export. In many Appalachian communities, poor laborers managed special jails that housed runaways or slaves awaiting the auction block. Customarily, slaveholders paid these jailers 30 cents to one dollar per day for each slave housed.[22]

Some poor whites were "slave catchers" who trained and used bloodhounds to track and capture runaways. When "bounty hunters" spotted blacks "working about as free men" who fit the description of runaways, they contacted owners and offered to return them for a fee. After a Wilkes County, North Carolina, master advertised a reward for a truant, he was contacted by such a slave hunter. "I have noticed him closely since I have seen your reward," he wrote. "He is hired out by the month, and he has every opportunity of running away, if he should suspect a discovery. The man who has him hired has agreed with me to keep him in his employ until you can come and get him." In another instance, B. W. Brooks offered to assist an owner if he came "in the night" to check the identity of a black who was "working about as a free man" who had not "yet obtained any Certificate of freedom from the Court." Brooks thought "it most prudent not to take him up and commit him to jail as he would in that event be certain to break jail and escape." John P. Chester wrote to an owner that "if there is no other hand I will kidnap them." Fearing that someone else would interfere and collect the reward, Chester added, "I am compelled to keep this secret from the world."[23]

Finally, poorer Appalachians dabbled directly in the human export business through the violent practice of kidnapping blacks. Nearly 4 percent of the Appalachian slave narratives describe incidents in which individuals were captured and sold illegally in this manner. This activity occurred often enough for regional newspapers to coin the term "blackbirding" when they reported such cases. Two poor whites in a buggy lay in wait on an isolated country road for fourteen-year-old Benjamin Washington. "One jumped out and tied his hands together," and the pair sped off to sell him to an itinerant speculator who was collecting a coffle for export to Mississippi. In McMinn County, Tennessee, free blacks were kidnapped and sold at Chattanooga. In Grayson County, Virginia, "five white men undertook to take five negroes." When the free blacks resisted, "two white men and two or three negroes were killed." While driving a wagon to an isolated West Virginia field, teenager Peter Wych "was overtaken by a 'speculator' and brought to Georgia where he was sold." Similarly, two middle Tennessee slave children "wuz stole" and exported to Georgia and Mississippi. Because middle Tennessee children "were often stolen by speculators and later sold at auctions" in Nashville, one Warren County master constructed "a tall lookout on the roof" of his mansion. From that vantage point, a "watchman" kept guard over "the carefree children who played in the large yard of the nearby quarters." Cherokees were also kidnapped and sold into slavery. Near Lookout Mountain, Tennessee, Sarah Red Bird, "a pureblood Indian," was sold to a Mississippi slaveholder after her family was killed "in an uprising wid de whites" who were "trying to drive dem out." Free Cherokees of mixed-Negro heritage were sometimes captured, and free blacks could be kidnapped in the Cherokee Nation and sold to traders.[24]

At Lexington, Virginia, an eight-year-old boy "was taken from the lower end of town by kidnappers, and carried off in a row boat." In West Virginia, "blackbirders" kidnapped slaves who had been hired out to the salt works and then sold them at Wheeling or Richmond. Promising their captives a march to freedom, Floyd County, Kentucky "slave rustlers" stole blacks at night and "hid them in Campbell's Cave." When their trail had cooled, the kidnappers exported the black laborers to Clarksville, Tennessee, where they would "sell them again on Mr. Dunk Moore's slave market." Similarly, Lewis Robards, a Lexington slave dealer, used the services of "slave stealers" in rural eastern Kentucky. Some blackbirders formed regional networks for their illicit traffic. In Rutherford County, North Carolina, for example, William Robbins colluded with poor whites to "rustle" slaves. In one instance, Robbins even convinced a free black that, by "stealing slaves," he could "make money much faster than he was doing" as a blacksmith. In Surry County, North Carolina, "a number of colored people" were "illegally held in bondage" after they were kidnapped and sold by a group of blackbirders. One company of slave and horse rustlers was made up of several men scattered through a four-county area along the eastern Tennessee and northwestern Georgia border. "They had stations in various parts of the country, at convenient distances, and when a member of the club succeeded in stealing away a negro or pony, he would pass him on as quickly as he could to the nearest station, from which point he would be forwarded to another, and so on, till the negro or horse was quite safely disposed of." By promising them freedom, another gang was able to attract slaves to leave with them voluntarily. In northern Georgia, Buck Hurd "used frequently to come round to [the] quarters of a night," to "try to entice" slaves away. This kidnapper bragged in his community that he "had got slaves to run from one master, and after selling them to another, would induce them to run from him, and then sell them to a third." In that way, "he had been known to sell the same [slave] three or four times over."[25]

Class and Ethnic Biases Against Poor Whites

Appalachian slaveholders culturally demeaned the poor white laborer "as being no better than a slave." Frederick Olmsted summarized the class prejudice he heard from a southwestern Virginia slaveholder who thought that "white hands [we]re not, in general, a bit better than the negroes." While the "white hands were seated with [them] at the breakfast table; coarse, dirty, silent, embarrassed," the mountain elite told his visitor that he

> employed several white hands and paid them ten dollars a month; and they wanted the same whether they were hired by the year or only for the summer. They didn't care to work for any great length of time without a change. They were very stupid at work, almost as much so as the negroes, and could not be set to do anything that required the least exercise of judgement, unless he stood over them constantly.... [T]here was much that was inconvenient and unpleasant in employing whitemen, especially where they were employed with negroes.

In the view of the Appalachian elites, "such white folks brought that opprobrium upon themselves by being too lazy to work and too thriftless to save."[26]

No wonder, then, that mountain slaveholders, like their Lower South peers, frequently lamented the "scarcity" of labor and bemoaned their difficulties in recruiting sufficient hands. In reality, however, Southern Appalachia experienced an empirical surplus of agricultural laborers, unlike the Northern states where there was less than one laborer for every two farms. Many Southern agricultural societies argued that "scientific systematization" could only be accomplished with workers under the total control of the slaveholder. According to John Horry Dent of Floyd County, Georgia, free labor was much less efficient on his small plantation because

> every year having a new set of hands we have the trouble of teaching them to do as we want them. But being indifferent and reluctant to fall into our system if it is in the least more troublesome to what they have been accustomed to, of course, they only half do, or do what you require in a way that does not answer. Hence the impossibility of farming with pleasure or with any confidence in your laborer.[27]

Throughout the antebellum period, wage rifts between free laborers and slaveholders were reported in Appalachian newspapers. Slaveholder control over local politics generated intense class conflict when land owners called for public regulation of wage rates. One West Virginia slaveholder believed that "a death struggle must come between the two classes, on which one or the other w[ould] be extinguished forever." Using a militia of forty men, a faction of northern Georgia slaveholders controlled local elections to ensure that poor whites could not vote against the proslavery policies of the governor and the Georgia legislature.

> The said band, from the day of their organization, never permitted a citizen of Murray County opposed to the dominant party of Georgia, to exercise the right of suffrage at any election whatever.... [T]he said band appeared at the polls with the arms of the State, rejecting every vote that 'was not of the true stripe,' they called it. They frequently seized and dragged to the polls honest citizens and compelled them to vote contrary to their will.... Appeals from the citizens of Murray County brought them no relief – and incensed at such outrages, they determined... to turn out and elect such Judges of the Inferior Court and county officers as would be above the control of [the slaveholding faction].

On election day, the slaveholders ordered the militia to open fire on the dissidents. Expecting "an appeal to the [state] judiciary on the part of the injured citizens," the controlling slaveholder "had a jury drawn to suit him" and appointed a new superior court clerk. Subsequently, the governor "rewarded him with an office in the Bank of the State."[28]

Many of the region's plantations and industrialists perceived the white laborer to be "a far greater pest" than blacks because he "charged too much" and "took offense at trifles." Moreover, slaveholders constantly feared that poor whites "incited unrest in blacks." Slaveholders of Frederick, Fauquier, and Loudoun Counties reported that they "found white labor unsatisfactory." Similarly, a middling western Carolina slaveholder was convinced that "the white men here who will labor, are not a bit better than negroes. you have got to stand right over them all the time, just the same." One northern Alabama master labeled poor whites "common, no account people," who were thieving, landless vagabonds who "make a heap of trouble." After he discharged a white laborer who "had often been seen lounging in the field," the slaveholder generalized that blacks "would come somewhere between white folks and such as he." Ethnic prejudices and class biases toward Irish immigrants were particularly rancorous. Railroad companies and extractive industries attracted large numbers into western Maryland and Blue Ridge Virginia through indenturement contracts with workers who were recruited in Europe and transported at the expense of the employer. One Appalachian iron forge operator managed an ethnically mixed labor force of slaves and recent immigrants. The manufacturer was convinced that the Irish "d[id] well at first . . . but after they'[d] been here a year or two, they g[o]t to feel so independent or keerless-like, you can't get along with 'em." Another Blue Ridge Virginian was even more explicit in his stereotypes. "You can order slaves about," he said. "You can make them do a job on Sunday, or any time when you want to; but the Irish, when they come to this country, get above themselves – they think they are free, and do just as they have a mind to! Then, again, they are very much given to drink, and they're very saucy when they're in liquor."[29]

Clearly, Appalachian slaveholders assigned lower economic value to their poor white laborers than to their slaves. Compare this owner's treatment of these two types of workers. On 31 January 1838, a western Maryland master wrote in his journal: "Isaac Widows [a white cropper] called and begged for 2 Bushel corn says the family has no bread." Two weeks later, he added: "Isaac Widow called wants meat Bread and money gave him none negro George came gave hime $1 to purchase a hat." Just as they controlled and punished slaves and free blacks, Appalachian counties used the sheriff, the courts, the poor farm, and the "pillory and stocks" to deal with poor whites who did not meet debt obligations or who were unemployed vagabonds. In Murphy, North Carolina, for instance, a poor white man was "stripped, whipped, and branded with a red hot iron for some petty crime."[30]

Living Conditions of Poor White Appalachians

More than a third of the Mountain households remained landless most of their productive years. Typical of this pattern was Isaac Brown of Rhea and Meigs Counties, Tennessee, who reported at the age of 80 that he had farmed all his life "mostly on rented land." A long-term analysis of landholding in mountainous Blount County, Tennessee, offers enlightening insight into the longevity of this pattern. Less than one-quarter of the Appalachian surname groups that were landless in 1801 had acquired land by 1860. More than three-quarters of these 1801 landless surname groups were either still unpropertied in 1860 or gone from the county. In addition, 16 percent of the 1801 land-owning surname groups lost their holdings by 1860. A similar pattern occurred in Greene and Johnson Counties, Tennessee, where three-fifths of the landless households tracked over a twenty-year period failed to acquire land, and 15 percent of the land owners lost their property. The ancestors of one eastern Tennessee woman "settled first in Pennsylvania" where they "cropped on shares before the Revolutionary War." Her great-grandfather "moved to Kentucky where he worked for a store owner. . . . After that, he lost what little he had saved to buy a farm. So he took up sharecropping for a family who owned about 500 acres someplace in southeastern Kentucky." Then about 1830, her grandparents "moved to east Tennessee where they took up sharecropping." Subsequently, two other generations of this agricultural family "never owned their own farm land." Typical of this pattern of intergenerational landlessness are the work histories of fifty-nine laborers on the Lenoir Plantations of western North Carolina. Several of these agricultural households initiated sharecropping arrangements before the 1820s, yet none of them experienced this form of land tenure as a transitory step toward ownership. In fact, it was not unusual for the Lenoir tenants to renew their annual contracts for twenty to thirty years or longer. Josiah Anderson, for example, leased from 1828 until 1858. Daniel Henson, who began sharecropping in 1820, saw two of his sons become tenants in 1826 and 1833; in 1837 all three were still landless Lenoir laborers.[31]

Poor White Families at Risk

In local economies that did not permit wealth accumulation for the bottom majority of the population, only a small minority of unpropertied whites became landholders between 1810 and 1860, and one-quarter or more of the region's households remained landless on an intergenerational basis. In reality, most poor mountain whites began and ended their work careers in households that could not improve their wealth, social status, or quality of life. Structurally, antebellum Southern Appalachia mirrored the economic conditions of the global economy so that a large number of laborers were "trapped permanently at the bottom" and "led economically precarious lives." Landless laborers "faced difficulties simply caring for their family's basic needs, much less establishing a position secure from the threat of poverty or deprivation." Never fully integrated into the local economy as independent producers and never completely proletarianized into wage occupations, much of the white Appalachian population was economically marginalized. They neither owned the means of production nor were they remunerated for their labor on a reliable or equitable basis. Facing erratic wages, few chances to locate rental farms, and limited educational opportunities, a sizeable segment of the white Appalachian population faced living conditions no better than those experienced by the region's slaves. Because control over land, the primary factor of production, was denied to them, the unpropertied majority of the white Appalachian population was transformed into an agricultural semiproletariat. By 1860, nearly 60 percent of all agricultural households in Appalachia owned no land, and the vast majority had no access to rented acreage. Only one-third of these households were tenants and sharecroppers. The rest were either short-term *day laborers* who resided off farms, annual *contract laborers* who lived in farm-owner households, or laborers indentured by county poorhouses.[32]

Most poor white wage laborers were engaged by slaveholders to complete specific short-term tasks or to assist with planting and harvest. The low, unstable wages of day laborers amounted to no more than food and shelter. The Civil War veterans indicated that it was not unusual for day laborers to be paid "in trade," rather than in "money wages." The Ferry Hill Plantation sometimes hired thirty or more such laborers at a time, some exchanging their work for firewood or for housing in the slaveholder's town properties. Eastern Tennessean John Sevier remunerated his farm laborers with provisions, like "an order to Millers store for half bushel salt." A small West Virginia plantation paid day laborers on a weekly basis in meat; for instance, one worker "had worked four days and a quarter got a shoulder fifteen pound." Only the large plantations ever paid money wages. On the Barbour Plantation, for instance, typical day laborer agreements required that the worker was "to have one dollar a day also finding himself" (i.e., supplying his own food and shelter). South Carolina's governor estimated in 1850 that at least one-quarter of these day laborers could "not gain a decent living." In some Appalachian counties, one-quarter or more of laboring men were "out of honest work." For instance, Marion County, Tennessee, was described as "full of pore men" who "had to wourk hard on farming to raise their family." A Hall County, Georgia, veteran reported that landless young men like himself "could not get a job." The observations of a western Carolina slaveholder provide a telling synopsis of the economic circumstances of the region's agrarian semiproletariat.

> Laborers wages were from 50 cents to one dollar a day or eight dollars a month.... [A]in't general for people to hire here only for harvest time; fact is, a man couldn't earn his board, let alone his wages, for six months in the year. But what do these men who hire out during harvest time do during the rest of the year; do they have to earn enough in those two to three months to live on for the other eight or nine? Well they gets jobs sometimes, and they goes from one place to another. But in winter time, when you say there's not work enough to pay their board? Well, they keeps a goin' round from one place to another, and gets their living somehow.

Such households moved about frequently in search of work, like one itinerant northern Georgia family who owned only "a cart but no horse. The man had a belt over his shoulders and he drew in the shafts – the son worked by traces tied to the ends of the shafts and assisted his father to draw the cart: the son's wife rode in the cart, and the old woman was walking, carrying a rifle and driving a cow."[33]

The vast majority of the surveyed Appalachian Civil War veterans described economic opportunities as very limited because slaveholders "kept the poor man down." Nine-tenths of the veterans whose parents were landless and four-fifths of the veterans whose parents were impoverished owners of small farms were convinced that the poor Appalachian had no chance of upward mobility because economic resources were so concentrated into a few hands. Olmsted "overtook upon the road three young men of the poorest class" in western North Carolina. They told the writer that "poor folks [did not] hardly make enough [wages] to keep [them] in liquor." Indeed Mountain landless agrarians "was vary pore men" who moved almost yearly, like an 1849 northern Georgia family that was escaping from one exploitative contract into another county "in search of a new location." Their meager material goods were packed into "a very small covered wagon... which was laden with corn husks, a few bedclothes, and several rude cooking utensils. Behind this team marched a man and his wife, five boys, & eight girls, and in their rear the skeleton of a cow and 4 hungry-looking dogs."[34]

Indeed, poor landless Appalachians lived in circumstances that paralleled or exceeded the worst ecological and nutritional conditions experienced by mountain slaves. One northern Georgia mistress described poor whites as households that "squat[ted] on other men's land till ejected. They [we]re hardly protected from the weather by the rude shelters they frame[d] for themselves." In 1850, Fredrika Bremer described northern Georgia's poor as "wretched white people, who live[d] in the woods without churches, without schools, without hearths, and sometimes, also without homes." Judging from manuscript sources and numerous published accounts, the dwellings of poor white Appalachians were very similar to the region's rough one-room slave cabins. Like the typical mountain slave cabin, the average house of a poor white Appalachian was a single floorless room open to the roof above, with a large fireplace at one end that was vented through a stick-and-mud chimney. Many poor white dwellings lacked the shuttered window openings that characterized slave cabins. In western North Carolina, Olmsted observed that "the great majority" of poor white Appalachians "live[d] in small comfortless log huts, two detached cabins usually forming the habitation of a family." In other words, those poor white laborers occupied the same type of ramshackle housing that mountain masters provided for their slaves. Housing provided at industrial sites was even smaller, paralleling once again the experience of mountain slaves at nonagricultural work sites. At the copper mines in Polk County, Tennessee, for instance, several hundred Cornish immigrants and slaves lived in tiny "miserable huts."[35]

Poor Appalachians were just as nutritionally endangered as mountain slaves. Corn bread and fat pork, subsidized by hunted game and fish, made up their basic diet. In slave cabin and poor white dwelling alike, a "dinner pot" hung over the fire, blending fat meat or game with whatever vegetables or wild plants were in season. Like slaves, white laborers received the scrap parts of the hog meat, so the boiling pot often included the head or feet of the pig. Like slave mothers, poor white wives baked cornmeal cakes in the ashes and boiled cornmeal mush for breakfast. Poor whites probably consumed even fewer fruits and vegetables than slaves. In the early spring, the only items for the dinner pot were lye hominy and roots or greens from the woods or pastures. Three-quarters of these poor white households were probably food-deficient, as were the majority of the region's landless farm operators. Traveling through the mountains of northern Georgia, European travelers described impoverished whites on the roads as "tall, thin, cadaverous-looking," or "dissipated," documenting the long-term effects of chronic malnutrition. One landless northern Alabama household was "right nigh starvin" because their only source of income was when they "worked all around," sometimes earning about a dollar a day for the labor of "the man, the woman, and children together." One small western North Carolina slaveholder "had plenty o' poor white trash help what wuked fer flour, meal, syrup, en fer anything else he'd give 'em as pay fer day wuk." Throughout Appalachia, landless whites were employed in sharecropping contracts as herdsmen, drovers, and cowboys for slaveholders who kept cattle in the mountains. According to Edmund Ruffin, "these capitalists hire[d] some of the poor population . . . to pay some attention to their stocks." This "peculiar class" of itinerants were "wretchedly poor" because they had no regular employment at "agricultural labor or regular industry of any kind." They suffered from malnutrition "every year & greatly by sickness." In comparison to the living conditions of these poor whites, Ruffin thought "that of the slaves [wa]s not only of greatly superior comfort and happiness, but also of respectability and dignity."[36]

Appalachian slaves recognized that poor whites struggled against threatening circumstances. Charles Ball wrote that "there [wa]s no order of men in any part of the United States who [we]re in a more debased and humiliated state" than poor whites of the South. With respect to food and living conditions, Frederick Douglass considered himself and his slave family "much better off... than many of the poor white children." Mountain slaves agreed with those assessments. One northern Alabama slave thought that

> poor white folks wouldn't never had a chance. De slave holders had most of de money and de land and dey wouldn't let de poor white folks have a chance to own any land or anything else to speak of. Dese white folks wasn't much better off dan we was. Dey had to work hard and dey had to worry 'bout food, clothes, and shelter and we didn't.

A Blue Ridge Virginia slave described his master as "more hard on them poor white folks" than he was on his own slaves. One family rented a small plot from his master, and they lived in the same kind of ramshackle cabin and endured the same food shortages as the slaves. "The poor white man had some dark and tough days," he believed. Moreover, "they were lashed and treated, some of 'em, just as pitiful and unmerciful" as slaves. Rachel Cruze was convinced that "the pore white folks... mostly had a harder time than the colored folks" and that "many poor white folks would have starved if it had not been for slaves who stole food from their masters to feed the white folks." John Brown recalled that slaves stole corn and chickens from the masters for poor whites who lived on the plantation with them. As an aging ex-slave, Julius Jones reported that he had never again in his life "seed the like of the poor white folks that lived" near the slaves on his Coffee County, Tennessee, plantation. "They was sure bad off," he commented. "When they moved, they put their belongings in little wagons and had dogs pull them. That sure was a sight seeing dogs pulling wagons, but they didn't have no other way to get from place to place."[37]

Poor White Women at Risk

Unlike their more well-to-do counterparts who had access to servants, poor Appalachian women carried the burden alone for reproduction, child rearing, household maintenance, and the care of ill or elderly relatives. In addition, these women were responsible for tending the family garden plot, poultry, and livestock. To finance the family's medical care, the wife usually raised an extra head of beef or a hog to be used in barter with the physician. If her household were to survive, however, the poor woman was required to overextend herself so that she also committed time and energy to several other economic activities. Virtually every poor Appalachian wife whose husband worked in close proximity to the home was expected to contribute labor in the fields. In this regard, poor farm women "went and helped the men folkes in the field," quite often to plant and "layby" crops, cut firewood, make hay, or even to plow.[38]

Though her labor contribution remained hidden behind that of her husband, the typical landless Appalachian farm wife was intricately controlled by the land tenure contract. She was expected – along with her children – to become an "unpaid employee of her husband" in the cultivation of the slaveholder's cash-crop fields or in the completion of other assigned tasks. When local slaveholders were short-handed at harvest or spring planting, "all worked alike"; so the husbands might sell more of their wives' labor time to neighbors, then collect the wages for their work. One northern Alabama wife maintained a ramshackle cabin, tended the family garden, cared for the children, and did housework – after working all day to increase the husband's share of production from a slaveholder's coal pit. "They were all clothed very meanly and scantily. The woman worked . . . as hard as the men. The children, too, even to the youngest – a boy of eight or ten – were carrying large lumps of ore, and heaving them into the kiln."[39]

In farm manager households, wives endured "extra-economic coercion" from husbands who contractualized their kinship and who negotiated in "the marketplace as the 'possessors' of their wives' labor." It was not unusual for the husband to obligate his wife to complete cash-crop tasks for the slaveholder. In an 1828 eastern Kentucky agreement, one husband contracted his wife's time "for her care and attention to the dairy and smokehouse" and to spin clothes for the owner's slaves. After the first year, one 1840 farm manager resisted the slaveholder's continued demands on his wife's labor. "She has not been inside a meeting house since I have been under employment," he protested. "She has been confined down and have exposed herself in attending to the dairy and the sick [slaves], cutting and making of your clothing until she has lost her health and has become so much reduced in strength." In other instances, the slaveholder brought pressure to bear directly on the landless wife so that she took on additional tasks, like sewing clothes for the owner's household, "weaving jeans and cotton goods," manufacturing tobacco twists, making rag rugs, or weaving cloth. Masters sometimes employed white midwives to deliver the babies of enslaved mothers. Slaveholders were also able to expropriate unpaid labor from the landless wives by requiring them to undertake additional tasks in exchange for food allocations. Rather than charging provisions against the husband's future crop production, the slaveholder could mandate a "pay-as-you-go" arrangement in which the woman traded "piecework labor" for rations. At a small plantation in eastern Kentucky, for example, the farm manager agreed "to purchase all the family's produce and provisions and furniture for their personal use" from the slaveholder who expected the wife's "spinning and milk in exchange for the wheat."[40]

The negative prejudices of Appalachian slaveholders toward white laborers extended to poor women. Even though recent Irish and German immigrant women could be hired "cheaper than slaves," western Maryland landowners still preferred hiring blacks because they could "order slaves about." One middling southwest Virginia slaveholder told Frederick Olmsted that "if they could get rid of slaves and obtain a sufficient number of white laborers to do their field work, they would still have to employ negro girls for the kitchen and household. The white girls who would go out to work were worse than their men, much worse than the negroes. He did not know a white girl who would hire out, whose habits were such that he could endure to have her in his house." The most visible class distinction between wealthy and middling landowners was the workload of women. In poor Appalachian households, females still worked the fields, and they were often seen plowing, hoeing, and harvesting crops. As he traveled southward through the Appalachian counties of Virginia, Tennessee, North Carolina, and Alabama, Olmsted claimed that in a single month he had "seen more white native American women at work in the hottest sunshine" than he had encountered in any other part of the country.[41]

Rachel Cruze, an eastern Tennessee slave, describes the vast gulf between the mistresses and poor white women. Though only a small slaveholder by Lower South standards, Rachel's owner was still a recognized member of the elite class in his community. Confined to the big house as a domestic servant, Rachel was very perceptive about the social distance between her mistress and a poor white seamstress.

> Fanny Oldsley was one of the pore whites who lived near Miss Nancy, and Miss Nancy would sometimes give her sewing to do, but she had to take it home to do it. Miss Nancy wouldn't have her around the place. I used to get lonesome sometimes because there wasn't a child of my age to play with. Fanny Oldsley had a little girl, who came with her sometimes, but do you think Miss Nancy would let me play with her? No, ma'm. I'd no more than sit down close to the little girl

than I'd hear, 'Rachel, you come here this minute.' And when I would go to her, Miss Nancy would say, 'Don't you sit near her. Why, she'll bite you and she'll get your head full of lice.' The pore child would look at me and I'd look at her, but I didn't want her to bite me, so I didn't get close to her.

Appalachian mistresses interacted much more frequently with slaves because they were members of a self-consciously elite class in which poor white women had no place, except the fields or the factories. Even when they attended the same churches, slaveholding women and poor whites did not socialize. Appalachian churches entrenched class distinctions by renting pews on a cost scale that put all the poor whites nearest the area reserved for slaves.[42]

Like enslaved women, poor white females worked at field labor, or they hired themselves to do some of the dirtiest industrial work. Faced with the crisis of "half-starved" children, one mother picked cotton alongside slaves on a nearby plantation. "She kept at it two days, and took her pay in corn." Women even mucked out canals and, when nothing else was available, joined the ranks of washwomen and prostitutes in the towns. Also like enslaved females, poor white women dressed their families in homespun clothing that they produced themselves. However, slaves had better access to looms and spinning wheels, for most poor whites could not often afford their own textiles-producing equipment. Wives of small farm owners were more fortunate. Like enslaved women, poor white Appalachian females endured poor diets and frequent hunger, and they received no medical treatment during pregnancy or childbirth except that delivered by midwives. Because of ecological risks, malnutrition, and physical labor during pregnancy, poor white women probably watched their children die with about the same high frequency as mountain slave women. If we could isolate their mortality rates in the census data, we would probably discover that, like their enslaved counterparts, poor white women experienced higher mortality rates than poor white males, especially during the childbearing years.[43]

6 Repression and Antisystemic Resistance on Mountain Plantations

> There comes a time when the cup of endurance runs over, and men are no longer willing to be plunged into an abyss of injustice where they experience the bleakness of corroding despair.
>
> – Dr. Martin Luther King, Jr.

Like their counterparts all over the New World, Appalachian masters recognized that they could never fully control those they held in bondage. As Orlando Patterson has observed, "there was more than despotic authority in this master-slave relationship." In an antebellum planters' magazine, one Appalachian slaveholder advised masters to rely heavily on "rewards to the most deserving" because "the cost [wa]s trifling" while the outcome was "manifestly beneficial." Positive incentives, he counseled, "inspire[d] gratitude to the master, and bec[a]me a stimulus to good conduct." The ingratiating paternalism of the slaveholder proved to be a more powerful motivating force than any whip, for masters utilized slave families themselves as a powerful means of social control over laborers. On the one hand, slaveholders proffered rewards and privileges and then withdrew them as punishment for unacceptable behavior. On the other hand, the entire household assumed liability (might even be sold) for the infractions of its members. As their most effective mechanism of social control nearly two-thirds of the time, masters dispensed and withheld privileges, such as family garden parcels, household opportunities to earn cash, and visits to abroad family. Through these devices, masters expanded their regulation to encompass slaves' "free time," those waking hours when laborers were not assigned to "the masters' work," and, thereby, acculturated them "to a discipline which wedded them still further to the overall slave system." Mountain masters implemented skillfully the philosophy that laborers who used their leisure hours to generate the survival needs of their families would simply be too exhausted to organize antisystemic resistance.[1]

Regulation and Control by Appalachian Masters

Like the rest of the South, Appalachian counties restricted the mobility of unfree laborers through a series of structured control mechanisms. To prevent unsupervised travel of unfree laborers, some Appalachian masters "neber 'lowed [slaves] out de cabin at night," and most limited visitations to adjacent farms. Slaves "had to have a pass ... to go from one place to another" because patrollers "would go out in squads at night and whip" any black Appalachians they caught without documents. Policing was not limited to the roads, towns, and rivers. Bursting into Alex Montgomery's family cabin, patrollers dragged his father outside, and "whupped him hard." At one of the iron forges, patrollers disrupted a slave wedding party and whipped the most respected hand so viciously that he was incapacitated eleven days. If slaves "run away, de overseer set de dogs on dem." Andrew Goodman's master used to train his bloodhounds "for fun. He'd git some the boys to run for an hour or so and then put the dogs on the trail. He'd say, 'If you hear them gittin' near, take to a tree.'"[2]

Many larger farms had their own guardhouses or joined with neighboring slaveholders to build a common jail. If Anderson Furr's owner thought slaves were unruly, he "slapped 'em in de guardhouse, widout a bite to eat." Silas Jackson's master built a two-room stone jail in the basement of his house. Other owners organized a neighborhood facility managed by a hired poor white, as in Macon County, North Carolina, and Hall County, Georgia. Such full-time jailers were paid to punish, "to handle," and to demoralize resistant slaves. Sheriffs collected fees at town jails for catching, housing, paddling, whipping, and "breaking the spirit" of slaves. The Ferry Hill Plantation Journal provides a rare description of the methods of these jailers. After a western Maryland slaveholder accused a neighboring slave of stealing $170 from his desk, the sheriff "lodged the Boy Charles in gale and Ironed him" in order "to extort a confession." Once admission of guilt was extracted, the sheriff scheduled a quick trial, at which the jury "pronounced him guilty" without "leav[ing] the Jury Box." Using the tactic of "divide and rule," Appalachian masters co-opted slaves to spy on their peers. One middle Tennessee woman recalled that owners taught them "to be against one another and no matter where you would go you would always find one that would be tattling and would have the white folks pecking on you." When one western Maryland family confronted their master's "confidential servant" about his treachery, the master "accused [them] of an attempt to resist," warning them that any future verbal assaults or gossip about the spy would earn them a public flogging. At Oxford Iron Furnace, the manager paid "trusty servants half a dollar for whipping each of those rascals" who had broken rules or destroyed property.[3]

When controls failed, mountain masters implemented several degrees of punishment. Verbal reprimands, belittling, and abuse were the most common forms of nonphysical punishment. Owners also withdrew privileges, such as family visitations or attendance at social gatherings. Shifting laborers to onerous tasks was another popular strategy. At the Oxford Iron Works, a female textiles producer "ha[d] for Sometime promised to improve" her declining output. When her work continued to "fall off," the owner assigned her to "digging of iron ore & raking it." After she was reassigned to weaving, the owner reported that the punishment had "greatly enlightened her weaving talents." By publicly exhibiting the "degrading submission" of the slave to authority, the master played upon the human "yearning for dignity." What the symbolic display of degradation denied the slave, the master hoped to "utilize as the major means of motivating" better behavior, and thereby, acquiescence to the owner's power. Appalachian masters often humiliated offenders with public displays. When they did not work fast enough, one West Virginia master made his slaves "bite off de heads o' baccer worms." Appalachian masters stigmatized men or women who left without passes to visit nearby families. A frequently truant slave "had to wear chains to de field" or "iron hobbles around each ankle." To call attention to the "shame" of a household slave who kept leaving to visit her absent children, a Staunton merchant installed "an iron collar around her neck, with horns or prongs extending out on either side, and up, until they met at something like a foot above her head, at which point there was a bell attached." One mountain slave was "so bad 'bout runnin' way" to visit his previous spouse that his master "made him wear long old horns," to mark him an adulterer in the eyes of his neighbors. "If one slave kilt another," one northern Georgia owner tied the body "to de one what kilt him, and de killer had to drag de corpse 'round." Several mountain slaves described the practice of requiring slaves to "say 'Oh, pray master'" while they were being lashed, to show the owner that they were now willing "to be humble."[4]

The worst form of punishment was not physical torture, as many writers have suggested. The threat of being "southed" or "sold down the river" was the most oppressive social control utilized by mountain slaveholders. An 1842 promotional booklet for eastern Tennessee commented that to threaten a slave "that if he does not behave better, he will be sent to Mississippi, ha[d] a much greater effect than to threaten an English rogue" with deportation. One industrial master instructed his supervisory personnel that "nothing but the lash or fear of being sold" kept "self-willed," stubborn, or resistant slaves "straight." Indeed,

Appalachian masters executed nearly 10 percent of their slave sales in order to rid themselves of social risks who had resisted authority or threatened community safety. Every Appalachian slave knew what the master meant when he angrily menaced "I'll put you in my pocket." Indeed, Appalachian ex-slaves reported slave selling twice as often as other WPA interviewees; thus, about one of every three mountain slaves was sold.[5]

Likewise, Appalachian ex-slaves reported frequent or obsessive physical punishment nearly twice as often as other WPA interviewees. In his analysis of a national sample of the WPA narratives, Crawford found that "roughly half of all slaves on frequent-punishment plantations were ever whipped. On infrequent-punishment plantations roughly one-quarter of the slaves were ever whipped. A best estimate of the percentage of people in the slave population as a whole ever whipped is 30 percent." Since two-thirds of the Appalachian ex-slaves reported frequent physical punishment, it is likely that one-half or more of all Mountain South slaves were whipped or physically abused. Another way to assess the extent of physical abuse by Appalachian masters is to examine the physical descriptions that were published for runaway slaves. Among 297 western North Carolina and Blue Ridge Virginia runaways, 40 percent bore scars from whippings; and one of every seven had large scars from dogbites.[6]

Heavy reliance on physical punishment was grounded in a racist philosophy about the biological, spiritual, and intellectual inferiority of blacks. Appalachian clerics counseled their slaveholder members that they were expected by God to guide their laborers with physical restraints. Eastern Tennessee's renowned Parson Brownlow admonished: "The Scriptures look to the correction of servants, and really enjoin it, as they do in the case of children. We esteem it the duty of Christian masters to feed and clothe well, and in the case of disobedience to whip well." In order to "make a dog like and follow you," a regional iron manufacturer admonished his forge manager, "you must whip him occasionally & be sparing of favors, or he will turn at last & bite the hand that feeds him." Such ideologies were ingrained in slaveholding children from an early age. One Greenbrier, West Virginia, parent acculturated his young son for future paternalism by teaching him the demeanor of oppression. The eight-year-old child "would swear at the slaves, and exert all the strength he possessed, to flog or beat them, with whatever instrument or weapon he could lay hands on, provided they did not obey him *instanter*." The father encouraged the outrageous attacks of the child until the slaves "fled from this young tyrant in terror."[7]

These findings from Appalachian manuscripts are supported by earlier studies; slaves on small plantations all over the world were physically punished and abused more often than their counterparts on larger holdings.

In addition to being punished more often, Appalachian ex-slaves reported masters who were obsessive about physical punishment nearly five times more frequently than their counterparts in the rest of the United States. Even when they employed overseers, the vast majority of Appalachian slaveholders administered physical punishment themselves. Nearly one-fifth of them were described as people who could not control their tempers, even in the face of economic damage to valuable human property. Jordon Smith told the WPA interviewer that a few ex-slaves thought "their white folks was good to them," but it had always been "a tight fight" on his northern Georgia plantation. Enslavement had been "skeery times" for Oliver Bell because his owner "never had no mercy fer nobody." Jim Threat and his peers "all hated" their northern Alabama master because he would "beat them for everything they done and a lot they didn't do." Anderson Furr's northern Georgia master "was all time knockin' on" his slaves. "He 'lowed dey didn't do dis, or dat, or somepin else right – he allus had to have some 'scuse to knock 'em 'round." According to Silas Jackson, "a meaner man was never born" than his "brutal, wicked and hard" Allegany County owner. Jackson had "seen men beaten until they dropped in their tracks or knocked down by clubs, women stripped down to their waist and cowhided." Easter Brown's northern Georgia owner "wuz real cruel." When he got angry, "he'd beat his hoss down on his knees," and he was no less brutal toward his slaves. One White County, Tennessee, master "wouldn't whip horses half as hard" as the slaves. Effie Cowan's owner "was beatin on some of his slaves all de time." If a punished slave resisted or sassed during the whipping, "he would put salt in dose raw places." When her master "sole a slave, dey was allus glad ter git away, but when he bought one, de first thing he done was brought de slave home and gives it a whippin', he calls him self puttin' de fear of God in him." Though an active member of the Methodist Church, one western Maryland owner "thought nothing of taking the shovel to [a slave's] head; or of knocking him [down], and stamping his head with the heels of his boots." On Andrew Goodman's farm, slaves "was afeared all the time and hated [their] vicious cruel master." When this owner retrieved a slave who had attempted to escape North, "he tied him and beat him for a turrible long time. Then he took a big, pine torch and let burnin' pitch drop in spots all over him. Old Charlie was sick 'bout four months and then he died." Cherokee slaveholder James Vann burned a slave to death for participating in a plot to rob his store.[8]

Women and children were physically abused just about as often as adult males. Many Appalachian masters "made a common practice of flogging females when stripped naked." According to one northern Georgia woman, her master "would tear your back all to pieces." Females "had no protection," so they "had to stand in fear" of an owner who would "take your clothes off and whip you like you was no more than mules." When Sarah Gudger's western Carolina owner would "get his dandah up," she "dassent look roun' at him." When he was infuriated, he tied her hands in front of her and whipped her haphazardly all over her body. An Albermarle County overseer threw a female slave into a fire twice. Some children were the victims of physical tortures that left them maimed for life. Bethany Veney was hired out to a Page County blacksmith who was "a man of most violent temper." When the young girl "was awkward one day," the employer struck her "with a nail-rod," causing her to be lame. When her owner complained about such treatment, the blacksmith called the child into a field and beat her severely, warning her never to tattle again. To punish a child for masturbation, her West Virginia master and mistress "would pinch her ears with hot tongs, and throw hot embers on her legs."[9]

Appalachian mistresses engaged in brutality toward enslaved women and children, just about as frequently as male owners. One West Virginia mistress would "beat the woman who performed the kitchen work" with a stick of stove wood, "striking her over the head, and across the small of the back, as she was bent over at her work." One Franklin County, Tennessee, household servant was hit "across the head with tongs and poker" by a mistress who "knocked [her] around so much [her] head and back stayed sore all the time." Perhaps she was like John Calhoun's wife, who managed her domestic slaves "not too skillfully." So she often "let things get out of hand" because she was "imperious and slightly panicky." Delia Garlic was repeatedly abused by a hot-tempered mistress. As the nurse to the white baby, she was punished when the baby would cry or when she committed social errors. On one occasion, the white woman "pick[ed] up the hot iron, an run it all down [the slave's] arm an' han', an' took off the flesh as she done it." Another day, the mistress flailed her head with stove wood for "mocking her betters," and the child "didn't know nothin' more till [she] came to lyin' on the floor."[10]

More Frequent Punishment for Noneconomic Infractions

Several scholars have focused upon economic infractions as the behaviors that accounted for most instances of slave punishment. Herskovits has argued that slave disobedience was "manifested chiefly through shirking, destruction of tools, stealing, malingering, spoiling of crops, slowdowns, and other deliberate forms of sabotaging production." Stampp described a wide array of devices that were invoked by slaves to frustrate the production goals of their owners and overseers. According to Genovese, the work rhythm and productivity of slaves "had to be hammered out as a compromise between themselves and their masters. The masters held the upper hand, but the slaves set limits as best they could." About one-third of the Appalachian slaves reported instances of punishment for low productivity or property destruction. John Finnely's master "'manded plenty work. Dat cause heap of trouble on dat plantation, 'cause whippin's am given and hard ones, too." If they did not keep pace with the driver in the fields, the overseer might "ride 'roun' . . . and blacksnake whip and give each slave a lick or two." Slaves were also whipped for "cumin' in too soon [from the fields] and unhitching the horses." On one northern Alabama farm, slaves caught stealing food "were chained to a tree and whipped." When three boatmen lost a cargo of slave clothing, the Oxford Furnace operator ordered his manager to "carry them with ropes around their necks to the boat landing where the load was lost & there have them stript naked & 39 stripes inflicted . . . on the bare backs of each of those Scoundrels."[11]

Herskovits, Stampp, and Genovese contend that U.S. slaves expressed resistance primarily through work slowdowns or withholding labor. Recently, Franklin and Schweninger have argued that most day-to-day slave resistance involved "crimes against property." Despite these overstated claims about economic sabotage, such infractions were not the primary reasons for whippings on U.S. plantations. Indeed, regional manuscripts provide numerous incidents in which owners fired or punished white overseers or black drivers for "over-using the whip" to try to spur higher productivity. For instance, the master of one slave driver "took [him] to the granary" to whip him because he "was harder on the servants than he wanted." Punishment was utilized much less often to motivate increased productivity or to protect property than to exert social control. In fact, inadequate production was the cause of less than one-fifth of the whippings reported by ex-slaves. Similarly, Appalachian masters administered less than one-third of their whippings to deter inadequate production, work deficiency, or property losses. Rather, two-thirds of the adult Appalachian slaves were whipped for social offenses.[12]

Mountain slaves were physically punished for verbal infractions more frequently than any other violation. Nearly one-quarter of the sample of incidents involved discipline for sassing, lying, disagreeing, or "back talking." Lizzie Grant's West Virginia master whipped them "real good" for "telling stories, getting sassy, or stubborn." James Pennington's western Maryland owner "would not tolerate a look or word from a slave like insubordination. He would suppress it at once, and at any risk. When he thought it necessary to secure unqualified obedience, he would strike a slave with any weapon, flog him on the bare back, and sell." According to Jordon Smith, "it was 'Hell 'mong the yearlings'" if any of the house servants verbally "crossed" the mistress. "She had a place in the kitchen where she tied their hands up to the wall and cowhide them." Because Oliver Bell's mother raised her voice in disagreement, the master "made her pull her dress down 'roun' her waist en made her lay down cross de do' en he taken er leather strop en whooped her." Cherokee missionaries routinely whipped their sassy domestic servant "into obedience." If a black woman was insolent or willful in her kitchen, one Rockingham County mistress "pinion[ed] the girl to a post in the yard ... scourge[d] her, put on the negro plaster, salt, pepper, and vinegar, le[ft] them tied." When the Etna Furnace clerk demanded that a slave go to work during his Sunday off-time, the worker replied "with some impudence." The clerk "collared him" and "struck him on the head with a rock." On top of his "Impudence and verbal abuse," the slave struck back at the white, causing the clerk to demand that the furnace master "have him corrected as he deserve[d]," with a public whipping.[13]

Unless we remind ourselves that owners interpreted such insolence as challenges to their authority, the severity of the punishments seems out of proportion to the verbal crimes. Since they were structures grounded in frequent daily interaction between owners and laborers, small plantations engaged in much more micro-management of slave behavior than their large holdings. The slave's deferential demeanor was critical, if masters were to maintain "the correct balance between social distance and social intimacy." Therefore, polite behavior always contained political concessions; it was through overt signs of deference and humility that the slave demonstrated "submission to the established order." To ignore the expected signals of deference or to push the intimacy boundaries too far was to "get out of place" in relation to the dominant white. Because the hierarchical structure was stabilized by the slaves' adherence to a deferential protocol, "the occasional miscreant could be, and was, dealt with by the naked and savage use of power." E. P. Thompson described as "theatres of control" those public performances in which the powerful act out their dominance in the belief that those they oppress will be intimidated into quiescence. Physical punishment was intended by slaveholders, then, as one of those theaters of control; these incidents were designed as much for their demonstration effect on nonoffenders as they were meant to deter future violations by the transgressor.[14]

The other social infractions were more serious than verbal confrontations with masters and mistresses. Physical assaults were the second most frequent noneconomic violation for which Appalachian slaves were physically punished. The third most frequent social infraction was temporary truancy (i.e., absence from the home plantation without a pass). Mountain slaves were physically punished for these three social infractions nearly three times more often than they were whipped for low productivity or work deficiencies. Moreover, they were not whipped for stealing or for property destruction much more often than they were physically punished for violations that involved unauthorized religious services, learning to read or write, possession of written materials, illicit communication with other blacks, spying on whites, socializing with free blacks or untrustworthy whites, and permanent escape attempts.

Mechanisms of Nonviolent Resistance by Individual Slaves

Up to this point, we have taken the master's regulatory perspective, but slaves did not acquiesce passively to their lot. As James Scott has documented, the powerless know they are dominated, but they initiate numerous subtle tactics to survive, avoid, resist, undermine, and confront. As Orlando Patterson has observed, masters were never fully successful at constructing authoritarian power relationships. "Powerless, isolated, and degraded in the eyes of nonslaves they may have been, but they struggled constantly to set limits beyond which they would not be expected to go. In so doing they could regularize their relationships with the persons who parasitized them and carve out some measure of predictability."[15]

Indeed, slaves were not recognized by masters as "active agents" until they behaved "in a criminal manner," that is, unless their actions questioned the superiority of their owners. If we shift the lens of inquiry, then, toward an examination of the slaves' stated reasons for their actions, we learn that all the infractions for which Appalachian slaves were physically punished or sold represented acts of day-to-day resistance. Scott describes everyday resistance as "undeclared, disguised" forms of "self-help" that "typically avoid any direct symbolic confrontation with authority or with elite norms." However, slaves were much more closely regulated and watched than the peasants described by Scott. Moreover, every act of resistance or disobedience pitted the deviant against the rules of oppressive elites and their agents, and slaves were *intentionally* opposing their masters' rules when they engaged in most of their acts of resistance. Furthermore, slaves on small plantations engaged in many more overt violations and much less economic sabotage than Scott claims is typical of everyday resistance. For these reasons, Scott's approach does not capture the degree of risk taken by slaves when they confronted their masters.[16]

We can find more useful insights in Gandhi's political and spiritual philosophy. In sharp disagreement with Scott, Gandhi argues that nonviolent resistance is not a "weapon of the weak," for such defiance requires "the pitting of one's whole soul against the will of the tyrant." Nonviolent resistance "is not a method for cowards," according to Martin Luther King, Jr., because there is likely to be "conscious suffering" as a result of their acts. Both Gandhi and King saw nonviolent resistance as *empowering* mechanisms, not as the only strategies available to the weak and oppressed. Nonviolent resistance can be the most constructive – and the most humanizing – channel for the frustrations of those who have been oppressed. "When tyranny is rampant much rage is generated among the victims. It remains latent because of their weakness and bursts in all its fury on the slightest pretext," Gandhi recognized. But nonviolent noncooperation is a "method of transmitting this undisciplined life-destroying latent energy into disciplined life-saving energy." Elihu Burritt saw political power in passive resistance. In spite of the access of the powerful to brutal force, he admonished antebellum abolitionists, "the steady bravery of the human heart looks gigantic despotism in the face with an eye that makes it cower." Gandhi identified two forms of resistance that seem particularly relevant to an analysis of slaves on Southern Mountain plantations: (a) offensive defiance and (b) defensive disobedience.[17]

Offensive Defiance by Individual Slaves

In his analysis of everyday resistance, Scott argued that public acts of defiance made little sense because safety and longevity were "built by a record of deferential behaviour." In the view of Gandhi and King, however, overt submission maintains the oppressive system, so the victim must force himself or herself "upon the attention" of the oppressor. Gandhi taught his followers that they "most effectively" kept in place the system that dominated them "by obeying its orders and decrees." Since an oppressive system cannot survive "if the people cease to serve it," Gandhi urged Indians to engage in aggressive or offensive "wilful disobedience." In his "Letter from the Birmingham City Jail," King reminded his white moderate critics that "history is the long and tragic story of the fact that privileged groups seldom give up their privileges voluntarily." Freedom "is never voluntarily given by the oppressor," he continued, so every small degree of liberation "must be demanded by the oppressed." By engaging in individual acts of noncooperation, the dominated party intentionally defies established procedures in order to "offend" or to "injure" the interests of the oppressor.[18]

Appalachian slaves utilized several overt methods of such aggressive disobedience. Nearly half the time, Appalachian slaves engaged in forms of resistance that were designed to cost the owner financially. Economic sabotage – such as labor slowdowns, property destruction, and escapes – threatened the financial position of owners. When industrial slaves were underfed or poorly clothed, they sometimes refused to work, knowing that the employer would weigh the lower cost of their survival needs against the drop in profits. When Etna Furnace worked one hired male "about the furnace," he was too far away to visit his family. To protest, "he laid up . . . very often & for long periods." The owner advised his manager to tell the hired hand that he would "put him in the wood chopping when he gets well." The manager was "guarantee[d]" the worker would soon be well because "he laid up very seldom when he could get a chance to run to his wife." Withholding labor was risky, and slaves were effective only when they maneuvered within narrow constraints. One case at Buffalo Forge offers insight into the politics of this form of resistance. During the dangerous summer heat, Sam Williams took a vacation, but he kept his protest within boundaries that would trigger the least retaliation from his employers. Sam's skills were crucial to the high productivity of the iron manufactory, and his past work history gave him a certain amount of leverage. Still, the artisan did not leave his work until he had been replaced by another laborer. According to Dew:

> This kept the situation from assuming potentially dangerous and threatening dimensions. . . . Ironmaking would not grind to a complete and costly stop. . . . Thus [the owners] would not be backed into a corner where they would be forced to crack down. . . . Sam knew just how far he could go with his resistance, and he was careful to keep the situation under control. At the same time, he had enough pride in himself to insist, through his actions, that there was a line beyond which he would not allow himself to be pushed. Months of steady labor, followed by forge work in temperatures reaching 100 degrees, comprised a step over that line. . . . Sam Williams won this confrontation, probably because of who he was and because his challenge to the system was guarded and oblique and had a limited objective – rest from work.[19]

However, most Appalachian slaves were not in such elite occupational positions, and they lacked the economic leverage that characterized the resistance of Sam Williams. Consequently, verbal insolence and playing whites against one another were the most frequent expressions of overt defiance. Appalachian masters often pinpointed lack of deference as one of the identifying marks of their runaway slaves. When "examined about anything," one West Virginia escapee was "apt to stare [whites] in the face and speak short." Similarly, a western Carolina male was "surly when interrogated." Isaac Bluefoot had "an impudent stubborn look when spoken to," according to his Blue Ridge Virginia owner. However, verbal resistance was most effective when the violator coupled "bad talking" with cunning, so that resistant slaves tested and pushed the fine line between deference and subtle manipulation of whites. Cleverly handled, verbal violations allowed slaves "to assert themselves and downgrade their masters without committing a crime." To try to avert their impending sales at auctions, Appalachian slaves called attention of prospective buyers to fictitious ailments or abnormalities. For instance, one eastern Kentucky slave halted her sale by staging an epileptic seizure on the auction block. After Robert Fall's mother was sold to speculators, "she begun having fits," so the traders returned her to her western Carolina owner and "demanded their money back." When the Bell family was finalizing its purchase at the auction block, a western North Carolina slave "made her braggs that if [they] kept her a hundred years she would never do [them] any good." Once she had been traded, she "ma[de] her words come true" by pretending "there was always something the matter with her." Pretty quickly, the new buyer claimed she was defective and demanded that the former owner take her back.[20]

Masters might underestimate the hostility of those who displayed the correct protocol of humility. The slave who was seen by masters and mistresses as too "quick and prompt in speech" was more likely to be punished than the slave who used a little more cunning. Flattering remarks, wide smiles, curtsies, bows, and effusive professions of affection comprised a "deference ritual" that was itself a strategy of resistance. Slowness, carelessness, stupidity, or fear could be "artfully cultivated, helping to disguise countless acts of willful subterfuge as inadvertent mistakes." One child nurse would "make like [she] was sleep, and would ease the cradle over and throw the baby out." The mistress would slap her and say, "Git on out of here and stay till you wake up," exactly the outcome the enslaved girl intended. Appalachian slaves coined the term "false teller" to refer to a slave who was skilled at lies to avoid work or to prevent masters from blaming them for infractions they had actually committed. Henry Johnson duped his mistress into giving him the turkey he had stolen and killed. The boy knew that a faulty "tally" of poultry would get the quarters in trouble, so he had to devise a tactic in which he accounted for "dat missin' bird." After wringing its neck, Henry "took out up to de big house" to tell his mistress that one of her "finest turkeys dead." Because he played his role as the white woman expected of a deferential slave, the owner replied, "[S]top cryin' Henry and throw him under de hill." That night, Henry's family "cooked him."[21]

Some Appalachian slaves played on the fears and ignorance of their masters and overseers. On a Roanoke, Virginia, farm, "the slaves used superstition to fool the white man." By sewing a huge bullfrog into his jacket, one male fooled his overseer into believing that he was a powerful conjuror. "He would hang the jacket on a nail, say something, squeeze it and the jacket would groan, moan and carry on. If anyone else touched it, the jacket didn't move." The ignorant overseer did not see that he was using a pin to make the frog jump, so he "gave the slave very few orders." Even children effected verbal charades to achieve change in their repressive regime. After her master died, one middle Tennessee girl told stories of seeing his ghost repeatedly on the plantation. "It got to be hinted around that his spirit was coming back tormenting" the mistress. While she was sitting in her bedroom, the ghost suddenly "appeared before her and such hollering you never heard." The mistress became "so nervous that she was afraid to stay in the house," so she left the plantation, thereby ending the child's daily physical abuse at her hands.[22]

Appalachian slaves frequently engaged in forms of resistance that were designed "to compel redress." One strategy was to manipulate a point of vulnerability, "a loophole in the patriarchal institution of slavery," by playing whites against one another. During crises that threatened the survival of their families, slaves forced themselves "upon the attention" of whites who might intervene to plead their cause or to stop the injustice. When facing sales or forced labor migrations that would remove kin, slaves plied the sympathies of selected whites. In Gandhian terms, they were skillful at evoking from one white "a sense of moral shame" for the brutal actions of white kin or neighbors. Deference was demanded on small plantations, but frequent interaction created a familiarity between the powerless and the elites who controlled them. Given the structure of daily work regimens in which owners knew every slave personally, masters and mistresses recognized them as human beings, and it was morally difficult for some whites to dehumanize them completely. On one Coosa, Alabama, plantation, abused slaves played on the concern of their Master to seek relief from the physical punishments administered by the Mistress. "De Marster have de fight wid her lots ob times 'bout de treatment ob weuns," Penny Thompson recalled. Fannie Tippin's mistress and her children "would hide [her] to keep [her] from being whipped" by her eastern Kentucky master. When a Warren County, Tennessee, overseer "whipped the blood" out of an enslaved child, "old Marster got a hickory stick and whipped her and said nobody aint got no business with [slaves] if they don't know how to treat them. He told her if she whipped [the child] again like that, he would cut the blood out of her." Mountain slaves frequently sought the intervention of whites when kin were about to be removed. A few slaves were able to prevent sales by appealing to whites who had known them over a long period of time. When Alfred Day was sold, his wife cried and begged the mistress "and took on so dat de master went after de men what had bought" the enslaved husband and brought him back.[23]

Because mistresses were less powerful, Appalachian slaves appealed much more often to white males who might mediate their causes with masters. Cornelia McDonald provides a direct example of the inability of a wealthy white woman to intervene effectively with a male of her own social status. In the absence of her husband, Cornelia was confronted "several times" by the slaveholder from whom they had hired a trusted household worker. Cornelia had "refused to give her up" but was "not sure that [she] ha[d] the right to do so." When Cornelia was first notified of the owner's intentions, she recorded in her diary that she thought it was "downright perfidy" for the master "to deceive the poor creature into consenting to go" back with him. The slaveholder did "not tell her there [wa]s a negro trader coming for her." Still Cornelia participated in the deceit, for she made no attempt to warn the servant or to aid her in contacts with kin. Recognizing that she was caught in the middle and could do nothing to influence the owner, Cornelia submissively wrote in her diary:

> Another painful scene with Lethea's owner. Poor Lethea must go. It is dreadful to see her tears and distress. I went up stairs into a room where she was busy tacking down a carpet. Her tears were falling on her hands as they held the hammer. . . . I could not tell her she had to go, dreading to witness her sorrow, but turned away, and waited for some other time.

After four days of such complicit silence, "Poor L. [w]as gone," and Cornelia lamented hypocritically that she "would not have believed that the sorrow of a poor servant and her departure would have made [her] so sad."[24]

Slaves could get more effective assistance when they pled their causes to male elites, as the following cases illustrate. When a middle Tennessee owner auctioned off a sibling, one slave "cried and cried till master's brother told me . . . that he would go and get him." After one elderly slave had been physically abused by the overseer, he ran away to his owner's brother. Convinced that their deceased father "would deplore" this mistreatment "with grief and anguish," the white felt that "sense of moral shame" of which Gandhi spoke. He wrote his brother tactfully:

> Old York has come to me this morning as a runaway and asks for my intercession in some way in his behalf. He complains of having rec[eive]d much ill treatment at the hands of [your overseer], and appears greatly distressed and dissatisfyed. Among other things, he is not regarded at your house as one of your negroes but as belonging to [our] Fathers estate. . . . [W]hether there is any truth in what he says I am entirely unable to tell. Permit me to say however as a matter of feeling, that he is an old man, that he was a favorite negro of his old master, on which account I think as much laxity ought to be extended to him as the nature of the case will admit barring entirely the question as to whom he may belong. . . . I am

willing that he may stay here upon any terms that may hereafter be considered right and equitable. If you do not approve of this, the negro is here and you can take such steps as you think. . . . I have advised [him] to return Home, He pointly refuses to do so. . . . Let me assure you that all I have said in this matter is in a Spirit of friendship and in accordance with what I believe would be the wishes of our Father on this subject.[25]

To escape punishment for resistance, some hired slaves manipulated "loopholes in the structure" of dominant hierarchies. One such loophole lay in the power struggles between employers of hirelings and owners. Employers sought to accumulate profits by maximizing labor output of hirelings, often under hazardous conditions and at great distances from their black families. Owners feared the loss of long-term profits if one of their laborers was permanently harmed while working on an annual contract. To resist forced labor migration from their families, two hired males went "with the person who hired them, work[ed] about a month," and then ran away, knowing that their master would permit them to stay at home during their truancy.[26]

In other instances, mountain slaves engineered resistance to be "so crisis-packed that it w[ould] inevitably open the door to negotiation." Slave carpenters at the Oxford Iron Works went over the heads of the managers and clerks to complain about dangerous conditions. The owner was enraged and ordered his agents to make immediate changes in the project design: "Everything is to be accomplished by the Main Strength of the Servants. They are compelled by the folly of their conductors to work up hill constantly & what little they accomplish is by treble labour." Convinced that railroad work was safer, one group of slaves threatened to run away if they were hired to an iron manufactory. After their owner contracted them to a foundry, the group refused to work, forcing the ironmaster to return them to their home. Appalachian slaves frequently ran away from employers to report brutal treatment to their owners. Hired to an abusive blacksmith, Bethany Veney appealed to her owner. After the slaveholder intervened by instructing the employer not to whip her, "that was the end of it." When one Charlottesville woman appeared at home "with a chain around her neck . . . fastened with a pad Lock," her owner terminated the contract, informing the employer that "she would rather be sold than go back."[27]

Another mountain master intervened on behalf of a runaway because the employer had assigned him to an ore bank that was "so dangerous that all [the company's] white hands had quit on that account." Another owner permitted a hired runaway to stay at home, after the slave "left [the employer's] Service . . . in consequence of not being fed well & other harsh treatment." This loophole in the annual contract was so counterproductive for one employer that he complained that mountain masters "let their [slaves] go pretty much where they please." This form of resistance occurred often enough in Appalachian counties to elicit special attention from Frederick Olmsted. If the mountain slave "is indisposed to work, and especially if he is not treated well, or does not like the master who has hired him," Olmsted wrote, the laborer "will sham sickness.... But a more serious loss frequently arises, when the slave, thinking he is worked too hard, [runs away] and comes back when he has a mind to. Often this will not be till the year is up for which he is engaged, when he will return to his owner."[28]

Defensive Disobedience by Individual Slaves

Gandhi argued that there was a second form of nonviolent resistance that involved unplanned, spontaneous instances of *defensive disobedience*. Such counteractions against oppression are involuntary or reluctant noncooperation with treatment that "would be inconsistent with one's self-respect or human dignity." Scott contends that oppressed people can only attain safety and longevity through "a record of deferential behaviour." In contrast, Gandhi recognized that "the risk of supineness in the face of a grave issue is infinitely greater than the danger" of punishment. "To do nothing is to invite violence for a certainty." Inaction might spur additional brutality or coercion from an oppressor who presumes that the victims have no willingness or resources to rebel. Moreover, passivity is permanently damaging to the victims' dignity, thereby keeping them powerless. My own father verbalized the motivation for defensive disobedience from the perspective of an ethnically mixed group of sharecroppers who were attacked by white Klansmen as they worked in the fields together in the 1940s. To explain why his small group took the risk of retaliating against the neighborhood Ku Klux Klan, he said: "Life without dignity is worse than physical death." King describes the circumstances just as poignantly. "There comes a time when the cup of endurance runs over, and men are no longer willing to be plunged into an abyss of injustice where they experience the bleakness of corroding despair." When the master caught Sarah Wilson's aunt picking up an object while cleaning the yard of the big house, "she just stood right up to him." When she faced the likelihood of punishment for retrieving a prized piece of trash, she recognized the hopelessness of her situation. Still she "run at him with her fingers stuck out straight and jabbed him in the belly." The owner immediately sold the woman and her son.[29]

Appalachian slaves most often destroyed their masters' property as a form of defensive disobedience that was motivated by noneconomic reasons. When John Wise decided to sell Jane, she tried to "burn down the place." Between 1850 and 1860, four Blue Ridge Virginia slaves were convicted of retaliatory arsons after each of them had despaired of any future relief from brutal conditions. Repeatedly denied visits to their children, hired women set hotel fires in Asheville, Warm Springs, and Staunton. When he was accused of stealing and his fate looked grim, a Pendleton, South Carolina, slave torched the small cotton mill that had accused him. In almost all these incidents, their "cups of endurance" had run over, their situations seemed hopeless of relief, and retaliation was the only small element of justice they could grasp.[30]

Appalachian slaves also developed a variety of strategies to elude patrollers. In mountainous Scott County, Tennessee, Anna Lee utilized the tactic that was probably typical of most slave resistance against patrollers. When the patrol would chase her for being truant, she would "run all the way back to [her] quarters and [be] in the bed when they got there." She would pretend to be "sound asleep," and they "finally went on cause they wasn't certain [she] was the negro they wanted." Slaves would also "tie rags on their feet to keep from making any noise that the paterollers might hear." When the Macon County, North Carolina, patrol caught him without a pass at a neighborhood hog slaughtering, Adam Angel turned a "pot of boiling lard" on them to escape. Roanoke County, Virginia, slaves would "run for the cornfield" when the patrol chased them. "They would run around or jump over the stumps," but the patrollers' horses often broke their legs. When a patroller taunted a Floyd County, Georgia, man, the slave "flew into him and give him the teribblest licking a man ever toted." One Franklin County, Tennessee, slave handed the patrol a forged pass. While they were examining the paper, he "give them the slip." When the patrollers would chase Henry Banner's mother, she ran home by way of gates they "couldn't get through." Patrollers would hide in a thicket near a middle Tennessee slave church, so they could whip them as they left. "Old Alfred Williams was the preacher, and he would send somebody after his master Andrew and he would sit there with his gun on his lap" to keep them from attacking churchgoers. In 1849, a Jefferson County, Alabama, slave defended himself against the patrollers with a knife. In the scuffle, he wounded one patroller and "so miserably lacerated" a second patroller that he died quickly. When a third patroller shot at him, the slave cut his own throat.[31]

However, the two most common forms of defensive disobedience were a lot less dramatic and much less risky. Males utilized truancy and laying out more often than any other defensive resistance strategies. When visitations to families or to social gatherings were denied, slaves tested the control limits of their masters and communities. Even in the face of

Capture of runaway slaves in a barn near Harper's Ferry, West Virginia. *Source:* Still, *Underground Railroad*, p. 51.

patrollers, whippings, or worse punishment, some slaves repeatedly left their plantations without the required passes. "Sometimes the slaves run off and go to dances without a pass. 'Bout the time they was kicking their heels together and getting set for a big time, a Pattyroller would come in. . . . If you didn't have a pass he'd have four or five men to take you out and when they got through with you you'd sho' go home." On a Floyd County, Georgia, farm, slaves "wukked all day Sadday 'cept once a month." Faced with limited family visits with abroad kin, "some of de slaves would slip off and stay half a day. . . . It was jus' too bad for any [slave] what got cotched at dat trick." On a small West Virginia plantation, slaves were "neber 'lowed out de cabin at night. But sum times de oldah 'uns wud sneak out at an' tak de hosses an' tak a leetle ride at night. An' man it wud bin jes too bad if ol' Marse John ketched 'em."[32]

When the weekend pass was withdrawn from an "impertinent" male who had been "very neglectful in his business," he left without a pass to visit nearby kin. When caught by patrollers, he "bore" his defiance like "an aspect of majesty." Still the master reacted with little punishment because the truant "begged to be excused," promising his master if he "would only try him once more" the master would "never have any trouble with him" again. Other Appalachian masters were more brutal in their punishment of frequent runaways, but their coercion had no more preventive effect than kinder treatment. Callie Elder's father and grandfather were repeatedly truant and frequently whipped, but they continued to resist. Every time Callie's father ran away, "Marse Billy sicked dem hounds on his heels and dey was sho' to ketch him and fetch him back. Dey had to keep knives from Pappy or when dem dogs cotch him he would jus' cut 'em up so dey would die. When dey got him back to de house, dey would buckle him down over a barrel and larrup him wid a plaited whup." Callie's grandfather "was so bad 'bout runnin' way" that her master "made him wear long horns." When the owner dropped his security and let him "take de horns off his head whilst he was in de meetin' house," the slave "lit a rag to de woods and it tuk de dogs to find him."[33]

Some slaves engaged in evasive truancy when punishments were about to be administered or forced labor migrations were pending. Sometimes slaves received less severe punishment if they were truant long enough for a "cooling off period." George Jones's father "would hide in the hay stacks at night because he was whipped and treated badly by his master who was rough and hard-boiled on his slaves." When "several fine shoats" were stolen on a Blue Ridge Virginia farm, the overseer gathered the slaves for "an examination." Certain that he would be accused and charged with the crimes, Wilson ran away, convinced that his "many acquaintances" in an adjacent county would "harbor him."[34]

Slave narratives, local newspapers, and slaveholder manuscripts all document the practice of *laying out.* Nearly one-fifth of the slave narratives described caves, underground pits, and isolated spots in rough terrain that were used to conceal truants from detection. Oliver Bell knew about three such hideouts on his plantation, "down by de burial groun," "on de river bank," and a mountain cave. After the master beat him and made other threats, Martha Showvely's uncle "went up in de woods an' dug him a hole in de ground an' covered it with leaves. He stayed dere two years. In de day he stayed up unda de ground an' at night he went about an' got food." On Jim Threat's plantation, there were five males who repeatedly ran away to escape the brutality of their master. Jim recalled that one male "would take and take till he couldn't stand it no longer and he'd run off," even though he knew he was likely to be caught and whipped. After being purchased without his family, a newly acquired slave ran away for six weeks and then returned to his Burke County, North Carolina, mistress, announcing to her his intention to "leave again whenever he please[d]." Forced to leave their families, William Johnson's two uncles "never worked more than four months during the four or five years that they were hired out. They would go with the person who hired them, work about a month, then steal off."[35]

Individual Forms of Defensive Violent Disobedience

Defensive resistance also took more violent forms on small plantations of the Mountain South. Some Appalachian slaves harmed themselves in order to subvert their owners' agendas. Self-directed violence infrequently occurred as acts of defensive resistance by slaves who had reached the limits of their endurance of oppression. Rather than see their children sold South in a few years, some enslaved mothers engaged in infanticide and abortion. Anna Lee reported that pregnant women "like to have depopulated" mountainous Scott County, Tennessee, of new slaves through their abortions, infanticides, and birth control methods. One hired slave hurled himself into the iron furnace rather than be whipped again. Another hanged himself because of the repeated brutality of the overseer. When it was clear that she would be sold away from her family, a Loudoun County woman poisoned herself. After "being cruelly whipped" by her mistress, "a Sullivan County, Tennessee, woman" leaped off a bridge and drowned, "thus ridding herself of a life which was rendered intolerable."[36]

However, Appalachian slaves directed a much higher incidence of violence toward whites than toward themselves. Most social historians of slavery have argued that criminal sanctions for major crimes were most severe in those areas where slaves represented the greatest numerical threat to whites. In light of that argument, we should expect a lower incidence of slave imprisonment and capital punishment in the Appalachian counties. In reality, however, the public records document a disproportionately high rate of court convictions of Appalachian slaves for violent resistance and for attacks against whites. Between 1821 and 1853, Appalachian slaves accounted for nearly one-fifth of the Alabama imprisonments of slaves for physical assaults on whites. Of all the Virginia slaves condemned for capital crimes between 1786 and 1845, nearly one-third originated from Appalachian counties. Indeed, mountain slaves accounted for more than one-quarter of the convictions for murders of masters or overseers, and more than two-fifths of the reported poisonings of whites. Moreover, mountain slaves disproportionately were condemned to death for violent acts against whites.[37]

Organized Resistance by Appalachian Slaves

Even though there were few insurrections, there was a pervasive "acute fear" of "militant concerted slave action" among U.S. slaveholders after 1830. Mountain slave populations may have been smaller, but Appalachian communities were just as unnerved by gossip about black rebellions as southern areas with large plantations. We can glean significant clues about organized resistance from the accounts in slaveholder manuscripts; however, we should not assume that every incident identified by Appalachian masters is evidence that there was a real organized rebellion. In most instances, owners were recording their overreaction to overt small group activism or their own racist fears of black violence. Thomas Jefferson's correspondence includes a warning about an 1808 "slave insurrection" in Amherst County. After the George Boxley slave plot of 1816, West Virginia salt manufacturers became worried that a rebellion would be easy because of the concentration of black laborers along the Ohio River. After a fiery preacher visited black gold miners, community anxiety rose in Burke County, North Carolina. As rumors of a possible insurrection became heated, one of the owners instructed his agents that "the great number of slaves employed about the mines would make vigilance among Managers and Patrollers proper at all times." After the Nat Turner Rebellion of 1831, Appalachian masters frequently verbalized their uneasiness about similar uprisings in the mountains. "Trouble" was reported with Albermarle County blacks in August 1831, and by October whites were spreading rumors that Nat Turner was in the county organizing slaves to revolt. Shortly before Christmas 1835, Roane County, Tennessee, was buzzing with "a great deal of talk and some dread of the negroes rising." Pressed "to be careful and watchful," one master observed, "It is a disagreeable state of living to be ever suspicious of those with whom we live." During the 1840s in eastern Tennessee, there were several mob actions against slaves suspected of violent conspiracies against whites. Lynchings were not uncommon, and six thousand people gathered to watch a slave burning in Jefferson County.[38]

After news of a foiled 1856 slave revolt at a Tennessee iron manufactory, mountain masters became panicky again. One newspaper commentary attests to the frenzy that settled on Appalachian communities during this period. "Fearful and terrible examples should be made," the editor warned his county. "If need be, the fagot and flame should be brought into requisition to show these deluded maniacs the fierceness and the vigor, the swiftness and completeness of the white man's vengeance. Let a terrible example be made in every neighborhood where the crime can be established, and if necessary, let every tree in the country bend with negro meat. Temporizing in such cases as this, is madness. We must strike terror, and make a lasting impression, for only in such a course can we find... future security." Reports of widespread "insubordination among slaves" in Albermarle County caused masters to sound the alarms to neighbors twice. In December 1856, fears about insurrections overshadowed conversation at local political debates; eight months later, a second conspiracy was rumored. During the same time period, the little town of Lexington, Virginia, was rocked by "excitement about some fears lest there should be a Negro riot." In the faraway small mountain community of Dandridge, Tennessee, there was "some Excitement about an insurrection among the negroes." Nonslaveholders believed that blacks were about to "rise against the whites" because "the patrol whipt" a respected black community leader. Several slaves of William McMinnis, the largest slaveholder in Carter County, Kentucky, were accused of plotting against whites, so the sheriff administered severe public whippings in town.[39]

Community apprehensions were fueled again when John Brown made his 1859 raid on Harper's Ferry, West Virginia. Dalton, Georgia, imprisoned thirty-six slaves, after they were accused of participating in an 1860 plot to burn the town and seize the Marietta train to effect a mass escape. During the same period, Habersham County, Georgia, documented its own "slave conspiracy" in such a way that we can see how easily white Appalachians overreacted to black preachers and white strangers. "The people in... the neighborhood of Walton's Ford, ha[d] been greatly alarmed for several days past by the discovery of a hellish plot among the negroes." A local mistress overheard "the talking of the arrangements." She thought she had heard blacks say that "they were going to pitch her into the well – Then how they were going to dispose of others in the neighborhood." A free black "had been talking and reading to them for sometime." Thus, he was identified as "the head leader" and tortured until he "was made to confess the whole lot of it." The suspected local slaves were "taken up and severely whipped," and the free black "was given five hours" to leave the territory. At Christiansburg, Virginia, vigilantes jailed and then ran out of town a Yankee peddler who was suspected of inciting slaves. Panicky Page Countians attacked whites who openly expressed "abolitionist sentiments," and a county judge intervened to stop a community lynching of a suspected abolitionist at Harrisonburg.[40]

Five days earlier, a Blue Ridge Virginia slaveholder wrote that "there [wa]s considerable excitement . . . throughout the Neighborhood in relation to some movement of the Negroes & some two or three white men that ha[d] been lurking about for some two weeks." Because they were strangers from Baltimore, "no person kn[e]w anything about them nor what they [we]re after. Negroes seem[ed] to be consulting and meeting together frequently." As the war opened, communities redefined small groups as dangerous "bands of blacks," so most small towns employed larger patrols to police black Appalachians with even closer scrutiny. As rumors spread "of the negroes intending to raise," a vigilante squad stormed Etna Furnace. The "Vigilance Committee" of Buchanan, Virginia, expelled two white Pennsylvanians, and they tried and imprisoned a gambler "who had said something about the negroes raiseing." In such a repressive, reactionary atmosphere, massive open rebellion was not a viable strategy. However, that did not mean that Appalachian slaves eschewed organized resistance entirely. Incidents involving organized small-group and family-based protest are common in manuscript sources. There was a widespread ethic of community solidarity and silence. In addition, underground cultural and religious activities were the points of origin for community building and opposition to masters.[41]

Mechanisms of Small Group Protest

About one-fifth of the incidents of resistance sampled from Appalachian manuscripts involved small groups. For example, mountain slaves reported food stealing three times more often than did other U.S. slaves, and much of this activity was engineered by cooperating groups. Slaves typically worked in small groups to steal livestock for the benefit of the community. On a small Putnam County, Tennessee, plantation, black laborers would kill one of their master's hogs at night, divide it up, and store it in the root cellars of their cabins. Gradually, they would add the meat to their regular evening meals, and the master "would never know nothin about it." In Grayson County, Virginia, Sarah Burke and the other slaves would work in small groups to steal meat when they "had a hard time getting food." Late at night, they would butcher livestock in the woods. "The wimmin folks would carry the pieces back to the cabins in their aprons while the men would stay behind and bury the head, skin, and feet. Whenever they killed a pig they would have to skin it, because they didn't dare to build a fire." Near the cabins, the women "would put the meat in special dug trenches and the men would come erlong and cover it up." On Josie Jordan's farm, the entire quarters were in on a scheme to fool their master into killing the meat they needed. After they hit seven hogs in the head with a heavy mallet, a trusted livestock specialist told their master the swine died of a mysterious disease called "malitis" and acted "like they don't want to touch the hogs." Not only did they fool their master, but they also belittled him with their play on words. Because they feigned the correct behavior, the master was "afraid to eat it hisself," so he instructed them to "dress them anyway" and "to keep all the meat for the slave families." In an even more complex scheme, "a big scrape" occurred after whipped slaves described a community-wide plot by slaves and free blacks to steal bacon for resale to whites.[42]

Small group labor protests at industrial sites were not uncommon. At Oxford Iron Works, the owner was forced to abandon the richest iron ore vein. After three hired miners were killed in a rockfall, slaves refused to go back into the pit. Due to food shortages, slaves threatened to "leave in a body" from an iron furnace unless the owner did "something to satisfy them." There are also a few reports of resistance organized among slave coffles. As one coffle was being marched out of Greenup County, Kentucky, they mutinied and escaped from the speculators. After forced removal from their families in Strawberry Plains, a group of eastern Tennessee slaves planned a mass suicide.

> A speculator had been around the neighborhood buying up [slaves] for the cotton fields down South.... As they walked together they talked about their future, and they all agreed that death would be preferable to the living death of the cotton fields.... When the [speculator] drove them onto the ferry... they all walked off into the deep of the [Holston] river.... If there was any among them who was lukewarm he was shoved in by the ones behind him. That [speculator] was nearly crazy because of the money loss. He had not bought all the men outright, but had paid some down on every one of them, with a signed contract to complete payment when he received his money from the cotton raisers.[43]

Escapes were quite often designed by small groups. One group of Loudoun County, Virginia, slaves escaped in "a two horse wagon" on Christmas eve. The owner offered a high reward of "$50 each, if taken in the state, and $100, if taken out of the state." After they were captured, some small groups of runaways planned jail breaks, often with outside assistance from blacks in the community. Though their jailers could not discover how they acquired the needed tools, a small group of Amherst County captives tunneled out of jail to freedom. Braving the stench and the filth, the inmates crawled out through "a deep sink dug out in the floor to be used for the purposes of a necessary." Working slowly, the group "got into this sink" and slowly "worked a hole under the Wall of the Jail and up to the surface of the ground on the outer side." Ralph eluded his owner for a year before he "was apprehended and put in Asheville Jail." With help from unknown parties, "in a few weeks he broke jail." Captured a second time, he "was returned to the same Jail" and claimed by his master. Almost immediately, Ralph sought help again and "ha[d] not been heard from" in nearly nine months when his owner advertised him as a runaway.[44]

About one-third of the successful escapes to the North were effected by small groups of Appalachian slaves. Using forged passes, three Botetourt County slaves escaped across the Ohio River. After they overheard information "that all the servants ought to be sent South," twelve Front Royal slaves stole three of their master's prize horses to aid their escape in the night. When word began to spread in the quarters that the group "was doing finely keeping a boarding house" in Pennsylvania, the mistress worried that the successful escape would "have the effect of inducing numbers to leave home." In northern Alabama, twenty-three slaves escaped from the railroad depot where they were working. They moved at night along the Coosa River, hoping to sneak onto a steamboat.[45]

Small groups of Appalachian slaves sometimes engaged in violent resistance. In 1808, a group of Albermarle County slaves plotted "a massacre" of whites on their plantation. In 1815, a small group of western Maryland slaves killed "a most barbarous planter... in a fit of desperation." The slaves retaliated for "his atrocities among their female associates" and because "he had deliberately butchered a number of his slaves." Despite the owner's brutality, the public demanded the deaths of the perpetrators. As he whipped one of their peers, a group of Tazewell County slaves attacked the overseer and escaped. After they were recaptured, the master sold them to Lower South traders. On one Staunton, Virginia, plantation, the entire slave community participated in the horrible execution of a brutal overseer. The overseer "was de meanes' po' white debbil dat ever drawed a breath." He had "beat an' beat" the slaves until they "made up [thei]r mind not to stan' it no longer." On a bright moonlight night, the master ordered the slaves to clean up a "plantin' patch," so the workers used the cover of darkness to implement their plan. The overseer had slaves "pile de tree limbs an' brush in de middle of de patch." After the bonfire was large enough, "some of de slaves crep up behin' an' all at once pushed him over in de fire." After he fell down on his face into the fire, they "kep' pilin' brush on top of him." Next morning, they "stood roun' makin' believe dey was waitin' fo' him." When their master inquired about the overseer's absence, one of the slaves responded: "Didn' see him no mo' after we finish clearin' up las' night." When the master discovered the man's remains, he believed that the overseer "had got sick while standin' dere and fell over in de brush an' got burnt up."[46]

Appalachian slaves sometimes retaliated against white patrollers with group violence. Alleghany County, Virginia, slaves killed two patrollers after they caught runaways who were sold to a Georgia trader. In Macon County, North Carolina, slaves would "stretch ropes and grapevines across the road where they knew the paterollers would be riding' then they would run down the road in front of them, and when they got to the rope or vine they would jump over it and watch the horses stumble and throw the paterollers to the ground." Jim Threat described a northern Alabama slave plot to retaliate against patrollers. Like the Macon County slaves, they stretched vines across the road and baited the patrollers to chase them. As "the horses run full into the vines," they turned "summersets." One patroller was killed, and three suffered broken limbs. According to Jim, several blacks "lost their lives over it, but patterollers was sorter scared in them parts from then on."[47]

Resistance and Family Persistence

Fox-Genovese contends that household membership "could not provide slaves with reliable bases of resistance." Appalachian slave families may not have been stable in composition or daily contact, but they were still the pivotal units in which resistance was taught, planned, and executed. Families survived and maintained kinship linkages because they acted as units that protected and supported members. Households concealed the low productivity of weaker members by "evening up." So that kin would not "come up short" and attract the ire of masters and overseers, more productive workers shifted part of their harvest into the workbaskets of the weaker laborers. When their western North Carolina overseer was about to "whup [her] mammy onct," Laura Bell's father "comes up an' takes de whuppin' fer her." Nearly all the instances of food stealing were acts of desperation meant to aid the household, and all members were complicit in the planning and consumption of the stolen goods. Common throughout the Mountain South, the root cellar was an important mechanism through which slave families successfully engineered nonviolent sabotage. These pits in the cabin floors were used by slaves to conceal stolen goods or forbidden items, like firearms, written materials, knives, and writing implements. Because the root cellar provided a means for hiding evidence of resistance, masters unsuccessfully tried to forbid their construction.[48]

Families as Units of Resistance

Children were trained in the arts of resistance within the family unit. According to Stevenson, slave kin emphasized to youngsters "the value of demonstrating respect for other slaves and, in complete opposition to the lessons of owners, instructed their youngsters in a code of morality that paid homage to blacks rather than whites. They preached against lying to and stealing from one another, the importance of keeping slave secrets, protecting fugitive slaves, and sharing work loads." By socializing children to respect all older slaves, whether kin or not, parents "taught them to hide slave feelings and beliefs from nonslaves," contended Gutman. Moreover, slave parents and kin "clandestinely challenged brutal lessons of owners about obedience, docility, submission, and hard work," by teaching slave youngsters "through stories and examples that it was possible to outmaneuver and manipulate whites." Civil disobedience, sabotage, and theft could not have remained covert if slaves had not agreed to an ethic of secrecy; as a result, families acculturated children into the community code of silence. Afraid that youngsters "would say something to give them away," adults taught children that they "were not supposed to see anything." That way, they "couldn't say nothing" that would alert whites. If children "come up and the old folks was talking," they were disciplined to leave so they "saw nothing" and "never knew anything went on at night." Perry Madden recalled that adults "didn't let [children] stan' and listen when they talked. If you did it once, you didn't do it again. They would talk while they were together, but the children would have business outdoors." Martha Showvely's mother trained her "to mind [her] own business an' don' meddle in older people's business." According to Frank Menefee, adults "used to scare up [slave children] 'bout Raw Head an' Bloody Bones gwine to ketch [them] iffen [they] didn't mind 'em." Callie Elder's mother used haunts and ghosts to deter her children from breaking the code of silence.[49]

One middle Tennessee woman described the stress of the code of secrecy for children who were caught between the antagonistic disciplines of family and master.

> Sometimes my mother would have a little meeting and some of the slaves from neighboring farms would come over. We children had better get out or at least make like we were not listening.... She used to call me to her and say, "Now don't you tell anybody."... She would caution me because she knew the white folks would be trying to pick some things out of me. Often, they would get me up

These Loudoun County, Virginia, slaves were very aggressive in their escape to the North. Women were included among this group, but most runaways were males aged 18 to 35. *Source:* Still, *Underground Railroad*, p. 312.

> in the big house and ask me [questions about activities in the quarters]. To all of this, I would either answer "I don't know" or "no." At the same time I would be trembling so that I could hardly speak because I knew if they caught me in a lie I would get a whipping and if I told, my mother would whip me. I was just in hell all the time.

Two examples illustrate the significance of such socialization. When several families stole and slaughtered a pig at night, "all de chillun was warned not to say nothin 'bout dis . . . 'cause this pig was stole to fill their bellies." When abolitionists tried to help slaves escape from her quarters, Penny Thompson broke the code of secrecy and endangered the entire black community. Penny fretted because she was "'fraid dat dey am gwine to takes [her] away." Confused and afraid, Penny "begin to cry" and went to ask her master what to do. "Now, de night w'en de men am 'spose to come," Penny's master removed all the slaves from the quarters. "De w'ite men am in de qua'ters wid de long pistols." After the shooting, "dat am de last" Penny's quarters were visited by abolitionists.[50]

Children were also trained by their families in the arts of reconnaissance and espionage. Trained to eavesdrop on whites when they worked in the big house, youngsters were taught the body language of "hearing 'em talk while they wuz eating," while giving the appearance that they were too naive to comprehend. Mothers taught preteen domestic servants "how to listen and hear and keep [their] mouth shut." One young nurse "used to hear [her] mistress talk," but she "better not be caught listening." By giving the appropriate signs of ignorance, she "saw and heard a lot more than they thought [she] did." While she tended the white baby, another nurse would spy on her master and mistress, but "didn't know what they was talking 'bout." She would collect the words and information, however, and carry it to her mother. The adult "made like it wasn't nothing, 'cause she was scared I'd tell them if she made like it was important." When another young girl cleaned, she would eavesdrop carefully to be sure that she "eased out befo' [they] could catch [her] lissenin'." Outdoors, "always playing around, and eavesdropping," boys "would steal up" in order to overhear whenever three or four whites were "in close conversation." In the evenings, the slave children "would go round to the windows and listen to what the white folks would say when they was reading their papers and talking."[51]

Resistance to Protect Family Ties

The struggle of mountain slaves was not revolutionary in the sense that they meant to overthrow the system of oppression that trapped them. Rather their everyday resistance was focused upon the amelioration of conditions of life for households and upon the protection of the family. Indeed, there was a noticeable connection between kinship and socially prohibited behaviors. In nearly half the sampled whippings of Appalachian slaves, the acts of defiance involved attempts by slaves to maintain or to protect their families. About half the incidents of spying on whites or illicit communication among slaves involved the transmittal of information about pending punishment, sales, or hires of family members. For instance, one Fauquier County slave ran away after "he apprehended an intention of sending him to a distant part of the country." Facing permanent separation, some couples planned effective escapes, like "Abram and Nelly, about 60 years old." Nearly one-third of the verbal infractions and more than half of the physical assaults on whites occurred when slaves interfered in the discipline or sale of family members, were trying to stop sexual exploitation of female kin, or were retaliating for a master's abuse of household members.[52]

Some scholars have argued that economic grievances were the underlying causes for running away. In their view, "slave flight was a tool used by those with no other redress to define acceptable working conditions and tasks." In sharp contrast to that view, impending sales or distant hires of family members triggered more than two-fifths of the successful escapes of Appalachian slaves to the North. "Forced away in consequence of bad usage," Joseph Taper and his entire family fled from Frederick County, ultimately settling in Canada. Furthermore, two-thirds of the incidents of truancy (absence from home plantation without a pass) were not escape attempts. Instead, most of the miscreants were traveling to visit abroad families, with every intent to return to their assigned work places. Running away to visit abroad family appears in slave narratives, newspaper advertisements, and slaveholder documents more frequently than any other form of resistance by Appalachian slaves. Regional manuscripts are filled with stories of truants who repeatedly tested the limits of the structured control mechanisms. Because of his habitual "slipping off at night to see his woman," one Scott County, Tennessee, man "had to wear a bell." Despite repeated beatings and sanctions, he would get others "to stuff that bell full of rags and leaves or something to keep it from clapping, then he would leave." The pain of separation from his recently sold sister was more painful to young Ben Brown than repeated punishment. Ben "ran away three times, but ev'ry time dey cum" and captured him. With his hands "tied crossways in front," Ben "had to run or fall down an' be dragged" behind the horses. Even though this treatment "wuz terrible" and even though he "wuz whipped ev'ry time" for the infraction, the young boy continued to run to his sister. Billy ran away from an Albermarle County plantation in an attempt to return to the family from which he had been sold more than a decade earlier. The owner was convinced that he would "make toward" those kin in an adjacent county, even though the slave had not seen them in many years.[53]

After forced labor migrations, Appalachian slaves often ran away to the area of their former residence. Unauthorized visits to family accounted for most runaways at Buffalo Forge and Etna Furnace. Etna Furnace closed down rather than "blowing through Christmas holy days" because hired slaves were anxious to return to their families. In order to visit abroad families, canal boaters extended their five day runs between the Oxford Iron Works and Richmond into twenty days. After a Nelson County owner "decided to see [a household servant] sold," the slave woman escaped twice to return to her husband. A Richmond master advertised for the return of a recently purchased mountain slave whom he believed "to be now lurking" in the Blue Ridge Virginia area "where her husband reside[d]." After her northeastern Kentucky owner sold her, one thirteen-year-old girl ran away "bare headed and barefooted . . . going to see her mother" who lived sixty-four miles away.[54]

Gender and Patterns of Resistance

Because of the absence of males from Appalachian slave households, there was a striking gender differentiation in patterns of resistance and punishment. Men and women were physically punished just about at the same levels of frequency; however, males and females committed different social infractions. Nearly two-fifths of the women were punished for verbal infractions while more than one-third of the men were whipped for absence without passes. Since females headed a majority of Appalachian slave households, they acted as lone parents to protect children against whites, and they resisted sexual exploitation without assistance from black males. Consequently, women engaged in sassing and verbal insubordination 1.3 times more frequently than males. However, males ran away nine times more often than females, reflecting the much higher probability that husbands, fathers, and sons would be removed from their families through forced labor migrations. Women were much less mobile than men, so males had more opportunities to engage in certain forms of resistance. Because they were more frequently hired out, men tried to escape permanently five times more often than women.[55] As a result of their greater employment in skilled occupations that permitted chances to learn to read and write, males were slightly more likely than females to be involved in attempts at literacy. Because of their high employment as nurses and caretakers for white children, women and girls were more frequently punished for spying on whites. Because of the high incidence of female-headed households, women were more frequently punished for illicit communication with other plantations, the only method they had to warn abroad spouses about family crises. Even though the few slave preachers were males, women were punished nearly three times more often than men for their participation in unauthorized religious services or nighttime singing. Women engaged in prayer meetings or singings while they completed their evening textiles production; thus, females were more likely to be caught at such forbidden activities. Consistently, women were more likely to be punished for infractions that involved family maintenance. Consider, for example, the gender difference with respect to physical assaults on whites. Surprisingly, women engaged in physical assaults on whites a little more often than males.

Gender and Violent Resistance

Men and women had different motivations for their violent resistance against whites. While women most often assaulted whites to protect family members or to resist sexual exploitation, males more frequently assaulted white males for their abusive treatment. In most of the court convictions, enslaved Appalachian men had defended themselves against personal assaults from white males. For example, a Bedford County slave resisted violently when "his master talked of carrying him off and selling him." When a Botetourt County master "picked up a bar of iron, the slave wrested it from his hand and struck [his master] on the head with it." When a Washington County master struck a slave for injury to a horse, the slave reacted and killed his master. When a Montgomery County master attacked a slave with a club, "he wrested the club from his master and afterwards struck him three or four times." Thomas Jefferson labeled a runaway a "bloodyminded villain" who had to be sold South because he had struck an abusive overseer "with a stone in each hand," then he "got his thumb in his mouth and [bit] it severely." After years of abuse, a northern Georgia slave plotted to kill his Cherokee owner. When a Loudoun County overseer "raised de whip," the slave "gave him one lick wid his fist and broke his overseer's neck." When an eastern Tennessee master attempted to punish a male for borrowing a horse, the slave "whipped ole Major" instead. A middle Tennessee slave described the breaking point that triggered resistance from many Appalachian males. He would acquiesce to repression up to the limit of his endurance. When the punishment seemed unjust or too brutal, he "wouldn't stand them over" him. Instead, he "would fight." An Overton County slave reacted in the same way. When the overseer threatened to punish him unfairly, the slave yelled back, "You come two inches nearer me [and] I'll give ye the lash! I'll stick this ax plumb through you." In an attempt to make her "hurry up

Slaves escaping by boat from a small plantation on the Tennessee River outside Knoxville. *Source: Harper's*, 1864.

with the work," a middle Tennessee mistress struck Josie Jordan's mother "with the broomstick." Her "mammy's mule temper boiled up all over the kitchen and the master had to stop the fighting."[56]

While males most often were convicted of capital offenses for engaging in self-defense, women more often assaulted their owners and employers for abusive behavior toward family members. A Sequatchie County master was "allus beatin'" on John Day's father. During one extended whipping, John's mother "gits a butcher knife and runs out dere and say, 'Iffen you hits him 'nother lick, I'll use this on you.'" When a middle Tennessee owner whipped a young girl because she "wouldn't keep her dress klean," the enslaved mother entered the master's house and "throwed [the mistress] out the kitchen door." As a young girl, Margaret Terry intervened when the mistress slapped her mother. On Mollie Moss's eastern Tennessee plantation, "one of the slave women 'bust de skull' of the head of her marster 'cause she was nussin a sick baby an' he tell her she got to git out in dat field an hoe." Perhaps he was referring to the high incidence of this type of verbal and physical resistance in defense of family when one Appalachian master generalized in the *Southern Agriculturalist* that "the negro women are harder to manage than the men."[57]

The second most important cause of female assaults on whites was their physical resistance against sexual exploitation by white males. Even though she was repeatedly whipped for resisting her overseer's sexual abuse, Minnie Folkes' mother taught her daughter, "Don't let nobody bother yo principle; 'cause dat wuz all you had." White males never "fooled wid" Chaney Mack's mother because "she'd grab a man by the collar, throw him down and set on him." Similarly, Anderson Furr's "ma would jump on anybody what looked at her twice." Even though such resistance represented "a bold, perhaps implicitly feminist contestation of patriarchal rule," such aggression against white sexual exploitation came at great cost to the enslaved woman. A Winchester, Tennessee, slave woman was sold six times because "no man could whip her." After she physically resisted his sexual advances, one Martinsburg, West Virginia, master sold a mother and her four children to a Richmond trader. When a Franklin County, Tennessee, woman fought her master's advances, she faced a "paddle with holes in it" and a switching. When drunk, one northern Alabama master would attack the prepubescent girl who "waited table" in the Big House. The young slave reported her first such encounter with sexual molestation as one in which the master utilized extreme force. "I was scared an' showed it," Delia Garlic reported. The master was enraged by the child's reluctance, "an' he said to the overseer, 'Take her out an' whip some sense in her.'" John Finnely reported that his sister Clarinda was violently beaten for resisting the sexual advances of their Jackson County, Alabama, master. After hitting "massa with de hoe" to try to stop his abuse, Clarinda was "put on de log" and whipped. She was "over dat log all day and when dey takes her off, she am limp and act deadlike. For a week she am in de bunk."[58]

Gender and Differential Punishment

The regional narratives indicate that masters usually punished resistant women, like the following cases, by whipping them. A middle Tennessee woman "just figured she would be better off dead and out of her misery as to be whipped all the time." So she "fought back and when the ruckus was over the master was laying still on the ground." Jenny McKee "wa'nt feared," so every time her eastern Kentucky overseer hit her, she "hit him." When a Clay County mistress dragged Sophia Word, the young slave woman waited "until she turned her back," then she "shook her until she begged for mercy." Surprisingly, women were whipped for physical assaults on whites a little more often than males were whipped. On the one hand, women assaulted whites more often than males. On the other hand, there was a marked gender difference in the reaction of white Appalachians to the crimes of resistance committed by the region's slaves. Enslaved males who engaged in similar acts of violence toward whites were more likely to be jailed, to be tried in courts, and to receive maximum public sanctions. In the Appalachian counties of Alabama and Virginia where enslaved adult women outnumbered males, two-thirds of the slave death penalties were levied upon males. Community racism was one explanation for this gender difference in punishment. Even though both genders assaulted whites, black males were viewed as greater societal dangers.[59]

The differential punishment of violence related to sexual assaults is instructive. Typically, enslaved women were whipped or sold when they physically harmed their white sexual attackers. In contrast, enslaved mountain males accounted for more than one-third of the rape convictions recorded in Alabama and Virginia. Since they did not represent this proportion of the slave populations in those states, why would this have been the case? Compared to blacks on large plantations, Appalachian male slaves interacted more frequently with white females on a daily basis, including members of their owners' households and poor women who worked alongside black men in the fields and industries. Because of that proximity, Appalachian males were more likely to be charged with "rape" for behaviors that were neither sexual nor criminal in orientation. Any act of verbal insolence or physical assault upon white females might be labeled rape because of the amplified fears of the general public. Moreover, Appalachian male slaves faced an added risk because they were hired out more frequently than their female counterparts. Black "men on the road" were likely to be viewed as "dangerous strangers" outside their home communities. There was a second, perhaps more significant, explanation for the gender difference in the public reaction to crimes of resistance. Enslaved women provided Appalachian counties the added economic benefit of reproduction of future laborer exports.[60]

7 Cultural Resistance and Community Building on Mountain Plantations

> The most active incendiaries among us, stirring up the spirit of revolt, have been the negro preachers.... Those preachers... have been the channels through which the inflammatory pamphlets and papers [are] brought... from other states, [and] circulated among the slaves.... Through the indulgency of the Magistracy and the laws, large collections of slaves have been permitted to take place... for the ostensible purpose of religious worship, but in many instances, the real purpose, with the preachers, was of a different character.... The public interest requires that the negro preachers be silenced.
>
> – John Floyd, Appalachian planter, governor of Virginia

Appalachian ex-slave Booker T. Washington described freedmen as "a simple people... with no past." Agreeing with that position, Orlando Patterson recently argued that "slaves differed from other human beings in that they were not allowed freely to integrate the experience of their ancestors into their lives, to inform their understanding of social reality with the inherited meanings of their natural forbears, or to anchor the living present in any conscious community of memory." Still African-American slaves were not the "genealogical isolates" these scholars have claimed. Contrary to the perception that "there was little opportunity for experiencing family life," there was an overwhelming tendency for slaves throughout the American South to live in two-parent households. Prior to disruption by their masters, more than three-quarters of Appalachian slaves also lived in two-parent households. Moreover, nearly half the slave families were left intact, while another 14 percent experienced labor migrations that did not cause permanent loss of family ties. What is even more remarkable than the extent of family breakups is the passion of Appalachian slaves to keep their kinship networks intact. Attempts by slaves "to maintain the integrity of family life amounted to a political act of protest." Reaching back for their family heritage required "struggling with and penetrating the iron curtain of the master, his community, his laws, his policemen or patrollers, and his heritage." Still Appalachian slaves routinely engaged in "acts which unsettled slaveowners by testifying to the family ties which the laws of slavery refused to honor." Far from being casual about their spouses, many black Appalachians unsuccessfully cajoled their masters, even to the point of punished unruliness, to register their marriages with county courts. Some emancipated slaves risked loss of freedom to remain near their enslaved family members. Abroad spouses were routinely beaten by the "patrollers" for traveling the roads at night to visit their families. Because of forced labor migrations, many Appalachian male slaves had more than one family. Torn between their present families and their past kin, male slaves frequently ran away to those households from which they had been forcibly removed. These attempts to maintain past family linkages were the cause of more whippings of Appalachian male slaves than any other form of resistance. Because they saw their distant parents only about once a month, separated children left without passes to return to their families. For instance, Ben Brown ran away repeatedly to see his sister even though he was dragged back, running on foot behind the mistress's horse, and beaten for every infraction. By organizing and behaving as families in ways that frustrated white beliefs and stereotypes, slaves shaped their kinship patterns to confront oppression.[1]

Diaspora History Construction as Antisystemic Resistance

Appalachian slaves kept alive their individual family histories, teaching young children about a past that belonged to them, even if they had never been permitted to experience it. The structural intervention of masters may have caused family diasporas, but their disruptive strategies did not obliterate family histories. Even though they lived in small Appalachian slave communities, participants kept alive their family histories and the pasts of several generations of "many thousands gone." Mary Barbour's mother "had sixteen chilluns," twelve of whom were sold during childhood by her master. Her youngest four offspring never knew their "disappeared" siblings, but the mother transmitted stories about the absent youngsters. After masters relocated family members, Appalachian slave households adopted "fictive kin." Thus, many dwellings were filled with "household clusters," comprised of unrelated persons from broken families. When parents "disappeared" in forced labor migrations, Appalachian slave women embraced the orphans and imparted to the foster children the histories of their kinship ties. In that way, Appalachian slaves knew about family linkages, even when they had never interacted with predecessors. Through oral rituals and images, the family storytellers documented the contributions and sacrifices of missing kin and of past generations of community members who had been removed. Unrelated slaves kept alive the oral history of Gip Minton's past, for he was removed westward at the age of ten. Although he never really knew them, Gip was told about his grandparents, his father, two sisters, a brother, and a mother who died when he was a baby. He felt their loss even though he "never did hear from none of them." Anna Lee was raised by her "old slave mam," an unrelated woman who told her about the sale of both her parents and their lineage. "I don't knows as I'se had any brothers or sisters," Anna lamented, "cause father and mother they were sold to another man before I'se old enough to remember." Anna "never heard tell of [her] parents no more," and she "don't know whatever became of them." C. O. Johnson "had no parents to rase" him, but he still knew about the history of extended kin. Alfred Smith knew his parents' names, but he had never "seen neither of them," and he did not "even know how or who raised [him] up into the teens." Delia Garlic "was the younges' of thirteen chillen an [she] never saw any of [her] brudders an' sisters," except one that was sold in a slave coffle with her and her mother. Later, however, Delia lost the two remaining members of her family when the master sold her for resisting his sexual advances.[2]

Recognizing the possibility of discrepancies between written history and the collective oral memories of the slave narratives, I checked the family backgrounds supplied by black Appalachians against public records. When compared to county tax records and federal census manuscripts from 1840 through 1870, the genealogical details provided by Appalachian slaves are found to be reliable. In all but two cases, Appalachian ex-slaves documented with unexpected accuracy the empirical information about their masters' families, about their own kinship networks, and even about the neighboring white families adjacent to their home plantations. Because most were illiterate during enslavement, Appalachian ex-slaves rarely could correctly report how many slaves their masters owned or how many acres there were in the plantations where they worked. However, they could relate with precision the births, marriages, and deaths in their masters' families, and they had constructed extensive oral documentation of the kinship networks and diasporas of their own families.[3]

One particularly interesting story among the WPA narratives illustrates the centrality of the oral tradition among Appalachian slaves. Still illiterate herself when she was interviewed in the 1930s, Sarah Patterson treasured a family Bible which she believed to contain the written record of her family ancestry. She recounted the oral history that "her old mistress kept the record and gave it to [her] mother after freedom." At the end of the narrative, the interviewer commented:

> I didn't have the heart to tell the old lady that her Bible record is not what she thinks it is. It is not the old original record.... From questioning, I gather that the old mistress dictated the original record to some one connected with her mother or might have written it out herself on a sheet of paper. From time to time, as new deaths and births occurred, scraps of paper containing them were added to the first paper, and as the papers got worn, blurred, and dog-eared, they were copied – probably not without errors. Time came when the grandchildren ... copied the scraps into the family Bible. By that time aging and blurring of the original lead pencil notes, together with recopying, had invalidated the record till it is no longer altogether reliable.

Despite the inadequacies of her written record, however, the elderly ex-slave had stored in her memory the correct information about her own kinship linkages and about her former master's family. Even though the slaveholder's documents had not survived the passage of time, the oral memory could be confirmed by public records.[4]

Black Appalachians and the Native American Diaspora

The Middle Passage and forced labor migrations were not the only diasporas that threatened black Appalachian families. Scholars have written about New World slavery as though the enslavement of Native Americans ended abruptly when African captives were introduced, and there has been a tendency to silence details about the overlap between Indian and African enslavement. As a result, there is a sharp dissonance between written history and the actual family histories of many black Appalachians. In truth, there was no sharp, identifiable break between the two forms of slavery in the Mountain South. Nearly 12 percent of the Appalachian ex-slaves reported that they had both African and Native American predecessors. Alongside information about African genealogy and culture, those households passed from one generation to another vague memories of an indigenous past in the Mountain South and of the government removal of their ancestors. Indeed, Appalachian slaves had Indian parents, were part-Indian, or were Indian themselves 4.5 times more frequently than other U.S. slaves. Ethnically mixed slaves described three experiences through which they had acquired their Native American heritage.[5]

About two-thirds of the ethnically mixed Appalachian slaves maintained an unwritten record that documents the historical overlap between Indian and African slavery in the United States. Enslaved Indians are not uncommon in regional archival records or slave narratives because more than 2 percent were Cherokees themselves or were children of enslaved Cherokees. One narrator reports that her mother, uncles, and aunts were kidnapped from their western North Carolina village and sold into slavery in Mississippi, and three other narratives document similar histories of Cherokee enslavements. Even though her parents died when she was very young, Ann Matthews knew their story. She did not "member much 'bout [her] mammy 'cept she wuz a sho't fat Indian 'oman wid a turrible tempah." Her father "wuz part Indian," and people thought he "couldn't talk plain" because he spoke a pidgin English combined with Cherokee. Maggie Broyles was the daughter of an indentured Irishman and "a full-blood Indian" mother; yet she was still enslaved. Maggie probably had a history similar to that of Harriet Miller who was the daughter of a Cherokee and a white woman. Harriet was enslaved because her mother gave her to a white slaveholder when she was three years old.[6]

The mother of one Bradley County, Tennessee, girl was "half Spanish and half Indian." Sarah Red Bird was enslaved after a frontier "uprising wid de whites," and she taught her part-African daughter Cherokee folklore, songs, herb medicine, and oral history about clashes between white settlers and Indians in the Appalachian mountains. Cherokees sometimes sold Indian war captives to white slaveholders, condemning them to a life of slavery very different from indigenous traditions. Joseph Carter was the son of a runaway slave girl and her Indian captor; his mother lived more than a year in a Cherokee encampment in the Cumberland mountains. Other accounts described a frontier era that ex-slaves had neither witnessed nor read about. Sarah Wilson's ethnically mixed grandmother was among those slaves owned by Cherokees who migrated to Arkansas in the early 1800s. Wylie Nealy's "father was a free man always" because he "was a Choctaw Indian." Wylie's mother was of African-Cherokee heritage, thereby causing him to be enslaved. Chaney Mack's mother "wuz a pureblood Indian" who had been born near Lookout Mountain in southeastern Tennessee. "De white people wuz trying to drive dem out and in an uprising wid de whites, all [her] mother's folks wuz killed but her." So the army officers took the young girl and "give her" to a local white slaveholder.[7]

Ethnically mixed slaves also described a second way in which they had acquired their Native American heritage. In addition to past family ties, black Appalachians had opportunities to interact with adjacent Indians, and intermarriages sometimes resulted from such contacts. Until the late 1820s, Africans who came to live among Cherokees were eligible for adoption, intermarriage, and equal citizenship. In 1824, for instance, Shoe Boots petitioned the National Council to recognize the legitimacy and the citizenship of his three children by a black slave. In 1825, one of every fifty Cherokees had African forbearers, and there were mixed black-Cherokee households in several western North Carolina villages. Northern Alabama slaves sometimes interacted with Indians who "just lived wild in the woods." In southeastern Tennessee, northern Alabama, northern Georgia, and western North Carolina, Cherokees worked alongside slaves. Because they worked for half the wages paid to whites, slaveholders hired Indians to pick cotton, but they punished their female slaves for socializing with male Indians. Still intermarriages were common enough that a distinct wedding ceremony emerged. Three-quarters of the Appalachian slaves were married in an informal ceremony in which the master had them step over a broomstick. When the spouse was a Cherokee woman, however, the ceremony was different. The female's town chief or an important male in her clan "would marry dem." As the couple stood in front of him holding hands, the Indian official recited: "He is black; she is yaller. Made out of beeswax, and no taller [tallow]. Salute your bride, you ugly feller!" (or devil)." Even though laws defined enslavement in terms of the legal condition of the mother, early court rulings refused to free black children who were descendants of Indian women. The enslaved offspring of these marriages merged Cherokee basketry, beadwork, cooking, clothing styles, and herbal medicine traditions with African methods.[8]

The third method through which black Appalachians acquired their Native American heritage was much more rancorous, for about one-third of the ethnically mixed slaves had been owned by Cherokee masters. The families of Eliza Whitmire, Sarah Wilson, and Eliza Hardrick had been owned by Cherokee masters, so they had been forced westward during the government removal. Whitmire recalled extensive detail about the Trail of Tears and the resettlement of Cherokees in Oklahoma.

> The weeks that followed General Scott's order to remove the Cherokees were filled with horror and suffering for the unfortunate Cherokees and their slaves. The women and children were driven from their homes, sometimes with blows and close on the heels of the retreating Indians came greedy whites to pillage the Indians' homes, drive off their cattle, horses, and pigs, and they even rifled the graves for any jewelry, or any other ornaments that might have been buried with the dead. The Cherokees, after being driven from their homes, were divided into detachments of nearly equal size and late in October, 1838, the first detachment started, the others following one by one. The aged, sick, and young children rode in the wagons, which carried the provisions and bedding, while others went on foot. The trip was made in the dead of winter and many died from exposure from sleet and snow.

Not all slaves marched across country with their Cherokee masters. Eliza Hardrick recounted the manner in which the wealthy Ross family speculated in slaves. "It was about 1838 that Louis Ross [brother of Chief John Ross] chartered a boat and shipped five hundred slaves from Georgia." Louis had preceded the rest of the Nation in order to establish the family plantation. Ross "met the boat with an armed guard of full-blood Indians and ox wagons and took them to this plantation" where he put them to work growing crops, assigned them to run the new salt works, or sold them to other Cherokees.[9]

Cut off from their Native American past, most black Appalachians constructed their ethnic identity from the community linkages in which they lived their everyday lives. Ethnically mixed black Appalachian slaves identified themselves first as African, as part of the collective black community where their day-to-day support networks lay. On the one hand, ethnically mixed slaves had heard folklore about instances in which Cherokees captured and returned slaves to whites. On the other hand, support networks among black kin and neighbors were the only line of defense during crises. Chaney Mack's narrative is instructive in this regard. Chaney retained much of the Indian oral history she had been taught by her mother, and she had to be bilingual to understand the Indian songs and the Cherokee dialect spoken by her mother. She recognized the powerful nostalgia of both her parents for their lost past communities. She described her father as always "homesick fer Africa." Chaney also recalled that her mother would "g[e]t to thinking about her [Indian] folks sometime." When she sang traditional chants, Chaney and her siblings would "all gether round her" because they would "know she wuz thinkin' bout" her lost ancestors. Chaney's Indian mother was not fully integrated into the slave community, for her black peers "wuz afraid of her." As an adult, however, Chaney identified herself as a "black" person with Indian roots, but she looked to Africa as her ancestral home. "Nobody fooled wid" her mother, but Chaney herself was "'authority' in her small circle of black folk."[10]

There was a third reason that ethnically mixed black Appalachians viewed themselves as African, for about one-third of the ethnically mixed Appalachian slaves had experienced Indian ownership. Because she was the daughter of one of her master's Cherokee brothers and a black woman, Sarah Wilson recognized the complexity of her family lineage. "When I say brothers and sisters," she said, "I mean my half brothers and sisters, but maybe some of them was my whole kin, anyways, I don't know." Sarah experienced slavery under an ethnically mixed Cherokee master whose sexual exploitation and brutality she despised. "If I could hate that old Indian any more I guess I would," Sarah stated. According to Eliza Whitmire, black Appalachians who survived the Trail of Tears or who "had parents who made it, will long remember it, as a bitter memory."

When their owners were relocated, slaves were forcibly severed from their black kinship linkages in Appalachian communities. Eliza Hardrick recalled with bitterness the economic hardships of her family. A few slaves with documented Cherokee heritage and names were permitted to "draw land" for permanent settlement in the Cherokee Nation. During the Civil War, however, most were driven off the Nation, and "there was no end to the hardships the slaves went through in Kansas after they were set free."[11]

Black Appalachians and the African Diaspora

Another evidence of long-term slave family persistence is the intergenerational transmission of stories about the African diaspora. William Brown recalled a song in which Appalachian slaves drew an historical parallel between the Middle Passage and their own forced migrations as part of the U.S. domestic slave trade. The verse lamented: "See these poor souls of Africa transported to America. We are stolen and sold to Georgia." Born in 1845, William Davis could remember that his father was a first-generation slave. Davis's father "come from Congo," and he had told his children about how "a big storm druv de ship somewhere on de Ca'lina coast." Davis's father explained to his offspring that the "scars on de side he head and cheek" were "tribe marks" to identify his family and clan linkages in Africa. Davis's family history is an accurate reflection of reality. The slave trade concentrated West Central Africans, including 40 percent of the slaves from the Congo, in South Carolina and Georgia. The marks on the father's head distinguished him as a person of wealth and social status in his homeland.[12]

Red cloth tales were widespread, probably reflecting African spiritual, religious, and cultural associations with the color red. The ancestor of a northern Georgia slave was reportedly enticed aboard a slave ship by bright red articles. Once aboard, he was bound in the hold of the ship and transported to America. John Brown's grandmother was an African, and his mother transmitted oral myths about how blacks were captured for the slave trade. Brown recalled:

> One day a big ship stopped off the shore and the natives hid in the brush along the beach. Grandmother was there. The ship men sent a little boat to the shore and scattered bright things and trinkets on the beach.... Grandmother said everybody made a rush for them things soon as the boat left.... Next day the white folks scatter some more.... The natives was feeling less scared, and the next day some of them walked up the gangplank to get things off the plank and off the deck.... Grandmother was one of them who got fooled, and she say the last thing seen of that place was the natives running up and down the beach waving their arms and shouting.... The boat men come up from below where

they had been hiding and drive the slaves down in the bottom. . . . The slaves was landed at Charleston. . . . Most of that bunch was sold to the Brown plantation in [Talladega County] Alabama. Grandmother was one of the bunch.[13]

Chaney Mack's African ancestors were landed in Georgia. Her myth is very similar in context to that of John Brown. According to Chaney's father:

When ships would land in Africa, the black folks would go down to watch them and sometimes they would show them beads and purty things they carried on the ship. One day when my daddy and his brother, Peter, wuz standing round looking de Boss-man axed dem if dey wanted to work and handed dem a package to carry on de boat. . . . [B]efore they know it the boat has pulled off from de landing and dey is way out in de water and kaint hep themselves, so they just brought 'em on over to Georgy and sold 'em.

While presenting a myth about how the slave trade occurred, her father transmitted accurate African cultural information. Chaney would "be settin' on [her] daddy's lap and he'd tell [her] all 'bout when he lived in Africa. He usta play de fiddle and sing about Africa, and den he would cry." He told his daughter that "his mother's name wuz Chaney and dats whar [she] gits [her] name." He kept alive music and dance from the past, as well, for he "made him self a fiddle outa pine bark," and he taught his children "to dance when [they] wuz little like dey did in Africa." Perhaps the best evidence of the authenticity of her family history, however, is the postbellum return of her father to Africa. In the 1880s, the A.M.E. church organized expeditions to create new communities of repatriated slaves in Liberia, and Atlanta was one of the pivotal cities for their activities, as Chaney Mack reports. "After Bishop Jones come to [thei]r church [in 1884] to talk about taking [blacks] back to Africa," Chaney's father "walk off de next day."[14]

Construction of a Counter-Hegemonic Culture

Appalachian slaves engaged in a number of day-to-day activities through which they built a sense of peoplehood and community solidarity. Following the *griot* traditions of Africa, elders kept alive a community knowledge about the past of its absent members. Myths about the African diaspora and stories about missing kin and quasi-kin were pivotal to slave child socialization by elders. Perhaps the most fundamental form of resistance in which slaves engaged was their struggle to preserve a community memory of those who had been removed. Kept illiterate by their owners, without written records of marriages, births, and deaths, black Appalachians constructed oral histories that were passed from

Following the African *griot* tradition, older mountain slaves told stories that preserved distinctive slave culture, mocked white character flaws, and idealized the resistant black spirit. *Source: One Hundred Years of Progress*, p. 333.

one generation to another. Fictive kin taught young children about missing parents, grandparents, siblings, and extended kin. When "dark come," Appalachian slaves "would all go to de quarters an' afte' supper [they] would set 'roun' an' sing an' talk." On Eli Davison's small West Virginia plantation, Sundays were the time when slaves "mostly would lay around and . . . tell tales." Rachel Cruze recalled that, as a youngster, she sat in the eager group of children to listen to stories of runaways and resistance. Anna Peek revered the old slave women who "would sit against doors in a comfortable position and tell stories." If the evening's discussion needed to be more confidential, adults "put the children to bed by sundown" so they could "set around the fire and talk."[15]

It was within the context of evening textiles work that mountain slave women taught their children about the past through stories, handed down cultural traditions and community secrets, sang songs, and formed their own alternative religious practices. Women socialized children while they produced their nighttime quotas of spinning, weaving, quilting, and crafts. Because most mountain slave women worked at their evening textiles production without white supervision, outsiders rarely interfered, as they wove their own view of the world. At the feet of mothers, grandmothers, aunts, and elderly neighbors, children learned tales about African heritage, about the heroism of missing community members, and about the deceit of their white oppressors. While younger women and girls worked, "the old women with pipes in their mouths would sit and gossip for hours." In this way, mothers captured an ideological terrain over which masters and mistresses had little control. For the same purpose, domestic servants used "the dirt porch" at the back of the Big House. "The women in the kitchen used to sit there when they would be preparing vegetables for dinner." During those moments, they transmitted genealogical information, critiqued their owners, and idealized the value of black solidarity. The significance of these intergenerational oral histories is seen in their longevity. Sold away from Upper South regions like Appalachia in great numbers, slaves carried with them the legacy they had acquired during storytelling. In spite of dramatic cultural differences between whites who resided in those geographical zones, Mountain South and Lower South slaves shared many basic beliefs and cultural practices.[16]

Community solidarity was also expressed through resource-sharing and work assistance. As I have discussed earlier, food stealing was quite often planned by small groups. Adults adopted children and cared for the elderly kin of slaves who were sold or hired from the community. Whether friends or strangers, fugitive slaves found sanctuary in the quarters, and those who possessed medical knowledge freely offered their skills to the ill and the pregnant. To protect community members from punishment, the most productive workers shifted part of their harvest to the baskets of the young, the old, and expectant mothers. Because Appalachian masters required slaves to cultivate much of their own food supply, the household garden parcel was crucial to family survival. "Nobody want[ed] ter feed a lazy person," Thomas Cole reported, "but if dey gots sick de rest would pitch in and work hit out fer dem." Community solidarity occasionally clashed dramatically with the economic agendas of their owners. To reproduce as many slaves as possible for export, Julia Brown's northern Georgia master encouraged forms of sexual exploitation that the slaves found unbearable. According to Julia, her black community expected its members to adhere to taboos against incest, even when it was encouraged by masters. When one father impregnated his young daughter, the wife and the quarters complained to the owner.

When the master refused to do anything, the community demanded that the master remove the adult male, or they would kill him in the night.[17]

Community Building Through Social Gatherings

Social gatherings were important arenas for the formation of collective ties that made the emergence of a counter-hegemonic culture possible. The significance of these activities for slaves on small plantations can be measured to some degree by examining the comments of ex-slaves who had been denied such interaction. Only about 2 percent of the Appalachian ex-slaves reported that they were not permitted to participate in social gatherings. Sally Brown lamented that sometimes her mistress "would walk [them] to church but [they] never went nowhere else." Delia Garlic's small plantation "didn't have no parties, nothin' like that." On one small West Virginia plantation, there were no Saturday evening socials, for the few slaves there worked all day Saturday. More than half of the ex-slaves who had never experienced antebellum social gatherings were concentrated in counties that produced greater amounts of cotton than the rest of the mountain region. One Warren County, Tennessee, woman recalled that quite a few slaves in her community "didn't have any pleasure at all." According to Julius Jones, "there wasn't no form of amusement, not even a corn shucking," no slave weddings, not even any Christmas celebration. "There wasn't much fun to be had in them times," recalled another slave who worked on a small cotton plantation. "They didn't have no church at all to go to. We didn't have time to study 'bout nothing but work." A fourth man offered a similar critique. "Some slaves mighta had special things give to 'em on Christmas and New Year's Day, but not on Marster's plantation; dey rested up a day and dat wuz all." For his small quarters, there was no recreational activity after work pooling. "All corn shuckin's, cotton pickin's, log rollin's, and de lak wuz when de boss made 'em do it, an' den dere sho warn't no extra sompin t'eat."[18]

Whether situated on small plantations or not, the vast majority of Appalachian slaves engaged routinely in social gatherings that presented opportunities for them to build a collective consciousness about their shared oppression. There was nothing regionally distinctive or peculiar about the recreational and cultural activities in which mountain slaves participated, for they replicated customs that were widespread among slaves and free blacks throughout the South. Appalachian ex-slaves described two very distinctly different types of social gatherings. One category of activities emerged within the context of the labor management strategies of their masters. Even though work parties were structured for the owners' benefit, Appalachian slaves – like their counterparts throughout the world – used the arenas of those labor-maximizing strategies to resist the ideological and cultural hegemony of their masters. Even though masters tried to inculcate into their laborers their own dominant culture and ideological patterns, Appalachian slaves reframed such gatherings so that they provided an ethnically distinct experience. Work parties were mentioned by more Appalachian slaves than any other type of owner-sponsored amusement, and most of these occurred during or after fall harvest or in the early winter. Widespread throughout the rural United States, the corn shucking was a popular labor-pooling mechanism that was not distinctly a slave activity. Music and dance were so central to the husking that Appalachian slaves referred to the work groups as "corn hollers." According to Callie Elder, laborers "sung all de time [they] was shuckin' corn." Masters would send out invitations to adjacent plantations, and as many as 200 blacks might attend. After the corn crop had been harvested from the fields, "large bonfires were built adjoining the cribs where several thousand bushels were to be shucked, by both colored & white." As the laborers arrived at the designated farm in Coosa County, Alabama,

> they went at once to the corn pile and began shucking, throwing the husked ear into the crib, and the shucks to the rear. They commenced at the outer edge of the pile of corn, and cleaned up the corn to the ground as they went. There were usually two or more recognized leaders in singing the corn songs, and as they would chant or shout their couplet, all the rest would join the chorus . . . the hands would fly with rapidity in tearing off the shucks, and the feet kick back the shucks with equal vigor.[19]

Whether the husking occurred in eastern Kentucky, West Virginia, or northern Georgia, the custom was that "a song-leader mounted the pile of corn and kept the shuckers busy, hand and tongue." In Blue Ridge Virginia, laborers would

> take their places along the pile, every man taking about two feet, the aim being to see who could husk his way through the pile soonest. White and black, slaves included, worked side by side. There was always a rather free supply of whiskey. . . . If there were negroes enough, as was almost always the case, they would sing a corn song. . . . One who had a gift in that line would act as leader. He would mount the pile and improvise; the rest, and many of the whites, joining in the refrain. Occasionally, the leader would select someone in the crowd, and improvise at his expense.

Booker T. Washington described the corn hollers he had witnessed in southwestern Virginia and West Virginia.

> When [they] were all assembled . . . some one individual who had already gained a reputation as a leader in singing, would climb on top of the mound and begin at once, in clear, loud tones a solo. . . . [T]he chorus at the base of the mound would join in, some hundred voices strong. The words, which were largely improvised, were very simple and suited to the occasion.

Accounts from eastern Kentucky, western Carolina, northern Alabama, the Shenandoah Valley, and Appalachian Tennessee provide more detail about the structure of the singing. According to John Van Hook, "the man designated to act as [corn] general would stick a peacock feather in his hat and call all the men together and give his orders. He would stand in the center of the corn pile, start the singing, and keep things lively for them." Initially, someone would "strike up and singly give a few rude stanzas, sometimes in rhyme, and sometimes in short expressive sentences, while the rest unite[d] in chorus, and this he continue[d], until some other improvisatore relieve[d] him." Dancing also played a central part in the corn husking. Northern Georgia, eastern Kentucky, and West Virginia accounts document two elements of dancing that were part of the husking tradition. "When the corn was shucked about two or three o'clock in the morning they would catch the owner and ring and dance around him." After everyone had eaten and toasted the master, group dancing might begin. "There was nearly always a negro there with a banjo, who could play and others dance."[20]

In addition to corn huskings, Appalachian masters organized other types of work parties to pool labor in large numbers from the wider community. When the work and the feast were finished, slaves "would sit up nearly the whole night." Storytelling, gossip, music, and dance would fill the evening, transforming the labor management strategy into an ethnically distinctive event that helped slaves construct and preserve a collective past and to plan resistance. In addition to corn huskings, Appalachian masters organized cotton pickings, log rollings, house or barn raisings, and cotton ginnings. A Warren County, Tennessee, man recalled that slaveholders "would give a big dinner and put up the frame of a house in one day." Callie Elder thought that cotton pickings were much more labor-intensive, "warn't planned for fun and frolic lak corn shuckin's." The only reward was that the owner would "give de 'oman what picked de most cotton a day off and de man what picked de most had de same privilege." Anna Lee of mountainous Scott County, Tennessee, explained why slaves tolerated the labor maximization. Anna's master "sold lots of shelled corn," as did other Appalachian slaveholders. When it was time for harvest, he "wanted to get his cotton picked and out of the field." However, slaves had a hidden agenda behind their willingness to work so intensively. Work parties occurred only a few times each year, and these

Corn huskings, like this Fauquier County, Virginia, gathering, were labor maximizing strategies. However, such work parties also offered opportunities for community building and cultural preservation. *Source:* Criswell, *Uncle Tom's Cabin Contrasted.*

were rare occasions when masters and patrollers freely permitted slaves to be on the roads. Consequently, the slaves gathered at neighboring plantations and worked extra hours, in Anna's words, "so's [the] negroes could have some way to get together and have some fun."[21]

Other than cotton pickings, which required all available hands, work parties were quite often gender-segregated. While the men shelled corn, raised buildings, ginned cotton, or rolled logs, women were engaged in other group activities, such as pea hullings, bean stringings, or textiles production. Some of the women prepared the "cakes and pies and all kind of good things to eat" that would follow the work. To produce enough clothing and bedding for their slaves to survive the winters, Appalachian masters pooled female slaves. Under the supervision of the mistress or black female driver, the women produced bedding. While male gangs completed other tasks, "it warn't nothing for 'omans to quilt three quilts in one night. Dem quilts had to be finished 'fore dey stopped t'eat a bit of de quiltin' feast." The master "[di]vided dem quilts out 'mongst de [slaves] what needed 'em most." Millie Simpkins remembered work parties in which large numbers of women spun and wove cloth, cut and sewed clothing, produced household crafts, or manufactured quilts, blankets, and mattresses. Such events may have been designed for labor maximization, but they were also important opportunities for young people. On one White County, Tennessee, farm, "de only fun de young folks had wuz w'en de ole folks had a quiltin'. W'ile de ole folks wuz wukin' on de quilts de young ones would git in 'nuther room, dance en hab a good time."[22]

In addition to work parties, Appalachian ex-slaves described a second category of social gatherings over which their masters had much less control. Attendance at Saturday night parties was one of the primary reasons that mountain slaves were in frequent conflict with local patrollers. These gatherings represented a collective assault on the control and the authority of the slave owner, so these public festivities were set apart from forms of everyday resistance that usually were solitary. As Hartman has noted, "both the enslaved and slave owners recognized the possibility and the danger enabled by these collective gatherings." Except during busy planting and harvest periods or foul weather, one-half to two-thirds of the Appalachian slaves participated in regular parties. Most mountain slaves were freed from the master's work regimen by noon on Saturday, so the weekends permitted the temporary return of nearby abroad spouses and time for courting on adjacent farms. Those two important activities benefited owners, so they were willing to tolerate such affairs, except when white fears of black rebellions or conspiracies ran high. Throughout the Appalachians, slaves "was 'lowed to git together and frolic" on Saturday nights. Masters would "have to tell the padderollers . . . so they wouldn't bother" the slaves who were on the roads. In Warren County, Tennessee, the black community had "some kind of doin's every Saturday night." Lizzie Grant attended "negro dances," but she "always had to go to another plantation" because her West Virginia master only owned a few slaves. In Andrew Goodman's northern Alabama community, a neighbor slave "could play a fiddle," and the slaves "cooked their chickens and made 'lasses candy." On Penny Thompson's plantation, "de place in de yard am cleaned off, san'wiches am fixed" prior to every Saturday night dance. Sometimes the slaves would organize an unauthorized party. "All would gather at one of the cabins and lock the door so the paterollers couldn't git in." Jim Gillard thought the "frolics on Sattidy night was fine" because the slaves would "dance 'twel mos' day." Appalachian slaves also scheduled late summer and fall gatherings. Throughout the Southern Mountains, "in August when it was the hottest [slaves] always had a vacation after [their] crops were all laid by." During that break before harvest, they "usually had several picnics." In Coffee County, Tennessee, slaves held dances in the woods in summer by putting lanterns in the trees. After harvest and hog slaughtering, whites and blacks gathered at one barbecue after another so that there was a circuit of parties before Christmas. Sports, games, races, dancing, and singing contests were a part of the day-long celebrations. John Finnely was a strong boxer, and he recalled that masters loved to bet on slave fights during community barbecues. The bouts were "more for de white folks' enjoyment but de slaves am 'lowed to see it." The fights were "held at night by de pine torch light. A ring am made by de folks standin' 'round in de circle." While the masters bet on winners, the fighters engaged in dangerous conflict in which "nothin' [was] barred 'cept de knife and de club."[23]

Christmas "frolics" represented the second form of social gathering initiated by Appalachian slaves. Because it was that time of year when hired family members returned temporarily, Christmas was a time of reunion for separated families. Booker T. Washington described the emotional strain caused for families by the annual leasing of male laborers to distant sites. "Christmas was a season of great rejoicing on account of the home-coming of a large number of coloured people who had been at work in different industries in different parts of the state. Some of them had been hired out to work on the farms, some were employed on the railroads, and others were mechanics." Such disrupted families were reunited briefly in December, only to be separated again when new contracts were executed in early January. Perhaps that is why Appalachian slaves filled the Christmas reunion period with as many social gatherings as possible. Most Appalachian slaves enjoyed Christmas Day through New Year's Day, in the words of Jim Gillard, "six days to frolic." "Things would continue lively in the neighborhood until New Year's Day," Julia Gurdner recalled. The customary break varied from three days to a week since Christmas was the only period that Appalachian masters allocated to slaves "for there own amusement and recreation." Anna Peek thought of Christmas as "the only time that [her] Maser allowed [them] to be together just among [them]selves." Anderson Furr recalled that "Christmas was de time when old marster let us do pretty much as we pleased." The week of activities included "corn sings," quiltings, and dances at different plantations. Even in communities with small numbers of slaves, the end of the year brought "Christmas visiting and big parties," and black Appalachians gathered for at least one community feast. However, the smallest plantations were more restrictive, usually freeing slaves from work only on Christmas Day, if at all. For those black

Appalachians, "Christmas warn't much diff'unt f'um other times. Just more t'eat." When the weather turned too snowy and cold for travel, one Appalachian master reported in his journal that he "had a good deal of Complaint during Christmas holidays . . . of an extra bad kind." Unable to visit or to hold their customary festivities, his slaves experienced "a gloomy, grunty, dull Christmas" with "no company," and they were not cheered by their master's promise of "preaching" by the white circuit rider on 26 December and 2 January.[24]

Most Appalachian slaves saw the holiday break as just reward for the forced labor migrations and the hard work their families had experienced all year. At Andrew Goodman's cotton plantation, slaves "worked awfully hard" in the fall, for the cotton had to be picked, cleaned, and baled before it could be shipped to market. Their master "had a gin run by horse power and after sundown when [workers] left the fields [they] used to gin a bale of cotton every night." Goodman's master "gave [them] from Christmas eve through New Years off to make up for the hard work." For about one-third of the slave households, Christmas was a bittersweet time, for slaves would leave their kin soon after New Year's to be hired out or sold. Early winter also meant continuing hard work, for cotton ginning continued well after New Year, and laborers would begin preparing beds and planting tobacco seeds twelve days after Christmas. Since most Appalachian slaves routinely experienced food shortages and malnutrition, Christmas was one of the few periods they "had all kinds of good things t'eat." One northern Alabama master "would give a big hog to every four families," and it was the only occasion on which most mountain masters issued biscuit flour, sugar, coffee, and candy. Only a few Appalachian slaves received monetary presents at Christmas, a custom that occurred much more frequently on large Lower South plantations.[25]

The third type of slave-initiated gatherings were organized to celebrate major family events in the quarters. In order to construct an oral history of an unrecorded slave marriage, neighbors and kin assembled at the quarters of the woman, following the "jumping the broom" ceremony. The union was often marked by a big feast, singing, and dancing at which slaves "had fine times." For Appalachian slaves, a funeral was not only an occasion for a community gathering but also "a context for the collective enunciation" of the pain of slavery. Perhaps that explains why Appalachian ex-slaves provide just as much detail about funerals as they do about wedding rituals. Elsie Payne recalled that the entire black community visited the family over one specified evening after the death. The body was laid out on a "cooling board," the deceased was dressed in Sunday clothing, and the family of the deceased "would have a setting-up party wid de coffin and pray and shout, lak at a meeting." Some middle

Funerals were a public exhibition of the persistent family ties and community bonds among mountain slaves. Following African tradition, the funeral procession set the pace with songs and wails. At this death, the master (left tophat) and the slave preacher (right tophat) walked on opposite sides of the wagon that bore the deceased laborer to the burial plot. *Source: Harper's New Monthly*, 21 February 1881.

Tennessee masters were more restrictive about funerals, so "de white folks wouldn't let nobody set up wid de body 'cept de [slaves] ob dat plantation, but urthur slaves would slip in atter dark, set up en den slip back ter dere plantation 'fore day." In two-thirds of the instances described, slave funerals occurred within two to three days after the death, but one-third of the informants indicated that slave funerals were conducted only on Sundays, so as not to interfere with work. In Lumpkin County, Georgia, all the slaves in Abner Griffin's community were permitted to "knock off" work for the funeral during the day. In Lizzie Grant's West Virginia, a slave funeral was "a sad affair," and "everyone for miles around quit work to come."[26]

The coffin was placed in a wagon, and people "walk[ed] in procession to de buryin' ground, singing." In some communities, slaves walked behind the wagon; in others, they walked in front of the coffin. In Macon County, North Carolina, slaves "funeralized the dead in their own homes, took them to the graveyard in a painted home-made coffin that was lined with thin bleaching made in the loom on the plantation." A slave artisan usually constructed the wood coffin. Typically, "slave parsons preached de funeral" at graveside, but whites often conducted an official church funeral several weeks after the burial. In one eastern Tennessee community, slaves "put the coffin in the spring wagon and took the long way round by road up to the burying ground on the hill," a custom that reflected the African tradition of carrying the dead person past every house in the community. Once the funeral procession started, "de preacher give out a funeral hymn. All in de procession tuck up de tune and as de wagon move along everybody sung dat hymn. When it done, another was lined out, and dat kept up 'till [they] reach de graveyard. Den de preacher pray and [they] sing some mo'." In four different parts of the Southern Mountains, slaves sang the same hymn as they marched to the grave: "We're travelin' to the grave, to lay this pore body down." Black Appalachians were either interred in a separate section of the plantation graveyard or segregated in a slave cemetery. Members of the immediate slave quarters usually dug the grave, as a token of respect for the family. In African tradition, Appalachian slaves often decorated the grave with personal items that had belonged to the deceased. There were no name markers, but "rocks was put up fer tombstones." According to Raboteau,

> Funerals were the last in a cycle of ceremonies during the life of a slave. Sunday worship, prayer meetings, revivals, Christmas, 'baptizing,' weddings, funerals, all came and went. . . . To the slaves these services and celebrations were special times, counteracting the monotony of life in slavery. Furthermore, the slaves asserted repeatedly in these seasons of celebration that their lives were special,

their lives had dignity, their lives had meaning beyond the definitions set by slavery.

More importantly, funerals and social gatherings were significant methods of preserving unwritten family history and of sharing a collective community past. Moreover, participation quite often required slaves to engage in covert resistance.[27]

Music and Dance of Appalachian Slaves

There was another significant way in which Appalachian slave gatherings, funerals, and weddings were ethnically distinct. It was during these activities that slaves developed and preserved their own forms of music and dance. There was a thread of similar songs and dances at work parties, social gatherings, marriages, funerals, and baptisms. These art forms provide evidence of the preservation in the Mountain South of African traditions that were challenges to the cultural and ideological hegemony of whites. On the one hand, music and dance served as community-building devices because they were methods of public discourse that permitted the performers to mock the dominant white culture. Through humor, satire, irony, mock praise and elation, sarcastic presentation of lyrics, and complex layers of multiple meanings and ambiguity, slaves sang about the inhumanity of slave owners in such ways that their targets were likely to misinterpret the intended meaning. Even at gatherings attended by whites, black Appalachians highlighted slave trading, family separations, sexual exploitation of slave women, owner brutality, and abuse from white patrollers. At ethnically mixed corn huskings in the mountains of North and South Carolina, travelers recorded the same slave song. The words pinpointed not only the frequency of slave trading but also an enigmatic reference to an escape plan using the master's horse.

> Johnny come down de hollow.
> De nigger trade got me.
> De speculator bought me.
> I'm sold for silver dollars.
> Boys, go catch the pony.
> Bring him around the corner.
> I'm goin' away to Georgia.
> Boys good-bye forever.

Another regional slave song simultaneously condemned family separations caused by masters and promised a future day of retribution.

See wives and husbands sold apart,
Their children's screams will break my heart.
There's a better day a coming.
Will you go along with me?
There's a better day a coming.
Go sound the jubilee!

Eastern Tennessee slaves publicly lamented the brutal oppression of their masters and their yearning for deliverance in a corn shucking song that went: "W'en de clouds hang heavy an' it looks lak rain, Oh Lawd, how long will de sun draw wautah from ev-e-ry vein, Oh Lawd, how long?"[28]

Clearly, such songs were subversive because they coalesced blacks around shared meanings that whites could not decode. Hidden and ambiguous meanings allowed Appalachian slaves to express openly in front of whites their "collective articulation of needs, solidarity, and possibility." At the same time, these songs reflect the belief of slaves that whites were relatively easy to fool and to manipulate. Popular at ethnically mixed corn shuckings were songs that ambiguously emphasized patroller surveillance, the stupidity of the riders, and the ability of slaves to trick them. A northern Georgia song depicted the ever-present danger for slaves on the road; "run, you'd bettuh git away" from nearby patrollers, warned the chorus. A Coosa County, Alabama, song described the patroller riding "up the hill and down the holler" late into the night while slaves "run and flew" away from them. An eastern Kentucky song demeaned the men who were required to work the roads for the wealthy slaveholders: "Poor white out in de night huntin' fer niggers wid all deir might. Dey don' always ketch deir game. De way we fool um is er shame." Fountain Hughes recalled that food shortages and lean times spurred the popularity of "We gonna live on milk and honey, way by and by." In a hymn that began "One day shall I ever reach heaven and one day shall I fly," Blue Ridge Virginia slaves ambiguously idealized freedom and escape.[29]

While economic and political liberation were unattainable, slave songs created "a discourse that represented freedom in more immediate and accessible terms." Mountain slave songs made public opposition to oppression politically possible, in ways that speeches, written materials, and group protests were not. By disguising them as music only meant to set the work pace, Appalachian slaves used field calls to communicate illicitly between squads working adjacent fields owned by different masters. As they worked, slaves concealed messages within the regularized words of their field hollers. A traveler on the road described such singing as an innocuous "harvest-home of the negroes" that could be heard all over town. In one instance, the medley of work chants hid the announcement of a night-time gathering within a chorus that seemed

The celebration of a slave wedding in the yard of a Franklin County, Virginia, plantation. Such gatherings offered mountain slaves opportunities to reach beyond the confines of small plantations to engage in community building and cultural celebration. *Source: Harper's*, 1867.

harmless to whites: "I take my text in Matthew and by revelation. I know you by your garment. Dere's a meeting here tonight." Whites were easily confused because the singing sounded like meaningless babble to them.[30]

Whites were not totally unaware that slave songs represented an ideological framework that was counter-hegemonic. They rightfully feared that black music was a means of communication between slaves and that their hidden meanings might signal resistance. As a result, Appalachian Presbyterians, Baptists, and Methodists were "particularly rigid in denying such amusements." Regional white churches preached against "the devils' music" of mountain blacks and undertook evangelical efforts to discourage slave dancing and singing. Appalachian owners also prohibited night-time singing, one of the most frequent causes of whippings endured by the region's slave women. Some plantations even punished field hollers. Hearing prohibited singing, one Asheville mistress yelled out: "What's all that going on [in] the field? You think we send you out there just to whoop and yell? No, siree, we put you out there to work." Then she "grab the cowhide and slash" the female song leader "'cross the back." To alert field hands that the master or overseer was unexpectedly entering their work areas, eastern Tennessee, West Virginia, and northern Alabama slaves sang out, "Sister, carry de news on, Master's in de field." When one elderly lookout saw the overseer or the master approaching, he would "sings a song to warn 'em so they not git whupped, and it go like this: Hold up, hold up, American spirit!" Specific songs were used to signal important events. For example, daytime singing of "Steal Away to Jesus" by the black preacher or woman prayer leader alerted slaves that "dere gwine be a 'ligious meetin' dat night."[31]

In addition to their significance as public resistance, slave music and dance were also important means of preserving African cultural memory. Appalachian slave songs were constructed in the traditional African patterns of improvisation and call-and-response. Singing styles, storytelling in song, derisive mimicking, and the use of songs to set work rhythms were all derived from African customs. The musical instruments most popular among Appalachian slaves were also African derivatives. Thomas Jefferson was convinced that "the instrument proper" to his mountain slaves was "the Banjar, which they brought hither from Africa." Numerous regional narratives described the use of the fretless banjo at black social gatherings, and the fiddle was the second most frequently mentioned instrument. In the African tradition, some Appalachian slaves played fiddles that were either "a long gourd with horsehair strings" or a combination of pine bark and animal hair. Even though state and local laws prohibited traditional African instruments, Appalachian slaves were

At this Fauquier County, Virginia, gathering, the group is preserving African traditions. The midground slave is "patting juba" to set the pace for the other two. *Source:* Criswell, *Uncle Tom's Cabin Contrasted*.

still utilizing African style drums in the 1850s; tin pan beatings were common; and some could "blow reed quills."[32]

In the 1840s and 1850s, Appalachian slaves were also still preserving African dance derivatives, and they drew sharp distinctions between traditional black dances and derivatives from white customs. When she "wuz little," Chaney Mack was taught to dance "like they did in Africa." According to her father, "dey dance by derselves or swing each other 'round. Dey didn't know nothing 'bout dese huggin' dances." The regional narratives describe the "four hand fatillion" (quadrilles), buck dancing, jigs, patting juba, and kitchen balls, all adaptations of traditional African steps. Appalachian slaves also "call[ed] de figgers for de dances," engaged in ring rituals, used cutting and breaking, and danced in separate gender-segregated lines in African fashion. Mollie Kirkland remembered a northern Alabama version of the traditional African ring ritual. Black Appalachians called it "'Oh, Sister Phoebe,' but dey didn't call hit dancin'." Men and women "would all be in a circle an' de one in the center would choose his partner an' den dey go through de game" while singing. Slaves in Blue Ridge Virginia and northern Georgia described how to "cut de buck" (i.e., the buck dance in which "a boy and girl would hold hands and jump up and down and swing around keeping time with the music"). Appalachian slaves also enjoyed the sixteen-hand reel and the cake walk, and domestic servants often participated in "kitchen balls" while they worked parties in their masters' homes or at the regional mineral spas. Dave Lowry described how Blue Ridge Virginia slaves "would line up to dance" and proceed through a series of routines that included "cashing the ring." Also depicted in numerous regional accounts is the African practice of "patting juba," involving intricate, rapid clapping of the hands against different parts of the body in "quite complex successions of rhythm." In the absence of musical instruments, one black Appalachian "pat Jubor," a percussive style that emerged after Southern states outlawed slave drums. While he "patt[ed] time on his apron and with his right foot," the others danced. "At first the time and the dancing would be moderate but they would both increase until the hands of the patter and the feet of the dancer would fly so that you could not follow them. When the dancer gave out, he would stop with a 'sh-e-uh.'"[33]

The Subculture of Resistance

Despite their small populations in Appalachian counties, mountain slave communities operated as "subcultures of resistance" grounded in noncooperation, sabotage, and the emergence of a counter-hegemonic culture and religion. At the heart of this *subculture of complicity* lay illicit information networks. To remain on the offensive against their owners, Appalachian slaves developed secret communication strategies. Despite great distances between work sites, slaves managed to spread important news from one plantation to another. Religious meetings, social gatherings, contacts with free blacks and poor whites, the return of hireouts, and the arrival of new slaves all proved to be effective mechanisms for moving ideas and, thereby, building community solidarity. To evade strict rules about transmitting information from one plantation to another, slaves in Ashbie's Gap "used to take the horns of a dead cow or bell, cut the end off of it." Then they "could blow" them with "different notes," and they could identify "who was blowing and from what plantation." Masters despised "tattlers," and espionage could result in a slave being sold "just as far as wind would carry." Even though spying on the big house was risky, women "would peep around" and collect information that was passed to warn others in the quarters. After dark, slaves collected inside one another's houses and "they'd talk in low whispers." Occasionally, secret speech and coded language would appear in local slave dialects. As a way of rejecting the identity imposed by whites, mothers often substituted forbidden "basket names" for the names assigned by owners to their offspring.[34]

An ethos of sanctuary for runaways was also a central part of the subculture of resistance. Mountain masters engaged in physical abuse of slaves, forced labor migrations, and the breakup of families much more frequently than owners of large plantations in the Lower South. To resist those forms of repression and control, mountain slaves routinely engaged in truancy and laying out. Two-thirds of the runaways were younger than thirty, and more than three-quarters of them were males. This pattern was caused by the structure of forced labor migrations, for young males were sold and hired out more frequently than any other sector of the slave population. Owners felt threatened by small communities of truants, for the mountains had been havens for runaways from the colonial period. In the 1720s, Tidewater escapees "formed a settlement of their own" near present-day Lexington, Virginia. The runaways "built a town of boughs and grass houses in the manner of the homes of their native land, and set up a tribal government under a chief." Using "many farming implements which they stole from their masters," the fugitives cleared fields and cultivated crops. Once they were located by whites, however, militias "mustered from all sections of the colony, moved on their settlement, killed their chief, and returned his followers to their masters." For more than three months in the eighteenth century, the Albermarle County slave community successfully concealed runaways from an adjacent county. When an overseer finally apprehended them, the black community aggressively rescued the runaways. Slaves disappeared into the Cherokee Nation so frequently during the colonial period that the British included their return as one of the conditions of every major treaty with the Indians. During the early 1800s, about 20 percent of the advertised runaways from eastern Tennessee, western Carolina, and northern Georgia were suspected of "making for the Cherokee Nation" where they would be "harboured" by roaming bands of fugitives.[35]

There was widespread community knowledge about hiding places that were designed to keep truants concealed near their families. One eastern Kentucky slave hid in the woods almost two years. On Jordon Smith's plantation, a runaway hid in the nearby woods six months. "He lived in a cave and come out at night and pilfer 'round and steal sugar, meat and stuff to eat. They put the dogs on him several times but didn't catch him." Slaveholders and newspapers recount similar long-term layouts. Antebellum medical journals claimed that slaves were afflicted with the disease "drapetomania," a form of mental illness that caused them biologically to be unreliable truants. According to a Murray County, Georgia, newspaper account, the sheriff accidentally discovered a "runaways den" inhabited by a man and a woman who "had been out about a year." Their hideout was "artfully concealed underground . . . in sight of two or three houses, and near the road and fields where there ha[d] been constant daily passing." Underneath a camouflage of straw and leaves was "a trap door and steps that led to a room about six feet square, comfortably ceiled with plank, containing a small fire-place the fire of which was ingeniously conducted above ground." Stored inside were "meal, bacon, potatoes, &c., and various cooking utensils and wearing apparel." Knowledge of these hiding places had to be fairly widespread in the black community, for family and friends slipped them food and clothing. Sally Brown recalled that truants would "live in caves," but "they got along all right – what with other people slippin' things in to 'em." Owners were quite often convinced that their missing slaves might be hiding with known "bands" or "gangs" in about 15 percent of the sampled accounts of runaways. For example, Thomas Jefferson feared that one of his truants had "joind. a gang of Runaways" who were "doing great mischief to the neighboring stock." The runaways remained "out," even though "considerable exertions ha[d] been made to take them." So many small groups escaped into the hills of Jackson County that local whites described the northern Alabama mountains as a "favorite lurking-ground for runaway negroes." The rugged terrain provided "covers for concealment" in daytime; at night, "the necessaries of existence" could be secured from nearby blacks.[36]

The slave community conspired in runaway schemes in other ways. In an attempt to prevent his frequent truancy to visit abroad family, Anna

Lee's master attached a large bell around the neck of her grandfather. To subvert the master's control, neighbors would "stuff that bell full of rags or leaves," so he could be off again. On Jordon Smith's farm, the master would whip a captured runaway and lock him up, warning the other slaves "if they give him anything to eat he will skin them alive." The master's threats were futile for "the old fo'ks would slip him bread and meat." Jim Threat reported that the slaves on his plantation "didn't let on" to their master when his runaway father would return to visit them at night. Martha Showvely's uncle "went up in de wood an' dug him a hole in de ground an' covered it with leaves. He stayed dere for two years. In de day he stayed up unda de ground an' at night he went about an' got food" from black neighbors. When they were hired away from families, Appalachian runaways managed to lay out for long periods because strangers gave them refuge. "Many a one has come in our house and we'd hide 'em," reported one middle Tennessee ex-slave.[37]

Mountain masters were aware that the free black community aided runaways. In 1847, Loudoun and Fauquier County owners petitioned the Virginia General Assembly to rid the state of free blacks because "in many instances" they provided food and shelter to runaways. Two slaveholder accounts detail the extent of community complicity in slave escapes. Using forged passes and aid from neighbors and strangers, a young Monticello male ran away repeatedly between 1805 and 1812. He managed to stay at large in Lexington, Virginia, for more than a year before Jefferson's agent located him. With the help of free blacks, he eluded capture, and the bounty hunters had to pursue him all the way into West Virginia. Back at Monticello, Jefferson ordered "him severely flogged in the presence of his old companions and committed to jail." The master had no illusions that he had broken the spirit of the young man, however. "Circumstances convince me he will never again serve any man as a slave," Jefferson warned his plantation overseer. The master knew that there was so much illicit support and sanctuary among other blacks that "the moment he is out of jail and his irons off he will be off himself." When Mose Otey was hired by his Floyd County owner to the Virginia and Tennessee Railroad, he did not report for work for nearly five months. Otey eluded bounty hunters because he was receiving aid from black strangers. Even though the railroad agent "bribed negroes" to keep "on the lookout for him," none ever betrayed Otey. When the runaway finally returned voluntarily, the employer ordered him to have a "sound whipping" in order to "Make him tell who harboured him all the while."[38]

Aiding runaways was not quite as risky for Appalachian slaves as another form of resistance, which required community collusion. High on the scale of punishable offenses were attempts to teach slaves to read and write. The extent to which mountain masters deterred literacy infractions is evident in the regional slave narratives. Only about 10 percent of adult mountain slaves could read, and less than 2 percent learned to write. Most mountain slaves were illiterate because they experienced repressive masters like the owner of Silas Jackson, who commented that "no one on the place was taught to read or write. No one could read the Bible," not even their slave preacher. Books and writing materials were rare among slaves on Appalachian plantations. One northern Georgia ex-slave recalled that they "never was allowed to have a piece of paper to look at. They would whip you for that." When Blue Ridge Virginia owners caught slaves learning to read, they typically administered twenty lashes each to teacher and student. According to Ben Brown, "de slaves wuz not allowed any learnin an' if any books, papers, or pictures wuz foun' among us we wuz whipped." Catherine Slim asked her mistress "to learn [her] a book and she sez... don't ask me dat no more. I'll kill you if you do." When a young western North Carolina slave was discovered teaching others to write, the master's sons shoved him into a bonfire. Another western North Carolina man reported "dey cut off a hand if dey caught you" teaching someone to read. In middle Tennessee, a slave's thumbs would be cut off if the slave was caught teaching others to write. When churches held "sabbath schools" for slaves, they could expect white reprisals. In 1832, the Georgia State Guard invaded the classroom of a missionary because her students included two black children. In the 1840s, Albermarle County Quakers and Floyd County, Virginia, Baptists were indicted for assembling blacks for instruction in their meeting houses. In eastern Kentucky, sixty vigilantes stormed a slave sabbath school "armed with clubs and guns, and thus the school was dispersed never to meet again!"[39]

Literacy made slaves dangerous because it empowered them to question the white religious instruction that posited God on the side of masters. Literacy also opened up for slaves the agenda of liberation propounded by abolitionist writings. Literacy was crucial to mountain slaves for another reason. Nearly twice as often as other U.S. slaves, black Appalachians utilized forged papers to effect their escapes. Out of a sample of 506 escapes, nearly 12 percent of the runaways carried forged passes, fake manumission papers, or other documents to evade patrollers and sheriffs. The vast majority of black Appalachians were illiterate, but runaways needed the assistance of that small group of slaves and free blacks, like Joe Sutherland. While he "hung round the courthouse" waiting to drive his owner's carriage, "Joe learned to read and write unbeknown to [his] master. In fact, Joe got so good that he learned how to write passes for the slaves." Because of his unquestioned access "around the court everyday, Joe forged the County seal on these passes and [three] slaves used them to escape to free states." After they acquired such documents, mountain runaways were aided by the ignorance of the patrollers on the roads; for the vast majority of these poor whites had little or no access to free public education.[40]

Of those mountain slaves who could read, only one-third had been taught by their owners or in white sabbath schools. Appalachian slaves knew the importance of reading and writing, as is clear in the manuscripts of missionaries in the Cherokee Nation. When the American Board opened its sabbath school, large numbers of slaves attended. "The greater part c[a]me six miles or more . . . and none less than two miles and a half." However, a majority of literate slaves acquired their skills illegally, most often by capitalizing upon their roles as nurses to white children. On trips to drive the master's children to and from school, "the chillun learned [Marshall Mack's] uncle to read and write. Dey slipped and done this, for it was a law among slave holders that a slave not be caught wid a book." Dan Lockhard would borrow the books of the white children he tended; then he "would carry [his] gun down into a hollow, and have a book." Tom McAlpin "useta tote" the white children to school, so he was able to sneak opportunities to use their books. Sarah Burke, Ruben Woods, Margaret Terry, Celia Singleton, and Maggie Pinkard tricked white youngsters into game playing that involved reading and writing.[41]

Those few slaves became the educators for the black community. Thomas Cole recalled that each slave who became literate "would larn another one ter read and write." Thomas Jefferson sought permission from the county court to have his carpenters taught to read and write. Each of them, in turn, secretly transmitted those skills to others in the Monticello vicinity. Black preachers had to "slip old planks and things," so they could teach others to "read from the light of the fire." When they had no wood for fires, they used beef tallow candles or rough iron lamps, fueled by rags dipped in grease. Literacy was infectious, according to Thomas Cole. "One of de slaves would larn ter read and he would reads de Bible ter de rest of dem." Soon another "would wants ter larn ter read and he would larn him." After unauthorized religious services, black preachers would teach, using "a Blue Back Speller an' a Bible." Pit schools also emerged. "De slaves would slip out o' de Quarters at night, an go to dese pits" in the woods where a literate slave "would have a school." On one western North Carolina plantation, a few slaves created their own makeshift writing implements by cutting "blocks from pine bark" for paper. "Git a ink ball from de oak trees, and on Sadday and Sunday slip off whar de white folks wouldn't know 'bout it." The scholars "use[d] stick fer pen and drap oakball in water and dat be [their] ink atter it done stood all night." To teach counting, Alfred Smith "gathered some straws and broke them into short pieces."[42]

Literacy was a powerful tool of resistance because it created new access to written ideas that might inflame a revolutionary spirit. In the minds of mountain masters, dissemination of abolitionist literature among slaves was insurrectionary. There were enough real cases of abolitionist activism to fuel slaveholder fears that antislavery literature would kindle resistance. In 1843, one mountain justice of the peace went to a Quaker meeting house "to examine some Negroes who had been engaged in a riot," the disturbance being a sabbath school and a singing in a setting where blacks might be exposed to antislavery literature and ideas. White strangers appeared in Penny Thompson's quarters, telling her "mammy an' some udder [slaves] dat . . . those dat wants freedom, deys am gwine to take wid dem an' warns dem not to says a word." Other instances describe mountain slaves who were assisted by abolitionists in their escapes to the North. With the aid of Harriet Tubman, Silas Jackson's grandfather escaped from Ashbie's Gap, Virginia, to Philadelphia, "saved $350, and purchased [his wife] through the aid of a Quaker." "The Chesapeake and Ohio Canal was a part of the route which received, on certain boats, fugitives brought over by the ferryman." As a depot along the Underground Railroad, a Loudoun County free black ferry operator assisted escaping slaves.[43]

Appalachian masters feared abolitionist influences when blacks were seen gathering in small clusters. According to one middle Tennessee ex-slave, whites "didn't 'low no two or three men to be standing about talking" because "they feared they was talking about being free." Because he spoke of liberation and repeated antislavery rhetoric, Martha Randolph warned Thomas Jefferson that slave John "incite[d] the hands." After abolitionist literature was found in their quarters, several West Virginia slaves were charged with an attempt to organize an 1818 slave insurrection. In 1839, a slave named Jarrett circulated a "certain writing denying the right of Masters to property in their slaves and inculcating the duty of resistance to such rights." The County Court sentenced him to be "transported and Sold beyond the Limits of the United States." Out of their fears of the abolitionist agendas of free blacks, most mountain masters "didn't 'low [slaves] to go around them. If they knowed they went around them they would cut they backs off nearly." In Staunton, participation "in a fashionable game of cards" was enough to warrant twenty lashes to each free black and five lashes to each slave. Spencer Mavin was a landholding free black who circulated "Anti-Slavery Papers" in Fauquier County. Charged with spreading insurrectionary materials meant "to array the Blacks against the whites with a view to the supremacy of the former," Mavin had helped several slaves to escape North. After owners found Northern abolitionist pamphlets among their slaves, Loudoun and Rockbridge Counties petitioned for ordinances restricting the movements of free blacks. Similarly, Greenbrier County petitioned the Virginia Legislature to change the law so that free blacks could legally remain in the state only one month after their manumission. In that way, they would have less time to "spread discord and disaffection" or to map the mountain roads that could be used to "purloin off [their] slaves and reach a free state."[44]

Construction of a Counter-Hegemonic Religion

Slaveholders knew they did not have hegemonic control over the culture and ideology of slaves; that is why they implemented such coercive restrictions. After 1830, public ordinances prohibited slaves from attending Quaker meetings where they might be exposed to Abolitionist notions and made illegal black participation in religious services where there was no white supervision. More then three-quarters of the mountain masters required enslaved families to participate in regular religious instruction conducted by whites, and the vast majority of Appalachian slaves attended regular services at the white churches where their masters were members. In 1860, there was one church for every 507 Appalachians; so mountain slaves were slightly more likely than their Lower South counterparts to receive white religious instruction. In addition, the Baptists and Methodists organized missionary outreach for slaves who resided in many parts of Southern Appalachia, especially eastern Tennessee, southwestern Virginia, and northern Georgia. In western North Carolina and northern Georgia, Moravian missionaries conducted Sunday schools and services for slaves who were owned in the Cherokee Nation.[45]

Antebellum church records document the routine membership of blacks in white Appalachian churches that included slaveholders on their rolls. According to black Appalachians, "de slave eider b'long to de chu'ch he master b'long to or none 'tall." Thomas Cole recalled that slaves on his farm were required to "walk bout five miles" in order to "allus goes ter church mos every Sunday." Similarly, Henry Johnson described "a great string of slaves in de road on Sunday," surrounded by "buggies wid de white folks" in front. At most churches, slaves were segregated in rows along the side, at the rear, or in the balcony. At small churches, slaves "had ter stay outside," sometimes forced to sit "on a log in de broiling sun." Sometimes the two audiences were "separated by a partition." In the Cherokee Nation, Springplace missionaries assigned blacks "special seats at communion" and passed them the cup "last of all." In other situations, white churches held segregated services for slaves. In Talladega, for example, "de white folks went to de church in de mawnin an de [blacks] at night." In Appalachian counties where there were few organized churches, slaves attended only irregular community meetings held by circuit preachers. In Warren County, Virginia, Hardshell Baptist ministers "travelled from one plantation to another." In one middle Tennessee county, "it was not often [they] had church" because their circuit preachers only "had meetings once in a while" on a community farm.[46]

Social Control Through the Slaveholder Religion

Appalachian masters sought to atomize blacks and to deprive them of any collective faith that might oppose the slaveholders' version of Christianity. Many Appalachian masters personally provided religious instruction to their slaves. Despite the social stigma, one female slaveholder organized prayer meetings and traveled around southwest Virginia evangelizing slaves. Penny Thompson's master distributed "two fingahs" of peach brandy with prayers "ever' mo'nin' an' night." When there were no formalized Sunday services, several mountain mistresses led prayer and singing "out of the doors, in the yard." Appalachian slaves were indoctrinated in specially designed plantation catechisms that emphasized faithful service, honesty, and loyalty to the master more than salvation. Published guides enumerated the statements to be memorized by slaves, the oral explanations to be read, and a list of interrogatives that the master was to repeat in each service. For instance, one Southern Presbyterian script read: "The fifth commandment is: Honor thy father and thy mother." Carefully omitted from Exodus 21:12 was the final phrase "that thy days may be long in the land which the Lord thy God has given thee." The master was then instructed to read the question: "What does this commandment require you to do?" Slaves were expected to respond that God required them "to respect and to obey my father and mother, my master and mistress, and everybody else that has authority over me."[47]

Because he believed them to be "in a degraded and dependent condition," one western North Carolina minister read his slaves the prescribed Presbyterian catechism, instructed them at length, and then "asked them Questions" to test their comprehension of "the right way." Like other mountain masters, he was convinced that "suitable" religious instruction would "make better servants." Appalachian ex-slaves consistently recalled the white clerical emphases upon obeying the slave laws and upon "serving the Lord" by behaving in ways that pleased masters. One middle Tennessee ex-slave reported that very few white clerics taught slaves "about religion." Instead the "biggest thing" they preached about was "Servants, obey your mistress and master." At a Chattanooga church, the minister taught slaves that "Sampson slayed the Abolitioners, not Philistines." A northern South Carolina ex-slave recalled clerical preoccupation with the tenet "the better you be to your master the better he treat you." Even though most of them were illiterate, Appalachian slaves comprehended the contradictions in the religious interpretations of white churches. Henry Buttler recalled that neighborhood slaves were required to attend a weekly sermon preached by a white minister who "was inconsiderate in the treatment of his own slaves." Thus, "his brotherly talk was not taken seriously." When a listener "laughed at the minister's remarks" during a discourse on kindness, the cleric "administered twenty-five lashes to the unfortunate negro."[48]

Offended by the lively antics and singing of blacks, white congregations created segregated services, with black class leaders, catechists, watchmen, and exhorters. Slave preachers earned credibility and trust from white communities through their service roles in white-supervised activities. Black ministers sometimes traveled the circuits with Baptist and Methodist clergymen and helped them conduct services for blacks and whites. A few slaves served as assistants to the clergymen who owned them. There are numerous accounts of white-sponsored churches for blacks, especially among the Baptists and Methodists. In Talladega County, for instance, the Baptists were eager for blacks to "have churches of their own with black preachers to lead them in a language of their understanding." So they constructed a small brick meeting house, started the African Cottonfort Church, and trained a local slave who ministered to 130 blacks. The Roanoke Baptist Association purchased a slave and trained him to "preach the Gospel." At Lexington, Virginia, the black Baptist church was "without the town and placed in a hollow, so as to be out of sight.... It was a poor log house, built by the hands of the negroes. [On Sundays,] the place was quite full, the women and men were arranged on opposite sides.... Two whites and two blacks were in the pulpit. One of the blacks...gave out [the first hymn]. They all rose immediately. They ha[d] no books, for they could not read; but it was printed on their memory, and they sang it off with freedom and feeling." Similar white-sponsored churches were created throughout Southern Appalachia, including Franklin County, Tennessee; Lumpkin County, Georgia; Greenbrier County and Kanawha County, West Virginia; Cumberland County, Virginia; and the towns of Franklin and Staunton, Virginia. While the Charlottesville African Church was led by a white minister, the Methodists trained eight black preachers and five exhorters in Winchester and another four exhorters in Frederick County. There were even free black ministers, like West Virginian John Chavis.[49]

However, the predominant pattern was the establishment of informal plantation chapels, with black preachers or exhorters leading services. During these official services, "there was always some white people around" who "just came to hear what was said and see what [slaves] were thinking about." In Jefferson County, West Virginia, one master "built [slaves] a church" and allowed them to have "a colored preacher and deacons." The typical plantation church was no more than "an old shed with seats made out of old slabs and fence rails." On Andrew Goodman's plantation, a neighbor's slave "used to git a pass Sunday mornin' and come preach," to them, and he "baptized in a little mudhole down back of [the] place." At an Alleghany County, Virginia, plantation, slaves would gather on Sundays at a large cabin "with one of the overseers present," and the illiterate coachman would hold church. "When communion was given the overseer was paid . . . with half of the collection taken up, some time he would get 25 cents."[50]

Resistance to White Religious Control

Appalachian masters designed their white-supervised religious instruction to extend their ideological dominance, but mountain slaves resisted their cultural hegemony in several ways. Even though a majority of Appalachian masters required slave participation in white church services, less than 10 percent ever joined those churches. Major Southern denominations boasted in 1860 that one-quarter of all adult slaves were church members, as were one-third of adult whites. According to these clerics, one million slaves were under the regular tutelage of white churches. On the one hand, these church estimates are outlandish reports of white religious participation, for the white working classes were largely unchurched before the Civil War. On the other hand, such optimistic claims are certainly not an accurate description of the white church membership of mountain slaves. Using manuscript records of the major denominations that operated in antebellum Southern Appalachia, it is possible to track a close count of black church membership. In eastern Tennessee, blacks made up less than 8 percent of the entire membership roll of the Holston Conference of the Methodists. The Holston Conference was even less successful in southwestern Virginia where only 2 percent of their members were black. The Virginia Baptist Association reported 8,207 black members, claiming that nonwhites made up more than half their entire membership roll in a few western counties of Virginia. In northern Georgia, only about 10 percent of Baptist church members were black. Those 13,348 blacks who had joined Methodist and Baptist churches accounted for only about 7 percent of all the African-Americans in the Appalachian counties of Tennessee, Virginia, and Georgia. Episcopalians and Presbyterians attracted a high percentage of slaveholders, but those churches enrolled far less than 1 percent of the entire black population of the states of Alabama, North Carolina, South Carolina, and Virginia, with very few of those black members situated in Appalachian counties. Mountain slaves recognized the hypocrisy of their owners' Christianity, and that awareness accounted for their reluctance to join white congregations. A Fauquier County slave expressed that attitude openly. "How can Jesus be just," he queried a white cleric, "if He will allow such oppression and wrong? Don't the slaveholders justify their conduct by the Bible itself, and say that it tells them to do so? How can God be just, when He not only permits, but sanctions such conduct."[51]

Even when Appalachian slaves attended white church services, they reformulated them to reflect their own worldview. According to Anderson Furr, "evvybody went to de [white] meetin' house on Sunday, and dere's whar [slaves] had a good time a-courtin'." Quite often whites would picnic on the grounds of the church, permitting slaves to convene in the nearby woods, away from close scrutiny. According to Horace Tonsler, slaves managed to escape the narrow constraints of the white meeting house because

> de white folks would go inside, an' de slaves would sit round under de trees outside.... Den sometimes ole [man] would git up outside an' start in to preachin' right along wid [the white preacher]. Softlike, of course, wid a lot of handwavin' an' twistin' of his mouth widdout makin' no noise. We would sit up an' listen to him an' laugh when he say just what de white preacher say. Dat was de start of de colored folks' religion, I guess. Whites got used to it arter while an' let us preach an' pray under de shade trees round de church. Didn't bother us so long as we didn't make so much noise an' didn't go out of sight. Old John Southern used to be our [slave] preacher. Lawd, he could talk better'n de old white preacher, leastwise us used to think so. Got so de white boys used come to service late so's dey could stay outside an' listen to de black preachin.' Preacher always got quiet when dey come; couldn't trust dem white boys. Dey go back home an' tell dey fathers dat de slaves plannin' to run away.

Opportunities to reunite with abroad kin constituted the primary reason that enslaved women joined white churches. In order to visit family and friends, slaves in the Cherokee Nation "came from considerable distance to public worship on Sundays.... [I]ndeed, there were instances of their walking twenty miles over the mountains and returning the same day." Hired out at a distance from her family, Bethany Veney feigned "religious fever" as a loophole through which she could clandestinely see her children. By playing on the new employer's religious convictions, the enslaved woman convinced him to permit her to go to church frequently, thereby creating a cover for her illicit family visits.[52]

Mountain slaves transformed owner-directed religious services into ethnically distinct social gatherings. A traveler described a black preacher conducting a service at a white Presbyterian church in Chattanooga, Tennessee. Some slaves "were standing, others sitting, others moving from one seat to another, several exhorting along the aisles. The whole congregation kept up one loud strain" of hand clapping and singing, the kind of noisy, spontaneous service that whites frequently descried as African barbarism. After harvest and New Year's, "the slaves would have their protracted meeting or their revival," usually without close white supervision. Using circuit riders, white churches sponsored prayer meetings on plantations, thereby encouraging legal assemblies of slaves. Camp meetings were even more popular because whites stayed at the designated site for two weeks to two months, permitting slaves many legitimate opportunities for travel. In the northern Georgia and eastern Tennessee communities where Tom Neal and Anna Peek lived, whites held a "pertracted meeting" every year. "Looked like a thousand people come and stayed." In Tom's words, slaves "had a big time" at such services. After the revivals each year, the white church would allow black preachers to "baptize in the creek," and these rituals were one of the most joyous occasions for music and dance. In Hall County, Georgia, "white folks and slaves was ducked in de same pool of water. White folks went in first and den de slaves." Anderson Furr never "forgot dem baptizin's" because the entire black community "went in dem days." Thomas Cole remembered baptizings as major events for slaves. "Whar de baptizings comes off it was almost lak goin ter a circus. People comes from ever whar, dat was de biggest crowd [he] ever seed." Oliver Bell recalled that the baptizings were "de good, old-time religion, and us all go to shoutin' and has a good time. . . . People come from all over and dey all singin' songs and everybody take dere lunch and have a good time."[53]

The Underground Slave Religion

Attendance at white churches and white-sponsored services conducted by black preachers were not the only forms of religious services, for black Appalachians developed their own underground religion. Because they seemed loyal during white-sponsored services, slave preachers maintained the privilege of movement between plantations. That mobility made it possible for them to emerge as the charismatic leaders in the underground slave religion. Julia Daniels described her Uncle Joe who served his owner by holding Sunday "meetin' in front de [big] house." During such official services, the black preacher "had to be careful what he said 'cause the white folks were there and listening to him, so that he couldn't have anything to say to cause uprising of slaves." Out of the sight of the master at night, however, Uncle Joe and another nearby preacher would "make it 'tween 'em" to hold secret meetings." According to one western North Carolina slave, "colored folks jes kinder raised 'em up a colored preacher" who was held in high regard in the slave quarters. As a young child, Thomas Cole idolized his Uncle Dan who"would read de Bible ter de rest of [them] and tell de meanin' of it." James Pennington's western Maryland community treated an illiterate slave with equal respect. After their master "sternly resisted" efforts by the Methodists "to evangelize the slaves," illicit services were organized by an exhorter who "could not read . . . but he knew a number of spiritual songs by heart, of these he would give two lines at a time very exact, set and lead the tune himself."[54]

Despite legal restrictions and close surveillance, mountain slaves probably participated to a greater extent in their underground religion than in white services. Indeed, participation in illicit prayer meetings and singings was one of the primary reasons for mountain slave whippings, and black Appalachians coined the phrase "stealin' the meetin'." After "Nat Turner's insurrection broke out," reported one Blue Ridge Virginia preacher, "the colored people were forbidden to hold meetings among themselves. . . . Notwithstanding our difficulties, we used to steal away to some of the quarters to have our meetings." Jerry Eubanks "heard plenty of [slaves] preach" near Rome, Georgia. Females were punished nearly three times more often than men for their participation in unauthorized religious services or nighttime singing. Women "would get the cloth spun during the time they were having prayer meeting," and the older female who was the textiles driver was quite often the individual who "organized secret prayer meetings." On one middle Tennessee plantation, the owner "would hit [women] fifty lashes for praying" at night. Silas Jackson reported an incident in which his master discovered the slaves "having a secret prayer meeting. He heard one slave ask God to change the heart of his master and deliver him from slavery so that he may enjoy freedom. Before the next day the man disappeared, no one ever seeing him again. . . . [J]ust before he died [Silas' master] told the white Baptist minister, that he had killed Zeek for praying and that he was going to hell."[55]

In addition to their meetings in the quarters, mountain slaves also constructed "brush arbor" churches or held night services in the woods. No white clergyman "ever preach ter" one western North Carolina community that "built a shelter of sticks wid a place fer de preacher ter stand;

th'owed little bushy trees on top of hit fer a roof." The brush arbor provided space to accommodate extra slaves who attended from all over the community, sometimes walking six to eight miles at night to attend. Soon after James Smith "was converted [he] commenced holding meetings among the people, and it was not long before [his] fame began to spread as an exhorter. [He] was very zealous, so much so that [he] used to hold meetings all night." Slaves took great risks to attend illicit prayer meetings, for patrollers spent much of their time seeking out and breaking up such services. In Warren County, Virginia, "beaten paths extended in all directions" to the brush arbor church that operated in Pierce Cody's neighborhood. Ann Ladly's neighbor did not permit his slaves to go to church, so her quarters held services "by de line fence" between the two plantations. To avoid detection, the adjacent slaves "would crawl on dere hands and knees . . . to de fence and hear de gospel singing."[56]

Like other whites, Olmsted thought that mountain slaves had a "heathenish, degraded" idea of religion that was "a miserable system of superstition" derived from Africa. When only a teenager, W. E. B. Du Bois witnessed an African ring shout at a Putnam County, Tennessee, revival. While the preacher "swayed and quivered," a woman "suddenly leaped straight into the air and shrieked." What followed was a variant of the ring ritual, described by Du Bois as "the mad abandon of physical fervor, – the stamping, shrieking and shouting, the rushing to and fro and wild waving of arms, the weeping and laughing, the vision and the trance." In a less demeaning fashion than Olmsted or Du Bois, an Appalachian slave exhorter portrayed the African response style that characterized black services. "The singing was accompanied by a certain ecstasy of motion, clapping of hands, tossing of heads, which would continue without cessation about half an hour; one would leaf off in a kind of recitative style, others joining in the chorus."[57]

The African vestige most often described by Appalachian slaves was the practice of using "the pot" during secret religious meetings. Rawick contends that West Africans used iron pots in religious rituals to symbolize divine protection. Convinced that the pot provided them a supernatural defense, New World slaves "had the courage to gather at night for prayer meetings to assert and develop their community, even though such meetings were prohibited." Pot rituals varied slightly from one community to another, sometimes used to prevent noise, other times to signal the location for a secret meeting. In two separate reports from Franklin County, Tennessee, slave women "would turn the kettle down" to signal that a meeting would convene that night at a particular place. "Dey would turn a pot down en meet at de pot in de night en sing en pray." Most frequently described by mountain slaves was the practice of turning the pot down

As in this Rabun County, Georgia, prayer meeting, Appalachian slaves constructed their own liberation theology and participated in illegal services and singings. *Source: Scribner's*, 1874.

outside the door of the cabin where the secret meeting occurred, the pot or wash tub was "raised so the sound c[ould] get under there" and not be heard by whites. A few slaves reported that they would either "stick [thei]r heads in a big iron pot to keep de noise away from de big house," or they bring the pot inside the cabin "and raise one side up a little from the ground."[58]

Perhaps the most feared agent of social change among Appalachian slaves was the black preacher. In 1831, Governor John Floyd, an Appalachian planter, called for laws that prohibited the unsupervised activities of black preachers. Floyd contended in his annual message to the Virginia Legislature that "the most active incendiaries among us, stirring up the spirit of revolt, have been the negro preachers." White Appalachians disparagingly referred to slave ministers as "chairbackers," to signify their movement from one plantation to another to conduct services, that mobility being a major source of white apprehension about them. Black preachers were often included among the newspaper advertisements for runaway slaves. A Yancey County, North Carolina, slaveholder offered a reward for David, a young preacher who had taken two others with him when he escaped. The owner warned readers that this "greatest rogue" would "cloak his villainy" by "pretend[ing] to be religious; is fond of singing and psalms." According to one newspaper, a missing twenty-two-year-old West Virginia slave "professed to be a baptist, pray[ed] very well." Masters feared not only the connection between runaways and black preachers but also their role in spreading literacy among slaves. Illicit religious meetings were the settings in which nearly half the tiny minority of literate mountain slaves learned to read and write. Some preachers also taught women how to keep their own record of births, deaths, and sales in a family Bible they kept hid in their root cellars.[59]

Black preachers were also a threat because they were better educated, quite often better dressed, than the poor white Appalachians who worked the road patrols. Seeking to cement their power through cultural terrorism, mountain masters targeted black preachers for punishment. For example, a Fauquier County runaway named Clem was depicted as having "a lump on his back, occasioned by a whipping he received for being a clerk to a negro preacher." According to one black Appalachian, "patrollers wuz mostly after de preacher 'cause he wuz de leader of de meetin' an' if dey caught 'im, he knowed dar wuz a beatin' fer 'im." The Pickens County, South Carolina, court found a slave "guilty of seditious language" and sentenced him to three hundred lashes, after he was overheard telling a group of blacks "that God was working for their deliverance." The preacher prophesied that God "would deliver them from their bondage as sure as the children of Israel were delivered from their Egyptian bondage." He assured his listeners that outsiders were "working by secret means . . . but did not know exactly how long it would be before they would be set free. There was no doubt that it would be soon. That they ought to pray for [it], and their prayers would go up before God and be answered." Some preachers were aggressive in designing strategies to protect themselves and their congregations. In Garland Monroe's community, night meetings were held in a location where slaves could defend themselves. "Dey had what dey called a stump preacher" who conducted illicit services at the foot of Hardware Mountain. The patrollers "would jus' run down de mountain side 'long paths dat de paterollers didn't know nothin' 'bout." As their horses neared the bottom of the ridge, slaves knocked them into the hidden creek and escaped. Alfred Williams was even more defiant toward Warren County, Tennessee, patrollers. If the white riders invaded his thicket service, Alfred "would sit there with his gun on his lap to keep them from whipping him."[60]

As one Appalachian slave noted, "the idea of revolution in the conditions of whites and blacks [wa]s the cornerstone of the religion of the latter." An oppositional discourse emerged in the illicit meetings of mountain slaves because "the heaviest emphasis in the slaves' religion was on change in their earthly situation and divine retribution for the cruelty of their masters." Perhaps that is why one youngster had heard so many northern Georgia slaves "morning and night pray for deliverance. Some of 'em would stand up in de fields or bend over cotton and corn and pray out loud for God to help 'em." Nan Stewart described how black preachers selected Bible passages from which they could construct a coded message of future liberation. A preacher who regularly visited her Charleston, West Virginia, plantation "liked to read Michah 4:4" because it held the promise that slaves "would soon be undah [their] own vine an' fig tree and hab no feah of bein' sold down de riber to a mean Marse." Thus, many black Appalachian preachers were the greatest threat to their masters because they used their secret underground religion to foment dissatisfaction with subjugation. They may have disguised their religious rhetoric at official services, but they transformed slaveholder Christianity into a liberation theology that framed the certainty of future deliverance and retribution.[61]

Conclusion

Berlin's conceptualization of a *slave society* would cause us to predict that slavery did not dominate a region characterized by a nonslaveholding majority and a low black population density. However, the political economies of all Mountain South counties were in the grip of slavery. Even in counties with the smallest slave populations (including those in Kentucky and West Virginia), slaveholders owned a disproportionate share of wealth and land, held a majority of important state and county offices, and championed proslavery agendas rather than the social and economic interests of the nonslaveholders in their own communities. Moreover, public policies were designed by state legislatures controlled and manipulated by slaveholders from outside the Appalachian region. In addition, every Appalachian county and every citizen benefited in certain ways and/or was damaged by the regional slavery system, even when there were few slaves in the county and even when the individual citizen owned no slaves. For example, slaves were disproportionately represented among hired laborers in the public services and transportation systems that benefited whites of all Appalachian counties, including those with small slave populations. Furthermore, the lives of poor white Appalachians were made more miserable because slaveholders restricted economic diversification, fostered ideological demeaning of the poor, expanded tenancy and sharecropping, and prevented emergence of free public education.[1]

If, then, the old stereotypes about Appalachian exceptionalism do not hold, how was mountain slavery different from other sections of the American South? The Mountain South can be distinguished from the Lower South around eight indicators:

- One of every 7.5 enslaved Appalachians was either a Native American or descended from a Native American. Thus, black Appalachians were 4.5 times more likely than other U.S. slaves to be Native American or to have Indian heritage, reflecting the presence of eight indigenous peoples in this land area.
- Mountain masters meted out the two most severe forms of punishment to slaves much more frequently than their counterparts in other

Southern regions. Appalachian ex-slaves reported slave selling twice as often as other WPA interviewees; thus, about one of every three mountain slaves was sold. Likewise, Appalachian ex-slaves reported frequent or obsessive physical punishment nearly twice as often as other WPA interviewees.[2]

- Mountain slaves were employed outside agriculture much more frequently than Lower South slaves. At least one-quarter of all mountain slaves were employed full time in nonagricultural occupations. Thus, slaves were disproportionately represented in the region's town commerce, travel capitalism, transportation networks, manufactories, and extractive industries.
- In comparison to areas of high black population density, mountain plantations were much more likely to employ ethnically mixed labor forces and to combine tenancy with slavery.
- Compared to the Lower South, mountain plantations relied much more heavily on women and children for field labor.
- Fogel has argued that "the task system was never used as extensively in the South as the gang system." Except for the few large slaveholders, Mountain South plantations primarily managed laborers by assigning daily or weekly tasks and by rotating workers to a variety of occupations. Moreover, small plantations relied on community pooling strategies, like corn huskings, when they needed a larger labor force. Since a majority of U.S. slaves resided on holdings with fewer than fifty slaves, like those of the Mountain South, it is likely that gang labor did not characterize Southern plantations to the extent that Fogel has claimed.[3]
- Mountain slaves almost always combined field work with nonfield skills, and they were much more likely to be artisans than other U.S. slaves.
- Most Mountain South communities were deeply divided politically, socially, and economically over the issue of slavery. However, about one-third of the Appalachian counties were very similar to the Lower South in their political leanings.

How Should We Rethink Small Plantations?

More than 88 percent of U.S. slaves resided at locations where there were fewer than fifty slaves. Indeed, more than half of all U.S. slaves lived where there were fewer than four slave families. In 1860, one-half of all U.S. slaves lived on plantations that owned fewer than twenty-five slaves, and they were cultivating crops other than cotton or working at nonagricultural sites.[4] What have we learned from the Mountain South that requires rethinking of assumptions about areas with low black population densities and small plantations?

- A region was not buffered from the political, economic, and social impacts of enslavement just because it was characterized by low black population density and small slaveholdings.
- As Berlin has observed, "the Africanization of plantation society was not a matter of numbers."[5] Thus, slaves on small plantations engaged in much more day-to-day resistance and counter-hegemonic cultural formation than has been previously thought.
- In areas with low black population densities, plantations are much more likely to rely on an ethnically mixed labor force and to utilize part of their land for white tenancy.
- Small plantations are much more likely to utilize slaves in nonagricultural occupations and to require slaves to combine field labor with artisan crafts.
- Small and middling plantations much more often assigned slaves daily tasks while large plantations relied heavily on gang labor. Unlike large slaveholdings, small plantation owners typically supervised field labor. However, contrary to popular perceptions, those masters rarely engaged in manual labor alongside slaves.
- On small plantations, slave women worked in the fields, engaged in resistance, and were whipped just about as often as men.
- There was greater brutality and repression on small plantations than on large plantations. Moreover, areas with low black population densities were disproportionately represented in court convictions of slaves for capital crimes against whites.[6]
- As on large plantations, small plantations punished slaves primarily for social infractions, not to motivate higher work productivity.

The Nature and Extent of Mountain Slave Resistance

Why did most mountain slave resistance stop well short of collective defiance? On the one hand, it was futile for slaves to attempt justice through violent rebellion, for they could not have peaked the moral concerns of nonslaveholding whites through guerilla warfare. On the other hand, "non-violence is a particularly strategic instrument for an oppressed group which is hopelessly in the minority and has no possibility of developing sufficient power to set against its oppressors." Moreover, according to Gandhi, nonviolent noncooperation "results in the long run in the least loss of life." In recent analyses of the emergence of social movements, two key findings are relevant to U.S. slave resistance. Oppressed groups have organized the most successful collective actions after their governing systems relaxed coercive sanctions or after the general public became more critical of government use of force against activists. Moreover, social movements cannot survive and sustain organized resistance unless they are able to mobilize widespread resources in the form of political allies, economic inputs, and linkages to community institutions. When constrained by systems of domination that are supported by the brutal force of the state and its legal systems, low-key and nonrevolutionary resistance is typically the only rational approach. For Appalachian slaves in communities that had smaller black populations, insurrection meant "certain destruction." In the face of political realities and the alignment of the legal system and brutal force on the side of owners, mountain slaves "revolted in the only way left to them." Cal Johnson, a northern South Carolina slave, assessed slave uprisings as a strategy. "I never knowed 'bout no slave uprisins," Cal said. To explain why rebellions did not occur, he added that slaves in his area would have "had to uprose wid rocks and red clods. The black man couldn't shoot. He had no guns." Despite the low black population densities of most Appalachian counties, mountain slave communities operated as *subcultures of resistance* grounded in noncooperation, sabotage, and the emergence of a counter-hegemonic culture and religion. Because it aimed at building long-term family and community solidarity, nonviolent covert resistance was probably the most effective strategy feasible to slaves on small plantations. Four findings about mountain slave resistance call into question previous assumptions about counter-hegemonic activism in areas characterized by small slaveholdings.[7]

- There was much more day-to-day resistance in communities with low black population densities than scholars have previously thought, and most of that resistance was noneconomic in motivation.
- The slave family – especially on small plantations – was the organizational center of resistance.
- In comparison to males, enslaved women resisted just as frequently, if not more often.
- There was actually a higher per-capita incidence of slave assaults on whites in an area characterized by a lower black population density and small plantations.

Noneconomic Motivations for Slave Resistance

Several scholars have focused upon economic infractions as the behaviors that accounted for most instances of slave punishment. Herskovits argued that slave disobedience was "manifested chiefly through shirking, destruction of tools, stealing, malingering, spoiling of crops, slowdowns, and other deliberate forms of sabotaging production." Stampp described a wide array of devices that were invoked by slaves to frustrate the production goals of their owners and overseers. Genovese contended that U.S. slaves expressed resistance primarily through work slowdowns or withholding labor. Recently, Franklin and Schweninger have argued that most day-to-day slave resistance involved "crimes against property." Despite these overstated claims about economic sabotage, such infractions were *not* the primary reasons for whippings on U.S. plantations, whether large or small. Even though one-third of the Appalachian slaves reported instances of punishment for low productivity or property destruction, most slaves were punished for noneconomic infractions. Punishment was utilized much less often to motivate increased productivity or to protect property than to exert *social control*. In fact, inadequate production was the cause of less than one-fifth of the whippings reported by ex-slaves. Similarly, Appalachian masters administered less than one-third of their whippings to deter inadequate production, work deficiency, or property losses. Rather, two-thirds of the adult Appalachian slaves were whipped for social offenses. Since they were structures grounded in frequent daily interaction between owners and laborers, small plantations engaged in much more micromanagement of slave behavior than large holdings. E. P. Thompson described as "theatres of control" those public performances in which the powerful act out their dominance in the belief that those they oppress will be intimidated into quiescence. Physical punishment was intended by slaveholders, then, as one of those theaters of control; for these incidents were designed as much for their demonstration effect on nonoffenders as they were meant to deter future violations by the transgressor.[8]

Consequently, mountain slaves were most often physically punished for *verbal infractions. Physical assaults* were the second most frequent violation for which Appalachian slaves were physically punished. The third most frequent social infraction was temporary *truancy* (i.e., absence from the home plantation without a pass). Mountain slaves were physically punished for these three social infractions nearly three times more often than they were whipped for low productivity or work deficiencies. Moreover, they were not whipped for stealing or for property destruction much more often than they were physically punished for violations that involved unauthorized religious services, learning to read or write, possession of written materials, illicit communication with other blacks, spying on whites, socializing with free blacks or untrustworthy whites, and permanent escape attempts. In addition to those individual forms of resistance, about one-fifth of the incidents of resistance involved small groups. Most small-group resistance was directed at food stealing and violent retaliation against patrollers, overseers, or brutal masters. For example, mountain slaves reported food stealing three times more often than did other U.S. slaves, and much of this activity was engineered by cooperating groups. Slaves typically worked in small groups to steal livestock for the benefit of the community.

Role of Slave Families in Resistance

The second surprising pattern that characterized mountain slave resistance involved the role of the family. Fox-Genovese contended that

> it is essential to recognize that the power of the master over the household in which slaves worked, lived and reproduced influenced the specific form and content of slave resistance.... The kin, co-residence, and domestic functions of household life were never entirely under the slaves' control. Under these conditions, the family life of slaves ... could not provide slaves with reliable bases of resistance.[9]

Appalachian slave families may not have been stable in composition or in daily contact with members, but they were still the pivotal units in which resistance was taught, planned, and executed. The struggle of mountain slaves was not revolutionary in the sense that they meant to overthrow the system of oppression that trapped them. Rather their everyday resistance was focused upon the amelioration of conditions of life for households and upon the protection of their families. Indeed, there was a noticeable connection between kinship and socially prohibited behaviors. *Illicit information networks* and an *ethos of sanctuary for runaways* lay at the heart of their subculture of resistance, both strategies that had to be taught and orchestrated within families. For example, children were trained in the arts of reconnaissance and espionage. As they worked in their owners' houses or tended white children, they overheard conversations, stole papers or books, and dropped misleading information to owners.

Nearly half the whippings were punishment for acts of defiance by slaves who were trying to protect their families. About half the incidents of spying on whites or illicit communication involved the transmittal of information by adult slave women about pending punishment, sales, or hires of family members. Some scholars have argued that economic grievances were the underlying causes for running away. In their view, "slave flight was a tool used by those with no other redress to define acceptable working conditions and tasks." In sharp contrast to that view, impending sales or distant hires of family members triggered more than two-fifths of the successful escapes of Appalachian slaves to the North. Furthermore, two-thirds of the incidents of truancy were not escape attempts. Instead, most of the miscreants were traveling to visit abroad families, with every intent to return to their assigned work places. Indeed, males utilized truancy and *laying out* more often than any other nonviolent resistance strategies. Even in the face of patrollers, whippings, or worse punishment, some slaves repeatedly left their plantations without the required passes. More than one-third of all mountain slaves were sold, hired out, or forced to migrate with owners every year. To avoid removal – the most serious threat to their families – resistant men hid out for extended periods. Nearly one-fifth of the slave narratives described caves, underground pits, and isolated spots in rough terrain that were used to conceal truants from detection while they remained near families. Sanctuary for such truants was part of the resistant ethic of mountain slaves, for laying out required the complicity of family and neighbors who slipped them survival essentials.[10]

Role of Women in Resistance

More than half of all mountain slave households were headed by women who stood alone to protect children against whites and to prevent their own sexual exploitation. Because of the absence of males, there was a striking gender differentiation in patterns of resistance and punishment. Men and women were physically punished just about at the same levels of frequency; however, males and females committed different social infractions. Consistently, women were more likely than men to be punished for infractions that were aimed at family protection or maintenance. Nearly two-fifths of the women were punished for verbal infractions, usually triggered by white threats toward children or extended kin. Consequently, women engaged in sassing and verbal insubordination 1.3 times more frequently than males. Because of their high employment as nurses and caretakers for white children, women and girls were more frequently punished for spying on whites. Women were more frequently punished for illicit communication with other plantations, the only method they had to warn abroad spouses about family crises. Even though the few slave preachers were males, women were punished nearly three times more often than men for their participation in unauthorized religious services or nighttime singing. Women engaged in prayer meetings or singings while they completed their evening textiles production; thus, females were more likely to be caught at such forbidden activities.

Males engaged in other forms of resistance that were meant to maintain family ties. More than one-third of the men were whipped for absence without passes. Males ran away nine times more often than females, reflecting the much higher probability that husbands, fathers, and sons would be removed from their families through forced labor migrations. Because they were more frequently hired out, men tried to escape permanently five times more often than women. As a result of their greater employment in skilled occupations that permitted chances to learn to read and write, males were slightly more likely than females to be involved in attempts at literacy. Men and women also had different motivations for their violent resistance against whites. Surprisingly, women engaged in physical attacks on whites a little more often than males. While women most often assaulted whites to protect family members or to resist sexual exploitation, males more frequently defended *themselves* against white abusive treatment.

Slave Assaults on Whites

Most slavery specialists have argued that criminal sanctions for major crimes were most severe in those areas where slaves represented the greatest numerical threat to whites. In light of that argument, we should expect a lower incidence of slave imprisonment and capital punishment in the Mountain South. In reality, however, the public records document a disproportionately high rate of court convictions and death sentences for Appalachian slaves. Can we conclude, then, that mountain slaves were more likely to engage in physical assaults on whites than blacks outside the Appalachian counties? Since Appalachian slaves were more likely than their counterparts in the Lower South to be physically abused by white owners, employers, and overseers, it is certainly likely that Appalachian slaves engaged more often in certain types of violence toward whites. In addition, Appalachian masters resorted to sexual exploitation of their slave women more often than did their counterparts in the rest of the South. To complicate matters, small Appalachian plantations disrupted slave families and separated kin to a much greater extent than larger operations.[11]

Because of that higher incidence of white brutality on small plantations, Appalachian slaves were more likely to engage in acts that criminologist Richard Quinney labels *crimes of resistance* against oppressive conditions in the workplace. Indeed, a majority of the convicted Appalachian slaves had engaged in either acts of self-defense or acts of retaliation against whites who had shown a history of abuse toward them at their assigned workplaces. Such acts of self-defense between whites were typically not criminalized by antebellum courts. Moreover, "extenuating circumstances" (such as the degree to which the victim's behavior triggered an assault) would have been an acceptable legal defense by whites. For many Appalachian slaves on small plantations, it was the very closure of all openings for *constructive agency* that drove them to engage in violence toward whites. Gandhi recognized that "the risk of supineness in the face of a grave issue is infinitely greater than the danger" of punishment. "To do nothing is to invite violence for a certainty." Inaction might spur additional brutality or coercion from an oppressor who presumes that the victims have no willingness or resources to rebel. Staying silent, being acquiescent, and doing nothing were so costly that their fears of whippings, death, or being sold did not deter slave retaliation.[12]

How Should We Conceptualize Slave Resistance?

Even though worker resistance does *not* characterize the modern workplace, scholars seem to have expectations that slaves should have engaged in insurgency at greater risk. In reality, most contemporary U.S. employees do not engage in organized resistance, formal complaints, or public confrontations nearly as often as slaves did. Aptheker argued that slave insurrections and conspiracies were much more numerous than previous scholars had assumed. Woodson contends that slaves aimed most of their organized resistance at literacy, religious freedom, and the acquisition of vocational skills. Despite those studies, it is clear that most U.S. slave resistance did not take the form of large rebellions. As Scott observed: "The rare, heroic, and foredoomed gestures of a Nat Turner or a John Brown are simply not the places to look for the struggle between slaves and their owners. One must look rather at the constant, grinding conflict over work, food, autonomy, ritual – at everyday forms of resistance."[13]

In a highly repressive system like slavery, marginalized groups cannot constructively engage in insurrection, so their resistance is driven underground. In such circumstances, repressed groups construct and preserve *hidden transcripts* that become the infrastructure of their antisystemic resistance. What is the content of such hidden transcripts? First, those alternative narratives provide a better understanding of a group's social condition than that which prevails in the dominant culture. However, hidden transcripts are subversive and unwritten, so their creators must rely on oral history to preserve what Bellah and his associates call a *community of memory*. Such oppressed communities

> have a history – in an important sense they are constituted by their past – and for this reason we can speak of a real community as a "community of memory," one that does not forget its past. In order not to forget its past, a community is involved in retelling its story, its constitutive narrative.... People growing up in communities of memory not only hear the stories that tell how the community

came to be, what its hopes and fears are, and how its ideals are exemplified in outstanding men and women; they also participate in the practices – ritual, aesthetic, ethical – that define the community as a way of life. We call these "practices of commitment" for they define the patterns of loyalty and obligation that keep the community alive.

The second element of hidden transcripts is the shared suffering of the oppressed. According to MacIntyre, knowledge about widespread injustice socializes members of the repressed group "to pursue both their own good and the good of the tradition of which they are bearers," even in situations defined by danger, crisis, or tragedy. Third, those narratives explain domination in terms of power relations rather than in terms of the dominant culture's stereotypes of the inferiority of their group. As Couto observed, "the awareness of economic subordination and political repression of a group by its members reminds them constantly of the inaccuracies of the prevailing explanations of these inequalities" by the dominant group.[14]

Why were hidden transcripts of a shared past so important for black Appalachians? Mountain slaves were not permitted to develop overt institutions that would allow them to produce and disseminate their knowledge freely. Illiterate and denied any written history of their group's past, they rooted themselves politically in an oral memory pool that refuted slaveholder myths that justified the oppressive system. According to Dubnow, "the soul of each generation . . . emanates from the soul of the (collective) 'body' of all the preceding generations, and what endures, namely the strength of the accumulated past, exceeds the wreckage, the strength of the changing present." Through their knowledge about the collective past and through their participation in an ethnically distinct culture, mountain slaves developed a sense of solidarity with other distant African-Americans. Oneness with others who shared the same oppression helped Appalachian slaves withstand the repeated separations, the brutality, and the cultural terrorism of masters who were more abusive than slaveholders in other sections of the South. Anchored in the assurance that their community persisted even when their families were endangered, individual members shared a collective past and an alternate culture that blanketed them from total domination and despair. By risking reprisals to construct and preserve their families, culture, and religion, black Appalachians engaged in acts of profound antisystemic resistance. On the one hand, the slave community of memory sustained and nurtured individuals by making them part of a common past that was constructed out of stories of suffering and injustice. On the other hand, the slave religion fostered a subversive dream for the overthrow of the oppressive system. In that sense, cultural resistance was a political force for liberation. For, in the words of Immanuel Wallerstein, the Appalachian slave community "held the banner high for an alternative vision of the world." In addition to providing them a sense of deeper identity, the counter-hegemonic culture and community gave slaves hope for a future day of retribution and lay a lasting infrastructure for a liberation struggle that would span several generations.[15]

On the one hand, it is important to document the hidden transcripts of slave resistance. On the other hand, it is crucial that we not romanticize that resistance or exaggerate the independence of slaves. Recent scholarly preoccupation with slave agency has caused some scholars to overstate the power of slaves to control their own destinies. As Kolchin observed, most scholars "have abandoned the victimization model in favor of an emphasis on the slaves' resiliency and autonomy." Like a number of other scholars, I have grown increasingly concerned that too many recent studies have the effect of whitewashing from slavery the worst structural constraints and of magnifying the degree to which its harmful impacts were overcome by resistant victims. Notions like "windows of autonomy within slavery" or an "independent slave economy" are colorful intellectual cliches. However, they seriously distort the degree to which U.S. slaves were self-governing, and they trivialize the brutalities and the inequities of enslavement. Patterson is scathing in his criticism of such approaches.

> During the 1970s, a revisionist literature emerged in reaction to the earlier scholarship on slavery that had emphasized the destructive impact of the institution on Afro-American life. In their laudable attempts to demonstrate that slaves, in spite of their condition, did exercise some agency and did develop their own unique patterns of culture and social organization, the revisionists went to the opposite extreme [and] . . . came "dangerously close to writing the slaveholder out of the story completely." Or as Kolchin more bluntly puts it, the old myth of decimated Sambos and Aunt Jemimas with no social life of their own was replaced by a new myth: "that of the utopian slave community." . . . [T]hey emerged triumphant with the academic news that slavery had no damaging impact on the Afro-American family, that indeed the Afro-Americans had emerged from two and a half centuries of powerlessness, sexual degradation, male emasculation, childhood neglect, legal nonexistence (in which being raped by anyone Euro-American was not a crime), and general racist oppression with their nuclear families intact, their gender relations unsullied, and their communities tightly knit and harmonious.[16]

In their haste to celebrate the resilience and the dignity of slaves, too many scholars have underestimated the degree to which slaveholders placed black families at risk. Fogel observed that "arguments that make the balance of power turn on the ineptness of masters and the cleverness of slaves, despite their romantic attachments, are difficult to sustain." Taken to its extreme, the search for individual agency shifts to the oppressed the blame for the horrors and inequalities of the institutions that enslaved them. If, for example, we push to its rhetorical endpoint the claim of Berlin and Morgan that slaves "manipulated to their own benefit the slaveowners' belief that regular family relations made for good business," then we would arrive at the inaccurate conclusion (as some have) that the half of the U.S. slave population who resided in single-parent households did so as an expression of personal agency, not because of any structural interference by owners. If we push to its rhetorical endpoint the claim that there was an independent slave economy, then we must ultimately believe that a slave who was poorly fed or clothed was just not exerting enough personal effort at the economic opportunities available to her. Such views are simply not supported by the narratives of black Appalachians. In fact, nowhere in the six hundred slave narratives that I have analyzed (within and outside the Mountain South) have I found a single slave who exaggerates or glorifies moments of independence or autonomy in the manner that many academics do. Many slaves did resist, but ex-slaves voiced their comprehension that they struggled with few resources against an awesome power and that resistance was more often than not quite costly for the dissidents.[17]

Mountain Slave Construction of a Counter-Hegemonic Culture

In many ways, plantations had two distinct cultures, the master's worldview and the counterculture of the oppressed. Slave "voices from the edge" kept "disturbing the centre" of plantation life. The secrecy of the underground culture made insurrection a constant fear, and dangerous aspects of African heritage reminded whites that their ideology had not brainwashed slaves. Those voices from the edge were constant reminders to masters that African-Americans had "held on to their own, secret souls" and that they were engaged in "the continual creation of a community whose primary function was to struggle against their oppressors." However, such conceptualizations of American slave culture and community building have been grounded in the complexity of plantations with fifty or more slaves, representing only about one-fifth of the North American slave population. For the remaining majority, according to Fogel, "we have only shadowy sketches of the quality and content of their lives." Fogel went on to argue that "slaves could develop a degree of cultural autonomy only if there was a community in which they could interact with one another," and he was convinced that small plantations simply did not permit such communities to emerge. According to Fox-Genovese, small numbers of slave families could "not anchor the development of Afro-American culture."[18]

These two slavery specialists would argue, then, that four factors forestalled culture formation in a region like the Mountain South:

- Low black population density
- Repression
- Unstable families in households shaped and controlled by masters
- Illiteracy and reliance on oral indigenous knowledge

These writers have certainly overstated the extent to which these factors prevented slave culture formation. Even though there was a greater degree of surveillance and brutality in areas with low black population densities, slaveholders were neither totalitarian nor consistent in their repression. First, cultural activities were not prohibited until they were perceived as threatening. Thus, most slave dances, music forms, and textiles artisanry were allowed to survive overtly. Second, slaveholders themselves transmitted and preserved elements of slave culture that were economically beneficial, for example, African foods, basketmaking, and textile dyeing. In other instances, masters tolerated a countercultural element as a matter of convenience, such as acquiescing to separate church services because they found slave chanting and emotionalism distasteful. Third, slave patrols were the front-line of repression, and we need to think about those policing tactics in two ways. On the one hand, slave patrols represent an acknowledgment by masters that their black laborers were too mobile. In other words, owners implemented patrols because they recognized that their slaves were engaging in the production of counter-hegemonic knowledge. Thus, the slave patrol system can be interpreted as evidence of the development of a slave culture, not as proof that repression stamped out such activity. On the other hand, the slave patrol was successful at social control only to the degree that its agents were skilled at surveillance. The fundamental weakness in mountain slave patrols lay in their composition, for poor uneducated whites were disproportionately represented among the patrollers. By pitting two illiterate groups against one another, mountain slaveholders were failing to clench an iron fist of domination. That is not to claim that mountain patrollers were totally ineffectual or benign, but their lack of knowledge (coupled with the greater travel experience of many black Appalachians) created loopholes for evasions and escape. For instance, how could an illiterate patroller confirm whether a slip of paper was indeed a pass that authorized a slave's movement on the roads?

Should we presume that unstable families or illiteracy acted as unsurpassable obstacles to culture formation? On the one hand, some U.S. slavery scholars are biased toward the notion that stability is measured by the degree to which a slave family or household was nuclear. In that sense, they are making claims that fly in the face of anthropological evidence from cultures in which the nuclear family is not the organizing construct. Why should we single out North American slaves to be treated analytically in ways that anthropologists and ethnographers do not treat other target groups? Families and households are simply not the only units in which cultural knowledge is produced or preserved. On the other hand, why should we presume that reliance on oral indigenous knowledge precluded culture formation among slaves? Anthropologists have documented hundreds of cultures in which peoples transmitted unwritten information over time and space. So we should dismiss these two factors as having derived from the cultural biases of the American writers.

Now we come to what I consider the real meat of the matter, for I contend that small plantations actually structured processes through which slaves transmitted and produced their counterculture. Indeed, such mechanisms existed in areas with low black population density to a much greater extent than they occurred in areas dominated by large plantations. In comparison to the Lower South, small mountain plantations were more often characterized by slave selling and hiring, abroad marriages, unsupervised travel privileges for profitable skilled artisans, and women's nighttime textiles production. All those strategies generated opportunities for alternative worldview construction and for networking and knowledge transmission across distances. As a part of the Upper South, this region participated in the domestic slave trade through interstate and local sales and hires. Those forced labor migrations generated two contradictory outcomes for mountain slaves. On the one hand, mountain masters disrupted and destabilized families much more often than Lower South owners did. On the other hand, that trading fostered cultural fusion by allowing hired slaves to travel to distant areas and by bringing new members into the slave community. Two findings about the Mountain South call into question claims that areas with low black population densities did not permit the emergence of a slave counterculture.[19]

- Even though they were located in areas with low black population densities, Appalachian slaves engaged in numerous collective activities through which they built a sense of peoplehood and transmitted cultural knowledge.
- Even though most of them resided on small plantations, the vast majority of mountain slaves participated in an underground liberation theology that fused African, Native American, and Christian elements.

Wide-reaching ties with all those who shared their oppressed station rooted mountain slave children in a collective past. As part of their socialization, youngsters were taught to identify all blacks as part of their community, distinct from the dominant white system. Gutman recognized that "teaching Afro-American children to call all adult slaves (not just blood kin) 'aunt' and 'uncle' converted plantation non-kin relationships into quasi-kin relationships binding together slave adults (fictive aunts and uncles) in networks of mutual obligation that extended beyond formal kin obligations dictated by blood and marriage." As a result, "community ties based on quasi-kin connections emerged, flowing upward and outward from the adaptive domestic arrangements and kin networks that had developed over time among the slaves themselves." Because of the high frequency of forced labor migrations, family bonds reached across plantations, so visiting patterns created a network of associations larger than any single plantation. Even for those on small plantations, the "black community" lay out there and was a collective, counter-hegemonic reality.[20]

The cultural imperialism of Appalachian masters was limited by the enduring ties of slave collectivities, both local and distant. Only about 2 percent of the Appalachian ex-slaves reported that they were unable to participate in social gatherings. By staging their own oppositional values and practices, mountain slaves formed a defensive "closed circle" of ethnically distinct community members. Conjurors, herb doctors, musicians, storytellers, and handicraft artisans were the cultural specialists who kept alive mountain slave traditions. Weddings, funerals, weekend and holiday gatherings, work parties, and religious meetings were important arenas that made possible the emergence of a counter-hegemonic culture. Through group activities, Appalachian slaves developed their "collective identification" with a larger community and with a subculture that was more far-reaching than the Southern Mountains.[21]

As Gramsci argued, all ruling groups seek to perpetuate their power, wealth, and status by rendering unchallengeable their own philosophy, culture, and morality. The struggle for religious hegemony is "a process of competition for control of behaviours," so the values, deportment, institutions, and identity of the oppressed people conform to the interests of the dominant class. Slaveholders knew they did not have hegemonic control over the culture and ideology of slaves; that is why they implemented coercive restrictions. More than three-quarters of the mountain masters required enslaved families to participate in regular religious instruction conducted by whites, and the vast majority of Appalachian slaves attended regular services at the white churches where their masters were members. Thus, mountain slaves were slightly more likely than their Lower South counterparts to receive white religious instruction. Gramsci contended that oppressed groups give only a superficial consent to dominant institutions, so their conversion to an alternative worldview is always possible. To construct a counter ideology grounded in liberation, subordinated groups must engage in organized cultural struggle, like the underground religion of mountain slaves. Even though a majority of mountain masters required slave participation in white church services, less than 10 percent of those black Appalachians ever joined white churches. Despite legal restrictions and close surveillance, mountain slaves participated to a greater extent in their underground religion than in white services. In fact, illicit prayer meetings and singings ranked high among the reasons for whippings. Perhaps the most feared agent of social change among Appalachian slaves was the black preacher. As one Appalachian slave noted, "the idea of revolution in the conditions of whites and blacks [wa]s the cornerstone of the religion of the latter."[22]

Mountain Slaves and the Interregional African-American Culture

To what degree did slaves on small plantations or in a region with a low black population density, like the Mountain South, share the African-American culture that has been attributed to large plantations? According to Fogel:

> In the case of U.S. slaves, a central issue which is more often implicit than explicit is the extent to which cultural norms that were common on plantations with large numbers of slaves . . . could have been transmitted to the majority of slaves who lived on relatively small plantations, which usually had fewer than five slave households and in which slaves were usually under the constant supervision and regulation of their masters.[23]

Despite the differences in size and geography, Mountain South and Lower South slaves shared many basic beliefs and cultural practices.

- Even though the Mountain South is situated in nine states that are culturally diverse, black Appalachians engaged in counter-hegemonic religious practices and a liberation theology that shared many common elements with slaves throughout North America.
- The *cultural specialists* among mountain slaves were commonly found throughout North America.
- Mountain slaves preserved counter-hegemonic music and dance traditions that were common among slaves throughout North America.

- Mountain slaves transmitted diaspora myths that were common throughout North America.

We can best measure the extent to which black Appalachians shared the broader African-American culture through a closer look at religious practices and diaspora myths.

A Shared Liberation Theology

Gomez argued that three-quarters of North American slaves were still unconverted in 1860 and that the explanation for low black membership in white churches lay in the persistence of African religious customs. Christianity emerged among U.S. slaves late in the antebellum period. Until 1830, African religious practices dominated among slaves because most whites were themselves unchurched. After the Nat Turner rebellion, the Southern states tightened their legal controls to outlaw secret meetings and unsupervised black religious assemblies. Because of the contradictory cultural consciousness of slaves, however, "the process of Christianizing the Afro-American was not one of abject surrender of Africa to the West. In the spirit of Afro-Americans, Christianity was converted to their needs as much as they were converted to its doctrine."[24]

Unique in the United States, the praise meeting in the quarters or woods was a syncretism of African and conventional Protestant beliefs. African vestiges included the roles of preachers, elders, and women, verbal responses during services, the conversion experience, water baptism, shouting, prayer beads, pot rituals, conjuring, and the notion of the funeral as a "home going." All these practices appear in Appalachian slave narratives and other primary documents, and African-style conjuring and charms are described frequently. In northern Georgia, ethnically mixed slave women wore blue and white beads that could have been adapted either from Cherokee wampum customs or from African Islamic traditions.[25]

A Shared Diaspora History Construction

Blassingame contended that memories of Africa "were important in the development of self-awareness in slave children. Along with family names, vague memories of a 'homeland' never seen were passed from one generation to another." It is quite remarkable that Appalachian slaves retained African cultural influences through intergenerational oral histories. By 1860, U.S. blacks were more likely to be American-born than were U.S. whites. According to Fogel and Engerman:

> U.S. slaves were not only in closer contact with European culture, they were also more removed from their African origins than were slaves in the Caribbean.... By the end of the American Revolution, the African-born component of the black population had shrunk to 20 percent.... By 1860 all but one percent of U.S. slaves were native-born, and most of them were second, third, fourth, or fifth generation Americans. These Americans not only had no personal experience with Africa but were generally cut off from contact with persons who had such direct experience. To a considerable extent, the word that reached them about their African origins was filtered through minds and emotions of parents, grandparents, and great-grandparents who had always walked on the North American continent.[26]

When I first read the Appalachian slave accounts of the international slave trade, I was astounded by the consistency of the myth presented by men and women who were separated by great distance. After I had compared their tales against analyses of such stories from all over the United States, I was even more excited about what I had found. It is clear from these accounts that black Appalachians were transmitting both genealogical facts and a "politically correct" version of the slave trade that was common in areas with large black populations. Even though most of them lived in rural areas with small nonwhite populations, black Appalachians preserved and retold slave trade accounts that were almost identical to the stories of African-Americans on large plantations of the Lower South. Such cultural transmission was possible because the parents and grandparents of Appalachian ex-slaves had been uprooted by sales and by owner migrations three to five times during their lifetimes, repeatedly compelled to integrate themselves into the collective memories of different communities in the Upper South and the Lower South. In addition, male slaves were routinely hired to commercial and industrial sites where they interacted with blacks from different sections of the country. Through their long-term preservation of oral myths, mountain slaves were "communicating their very high regard of and a deep yearning for Africa to their descendants." By tracing their ancestral claims back to Africa, they were forging ideological weapons of resistance. Moreover, their transmittal of a standardized community myth of the slave trade demonstrates that black Appalachians participated in a culture common to other African-Americans.[27]

The omission of certain historical "fact" is less significant than the reality that slaves all over Appalachia and throughout the United States somehow constructed and reached consensus about the political parable that white Europeans tricked Africans onto the slave ships. On the one hand, African-Americans cast their slave trade account in the genre of trickster tales that depict characters gaining dominance over others through guile and lies, a political choice that permitted them to emphasize the moral responsibility of the oppressors. On the other hand, African-Americans were not simply fantasizing their explanation; they did indeed ground it in the real-life experience of some slaves. The kinds of practices described by black Appalachians had indeed occurred. Though infrequent, kidnapping had been one of the acquisition strategies of slavers. After the mid 1700s, European purchases of slaves were more often made in little boats detached from the main slave ship. In some instances, parties of sailors used canoes to work inland rivers. In a manner that echoes the details of black Appalachian accounts, they waited on land and ambushed or enticed stragglers. Since such small groups of whites could not defend themselves against captives, they quite often utilized red textiles, alcohol, or trinkets to trick them onboard. According to the journal of one such slaver, they would sometimes "leave goods a whole night" on the river banks. Slavers also used trickery to kidnap Africans whose families or clans were told that they were being hired to work near their homes. Payments were made in red wool, beads, metal tools, and bracelets. According to Michael Gomez:

> The stylized and sanctioned version of the initial capture, a well-known tale widely circulated throughout the South, excluded African agency and collusion.... The development of an initial capture account that points the finger exclusively at the European and excludes any mention of his African counterpart is highly significant, for it marks an important stage in the emergence of the African American aggregate identity and signals the fording of a major divide in the journey from ethnicity to race as the principal determinant of collective self-perception. For what the sanctioned version is fundamentally conveying is the idea that, notwithstanding the involvement and betrayal of African political and familial entities, the Atlantic trade in slaves was first and foremost the idea of Europeans; they initiated it; they had the ships, they made the voyage, they supplied the commodities, they transported the victims. It was the New World plantation complex that mercilessly drove the exchange.... By way of the domestic slave trade... slaves throughout the South exchanged data and created syntheses. The white man was found guilty of guile, guilty of violence, guilty of horrors unimaginable. This is the fundamental truth that the African-born wanted their offspring to understand about the initial capture.[28]

Why, then, would African-Americans and black Appalachians censor from their collective memory all reference to the collaboration of Africans in the slave trade? It is now clear that African-Americans developed two folkloric traditions. When the audience included whites, blacks focused upon Europeans; but there is clear evidence in antebellum manuscripts that African-Americans preserved much oral history about the complicity of Africans in the international slave trade. Kidnapping required the assistance of a special type of African middleman whose betrayal is documented in African-American accounts other than the WPA narratives. In the view of African-Americans, the middleman was "lower dan all other mens or beasts" because he had helped whites to "betray thousands into bondage." The role of the African middleman was "to entice 'em into [a] trap." By disarming unsuspecting blacks, "he'd git 'em on [the] boat" so that the "white folks could ketch 'em an' chain 'em." Indeed, the emergence of two separate accounts demonstrates the extent to which African-Americans and black Appalachians were constructing a new collective identity as one people with a shared exploitation. In their real life in the United States, Africans were not their oppressors, so the political parable was directed outwardly toward whites.[29]

Indeed, we can utilize the dissonance between official academic history and African-American mythology about the international slave trade to map slave resistance. To recover the "insurgent consciousness" of slaves from the historical silence, we must pay attention to many texts that traditional history discards as "not factual" and, therefore, irrelevant. Gramsci argued that such folklore was worthy of intellectual analysis because it was a "conception of the world and life" that was constructed by subordinated groups "in opposition to 'official' conceptions of the world." In the words of E. P. Thompson, the slave counternarrative was "valid in terms of their experience." Wallerstein argued that "pastness is central to and inherent in the concept of peoplehood." That past takes a moral and political dimension because it can be used to construct or to undo political solidarities, to legitimate or to undermine existing institutions, to induce quiescence or resistance. "Pastness is a mode by which persons are persuaded to act in the present in ways they might not otherwise act." Pastness is, in short, a tool that people use to resist domination and cultural hegemony.[30]

If we look beyond the "error of memory," we discover the exciting "historical fact" that African-Americans and black Appalachians were defining their peoplehood. Denied written or public communication, these illiterate subalterns constructed and reached community agreement about a counternarrative to the dominant worldview. Despite their powerlessness, they found a way to speak, to reclaim part of their past that had been torn away by the capitalist system, and "to speak that past – not in unison, but in harmony with one another," as a people who recognized their common exploitation. On the one hand, that myth identified all black American slaves as one people, even though they had originated from a wide diversity of African ethnicities. On the other hand, that political parable laid the moral responsibility at the feet of whites, for the international slave trade was driven by the greedy expansion of the European-based capitalist economy. As Wallerstein observed, peoplehood is "in no sense a primordial stable social reality, but a complex, clay-like historical product of the capitalist economy through which the antagonistic forces struggle with each other." The persistence and the broad reach of such an important counternarrative is testimony to the adherence of mountain slaves to the shared African-American worldview that stood in opposition to dominant white ideology. It is clear that black Appalachians identified themselves to be part of the same international diaspora and the same internal forced migrations as other African-Americans. It is also clear that black Appalachians shared ideologically the collective grievance of that emergent people and that they participated in the transmission of the community memory of injustices that the white system had heaped upon them.[31]

Notes

These locator codes are used to refer to collections of slave narratives. See the bibliography for the complete citations. Each locator code is followed by volume number and page numbers. For example, *Slave* 6 (a): 382 should be read *Slave*, vol. 6, part a, p. 382.

CWVQ	*The Tennessee Civil War Veteran Questionnaires*
Fisk	Egypt, Masuoka, and Johnson, "Unwritten History of Slavery," Fisk University Archives
Great Slave Narratives	Bontemps, *Great Slave Narratives*
Slave	Rawick, *The American Slave*
Slave I	Rawick, *The American Slave: Supplement I*
Slave II	Rawick, *The American Slave: Supplement II*
Slavery Time	Killion and Waller, *Slavery Time*
Slave Testimony	Blassingame, *Slave Testimony*
Website	http://scholar.lib.vt.edu/vtpubs/mountain_slavery/index.htm
Weevils	Perdue, Barden, and Phillips, *Weevils in the Wheat*

INTRODUCTION

1. Wallerstein, *Modern World-System II*, pp. 167, 233–34. Dunaway, *First American Frontier*, pp. 11–12.
2. Dunaway, *First American Frontier*, pp. 196–97. Regarding other peripheries, see Wallerstein, *Modern World-System III*.
3. Dunaway, *First American Frontier*, pp. 196–97.
4. Ibid., p. 120. Phillips, "Incorporation," p. 802.
5. Dykeman, "Appalachia," p. 29. Banks, "Emergence," pp. 189–90. Campbell, *Southern Highlander*, p. 94. Woodson, "Freedom," p. 136. West, "Freedom," pp. 19–21.
6. Trouillot, *Silencing*, p. 147. Eller, *Miners*, p. 9. Woodson, "Freedom," pp. 132–50. In his analysis of western North Carolina slavery, Inscoe, *Mountain Masters*, p. 94, utilized slaveholder manuscripts to come to the foregone conclusion that there was a "heightened sense of duty on the part of mountain slaveholders toward their slaves." Phifer, "Slavery," pp. 137–65. Perdue, *Slavery and Evolution*. Smith, "Historical Geography," pp. 17–20. Murphy, "Slavery," pp. 151–69. Williams, "Georgia's Forgotten," pp. 76–89. Dew,

Bond, pp. 110–11. Stealey, "Slavery," pp. 105–31. Noe, *Southwest Virginia's Railroad*, p. 47.

7. For example, Berlin, *Many Thousands*, p. 9, states that "slavery became exclusively identified with people of African descent in the New World." Fogel, *Without Consent*, pp. 178–82. Crawford, "Quantified Memory," p. 47. Gray, *History*, vol. 1, pp. 530–31.
8. Berlin, *Many Thousands*, pp. 8–10.
9. Ibid. McKinney, *Southern Mountain*, pp. 70–71. Dunaway, *African-American Family*, Ch. 13. For Southern trends, see Wilson and Ferris, *Encyclopedia*, p. 21; Anderson, *Race and Politics*, p. 25. For Mountain trends, see Chapter 1. For a map of U.S. slave trading routes, see Fox, *Harper's Atlas*, p. 42.
10. For extensive discussion about the debates over regional definition, see Dunaway, "Incorporation," pp. 989–91. For explanation of Appalachian terrain types, see Appalachian Regional Commission, *Appalachia*, pp. 17–28. Regarding terrain as precluding slavery, see Gray, *History*, vol. 1, pp. 308–10.
11. In response to a critique from an Appalachian scholar, I counted the number of citations I selected from planters. There are twelve for Thomas Jefferson, three for John Calhoun, and twenty-one from other planters.
12. Berlin, *Many Thousands*, p. 97. McKinney, *Southern Mountain*, pp. 53–62.
13. This massive regional data set was constructed during research for Dunaway, *First American Frontier*.
14. For details, see "Methodological Issues," website. Trouillot, *Silencing*, pp. 149, 153, 26. Published sources of slave narratives are *Slave*, *Slave I*, *Slave II*, and *CWVQ*. The Fisk collection is archived as Egypt, Masuoka, and Johnson, "Unwritten History of Slavery." The Kentucky collection is archived as UK, "Slave Narratives, Notes and Data," Typescripts, J. Winston Coleman Papers. A detailed discussion and the list of Mountain slave narratives is available at the website.
15. Yetman, "Background," pp. 534–35. Woodward, "History," p. 472. Narratives were located for Appalachian counties of Alabama (32), Georgia (45), Kentucky (26), Maryland (13), North Carolina (13), South Carolina (2), Tennessee (57), Virginia (80), and West Virginia (25).
16. Fisk, p. 143. Trouillot, *Silencing*, pp. 26, 29, 49. Woodward, "History," p. 475. To view the list of Mountain slave narratives, see the website.
17. That forthcoming book is *The African-American Family in Slavery and Emancipation* (Cambridge University Press).

CHAPTER 1

1. Opening quote is from *Records in British*, 5: 197. Hudson, *Juan Pardo Expeditions*, pp. 20–73. Hudson and Tesser, *Forgotten Centuries*, pp. 74–103. Mooney, "Myths," pp. 23–29. Walls, "On the Naming of Appalachia," pp. 57–60. Lauber, "Indian Slavery," pp. 68–70, 173–74. Dunaway, "Southern Fur Trade," pp. 216–18. Snell, "Indian Slavery," p. 94. Sellers, *Charleston Business*, p. 174. Thornton, *The Cherokees*, p. 19. Milling, *Red Carolinians*, p. 269n. Winston, "Indian Slavery," pp. 435–36. Baine, "Indian Slaves," pp. 422–23. Illustration 1.1, website.

2. In their journals of these early expeditions, the Spanish recorded that the mountains dwellers, like several other Southeastern groups, enslaved other Indians who had been taken as prisoners of war; see Malone, *Cherokees of Old South*, p. 20. Perdue, "Cherokee Planters," pp. 110–11. Perdue, *Slavery and Evolution*, pp. 31, 110–12. *Records in British*, 5: 197. *Carolina Chronicles of LeJau*, pp. 59–60. *Adair's History*, p. 407. Crane, "Tennessee River," p. 15. Lauber, *Indian Slavery*, pp. 68–70.
3. *Mississippi Provincial Archives*, 2: 573–74.
4. Koning, *Conquest of America*, pp. 17–55. Wolf, *Europe and People*, pp. 195–231. Williams, *Early Travels*, pp. 142–43. *DeBrahm's Report*, p. 109. Table 1.4, website.
5. Table 1.1, website.
6. Table 1.2, website. Fogel and Engerman, *Time*, vol. 1, pp. 33–34. Parrillo, *Strangers to These Shores*, pp. 126–61. Bailyn, *Peopling of North America*, pp. 40–58. Kivisto, *Americans All*, pp. 112–43.
7. Corkran, *Cherokee Frontier*, pp. 258–83. Allman, "Yeoman Regions," pp. 50–79. Lee, "Westward Movement," pp. 67–85. Illustration 1.2, website.
8. Dunaway, *First American Frontier*, pp. 157–94. Regarding export of slaves, see Tables 5.1 to 5.5, website.
9. Table 1.4, website. Fogel and Engerman, *Time*, vol. 1, pp. 43–52. Tadman, *Speculators*, pp. 225–47.
10. One of every 2.8 ridge-valley laborers was enslaved; see Dunaway, *First American Frontier*, p. 111. Table 1.3, website.
11. Wahl, "American Slavery," pp. 281–316. Walker, "Legal Status," pp. 382–95. Flanders, "Free Negro," pp. 250–72. Taylor, "Free Negro," pp. 5–26. Craven and Hay, "Criminalization," pp. 71–101. Dunaway, *First American Frontier*, p. 75. Soltow, *Men and Wealth*, Ch. 2, established $300 household wealth as the 1860 poverty line. See also for methods to calculate annual income from wealth. Data about free blacks derived from analysis of a systematic sample of one thousand free black Appalachian households drawn from the 1860 Census of Population enumerator manuscripts.
12. "Employment of the Indigent," *Journal of Commerce*, 20 November 1847. Townsend, "Dissertation on the Poor Laws," pp. 403–04, 415. *Mechanics Free Press*, 18 October 1828. *Journal of Commerce*, 20 November 1847. Klebaner, "Public Poor Relief," pp. 310–15. Information was located in the 1860 Census of Population manuscripts (NA) for the following Appalachian poorhouses (which averaged two to eleven inmates): Calhoun, AL; DeKalb, AL; Jackson, AL; Letcher, KY; Cherokee, NC; Rutherford, NC; Surry, NC; Pickens, SC; White, TN; Fauquier, VA; Warren, VA; Wythe, VA. Only two counties reflected a tendency to institutionalize paupers; the poorhouses in Allegany and Frederick, MD, housed ninety-eight and forty-one inmates, respectively.
13. Crowther, *Workhouse System*, pp. 37–49. Morris, *Government and Labor*, pp. 314–89. FHC, Bradley County, Tennessee Poor Commission Records. WV, Overseers of the Poor, 1850–54, Raleigh County Archives. WV, Record of Poor Funds, 1859, Summers County Archives. WV, Record of the Overseer of the Poor, 1835–57, Marshall County Archives. WV, Poor Funds, 1831–32, Harrison County Tax Book. WV, Overseers of the

Poor, 1861, Brooke County Archives. DPL, Poor Relief Records, Augusta County, Virginia, 1791–1822. DPL, Vincent Tapp Papers. DPL, Staunton, Virginia, Poor Records, 1770–1872. Scharf, *History*, vol. 2, p. 1347. WV, correspondence of Florence Fleming, 1858–63, Fleming Family Papers. DPL, Apprenticeship Indentures dated 1828 and 1846, Henry Clay Krebs Papers. See, for example, 18 November 1794 indenture of orphan by John Sevier, chairman of the Washington County Court in UT, John Sevier Papers. Sevier indentured a nine-year-old boy to work as servant and wheelwright apprentice until the age of twenty-one. At the end of his service, the orphan was to receive five dollars in cash and part of the needed wheelwright tools. The indenturement also instructed the employer to teach the orphan to read; the court, however, imposed no penalties for the employer's failure to meet the stated requirements. Johnson, *Antebellum North Carolina*, pp. 257, 690–96, 704. Taylor, *Antebellum South Carolina*, p. 86.

14. Craven and Hay, "Criminalization," pp. 71–101. Johnson, *Antebellum North Carolina*, p. 584. Weld, *American Slavery as It Is*, p. 52. Taylor, *Antebellum South Carolina*, p. 87. Johnson, *Antebellum North Carolina*, pp. 584–85.
15. Indenturement of free blacks appears routinely in poorhouse records. See WV, Overseers of the Poor, 1850–54, Raleigh County Archives; WV, Record of Poor Funds, 1859, Summers County Archives; WV, Record of the Overseer of the Poor, 1835–57, Marshall County Archives; WV, Poor Funds, 1831–32, Harrison County Tax Book; WV, Overseers of the Poor, 1861, Brooke County Archives. Bushman, *Registers of Free Blacks*, Augusta entries numbered 1, 29, 39, 48, 50, 51, 52, 85 and Staunton entries numbered 6, 29, 31, 33, 52, 63, 79. WV, Free Negro Register, WV, Monroe County Archives.
16. UT, Apprenticeship Indenture, Temple Typescripts, O. P. Temple Papers. Thwaites, *Travels West*, p. 301. Wallace, *South Carolina*, p. 382. *Slave*, 10 (a): 211. *CWVQ*, pp. 1705, 996–97, 1560.
17. Derived from analysis of a systematic sample of one thousand free black Appalachian households drawn from the 1860 Census of Population enumerator manuscripts (NA).
18. Table 1.4, website.
19. Table 1.5, website. Ratio of slaveholders to number of families from published Census of Population, 1860 (NA).
20. In these Appalachian counties, one-fifth to one-quarter of the families held slaves: Banks, Cass, Gordon, and Whitfield in Georgia; McDowell and Rutherford in North Carolina; Coffee, McMinn, and Warren in Tennessee; Augusta, Botetourt, Craig, Loudoun, Montgomery, Patrick, Pulaski, and Rockbridge in Virginia. These Appalachian counties were near the Southern average in slaveholding patterns: Coosa, Shelby, and Talladega in Alabama; Chatooga, Floyd, and Polk in Georgia; Madison, Kentucky; Franklin, Tennessee; Jefferson, West Virginia; and Albermarle, Amherst, Bath, Bedford, Clarke, Fauquier, Franklin, Greene, Madison, Nelson, Rappahannock, Roanoke, and Warren in Virginia.
21. Tables 1.1 and 1.4, website.
22. Wooster, *Politicians*, pp. 210–50. Dunaway, *First American Frontier*, pp. 123–56.

23. Wallerstein, *Modern World-System III*, pp. 166–67. Table 1.6, website.
24. Table 1.7, website.
25. Tables 1.8 and 1.17, website. For regional stereotypes, see Eller, *Miners*, pp. 11–12. Campbell, *Southern Highlander*, p. 94. Banks, "Emergence," pp. 189–90. Dykeman, "Appalachia," pp. 28–42. This historical misperception is corrected in Dunaway, *First American Frontier*, Ch. 5.
26. Table 1.9, website. In 1860, 8.2 percent of all Southern farms were large plantations. In the nation as a whole, one of every forty-two farms was a large plantation.
27. Braudel, *Civilization and Capitalism*, vol. 2, p. 272. *Weevils*, p. 9. Bouwman, *Traveler's Rest*, pp. 127–28. *Ferry Hill*, pp. 59–60. Wilms, "Cherokee Land Use," pp. 168–69. Betts, *Jefferson's Farm Book*, pp. xxxii–xxxix. NA, 1860 Franklin County, Virginia Census of Agriculture enumerator manuscripts.
28. *Slave*, 13 (a): 268. NA, 1860 Kanawha County, Virginia, manuscript Census of Agriculture, Census of Population, Census of Manufacturing, and Slave Schedule. Illustration 1.3, website.
29. Tables 1.6, 1.8, and 1.10, website.
30. Table 1.6, website. *Slave II*, 5: 1553. Occupations derived from analysis of a systematic sample of farms (n = 3,447) and a systematic sample of 3,056 households drawn from the 1860 Census of Agriculture and Census of Population enumerator manuscripts (NA).
31. Wallerstein, *Historical Capitalism*, pp. 27–28. Wallerstein, *Modern World-System III*, p. 138. This diversity was replicated all over the region; not a single county was composed entirely either of subsistent or surplus producers; see Dunaway, *First American Frontier*, pp. 123–56. Worsley, *Three Worlds*, p. 94. Table 1.6 and Illustration 1.4, website.
32. Table 1.11, website. Moore, *Mountain Voices*, p. viii. Dunaway, *First American Frontier*, p. 129.
33. Weld, *Travels*, p. 113. Analysis of questionnaire responses by all Civil War veterans from Appalachian counties (N = 474) in *CWVQ*. Wilms, "Cherokee Land Use," pp. 161–62.
34. Dunaway, *First American Frontier*, p. 129.
35. Pudup, "Social Class," pp. 248–49. Analysis of all Monroe County farms (N = 1,238) enumerated in the 1860 Census of Agriculture manuscripts (NA). Landholding patterns derived from analysis of all farm owners included in the sample of farms (n = 3,447) drawn from the 1860 Census of Agriculture enumerator manuscripts (NA).
36. Dunaway, *First American Frontier*, p. 79. Slaughter, *Whiskey Rebellion*, p. 65. Henretta, "Families and Farms," p. 7.
37. Dunaway, *First American Frontier*, pp. 73–77.
38. Ibid., p. 295. Table 1.12, website.
39. Dunaway, *First American Frontier*, pp. 56–66, 316–18. These economic activities are evident in numerous Appalachian slaveholder manuscripts. Illustration 1.5, website.
40. Soltow, *Men and Wealth*, p. 112. Dunaway, *First American Frontier*, pp. 294–95.
41. Dunaway, *First American Frontier*, pp. 308–15.
42. Ibid., pp. 145–52.

43. Table 1.13, website. Regarding disarticulation, see Amin, *Accumulation*, pp. 175–77, 393–95.
44. For Northeastern growth, see *DeBow's Review* 29 (1860), 269. Amin, *Accumulation*, p. 177.
45. Table 1.14, website.
46. Wallerstein, *Modern World-System III*, p. 84. Dunaway, *First American Frontier*, pp. 257–62.
47. *CWVQ*, pp. 911, 1448, 317, 1670. Glickstein, *Concepts*, pp. 217–19. See also Olmsted, *Back Country*, p. 238. Carpenter, "Henry Dana Ward," 10 July 1846 entry, p. 42. McDonald, *Woman's Civil War*, p. 238.
48. Dunaway, *First American Frontier*, pp. 257–62. *CWVQ*, pp. 801, 1235.
49. McDonald, *Woman's Civil War*, pp. 80–81. Olmsted, *Seaboard*, p. 84. "Lonaconing Journals," pp. 30–38, 44. *Baltimore Sun*, 9 January and 21 April 1854. When the Chesapeake and Ohio Canal Company paid differential wages to laborers based on ethnicity, labor riots erupted in 1838. The "military [was] sent off to quell" the unrest, in the process burning the laborer shantytown in Washington County, Maryland. Subsequently, state courts convicted twenty immigrant labor leaders; see *Ferry Hill*, p. 49, and Sanderlin, *Great National Project*, pp. 118–22. *CWVQ*, pp. 698–99. Appalachians paralleled capitalist views dominant throughout the United States and Europe in this era; see Glickstein, *Concepts*, pp. 32–52, 86–92.
50. Table 1.15, website. Whisnant, *Native and Fine*, p. 260. Wallerstein, *Historical Capitalism*, pp. 84–87. For an extensive discussion of this ideology about laborers, see Glickstein, *Concepts*, pp. 32–52, 86–92. Grund, *Americans*, pp. 172–73.
51. Clark, *Roots*, pp. 306–07. Dunaway, *First American Frontier*, pp. 82–83.
52. *CWVQ*, pp. 1063, 1, 801, 940, 966, 1946, 2165, 878.
53. Clark, *Roots*, pp. 306–07. Landless Appalachians moved frequently; 40 to 50 percent of the families disappeared from county tax lists about every five years. See Dunaway, *First American Frontier*, pp. 83–84; Soltow, "Land Inequality," pp. 283–85; Hsiung, *Two Worlds*, pp. 110–17. *CWVQ*, pp. 699, 801, 22, 1235, 94, 1946.
54. Innes, *Work and Labor*, pp. 251, 127. Almost all the Civil War veterans report the same pattern of schooling in every section of Southern Appalachia; see, for example, *CWVQ*, pp. 5, 9, 13, 20, 897, 1080, 1229, 1360, 1922, 2013, 2086. Also see WV, contract for subscription school, 7 July 1845, Freeman Family Papers. Hamer, *Tennessee*, pp. 356–57. *North Carolina Standard*, 3 August 1853.
55. Tables 1.16 and 1.4, website. For discussion of the relationship between slaveholding and the vote of Appalachian counties on secession, see Wooster, *Secession*, pp. 50, 138, 174, 194, 201, 206; Doyton and Hodler, "Secessionist Sentiment," p. 328.
56. *Raleigh Register*, 10 July 1850. Johnson, *Antebellum North Carolina*, pp. 76–79. Taylor, *Antebellum South Carolina*, Ch. 1. Ambler, *Sectionalism*, Ch. 9. Lacy, *Vanquished Volunteers*, Ch. 4. Coleman, *History*, p. 121. Norris, *Lower Shenandoah*, pp. 213–20. Heath, *Constructive Liberalism*, Ch. 13. Rohrbough, *Trans-Appalachian Frontier*, pp. 57–60, 309. Williams, *History*, pp. 226–53.

Olmsted, *Back Country*, pp. 331–37. *CWVQ*, pp. 51, 270, 461, 530, 819, 970, 1230, 1235, 1302, 1387, 1417, 1419, 1423, 1435, 1544–45, 1609, 1611, 1749, 1786, 1904–05, 1944, 1995, 2035, 2247. Dunaway, *First American Frontier*, p. 292.

57. *Kanawha Valley Star*, 2 December 1856, 12 July 1859.
58. *Kanawha Republican*, 25 January 1842. "Account of the Clarksburg Educational Convention of September 8–9, 1841," in *U.S. Commissioner of Education Report*, vol. 1, p. 435.
59. Ashe, *History*, p. 324. *Jonesborough Whig*, 8 December 1841. Lacy, *Vanquished Volunteers*, p. 110. Weaver, "Internal Improvements." Ambler, *Sectionalism*. Spencer, "Transportation." Verhoeff, *Kentucky Mountains*. Verhoeff, *Kentucky River*. Littlefield, "Maryland Sectionalism." Rice, "Internal Improvements." Fischer, "Internal Improvement." Boughter, "Internal Improvements." Delfino, "Antebellum Elites." Jeffrey, "Internal Improvements." Martin, "Internal Improvements." Heath, *Constructive Liberalism*. Folmsbee, *Sectionalism*. Hunter, "Turnpike Construction." Folmsbee, "Turnpike Phase." Allen, "Turnpike System." Brown, *State Movement*.

CHAPTER 2

1. Opening quote is from *Slave*, 12: 309. Dunaway, *First American Frontier*, pp. 123–56. Chase-Dunn, *Global Formation*, p. 210. National and Southern per-capita crop production averages were calculated using the published 1860 Census of Agriculture (NA): corn = 26.7 bushels; wheat = 5.5 bushels; cotton = 0.17 bales; tobacco = 13.8 pounds; hogs = 1.1; cattle = 0.7. Southern per-capita crop production aggregated using published 1860 Census of Agriculture (NA): corn = 8.1 bushels; wheat = 0.9 bushel; cotton = 0.13 bales; tobacco = 6.5 pounds; hogs = 0.5; cattle = 0.3.
2. Dunaway, *First American Frontier*, pp. 123–56.
3. Ibid. No Appalachian county consumed all of its food crops. The seven low-export counties were shipping agricultural surpluses to distant markets at a level below the global average, but they were not subsistent. Fannin, Lumpkin, and Rabun Counties in Georgia; Wilkes, North Carolina; Cumberland, Tennessee; Buchanan, Virginia; and Webster, West Virginia, exported less than one-fifth of their total grains and livestock, and they cultivated little or no staples.
4. Tables 1.6, 2.1, and 2.6, website. Dunaway, *First American Frontier*, pp. 123–56. Moore, *Mountain Voices*, p. 41.
5. Tables 1.6, 2.1, and 2.6, website. Dunaway, *First American Frontier*, pp. 76–80, 53–56. Moore, *Mountain Voices*, p. 41.
6. Table 2.2, website.
7. Dunaway, *First American Frontier*, pp. 87–122. Using the ratio from Table 2.2 (website), I estimated that 45 percent (928) of the region's 2,061 free black households were engaged in agriculture. Derived from analysis of a systematic sample of 1,000 free black Appalachian households drawn from the

1860 Census of Population manuscripts (NA). I checked for white households adjacent to the sampled free black households.

8. Dunaway, *First American Frontier*, pp. 87–122. UVSC, Hubard Family Papers, several 1827 diary entries.
9. From the sample of free black households, I know that 6.4 percent (131) of all the free black households were farm owners and that 5.8 percent (120) of the region's free black households were sharecropping. There were at least 17,260 sharecroppers in Southern Appalachian in 1860; see Dunaway, *First American Frontier*, pp. 79, 94, 328. *Code of Georgia*, pp. 436–38. Brooks, *Agrarian Revolution*, p. 67. Orser, *Material Basis*, pp. 56–57. Lenoir Plantation contracts in Reid, "Antebellum Rental Contracts." Betts, *Jefferson's Farm Book*, p. 166. Betts, *Jefferson's Garden Book*, pp. 202, 265, 267, 270. Numerous account entries, Miller Farm Records. *CWVQ*, pp. 293, 621, 665, 769, 1460, 2174. Several contracts in UK, Wickliffe-Preston Papers. Several 1840s contracts and account entries, WV, Wilson-Lewis Papers.
10. Free black patterns were derived from analysis of a systematic sample of 1,000 free black Appalachian households drawn from the 1860 Census of Population manuscripts (NA). I checked for white households adjacent to the sampled free black households. The following farm account books were useful: WV, Plantation Accounts of Alexander Henderson, 1798–1810, Henderson-Tomlinson Families Papers; WV, 1853 Farm Account Book, Edward E. Meredith Papers; WV, Correspondence and Receipts, 1841–50, John McClaugherty Papers; WV, Farm Account Book, 1831–50, Courtney Family Papers; DPL, Plantation Account Books, Campbell Family Papers; WV, Diary of farming operations, 1851–60, John P. Clarke Papers. Patterns of tobacco and cotton sharecropping are evident in these manuscripts: SHC, Mallory Diary (Talladega, AL), 1843–60; DPL Ridgeway Plantation (Albermarle, VA) Diaries, 1828–29, 1830–34, 1838–39, 1842–44 in Hugh Minor Notebooks; DPL, Frederick Co., Virginia, Plantation Account Books, 1810–50, in Bryarly and Rowland Papers. Patterns of sharecropping in connection with livestock operations (Haywood, NC) are evident in 1840–58 letters in DPL, Thomas Lenoir Papers.
11. NA, 1860 Census of Population manuscripts for Greene County, TN. For methods to calculate family subsistence requirements, see Dunaway, *First American Frontier*, pp. 323–32.
12. For overall indentured count, see Ibid., p. 89.There were at least 3,184 indentured farm laborers in Southern Appalachia in 1860; see Dunaway, "Incorporation," Table 3.11. Using the ratio from Table 2.2 (website) and the published Census count (NA), I estimate there were 204 indentured black farm laborers. Johnson, *Antebellum North Carolina*, pp. 584–85. Taylor, *Antebellum South Carolina*, p. 87. Jackson, *Free Negro Labor*, pp. 63, 75.
13. Bushman, *Registers of Free Blacks*: Augusta entries numbered 1, 29, 39, 48, 50, 51, 52, 85 and Staunton entries numbered 6, 29, 31, 33, 52, 63, 79. WV, Free Negro Register, Monroe County Archives. Indenturement of free blacks appears in the poorhouse records for the following counties: Raleigh, WV; Brooke, WV; Bradley, TN. Franklin, *Free Negro*, p. 227.
14. 1860 Census of Agriculture enumerator manuscripts: Calhoun, AL, entry 719; Wayne, KY, entry 590; Magoffin, KY, entry 311; Rockbridge, VA, entry

802. UVSC, indenture dated 10 April 1832, Bell Family Papers. Sellers, *Slavery*, p. 171; DPL, Letterbook, 1839–40, pp. 132, 140, William Holland Thomas Papers. *Cambridge Chronicle*, 24 January 1835. Brackett, *Negro in Maryland*, p. 265. Indenture dated 3 August 1836, SHC, Hamilton Brown Papers. 1860 Census of Population manuscripts for Greene, Monroe, and White Counties, TN (NA).

15. Trends derived from analysis of a systematic sample of 1,000 free black Appalachian households drawn from the 1860 Census of Population manuscripts (NA). *Slave*, 16: 78. SHC, letter dated 8 May 1840, Hamilton Brown Papers. Illustration 2.1, website.
16. Table 2.3, website. Betts, *Jefferson's Farm Book*, many 1797 entries. *Slave II*, 6: 2240.
17. *Slave*, 11 (a): 168, 229, 14 (a): 353. Fisk, pp. 156, 51.
18. Fox-Genovese, *Plantation Household*, p. 186. *Slave*, 12 (a): 196. SHC, James Hervey Greenlee Diary, 21 May 1849, 1848–53. *Slave II*, 6: 2276. Illustration 2.2, website.
19. Fisk, p. 217. *Slave II*, 5: 1554; 6: 2273, 2276. *Slave I*, 1: 151, 18, 432. *Slave*, 10 (b): 254.
20. *Ferry Hill*, pp. 53, 15–17, 19, 22, 25, 33, 41, 65. Betts, *Jefferson's Garden Book*, p. 200. SHC, James Hervey Greenlee Diary, 17 April 1849, 13 September 1850. Dunaway, "The Disremembered," pp. 90–97.
21. Roughley, *Jamaica Planter's Guide*, pp. 109–10. Crawford, "Quantified Memory," pp. 11–22. Illustration 2.3, website.
22. *Slave II*, 3: 784, 6: 2257. Child labor patterns derived from analysis of Appalachian slave narratives. *Slave I*, 5: 216, 9: 1525.
23. *Slave*, 12 (a): 196. Smyth, *Tour*, vol. 2, p. 130. Fisk, p. 156.
24. *Slave II*, 9: 3638. *Slave I*, 5: 448, 11 (b): 206, 14 (a): 354, 11 (a): 166. Oral history collected by the author. Drew, *North-side View*, p. 280.
25. *Slave II*, 1: 346–47, 3: 784. *Slave*, 4 (b): 75, 225. Jones, *Labor of Love*, p. 37. *Slave I*, 3: 94.
26. Table 2.4, website. Dunaway, *First American Frontier*, pp. 87–122.
27. *CWVQ*, pp. 1682, 1301, 621, 560, 1078, 1435, 1655, 587. *Slave*, 4 (a): 303, 11 (a): 168, 1: 425. *Slave I*, 5 (b): 306.
28. *Slave*, 16: 29–30, 4 (b): 35, 12: 143. *Slave II*, 9: 3871, 3: 498, 5: 1560–62.
29. *Slavery Time*, p. 99. *Slave*, 6: 155, 16 (a): 1, 88. Fisk, p. 199. *CWVQ*, p. 1022.
30. *CWVQ*, p. 1179. VHS, James Lawrence Hooff Diary, 1855–60 lists. *Slave II*, 3: 669, 6: 2276.
31. Fogel, Galantine, and Manning, *Without Consent*, vol. 3, p. 93. *Papers of Calhoun*, 14: 85. Flanders, *Plantation Slavery*, p. 99. *Slave*, 3: 498, 12: 312.
32. *Slave II*, 5: 1864, 3: 799, 2: 77. *Slave*, 12: 309. St. Abdy, *Journal*, 2: 291.
33. Fogel, Galantine, and Manning, *Without Consent*, vol. 3, p. 117. *Slave*, 12 (a): 196, 7: 142. SHC, James Mallory Diary, 1850 entries. For Deep South labor management styles, see Morgan, "Task," pp. 189–220. *CWVQ*, pp. 1670–71.
34. *Slave II*, 3: 797–98. *Slave*, 16: 23. *Weevils*, pp. 156–67.
35. Schlotterbeck, "Internal Economy," pp. 168–69. Janney and Janney, *Janney's Virginia*, pp. 75–76. *Weevils*, pp. 156–57. *Slave*, 14 (a): 353.
36. *Slave II*, 3: 787. For an extensive discussion of livestock production and meat processing by mountain slaves, see Slave Narratives, Excerpts, website.

37. Dunaway, *First American Frontier*, pp. 226–27. *Slave*, 13: 77.
38. SHC, James Hervey Greenlee Diary, February to April 1847. Bouwman, *Traveler's Rest*, pp. 119–21. Janney and Janney, *Janney's Virginia*, p. 3. UVSC, entry dated 31 December 1801, Benjamin Johnson Account Book; Barbour Family Papers. WV, letter dated 1 November 1820, McNeill Family Papers. Betts, *Jefferson's Farm Book*, pp. 219–20. *Slave II*, 3: 498, 787. Illustration 2.5, website.
39. *Slave II*, 3: 787. Fisk, p. 11. *Slave*, 16: 11. *Slave I*, 3: 482–83.
40. *Slave II*, 3: 787. *Slave I*, 3: 483. SHC, James Hervey Greenlee Diary, 2 December 1847. Janney and Janney, *Janney's Virginia*, p. 27.

CHAPTER 3

1. The opening quote is from *Slave*, 1: 56. Dunaway, *First American Frontier*, pp. 225–48. Wallerstein, *Modern World-System III*, pp. 148–49. Meillassoux, *Development*, 96–98. *Slave II*, 9: 3878–81.
2. "Letters to Jefferson," p. 130. *Railroad Advocate*, 4 July 1831. Illustration 3.1, website.
3. For the concept of bulking centers, see Wallerstein, *Modern World-System III*, p. 148. Dunaway, *First American Frontier*, pp. 204–08.
4. Tables 3.1 and 3.3, website. For Southern trends, see Levine, *Half Slave and Half Free*, p. 23.
5. Table 3.2, website.
6. Table 3.4, website. Regarding slave hiring, see Table 5.9, website.
7. Tables 3.5 and 3.1, website. Fogel and Engerman, *Time*, vol. 1, p. 43. *Slave II*, 3: 918. Fogel, *Without Consent*, pp. 41–58. Compare with Fogel and Engerman, *Without Consent*, pp. 139–45.
8. Tables 3.3, 3.4, and 3.6 and Illustration 3.2, website. Dunaway, "Incorporation," Table 8.1, p. 1098. Analysis of 2,012 indentures of free blacks between 1820 and 1860 in WV, Free Negro Register, Monroe County Road Records; WV, Overseers of the Poor, Raleigh County Archives; FHC, Bradley County, Tennessee Poor Commission Records; DPL, Augusta County Poor Relief Records, Vincent Tapp Papers; DPL, Staunton, Virginia, Poor Records.
9. Jackson, *Free Negro Labor*, p. 25. *Knoxville Standard*, 12 May 1846. Ash, *Past Times*, p. 8. McDougle, "Slavery," p. 245. Henry, "Slave Laws," pp. 179–81. Eslinger, "Liquor Reform," pp. 171–73. Stroud, *Laws*, pp. 159–73. Wade, *Slavery in Cities*, pp. 62–66, 106–10, 204–06. Craven and Hay, "Criminalization," pp. 71–101. Dunaway, *First American Frontier*, pp. 111–14.
10. Wade, *Slavery in Cities*, pp. 44–45. Starobin, *Industrial Slavery*, p. 31. Bishir, "Black Builders," pp. 433–40. Johnson, "Recreational," pp. 377–82. Inscoe, *Mountain Masters*, p. 78. Darst, "Benjamin Darst," pp. 72–73. VS, entry dated 25 December 1854, Auditor of Public Accounts: Slaves Condemned, Executed and Transported. Stroud, *Laws*, pp. 88–93. Henry, "Slave Laws," p. 191. Womack, *McMinnville*, pp. 149–51. Virginia Writers Project, *Roanoke*, pp. 220–21. Pentecost, "Corporate History," pp. 116–17.

Irwin, "Negro," 92–99. Booker, *Black Culture*, p. 13. *The South*, p. 319. Buck, *Sad Earth*, p. 241.

11. Tables 3.3 and 3.4, website. *Alexandria Gazette and Virginia Advertiser*, 6 January 1858. *Slave*, 10 (b): 254. *Weevils*, p. 165. Parkhurst, "Negro Mammy," pp. 349–69. Knox County, Tennessee, 1860 Census of Population enumerator manuscripts (NA). *Jacksonville Republican*, 11 April 1854. Ebert, "Window," pp. 37–38.
12. WV, 1850–60 account books, McNeel Family Papers. SHC, letter dated 11 February 1861, Calvin J. Cowles Papers. Inscoe, "Mountain Masters," pp. 84–100. DPL, letter dated 5 January 1860, William Holland Thomas Papers. Bouwman, *Traveler's Rest*, p. 165. Stokely and Johnson, *Encyclopedia*, p. 377. *CWVQ*, p. 684.
13. Tables 3.3 and 3.1, website. *Great Slave Narratives*, p. 208. *Slave*, 7: 138. *Lexington Intelligencer*, 31 May 1823. Darst, "Benjamin Darst," p. 67. LC, letter dated 25 August 1830, American Colonization Society Papers.
14. Ebert, "Window," p. 50. NA, 1860 Census of Population manuscripts for western North Carolina counties. NA, Sullivan County, Tennessee, 1860 Census of Population manuscripts. Russell, *Free Negro*, p. 150n. Jackson, *Free Negro Labor*, p. 80. *Ferry Hill*, p. 26.
15. Table 3.3, website. Free black trends derived from analysis of a systematic sample of 3,056 households drawn from the 1860 Census of Population enumerator manuscripts (NA). NA, Knox County, Tennessee, 1860 Census of Population manuscripts. Ash, *Past Times*, p. 29. *Chattanooga Times*, 3 September 1896, p. 3.
16. For a detailed list of mineral spas, see Dunaway, "Incorporation," Table 8.5. For a map of county dependence on travel capitalism, see Dunaway, *First American Frontier*, Map 10.3. For livestock trail maps, see Henlein, *Cattle Kingdom*, pp. 101, 138. Illustration 3.3, website.
17. *DeBow's Review* 10 (January 1851), p. 107; 21 (September 1856), p. 323. *Southern Literary Messenger* 17 (June 1851), p. 378.
18. Brewster, "Summer Migrations," pp. 40–63. Reniers, *Springs*, pp. 96–113. Berdan, "Spa Life," p. 113. For a typical diary of such an elite tour, see Shepard, "Trip," pp 193–212. Featherstonhough, *Excursion*, vol. 1, p. 94.
19. *DeBow's Review* 14 (1853), pp. 49–50. Moorman, *Virginia Springs*, p. 1, map. *Richmond Whig*, 19 June 1837. Dunaway, *First American Frontier*, p. 307.
20. Dunaway, "Incorporation," pp. 567–86. WV, 1830–31 Account Book, White Sulphur Springs Company Records. WV, Berkeley Springs Hotel Company Records, Stephen B. Elkins Papers. Dunaway, *First American Frontier*, pp. 305–07. Dunaway, "Incorporation," pp. 570–71. *Richmond Daily Enquirer*, 13 May 1853, 27 June 1853. Playfair, *Recollections*, p. 174. *Alexandria Daily Advertiser*, 27 July 1808. Inscoe, *Mountain Masters*, pp. 66–67. Illustration 3.4, website.
21. Stokely and Johnson, *Encyclopedia*, pp. 44–45. *Tri-Weekly Commonwealth*, 21 June 1852. *Knoxville Register*, 3 June 1858. *Knoxville Whig*, 27 August 1853. SHC, letter dated 20 December 1832, Hamilton Brown Papers. *Slave*, 4 (a): 109. *Charleston Daily Courier*, 14 April 1850. Lanman, *Letters*, pp. 314,

434–35, 439–44. Featherstonhough, *Canoe Voyage*, p. 317. *Harper's Monthly* No. 55 (1854).

22. Coffey, "Into the Valley," pp. 165–66. Darst, "Benjamin Darst," p. 73. Gaines, "Going Underground," pp. 26–27. Lanman, *Letters*, 434–35, 439–44. Featherstonhough, *Canoe Voyage*, p. 317. *Knoxville Register*, 3 June 1858. *Knoxville Whig*, 27 August 1853. *Asheville News*, 8 June 1854. Schwarzkopf, *History*, pp. 42–43. *Papers of Zebulon Vance*, vol. 1, pp. 37–38. *Chattanooga Gazette*, 10 May 1856.
23. Buckingham, *Slave States*, vol. 2, p. 193. NA, 1860 manuscript Census of Population and Slave Schedules for Sevier County and Warren County, Tennessee. Day and Dickinson, "Netherland Inn," pp. 67–77. Inscoe, *Mountain Masters*, pp. 66–67. Bouwman, *Traveler's Rest*, p. 164. *Weevils*, pp. 81, 82. *Slave*, 16: 67. Analysis of systematic sample of one thousand free black households drawn from the manuscript 1860 Census of Population (NA).
24. Ambler, *History of West Virginia*, p. 201. Henlein, *Cattle Kingdom*, p. 102. Leavitt, "Meat and Dairy." Hilliard, *Hog Meat*, p. 194. Dunaway, "Incorporation," Table 11.2. Dunaway, *First American Frontier*, pp. 138–42. Henlein, *Cattle Kingdom*, p. 119. SHC, letter dated 10 October 1849, Hamilton Brown Papers. Shadburn, *Cherokee Planters*, pp. 259–61. *Alexandria Gazette*, 12 January 1819.
25. Estimated using Table 3.3, website, and Dunaway, "Incorporation," Table 11.2. Shadburn, *Cherokee Planters*, pp. 259–61. Olmsted, *Back Country*, pp. 268–69. *Cherokee Phoenix*, 23 October 1836. *Tennessee Historical Markers*, pp. 12, 92, 107. Siler, *Tennessee Towns. WPA Guide to Tennessee*, p. 312. Smith, *Review*, p. 27. Burnett, "Hog Raising," p. 99. Dykeman, *French Broad*, pp. 147–49. Searight, *The Old Pike*, pp. 142–43. SHC, letter dated 26 October 1860, James Gwyn Papers. SHC, James Hervey Greenlee Diary, December through March, 1849–50.
26. Gilchrist, "Virginia Springs," pp. 98–110. Stuart, *Three Years*, vol. 2, p. 244. Shadburn, *Cherokee Planters*, pp. 260–62.
27. Stuart, *Three Years*, vol. 2, pp. 243–47.
28. Tables 3.4 and 3.1 and Illustration 3.5, website. DPL, letter dated 19 February 1856, William Weaver Papers. *Fredericksburg Herald*, 3 January 1859.
29. Haites, Mak, and Walton, *Western River*, p. 11. For a map, see Dunaway, *First American Frontier*, p. 210. Bouwman, *Traveler's Rest*. Banta, *Ohio*. Verhoeff, *Kentucky River*. Clark, *Kentucky*. Wiley, *Monongahela*. Bissell, *Monongahela*. Pease, "Great Kanawha." Spencer, "Transportation." Westfall, "Internal Improvements." Murphy, "Transportation." Ambler, *History of Transportation*. Douglas, *Steamboatin'*. Gauding, "History." Rollins, "Tennessee River." Tennessee Valley Authority, *History*. Davidson, *The Tennessee*. Campbell, *Upper Tennessee*. Hulbert, *Historic Highways*, vol. 13, pp. 81–85. Reynolds, *Coosa River Valley*. UVSC, letters dated 22 September 1836 and three undated reports regarding Rivanna Navigation Company, Randolph Family Papers. UVSC, numerous 1820s and 1830s letters about the Roanoke Navigation Company, Bruce Family Papers. Starobin, *Industrial Slavery*, pp. 28–29.
30. *Knoxville News Sentinel*, 3 January 1993, p. B-1. Trout, "Goose Creek and Little River," pp. 31–34. Simms, "John Jordan," p. 23. Niemi, "Further

Look," p. 515. Dupre, "Ambivalent Capitalists," pp. 215–40. Druyvesteyn, "James River." *Ferry Hill*, intro. *History of Etowah*, p. 19. Coleman and Hemphill, "Boats," pp. 8–13. Woodlief, *In River Time*. WV, Harper's Ferry Typescript. Gauding, "History," pp. 72–75. *American State Papers*, Misc., vol. 1 (1834), pp. 73, 809. Tennessee Valley Authority, *History*, pp. 58–65. *Huntsville Democrat*, 5 September 1833.

31. Stevens, *Shenandoah*. Davis, *Shenandoah*. Niles, *The James*. Gutheim, *Potomac*. Dunaway, "History." Pinchbeck, "Virginia Negro Artisan," pp. 64–65. *Richmond Enquirer*, 10 April 1838. Lewis, *Coal*, p. 29. Bruce, *Virginia Iron*, p. 273. Gilliam, "Jordan's Point," p. 117. March 1865 minutes, UVSC, James River and Kanawha Canal Company Papers. VS, Virginia Board of Public Works Report, 1854, pp. 388–89. Harlow, *Old Towpaths*. Woodlief, *In River Time*, pp. 100–25. Jones, "Study," pp. 83–90. *DeBow's Review*, 18 (1855), pp. 350–51. Starobin, *Industrial Slavery*, 165–68. Lewis, *Coal*, p. 163. Illustration 3.6, website.
32. *CWVQ*, pp. 1009, 624–25. Davidson, *Tennessee*, pp. 209–12. Coffey, "Into the Valley," p. 162. *Ferry Hilll*, p. 39. Lewis, "Valley," pp. 313–22. Ahern and Hunt, "Boatyard Store," pp. 257–77. Gauding, "History," pp. 41–44. Hunter, "Studies," pp. 51–57. Gilliam, "Jordan's Point," pp. 116–19.
33. Carson, "Transportation," pp. 26–38. Terrell, "James River," pp. 180–91. Haites and Mak, "Ohio and Mississippi." Haites and Mak, "Social Savings." Haites, Mak, and Walton, *Western River*.
34. Advertisements for slave runaways from Albermarle and Rockbridge Counties, *Richmond Enquirer*, 22 November 1805, 5 October 1810, 9 April 1813. *Richmond Enquirer*, 22 August 1809. *Alexandria Gazette*, 8 June 1816. *Alexandria Gazette and Daily Advertiser*, 30 April 1818. UVSC, two 1803 letters, Richard Foster Papers. *Richmond Enquirer*, 26 July 1815. Jackson, *Free Negro Labor*, pp. 101, 77. Callahan, *Semi-Centennial History*, p. 87. Betts, *Jefferson's Farm Book*, p. 19. Hughes, *Thirty Years*, p. 5. Letter dated 20 January 1813, *Ferry Hill*, p. 55.
35. Knapp, "Trade," p. 221. Wayland, *Twenty-Five Chapters*, pp. 420–21. Lambert, *Undying Past*, pp. 97–98. Bouwman, *Traveler's Rest*, pp. 160–66. An antebellum watercolor of seven slaves running a bateau through the rapids of the New River was published in *Harper's Weekly*, 21 February 1874, p. 153. Kirby, "Canalization," p. 269. Tennessee Valley Authority, *History*, pp. 155–57. Local history buffs do not agree with the scholarly perception of the French Broad. Older local residents recall that small boats regularly took tourists on excursion trips during the summer months. In addition, a small steamboat, the *Mountain Lily*, operated between Asheville and Brevard between 1881 and 1885; Patton, *Story*, pp. 192, 245–46. *Slave*, 3: 66, 68–69, 71.
36. Gamble, "Steamboats." Burford, "Steam Packets." Teuton, "Steamboating." Coleman, "Kentucky River." Spencer, "Transportation," pp. 12–15. *Rome Courier*, 3 March 1860. *History of Etowah*, p. 19. Norris, *Lower Shenandoah*, Ch. 20. Reynolds, *Coosa River*, pp. 101–10. Limited and irregular steamboating on Tennessee, Kentucky, Big Sandy, and Kanawha until after 1830s; see Haites, Mak, and Walton, *Western River*, p. 51. Campbell, *Upper Tennessee*. Hunter, *Steamboats*, p. 217. Mak and Walton, "Steamboats," p. 623. Hall,

Notes, p. 249. Shadburn, *Cherokee Planters*, pp. 260–62. Davidson, *Tennessee*, pp. 209–12.

37. Starobin, *Industrial Slavery*, p. 30. WV, Thompson v. Ruffner, Ruffner, Brooks, and Donnally, County Court, 1835; Capehart v. Norton and Coleman, Circuit Superior Court, 1846 in Kanawha County Court Records. *The South*, p. 312.
38. Watson, "Ferry," pp. 249–50. "West Virginia River Ferries," pp. 172–73. Spencer, "Transportation," pp. 12–13. Wayland, *History*, p. 266. Holmes, "Last Eight," p. 68. Moore, "Role of Ferry," pp. 76–80. *Alexandria Daily Advertiser*, 27 April 1805. These pre-Removal Cherokees were Joseph Vann, A. McCoy, Michael Hilderbrand, William Blyth, Jonathan Mulkey, John Ross, Lewis Ross, Peter Hilderbrand, Nicholas B. McNair, John Hilderbrand, William Grimmett, James Lassley, Lewis Blackburn, Martin Brannon, Major Ridge, John Ridge, and George M. Waters; see Shadburn, *Cherokee Planters*, especially p. 62. VS, Virginia Board of Public Works Report, 1858, pp. 189, 310. Bouwman, *Traveler's Rest*, p. 150.
39. *Slave*, 16: 57. 10 (b): 254. 5 (a): 214. *Ferry Hill*, pp. xi–xii, 129, 88, 18, 27, 34, 55, 86, 100, 97.
40. For a map, see Dunaway, *First American Frontier*, p. 216. For an early map of major roads for the entire region, see Melish, *Traveler's Directory*. For maps of major livestock drover routes, see Henlein, *Cattle Kingdom*, p. 102, and Hilliard, *Hog Meat*, p. 194. For turnpike information, see the following sources: Ierley, *Traveling*. Rouse, *Great Wagon Road*, map. Bouwman, *Traveler's Rest*. Davis, *Shenandoah*. Dykeman, *French Broad*. Folmsbee, "Turnpike Phase," p. 46. Harlow, *Old Towpaths*. Heath, *Constructive Liberalism*, p. 251. Hulbert, *Historic Highways*, vol. 9. Hunter, "Turnpike Construction," p. 193. Kincaid, "Wilderness Road," p. 45. Kirby, "Canalization." Niles, *James*. Reynolds, *Coosa River*. Bissell, *Monongahela*. Spencer, "Transportation." Templin, "Making a Road," pp. 80–87. Tennessee Valley Authority, *History*. Verhoeff, *Kentucky River*. Lord, *Blue Ridge Guide*. Martin, "Internal Improvements," pp. 21–25. Verhoeff, *Kentucky Mountains*, pp. 100–33. Williams and McKinsey, *History*, p. 181. Durrenberger, *Turnpikes*. Norris, *Lower Shenandoah*. Wayland, *History*, pp. 261–75. Hunter, "Turnpike Movement." Pawlett, *Brief History*. Wayland, *Valley Turnpike*. ter Braake, "Postal History," pp. 27–54.
41. Table 3.5, website. TS, Knox County Road Commissioners Minutebook. WV, letters dated 12 September 1832, 19 April 1844, 3 July 1858, Monroe County Archives. UVSC, letters dated 10 December 1853, 8 January 1849, Massie Family Papers. VS, Virginia Board of Public Works Report, 1854, pp. 128–54; 1858, pp. 297–310. Starling, "Plank Road Movement," pp. 16–17. VS, Virginia Board of Public Works Report, 1854, p. 187. WV, letter dated 16 September 1851, Frederick B. Lambert Papers. UVSC, letter dated 6 July 1857, Watson Family Papers. VS, Virginia Board of Public Works Report, 1854, pp. 133–34. Gilliam, "Jordan's Point," p. 115. Bouwman, *Traveler's Rest*, p. 163–64. Andrews and Young, "Plantations," p. 7. UK, contracts and plat map, 1857–59, Wickliffe-Preston Papers.
42. Such transactions are detailed, for example, in a Claiborne County, Tennessee, Stage Coach Book, 1846–48 (FHC). Rouse, *Great Wagon Road*,

p. 195. SHC, letter dated 15 July 1853, Hamilton Brown Papers. Advertisement for runaway slave, *Richmond Enquirer*, 8 November 1815. Patton, *Story*, p. 101.

43. Rouse, *Great Wagon Road*, pp. 167–75. *Hagerstown Mail*, 31 March 1837. *Harper's* 59 (November 1879), p. 804. Allman, "Yeoman Regions," p. 428. Gauding, "History," pp. 26–31. UVSC, letters dated 24 July 1833, 12 February 1860, 12 September 1860, 7 February 1839, 15 May 1849, Holland Family Papers. Merchant to Philadelphia about once a month in WV, Thomas P. Ray Diary, 1829–52. Regular 1830s trading trips in WV, William G. Dickinson Papers. WV, letter dated 15 November 1854, Chapin Family Papers. FC, John Wallace Journal, 1786–1802. *CWVQ*, p. 1272. *Knoxville Standard*, 31 March 1846. Royall, *Southern Tour*, vol. 1, May 1, 1828. "Thomas Lenoir's Journey," p. 158. Hilliard, *Hog Meat*, p. 281. Taylor, *Antebellum South Carolina*. Gray, *History of Agriculture*, vol. 1, pp. 123–24. Williams, "Washington County," p. 353. Malone, "Falmouth." Smith, *Review*, pp. 24, 54. NA, 1860 Census of Population manuscripts for Knox County, Tennessee, and Botetourt County, Virginia; Ebert, "Window," p. 50.

44. Clark, "Trade," p. 44. Dolan, *Yankee Peddlers*, pp. 250–51. Letter to Editor, *Southern Planter*, 11 (1851), pp. 355–56. DPL, letters dated 1830–45 about peddling of manufactured tobacco, Green W. Penn Papers. Robert, *Tobacco Kingdom*, p. 222. Olmsted, *Back Country*, p. 267. *Carolina Planter* 1 (1844–45), p. 42. *Farmer's Register* 4 (1802): pp. 711, 6, 93. Advertisements for runaway slaves, *Alexandria Gazette and Daily Advertiser*, 19–24 December 1816, 1 May 1817. DPL, "List of Slaves at Oxford Iron Works," William Bolling Papers. Salmon, *Washington Iron Works*, p. 53. DPL, letter dated 5 January 1860, Scoot's Creek Ledger, 1839–44, pp. 486, 494, William Holland Thomas Papers. Bouwman, *Traveler's Rest*, pp. 198–99. McKivigan, *Roving Editor*, p. 209.

45. SHC, James Hervey Greenlee Diary, 16 March 1847, 31 May 1847, 22 November 1847, 17 December 1847, 12 January 1850.

46. Dunaway, *First American Frontier*, pp. 215–17, 293. Dunaway, "Incorporation," Table 12.7. For a detailed map of all Southern railroads, see Phillips, *History of Transportation*, back pocket. *Alexandria Gazette*, 4 January 1859. WV, numerous letters between 1854 and 1862, John Bassel Papers. *Richmond Daily Dispatch*, 18 and 31 December 1853, 22 December 1856, 1 January 1857. UVSC, eight letters between 1847 and 1848, Randolph Family Papers. *Asheville News*, 12 December 1861. NC, letter dated 12 May 1862, Walter Clark Papers. *Dallas Gazette* (Alabama), 22 July 1859. *Huntsville Confederate*, 28 January 1863. Illustration 3.7, website.

47. SHC, letter dated 14 September 1838, Hamilton Brown Papers. Inscoe, *Mountain Masters*, p. 79. NA, 1860 Manuscript Slave Schedules, Talladega County, Alabama.

48. Starobin, *Industrial Slavery*, pp. 293–97, 139, 31. UVSC, Blue Ridge Railroad Receipts and Accounts, 1828–29, Randolph Family Papers. Burt, "Nashville and Chattanooga," pp. 58–76. UVSC, many letters regarding slave hires, 1851–60, Letters dated 21 December 1851, 10 July 1857, 27 November 1860, 20 February 1861, John Buford Papers. DPL, letter

dated 3 November 1853, William Weaver Papers. *Petersburg Daily Express*, 28 December 1859. Noe, *Southwest Virginia's Railroad*, p. 82. Smith, "Building," pp. 53–56. Holland, "History," p. 128.

CHAPTER 4

1. Opening quote is from *Booker T. Washington Papers*, vol. 1, p. 418. Dunaway, *First American Frontier*, pp. 157–224. Wallerstein, *Modern World-System III*, p. 78.
2. In 1860, only about 5 percent of the U.S. slave population was employed in industry; see Starobin, *Industrial Slavery*, p. 11. Nearly 14 percent of Appalachian slaves were employed in industry and extractive production. Tables 3.1, 3.3, 3.4, 3.5, and 5.9, website.
3. Dunaway, *First American Frontier*, pp. 145, 149–52, 165–66.
4. Bouwman, *Traveler's Rest*, pp. 141, 163–66. Malet, *An Errand*, p. 242. Andrews and Young, "Plantations," p. 7. Inscoe, *Mountain Masters*, pp. 75–76. UVSC, Distillery Records, Baumgardner Family Papers. *Alexandria Daily Advertiser*, 3 May 1813.
5. Table 3.1, website. Andrews and Young, "Plantations," p. 7. Dunaway, "Rethinking Acculturation," pp. 160–65. *Slave I*, 7: 689.
6. UVSC, Noland Mill Ledgers, 1817–18, 1828–29, 1838–39, Berkeley Family Papers. *Slave*, 13: 73, 85, 6: 234, 4 (b): 235. Inscoe, *Mountain Masters*, p. 74. Lambert, *Undying Past*, pp. 71–72. UVSC, Mill Ledger, 1817–18, Berkeley Family Papers. Dunaway, *First American Frontier*, p. 147. Janney and Janney, *Janney's Virginia*, p. 39. *Slave*, 4 (b): 35. Troy, John Horry Dent Farm Journal, July 1862. *Slave II*, 9: 3871. *Richmond Enquirer*, 11 May 1816. Table 3.5, website.
7. Dunaway, *First American Frontier*, p. 147. *Slave II*, 3: 918, 4: 1432. *CWVQ*, pp. 1823–24. Inscoe, *Mountain Masters*, p. 71.
8. Table 3.5, website. UVSC, Blacksmith Shop Book, 1800–18, Berkeley Family Papers. *Niles Weekly Register*, 15 (1818), p. 80. *Slave*, 4 (b): 35, 1: 55. Fletcher, *Ashe County*, p. 233. *Slave II*, 4: 1163. Ford, *Writings of Jefferson*, vol. 7, pp. 14, 49–51, 62–63, 271, 288, 377, 387–88. Betts, *Jefferson's Garden Book*, pp. 228, 230. *Slave II*, 3: 797. DPL, letter dated 5 January 1860, William Holland Thomas Papers. UVSC, Memorandum Book and Diary, 1851, Barbour Family Papers. Jackson, *Free Negro Labor*, p. 91n. *Slave Testimony*, p. 478. Inscoe, *Mountain Masters*, p. 74. Lambert, *Undying Past*, pp. 71–72. SHC, letter dated 19 June 1835, Hamilton Brown Papers.
9. Buckingham, *Slave States*, vol. 2, p. 411. Dunaway, *First American Frontier*, pp. 145–46. *Huntsville Democrat*, 26 July 1836, 4 April 1837. Runaway slave advertisement, *Alexandria Daily Advertiser*, 8 April 1811.
10. Dunaway, *First American Frontier*, p. 147. Morgan, *Emancipation*, p. 72. *Weevils*, p. 82. *Richmond Daily Dispatch*, 5 January 1853, 22 December 1856, 10 December 1858, 6 April 1859. Inscoe, *Mountain Masters*, p. 71. *DeBow's Review* 9 (1840): 325. *Slave I*, 8: 912. Illustration 4.1, website.
11. Dunaway, *First American Frontier*, pp. 148–49. *Richmond Enquirer*, 7 October 1827. DPL, letters dated 5 December 1830, 5 February 1856, William

Weaver Papers. SHC, letter dated 18 May 1833, Lenoir Family Papers. *Huntsville Democrat*, 20 January 1836. *Richmond Compiler*, 16 November 1843. Inscoe, *Mountain Masters*, pp. 71–72. Lander, "Slave Labor," pp. 163–64. *CWVQ*, p. 1961.

12. Dunaway, *First American Frontier*, p. 148. SHC, James Hervey Greenlee Diary, 12 March 1850. SHC, letter dated 17 August 1849, James Gwyn Papers. NA, 1860 Census of Population enumerator manuscripts and manuscript Slave Schedules for Franklin County, Tennessee.
13. Dunaway, *First American Frontier*, pp. 148–49. Hopkins, *Hemp Industry*, p. 136. Inscoe, *Mountain Masters*, pp. 71–72. Illustration 4.2, website.
14. Dunaway, *First American Frontier*, pp. 166–69.
15. Ibid., p. 169.
16. Ibid., p. 175. White, "Salt Industry of Clay," p. 238. *Wheeling Intelligencer*, 27 December 1854. WV, Donnally and Steele Kanawha Salt Works Records, 1813–15. Goodall, "Manufacture," p. 235. "General Slade's Journal," p. 45. Lanman, *Letters*, p. 158. *Knoxville Register*, 30 April 1834. *Hunts Merchants Magazine* 39 (1858), pp. 430–33. Illustration 4.3, website.
17. Dunaway, *First American Frontier*, pp. 176–77.
18. Ibid., pp. 176–77. *DeBow's Review* 18 (1855), p. 680.
19. Pease, "Great Kanawha," pp. 192–93, 180. Carpenter, "Ward Diary," p. 45. Cohen, *Kanawha Images*, p. 37. Mosby, "Salt Industry," p. 133. "Salt Manufacturing in Mason County, West Virginia." Dunaway, *First American Frontier*, p. 1777. WV, petition dated 27 January 1835, Legislative Petitions of Kanawha County, James M. Crump Typescript.
20. Billings and Blee, "Agriculture," p. 238. UVSC, numerous letters between 1808 and 1838, White Family Papers. WV, letter dated 30 December 1835, Wilson-Lewis Papers. UVSC, entries dated 31 January 1855, Etna Furnace Papers. UVSC, Virginia and Tennessee Railroad Company check rolls, 1851–60, John Buford Papers. UVSC, Negro Book for 1839–59 and 1863 estate inventory, Weaver-Brady Iron Works and Grist Mill Papers. UVSC, letter dated 9 February 1844, 1845 and 1858 hiring bonds, William W. Davis Iron Manufacturing Company Papers. UVSC, March 1865 Minutes of Stockholders' Meetings, James River and Kanawha Company Papers. WV, James Cowey deposition dated 31 August 1854, Circuit Superior Court, Mason County Court Records. Stealey, "Salt Industry," pp. 114, 473–76. Stealey, "Slavery," pp. 105–31. WV, petition dated 27 January 1835, Legislative Petitions of Kanawha County.
21. Stealey, "Salt Industry," pp. 436–37. These documents in WV, Circuit Superior Court, Kanawha County Court Records: Turner v. Early, 1848; Lewis v. Arnold, 1857; Hannah v. Billings, 1844. WV, ten letters dated 1834–50, Nathaniel V. Wilson Correspondence. UVSC, letter dated 2 December 1857, Holland Family Papers. These documents in WV, Circuit Superior Court, Kanawha County Court Records: William Cobb v. David Ruffner and Company, 1828; George M. Woods v. Andrew Donnally, 1844; Martha Stone v. William D. Shrewsbury and Henry H. Wood, 1852; Deposition of Jacob Runyon in George W. Clarkson v. David J. W. Clarkson. WV, petition, 27 January 1835, Legislative Petitions of Kanawha County. WV, letter dated 26 November 1838, William Tompkins Papers.

22. WV, deposition dated 1 September 1859, Taylor v. Waid, Circuit Superior Court, Kanawha County Court Records. WV, Cowey deposition dated 31 August 1854; Lewis depositions dated 23 February 1855, 28 February 1855, Circuit Superior Court, Mason County Court Records. WV, deposition of John D. Lewis dated 31 August 1854, Circuit Superior Court, Mason County Court Records.
23. Dunaway, *First American Frontier*, pp. 169–70.
24. *DeBow's Review*, 18 (1855), p. 241. *Medical Repository*, 2nd series, vol. 6 (1807), p. 193. Censer, *North Carolina Planters*, p. 12. Green, "Gold Mining of North Carolina," pp. 12–15. Phifer, "Champagne," pp. 489–500. Inscoe, *Mountain Masters*, p. 72. SHC, letter dated 26 September 1831, Lenoir Family Papers. UK, Francis M. Goddard Diary, 1833 entry. Illustration 4.4, website.
25. *State Rights Sentinel*, 16 February 1836. Some western North Carolina slaveholders cultivated cotton until the early 1840s when they shifted to tobacco; see published Census of Agriculture, 1840, 1850, 1860 (NA). Nitze and Wilkens, "Present Condition," p. 681. SHC, "Report on Baker Mine," October 1857, Calvin J. Cowles Papers. SHC, James Hervey Greenlee Diary, vol. 1, pp. 79, 100, 103, 230. Green, "Gold Mining of North Carolina," p. 146. Featherstonhough, *Canoe Voyage*, p. 233.
26. Vigne, *Six Months*, vol. 1, p. 138. NA, U.S. Congress, Report No. 39, Twenty-second Congress, p. 23. Green, "Gold Mining of North Carolina," p. 155. SHC, Record of W. W. Avery and Company, 4 November 1844, George Phifer Erwin Papers. Phifer, *Burke*, p. 214.
27. UVSC, Memorandum and Diary, March 1851, Barbour Family Papers.
28. *American Farmer*, 11 (1829), pp. 200, 222–23. *United States Telegraph*, 23 December 1833. Silliman, "Remarks," pp. 127–28, 117. Green, "Gold Mining in Virginia," pp. 227–35. Featherstonhough, *Excursion*, vol. 2, pp. 353–54. *Harper's Monthly* 32 (1866), pp. 35–37. *CWVQ*, pp. 2239–40. *DeBow's Review* 18 (1855), pp. 241–42. U.S. Census Office, *Special Reports*, pp. 168–69, 200–01. Lewis, *Coal*, p. 87. SHC, letter dated 28 September 1843, James Gwyn Papers.
29. *Niles Weekly Register* 39 (1830), p. 106; 41 (1831), p. 224. *DeBow's Review*, 18 (1855), p. 241. U.S. Census Office, *Special Reports*, pp. 276, 307, 317. Brewer, "Gold Regions," pp. 570–74. Roberts, *Gold Seekers*, pp. 59–65, 150. Van Benthuysen, "Sequent Occupance," p. 26.
30. *Western Herald* (Auraria, GA), 9 April 1833, 31 January 1834. *Tarborough Free Press*, 11 January 1831. *Macon Advertiser*, 21 June 1833. *Atlanta Journal*, 13 March 1832. SHC, letter dated 25 September 1832, Hamilton Brown Papers. Wilson, *Papers of Calhoun*, vol. 12, p. 555. *Slavery Time*, p. 99. Jackson, *North Georgia Journal*, pp. 158–59.
31. Bouwman, *Traveler's Rest*, p. 156. Mooney, "Myths," pp. 220–21. Peterson and Flynn, "Walhalla District," pp. 380–83. Lanman, *Letters*, p. 15. *Southern Banner*, 13 April 1933. *Engineering and Mining Journal* 94 (1915), p. 170. Grant, *The Way It Was*, p. 71. Head and Etheridge, *Neighborhood Mint*, p. 33. *Dahlonega Nugget*, 1 June 1917.
32. Values of gold are expressed in contemporary dollars. *Niles Weekly Register* 39 (1830), p. 106. Dahlonega, Georgia, Gold Museum. Green, "Georgia's

Forgotten Industry." Green, "Gold Mining of North Carolina." Green, "Gold Mining in Antebellum Virginia." *DeBow's Review* 18 (1855), pp. 241–42.

33. Dunaway, *First American Frontier*, pp. 170–75.
34. Wayland, *History*, p. 244. Smith, "Historical Geography," p. 106. Lewis, *Coal*, pp. 27–29. DPL, account books, Sanders-Greene Pig Iron Furnace, Richard W. Sanders and John W. Greene Papers and Notebooks. DPL, numerous letters dated 1849–61, N. L. Blakemore Papers. DPL, correspondence regarding Cloverdale Furnace, 1850–58, Francis Thomas Anderson Papers. WV, Iron Furnaces Typescripts. WV, Account Book of Monongalia Iron Forge, Lewis Maxwell Papers. UVSC, "Negro Book, 1839," Weaver-Brady Papers. WL, Etna Furnace Company Account Book, 1854–57. Starobin, *Industrial Slavery*, pp. 165–68. Dunaway, *First American Frontier*, p. 173. Smith, "Historical Geography," pp. 98–103. For an excellent discussion of Virginia iron plantations, see pp. 91–123. For a map of the Glenwood Plantation, showing locations of furnace, several farms, and landholdings in three counties, see p. 95.
35. UVSC, Negro Book, 1839–59, Weaver-Brady Iron Works and Grist Mill Papers. Dew, *Bond of Iron*, pp. 9–10, 245.
36. WV, Ice's Ferry Typescripts. *Atlanta Daily Intelligencer*, 8 April 1859. Jackson, *North Georgia Journal*, p. 13. Smith, "Historical Geography," p. 103.
37. *Richmond Times*, 15 January 1851. Bruce, *Virginia Iron*, p. 463. Lewis, *Coal*, pp. 20–35, 88. UVSC, letter dated 29 December 1855, Weaver-Brady Iron Works and Grist Mill Papers. *Richmond Dispatch*, 22 November 1862. For courthouse auctions, see *Louisville Daily Journal*, 22 and 28 December 1855. For iron furnace, see UVSC, letter dated 5 January 1856, William W. Davis Company Iron Manufacturing Papers. UK, Hiring Bonds, Buckner Family Papers. *Huntsville Confederate*, 28 January 1863. VS, letter dated 25 December 1860, Tredegar Letterbook.
38. Smith, "Historical Geography," pp. 106, 306. Dunaway, *First American Frontier*, pp. 173–74. "Furnaces and Forges," p. 191. Bouwman, *Traveler's Rest*, p. 155. *Rome Courier*, 3 March 1860.
39. Lewis, *Coal*, p. 51. Weld, *Travels*, p. 179. Harvey, *Best-Dressed Miners*, pp. 8–15. Smith, "Historical Geography," pp. 231, 235, 245.
40. Salmon, *Washington Iron Works*, p. 57. VS, letter dated 3 January 1848, Tredegar Letterbook. UVSC, Buffalo Forge Time Book, 1843–53 and Buffalo Forge Negro Book, 1850–58, Weaver-Brady Iron Works and Grist Mill Papers. DPL, List of Slaves at the Oxford Iron Works, William Bolling Papers. VHS, Letter dated 25 July 1813, David Ross Letterbook.
41. *Slave*, 2 (b): 6–7. For elite iron slaves, see Bradford, "Negro Ironworker," pp. 197–98.
42. For an overview of antebellum coal mining, see Dunaway, *First American Frontier*, pp. 178–80. Lewis, *Coal*, pp. 46–51. Scharf, *History*, vol. 1, pp. 1342, 1441. Jillson, "History," p. 1. Harvey, *Best-Dressed Miners*, pp. 8–15. Sellers, *Slavery*, p. 202. AL, George M. Figh Report, 21 July 1864, Montevallo Coal Mining Company Papers. SHC, James Hervey Greenlee Diary, many 1848 and 1849 entries. *Slave I*, 1: 433.
43. Pease, "Great Kanawha," p. 183. Stealey, "Salt Industry," p. 392. Lewis, *Coal*, p. 46. Rogers, *Report*, p. 123. Toothman, *Great Coal Leaders*, p. 260. UVSC, letter dated 9 October 1858, Holland Family Papers.

44. *Richmond Semi-Weekly Enquirer*, 16 January 1857. *Kanawha Valley Star*, 10 October 1859. *Richmond Daily Dispatch*, many ads in December and January, 1855–59. Lewis, *Coal*, pp. 168–72. Starobin, *Industrial Slavery*, p. 166. *Kanawha Valley Star*, 26 September 1859, 31 May 1859, 9 June 1857. *Charter of Coal River and Kanawha Mining*, p. 39. WV, Company Ledger, 1851–58, Winifrede Mining and Manufacturing Company Documents. Cannel Coal Company, *Report*, p. 9.
45. Lewis, *Coal*, p. 48. Scharf, *History*, vol. 1, pp. 1342, 1441. Jillson, "History," p. 1. UK, Francis M. Goddard Diary, pp. 12–13. UK, letter dated 6 January 1822, Wickliffe-Preston Papers.
46. Jillson, "History," p. 30. *Kentucky House Journal* (1837–38), p. 468. Verhoeff, *Kentucky River*, pp. 172–79. *Kentucky House Journal* (1838–39), Appendix, p. 24. Moore, "Historical Geography," pp. 52–56. WV, 1858 bill of lading in Maysville, Kentucky, Papers. UK, letters dated 28 November 1833, 7 February 1837, 29 August 1861, Cyrenius Wait Papers.
47. Hecht, "Lead Production," p. 174. *Journals of Continental Congress*, vol. 4, p. 185. *American State Papers*, 5: 139.
48. Ashe, *Travels*, p. 74. Thomas Jefferson held an interest in Westham Foundry. "Letters to Jefferson," p. 124. Dunaway, *First American Frontier*, p. 185. Kohler, "Lead Mines," Kohler Papers. "Statement Relating to Lead Interests in Virginia, Campbell-Preston Papers.
49. Dunaway, *First American Frontier*, pp. 158–93. Veney, *Narrative*, pp. 36–41. *Hunts Merchants Magazine and Commercial Review* 5 (1841), p. 54. Wayland, *History*, p. 291. Veney, *Narrative*, pp. 33–34. Marlin, *History*, pp. 149–50. UVSC, Peach Bottom Mine Records, Graham Family Papers. UVSC, "Lead Mines" Typescript, pp. 17–21, Kohler Papers. Noe, *Southwest Virginia's Railroad*, pp. 73–78.
50. Olmsted, *Back Country*, p. 242. *DeBow's Review* 14 (1853), p. 620; 18 (1855), p. 408. *Goodspeed's History*, p. 805. Pearre, "Mining for Copper," pp. 21–22. Mellen, "The Old Copper Road." *Knoxville Sentinel*, 22 October 1921. Campbell, *Upper Tennessee*, pp. 25, 46. Young, "Origins," p. 133. *DeBow's Review* 18 (1855), p. 408. NA, 1860 manuscript Census of Manufacturing and manuscript Slave Schedules for Polk County, Tennessee. *DeBow's Review* 14 (1853), p. 620. DPL, letter dated 24 October 1859, William Holland Thomas Papers. Stampp, *Peculiar Institution*, p. 68. Inscoe, *Mountain Masters*, pp. 170–71.
51. Stealey, "Salt Industry," pp. 385–86. Howe, *Historical Collections*, 383–84. *Richmond Whig*, 9 January 1849.
52. Lambert, *Undying Past*, pp. 160–61, 76–77. *Ferry Hill*, pp. xii, 8, 12, 27, 54, 59, 98. SHC, Folder 93, 1853–56, Hamilton Brown Papers. Illustration 4.5, website.
53. *One Hundred Years*, p. 196. Martin, *New and Comprehensive Gazetteer*, p. 60. WV, Sawmill Account Books, William Hall Papers. WV, Sawmill Account Books, James Rogers Moreland Papers. Clarkson, *Tumult*, p. 17.
54. Williams, *Americans and Forests*, pp. 177–81. Coleman, *History*, p. 170. Eisterhold, "Charleston," pp. 61–73. Eisterhold, "Savannah," pp. 526–45. Eisterhold, "Lumber," pp. 61–73.

55. Lambert, *Undying Past*, p. 97. Wayland, *History*, p. 267. Low, "Merchant," pp. 308–18. *Louisville Democrat*, 1 May 1860. Ambler, *History*, p. 198. Murphy, "Transportation," pp. 17–19. WV, 1856 tally book of rafts floated down Little Kanawha River, John R. Lynch Papers. WV, Bradford Noyes Recollections. WV, James B. Shahan Letter. WV, 1860 diary entries and letters, George W. Johnson Papers. WV, Barbour County Typescript. Hulbert, *Historic Highways*, 9: 76. Hunter, *Steamboats*, p. 108. Clarkson, *Tumult*, p. 17. Hunter, *Steamboats*, p. 58. Verhoeff, *Kentucky River*, pp. 187–92. FC, Willis and Lafayette Green Papers, 1818–60. Clark, "Early Lumbering." *Western Sentinel*, 3 June 1859. *People's Press*, 17 June 1859. Campbell, *Upper Tennessee*, p. 7. Livingood, "Chattanooga," p. 160. Hunter, *Steamboats*, p. 58. Hoskins, *Anderson County*, p. 36. Coleman, *History*, p. 170. Illustration 4.6, website.
56. Tarkington, "Saltpeter Mining." Hill and DePaepe, "Saltpeter Mining," p. 262. Donnelly, "Bartow County." Jenkins, "Mining," p. 81. Dunaway, *First American Frontier*, p. 162. *Slave I*, 5 (a): 230. Jenkins, "Mining," pp. 78–87. SHC, James Hervey Greenlee Diary, January through 23 February 1847. Gauding, "History," pp. 99–100. "Fairfax in the Mid-1800s," *Knoxville News-Sentinel*, 30 July 1989. TS, typescript, p. 68, Chris D. Livesay Papers. Plater, "Building North Wales," p. 49n. *WPA Guide to Tennessee*, p. 434. Semes, "200 Years," p. 49.

CHAPTER 5

1. Opening quote is from *Slave I*, 5 (b): 320–21. The bottom half of Appalachian households had accumulated less than $200 in assets; see Dunaway, *First American Frontier*, pp. 70–75, 90–115, 290. Slaughter, *Whiskey Rebellion*, p. 65. Henretta, "Families and Farms," p. 7. Dunaway, "Incorporation," pp. 1069–70, 1142–43, 1151. In 1860, families with less than $300 in assets earned $100 yearly or less, and they were impoverished by national standards. See Soltow, *Men of Wealth*, pp. 63–65.
2. A sample of 3,447 households was systematically drawn from the 1860 Census of Agriculture manuscripts (NA). Names of farmers adjacent to slaveholders were cross-checked in the enumerator manuscripts for the 1860 Census of Population and Slave Schedules (NA). All McMinn County, Tennessee, farms were recorded in the precise order that they appeared in the 1860 Census of Agriculture manuscripts. Farm operator names were then cross-checked with the manuscript Census of Population and Slave Schedules.
3. Olmsted, *Back Country*, p. 208. The two slaveholders were identified in the 1860 manuscript Slave Schedules for Buncombe County, North Carolina (NA). Then their names were cross-checked in the manuscript Censuses of Agriculture and Population (NA). Three slaveholding Coles were identified in the 1860 manuscript Slave Schedules for Albermarle County, Virginia (NA). Then their names were cross-checked in the manuscript Censuses of Agriculture and Population.

4. Dunaway, *First American Frontier*, pp. 101–23. NA, entry for William N. Berkeley, Aldie District, Loudoun County, Virginia, 1860 Census of Population manuscripts.
5. FC, Edward Harris Letter, 11 April 1797. Riordan, "Albermarle," pp. 44–45. Jefferson recorded extensive detail about his relationship with tenants; see five plat maps in Betts, *Jefferson's Farm Book*, following page 336. Olmsted, *Back Country*, pp. 258–59. For another example of tenant parceling; see UVSC, entries dated 17 December 1806 to 21 January 1807, Col. Benjamin Johnson Account Book, 1801–07, Barbour Family Papers. The following slaveholders, drawn from the 1860 Census of Agriculture manuscripts (NA), are typical of Appalachian gentleman farmers: J. J. Woodward, lawyer (Talladega, AL); William Henderson, minister (Cass, GA); James Hoff, physician (Mason, WV); Robert Elsom, merchant (Albermarle, VA); James Smith, manufacturer (Franklin, VA); W. S. Reed, physician (Warren, TN); Amos Harrill, merchant (Rutherford, NC); Lewis Brummer, miller (Frederick, MD); Nelson Read, merchant (Allegany, MD); William Long, physician (Clinton, KY). Usually among the wealthiest households in their communities, these men averaged owning twenty-two slaves and holding estates other than farms valued at an average of $23,425. Reid, "Antebellum Rental Contracts," p. 76. *CWVQ*, pp. 621, 625. *Ferry Hill*, intro.
6. Buckingham, *Slave States*, vol. 2, p. 266. Archival records validate Buckingham's impression that much of the vast acreage was cultivated by tenant farmers; see Bouwman, *Traveler's Rest*, p. 139. For conversion of barrel to bushels, see Battalio and Kagel, "Structure." Antebellum reports from this area reported an average yield of forty bushels per acre on this type of river bottom land in 1850; see *Report of the Commissioner of Patents*, pp. 400–01. For subsistence requirements, see Dunaway, "Incorporation," Table 5.7. For grain waste, see Dunaway, *First American Frontier*, p. 330.
7. UK, 1857–59 contracts and plat map, Wickliffe-Preston Papers.
8. *Slave II*, 3: 672. Traveler's Rest is now a Georgia state park located on Highway 123 about six miles southwest of the town of Toccoa. Descriptive details were drawn from a visit to the site and from Bouwman, *Traveler's Rest*, especially Ch. 8. Details about wealth, slaves, and crop production from 1860 Census manuscripts for Habersham County, Georgia.
9. *CWVQ*, pp. 542, 13, 595, 698, 819, 1022, 1913. *Slave*, 14: 332. Olmsted, *Back Country*, pp. 273–74. *Ferry Hilll*, pp. xiv–xvi, 72. Oral history collected by the author and verified in family records.
10. *CWVQ*, pp. 542, 13, 595, 698, 819, 1022, 1499, 1913. *Slave*, 14: 332. Olmsted, *Back Country*, pp. 273–74. *Ferry Hill*, pp. xiv–xvi, 72. Oral history collected by the author and verified in family records.
11. Dunaway, *First American Frontier*, p. 94. *Slave*, 16: 23. SHC, James Hervey Greenlee Diary, January through March and 18 February 1847.
12. Dunaway, *First American Frontier*, pp. 51–86. Mason, *John Norton*, pp. 486–88. Hofstra, "Land Policy," pp. 120–22. Correspondence with overseers in SHC, Benjamin Cudworth Yancey Papers, 1835–60; in SHC, Farish Carter Papers, 1825–58, in SHC, John McPherson Berrien Papers, 1851–55. *Slave I*, 8: 127.
13. Moore, *A Calhoun Boy*, pp. 5–8.

14. Boydston, "Daily Bread," p. 22. UK, agreement dated 1 November 1828, letter dated 26 May 1840, Wickliffe-Preston Papers. Bouwman, *Traveler's Rest*, pp. 151, 161–64.
15. Fedric, *Slave Life*, pp. 48–49. UK, Judge Cabell Chenault Diary.
16. *Slave*, 7: 45–47, 13: 81.
17. Oral history collected by the author.
18. Janney and Janney, *Janney's Virginia*, p. 89. *Slave*, 12: 350. Fisk, p. 10. *Slave II*, 6: 2282, 2 (b): 50, 12: 350, 311–12. Wiggington, *Foxfire 3*, p. 112. Wiggington, *Foxfire 2*, p. 189. SHC, James Hervey Greenlee Diary, 30 December 1848.
19. *Slave I*, 1: 361, 12: 325. Dupre, *Transforming*, pp. 212–13. Henry, "Slave Laws," p. 179. Catterall, *Judicial Cases*, vol. 2, p. 172. *Laws of Cherokee Nation*, pp. 24–25. Moore, *A Calhoun Boy*, pp. 5–8. *Slave*, 16: 25, 31; 12: 311.
20. *Slave*, 4 (a): 273, 16 (a): 32, 10 (a): 42.
21. *Slave II*, 5: 1864, 3: 501, 4: 1433. Fisk, pp. 132–33. McKivigan, *Roving Editor*, p. 141. *Slave I*, 5 (b): 299.
22. *Slave I*, 8: 128.
23. SHC, letters dated 18 November 1835, 20 December 1836, 13 September 1837, Hamilton Brown Papers. Letter dated 29 December 1845, SHC, James Gwyn Papers.
24. Pease, "Great Kanawha," p. 198. *Staunton Spectator*, 3 February 1858. *Slave*, 11 (a): 47, 16 (a): 2, 13 (a): 118. SHC, Entry dated 14 August 1851, James Gwyn Diary, p. 271, James Gwyn Papers. *Slave I*, 5: 461, 10: 2175, 12 (a): 196, 9: 1419–20. *Slave II*, 1: 68. NA, Records of Cherokee Agency, 29 July 1805, 18 August 1805.
25. *Alexandria Gazette and Daily Advertiser*, 8 August 1818. Pease, "Great Kanawha," p. 198. UK, Eaves narrative, J. Winston Coleman Papers. Coleman, *Slavery Times*, p. 211. *Western Citizen*, 30 April and 3 May 1848. *Asheboro Southern Citizen and Man of Business*, 6 May and 3 June, 1837. Franklin, *Free Negro*, p. 54. Brown, *Slave Life*, pp. 49–50.
26. Olmsted, *Back Country*, 275–76. *CWVQ*, p. 107. For the dominant view of the landless poor on the frontier, see Klein, "Ordering the Backcountry," pp. 678–79. Ball, *Slavery*, pp. 290–91.
27. For instances of Appalachian farmers commenting about labor scarcities, see: *Ferry Hill*, 8, 13, 19, 36, 44, 47, 52, 58, 62; Tilley, "Journal," pp. 497–98. SHC, James Mallory Diary, 12 April 1847, 1 August 1853. UVSC, letter dated 6 July 1852, Holland Family Papers. UVSC, entries dated 5 December 1837 and 18 December 1849, Aldie Memorandum Book and 14 November 1856 entry, William N. Berkeley Ledger, Berkeley Family Papers. UVSC, Benjamin Johnson Barbour Memorandum Book, 23 October 1858, Barbour Family Papers. WV, letter dated 30 December 1835, Wilson-Lewis Family Papers. WV, Farming Diary, 19 October 1852, 14 December 1858, John P. Clarke Papers. UK, Graham Account Book, 1 December 1812. UK, 1849 Browning account settlement, Forsythe Family Papers. For northern farm labor, see Wright, *Political Economy*, 46. Troy, John Horry Dent Farm Journal, 22 March 1869.
28. Martin, *Virginia Gazetteer*, p. 210. McKivigan, *Roving Editor*, p. 99. *Georgia Messenger*, 25 August 1837.

29. Wright, *Free Negro*, pp. 17, 43. *Richmond Whig*, 25 January 1853. Ruffin, *Slavery and Free Labor*, p. 20. *Farmers Register*, 5 (1837): 474; 6 (1838): 458. Olmsted, *Back Country*, pp. 228, 210–11, 219, 207. Gawalt, "James Monroe," pp. 251–72. McKivigan, *Roving Editor*, pp. 196–97.
30. *Ferry Hill*, pp. 13, 19. Olmsted, *Back Country*, p. 246.
31. Calculated from a systematic probability sample of 3,056 households drawn from the 1860 Census of Population manuscripts for all nine state subregions (NA). Of the 1,398 landless households, 14.2 percent were age twenty-four or younger; 32.9 percent were between twenty-five and thirty-four; 19.2 percent were between thirty-five and fotry-six; 15.9 percent were between forty-seven and fifty-four; and 17.8 percent were fifty-five or older. Atack, "Agricultural Ladder Revisited," p. 16, argued that "[r]ising entry costs seem the most likely explanation for why starting out as an owner-occupant was an increasingly remote dream for the young, but as these farmers aged they seem to have been able to advance more rapidly up the ladder than earlier generations." For Brown, see *CWVQ*, p. 392. Blount County's 1801 tax list (Creekmore 1959-60) and 1860 Census of Population manuscripts (NA) were computerized and alphabetized to permit longitudinal tracking. Households were grouped by surname, and each surname group was tracked in both sets of records. To check for inheritance, 1801 landless heads of household with the same surname as landholders were tracked again in the 1860 Census. McKenzie, "From Old South," p. 120. Quote from oral history collected by the author. For the Lenoir leases, see Reid, "Antebellum Rental Contracts," pp. 71–73.
32. Dunaway, *First American Frontier*, pp. 87–121. Innes, *Work and Labor*, p. 250. Dunaway, "Incorporation," pp. 1057–60.
33. *CWVQ*, pp. 64, 1932, 1057, 243, 395, 780, 801, 940, 1387, 1435, 1670, 1858, 1404. Lambert, "Oconaluftee Valley," p. 421. Olmsted, *Back Country*, p. 278. Smith, *Review*, p. 57. *Ferry Hill*, pp. xiv–xvi, 46, 55, 58–59. "Journal of John Sevier," p. 246. WV, 1846 diary, Wilson-Lewis Family Papers. UVSC, advances of food charged against wages, Col. Benjamin Johnson Account Book, 1801–06 and 13–14 January, 1858 entries, Benjamin Johnson Barbour Memorandum Book, Barbour Family Papers. Data about unemployment of day laborers derived from analysis of Census of Population manuscript sample (NA). Wallace, *South Carolina*, pp. 498–99.Olmsted, *Back Country*, p. 260. *Augusta Chronicle*, 24 September 1819.
34. Dunaway, "Incorporation," Table 4.4, p. 1062. Olmsted, *Back Country*, p. 265. *CWVQ*, p. 45. Lanman, *Letters*, p. 62. Thwaites, *Travels West*, pp. 279–80.
35. Kemble, *Journal*, pp. 110–11. Bremer, *Homes*, vol. 1, p. 373. Olmsted, *Back Country*, pp. 200–01, 205, 220, 230, 243–44. Irwin, *Alex Stewart*, p. 251. Craven, "Poor Whites," pp. 14–25.
36. Olmsted, *Back Country*, pp. 201, 210. Kemble, *Journal*, pp. 110–11. Janney and Janney, *Janney's Virginia*, pp. 19–20. Jefferson, *Notes*, p. 152. Dunaway, "Incorporation," p. 1069. Featherstonhaugh, *Canoe Voyage*, p. 226. Buckingham, *Slave States*, vol. 1, pp. 210–11. *Slave I*, 5: 285–86. Dunaway, *First American Frontier*, pp. 95–108. Mathew, *Agriculture, Geology*, p. 182. For a discussion of the health risks associated with this type of diet, see Dunaway, *African-American Family*, Ch. 2.

37. Ball, *Slavery*, p. 249. Douglass, *Narrative*, pp. 40–41. *Slave*, 7: 354. Botkin, *Lay My Burden Down*, p. 268. *Slave I*, 5 (b): 31, 8: 1221–22. Brown, *Slave Life*, p. 54.
38. Oral history collected by author. Also numerous entries of livestock or produce received by physicians in payment of annual medical accounts; see, for example, WV, Physician's Account Book, 1833–39, Laisley Papers and Physician's Daybook, 1855–60, Marmaduke Dent Papers. *CWVQ*, pp. 1229, 1609, 1640, 1682. *Ferry Hill*, pp. 22, 66.
39. *CWVQ*, p. 1229. *Ferry Hill*, p. 73. Olmsted, *Back Country*, pp. 208–09.
40. Boydston, "Daily Bread," p. 22. *Ferry Hill*, pp. 15–17, 19, 22, 25, 33, 41, 65. UK, agreement dated 1 November 1828, Letter dated 26 May 1840, Wickliffe-Preston Papers. For example, Aldie Plantation (Loudoun, VA) hired the wives of adjacent tenants to sew clothing for slaves. In 1841, the slaveholder charged an adjacent seamstress $17.55 for advances of food, salt, and candles against her $12.87 in annual wages for producing and repairing slave clothing; see UVSC, 1841 account of Mrs. Foster, Aldie Plantation Ledger, Berkeley Family Papers.
41. McKivigan, *Roving Editor*, pp. 196–97. Olmsted, *Back Country*, pp. 275–76, 298. Helper, *Impending Crisis*, p. 300. McCurry, *Masters*, pp. 80–83.
42. *Slave I*, 5 (b): 31–32. Isaac, *Transformation*, pp. 202–06.
43. Olmsted, *Back Country*, pp. 219–20. Dunaway, "'Disremembered,'" pp. 89–106. Irwin, *Alex Stewart*, p. 43. Stevenson, *Life*, pp. 102, 105. For discussion of health risks during pregnancy, see Dunaway, *African-American Family*, Ch. 4.

CHAPTER 6

1. Opening quote is from Lynd, *Nonviolence*, p. 467. Patterson, *Slavery*, p. 11. Throughout this chapter, discussion of physical punishment and forms of resistance is derived from an analysis of 383 incidents in which adult slaves were severely punished for their actions. Those cases were recorded in regional slave narratives and slaveholder manuscripts. Of the incidents, 189 involved female slaves; 194 involved males. Genovese, *In Red and Black*, p. 112. Fogel and Engerman, *Time*, vol. 1, p. 142. Genovese, *Roll*, pp. 451–52. "Address of James Barbour," p. 291. Fogel and Engerman, *Without Consent*, vol. 2, pp. 544–50. Walvin, "Slaves," p. 12.
2. Fisk, p. 239. *Slave*, 13: 79, 89, 16: 21, 11 (a): 167, 4 (b): 77. *Slave I*, 5 (b): 299. *Slave II*, 3: 669, 5: 1790–91, 1864, 10: 4273–74, 12: 144. *Great Slave Narratives*, p. 208. For the example of a slave pass, see Betts, *Jefferson's Farm Book*, p. 46. *Slave I*, 9: 1524. UVSC, entries dated 3 through 15 December 1859, Daniel C. E. Brady "Home Journal," 1858–60, Weaver-Brady Iron Works and Grist Mill Papers. Illustration 10.1, website.
3. *Slave*, 12: 309–11, 348, 13: 77–78, 16: 30–31. *Slave II*, 5: 1795–96, 1791. UVSC, letter dated 23 December 1849, Socrates Maupin Papers. UVSC, 1826 arrest warrant for slave, Gen. Joel Leftwich Papers. UVSC, letter dated 16 April 1856, Mathews-Dundore Papers. SHC, letter dated 6 February 1859, Thomas George Walton Papers. *Staunton Spectator*, 21 April 1858. *Ferry Hill*, pp. 88–89. Jones, *Born a Child*, pp. 98–128. Fisk, p. 9. *Great*

Slave Narratives, p. 214. VHS, letter dated 14 January 1813, David Ross Letterbook.

4. *Ferry Hill*, p. 65. *Slave*, 16: 88, 21, 12: 309–10. *Slave II*, 6: 2276–78, 5: 1864, 6: 2278. VHS, letter dated 9 January 1813, David Ross Letterbook. Patterson, *Slavery*, pp. 95, 101. *Staunton Spectator*, 27 September 1838. Weld, *American Slavery*, p. 74. Fisk, p. 6. *Slave I*, 12: 330.
5. Regarding Appalachian slave selling, see Table 5.10, website. Fogel and Engerman, *Without Consent*, vol. 2, pp. 536–50. Smith, *Review*, p. 21. DPL, letter dated 26 October 1860, William Weaver Papers. See narrative of eastern Kentucky slave Amelia Jones in *Slave*, 16 (b): 38. For a nonmountain narrative reporting this phrase, see *Slave*, 2 (a): 58.
6. Of U.S. ex-slaves, 34.5 percent reported frequent physical punishment; see Fogel, Galantine, and Manning, *Without Consent*, p. 357. In contrast, 68.2 percent of the Appalachian ex-slaves described their masters as frequent punishers. Fogel and Engerman, *Without Consent*, vol. 2, p. 550. Calculated using 297 newspaper advertisements for slaves who ran away from masters who lived in the Appalachian counties of North Carolina and Virginia. These ads were found in Meaders, *Advertisements* and Parker, *Stealing*.
7. Brownlow, *Sermon*, p. 17. UVSC, letter dated 5 January 1856, William W. Davis Iron Manufacturing Company Papers. Weld, *American Slavery*, p. 52.
8. Patterson, *Slavery*, p. 206. Crawford, "Quantified Memory," pp. 32–48. Fogel, *Without Consent*, p. 178. Of U.S. ex-slaves, 3.6 percent reported masters who were obsessive in their frequency of physical punishment; see Fogel, Galantine, and Manning, *Without Consent*, p. 357. In contrast, 17.2 percent of the Appalachian ex-slaves described abusive owners. *Slave II*, 9: 3642, 3: 798–800. *Slave*, 1: 58, 12: 348, 137, 16: 30, 4 (b): 77. *Slave I*, 12: 328. Fisk, p. 216. Still, *Underground Railroad*, p. 136. NA, entry dated 23 October 1808, Records of the Cherokee Indian Agency.
9. Still, *Underground Railroad*, p. 260. Fisk, p. 105. *Slave*, 14 (a): 353. UVSC, letter dated 11 January 1827, Randolph Family Papers. Veney, *Narrative*, p. 27.
10. Weld, *American Slavery*, pp. 85–88. *Slave*, 19: 205–07. Wiltse, *John C. Calhoun*, p. 116. *Slave I*, 1: 149–50.
11. Herskovits, *Myth*, pp. 99–102. Stampp, *Peculiar Institution*, p. 108. Genovese, *Roll*, pp. 303, 286, 291–92, 311–15. *Slave*, 4 (b): 36–37, 4 (a): 227, 273–74, 12: 136–37, 309–11, 16: 23, 30–31, 1: 425. *Slave II*, 9: 3642, 10: 4342–48, 2: 77, 3: 798. Fisk, p. 209. VHS, letter dated 14 January 1813, Ross Letterbook.
12. Franklin and Schweninger, *Runaway Slaves*, p. 2. Drew, *North-side View*, 45. *Slave II*, 3: 798. Fogel and Engerman, *Without Consent*, vol. 2, p. 543. Fogel, *Without Consent*, pp. 159–60. Discussion of reasons for physical punishment of Appalachian slaves is derived from an analysis of 383 incidents in which adult slaves were whipped or received severe physical punishment that were recorded in regional slave narratives and slaveholder manuscripts. Of the whippings, 31.9 percent were administered because of work deficiencies, property destruction, or food stealing; 68.1 percent involved social infractions. Of the victims, 189 were females; 194 victims were males. Of the incidents, 19.7 percent involved work deficiencies; 7.4 percent, stealing; 4.8 percent, property destruction. The social infractions included verbal violations, 22.7 percent; physical assaults on others, 20.9 percent; absent

without passes, 13.3 percent; illicit communication or spying on whites, 5.5 percent; unauthorized religious services, 3.3 percent; attempts to become literate or possession of written materials, 0.7 percent; attempts at permanent escape, 0.5 percent; socializing with free blacks or untrustworthy whites, 0.2 percent.

13. *Slave II*, 5: 1557, 9: 3639. *Great Slave Narratives*, pp. 121–213. *Slave*, 1: 56–57. McLoughlin, *Cherokees and Missionaries*, p. 52. Weld, *American Slavery*, p. 178. DPL, letter dated 30 July 1854, William Weaver Papers.
14. Newby, "Deferential Dialectic," pp. 157–59, 163–64. Bourdieu, *Outline*, p. 95. Thompson, "Folklore," pp. 254–55.
15. Scott, *Domination*, pp. 111–32. Patterson, *Slavery*, p. 206.
16. Patterson, *Slavery*, p. 200. Scott, *Weapons*, p. 29.
17. Scott, *Weapons*, p. 29. Gandhi, *Non-violent Resistance*, pp. 24–26, 239, 175. Lynd, *Nonviolence*, pp. 107, 391.
18. Scott, *Weapons*, p. 29. Gandhi, *Non-violent Resistance*, pp. 169, 116, 175, 239, 24. Lynd, *Nonviolence*, p. 466.
19. Lewis, *Coal*, pp. 127–38. Dew, *Bond of Iron*, pp. 276–77. *Slave*, 6: 269, 7: 139. UVSC, letter dated 22 March 1862, Weaver-Brady Iron Works and Grist Mill Papers. Dew, *Bond of Iron*, pp. 278–79.
20. *Alexandria Daily Advertiser*, 16 September 1805, 21 September 1810. *North Carolina Spectator and Western Advertiser*, 18 June 1830. Reed-Danahay, "Talking," pp. 222–23. Wood, "Slave Resistance," pp. 146–47. Tadman, *Speculators*, pp. 101–07. Coleman, *Slavery Times*, pp. 128–30. *Slave*, 16 (b): 13. DPL, letters dated 11 March and 17 March 1864, Alfred W. Bell Papers.
21. Ad for an Overton County, Tennessee, runaway, *Tennessee Republican Banner*, 6 January 1838. Jones, *Soldiers*, pp. 118, 148–49. Fisk, p. 117. *Weevils*, p. 347. *Slave*, 11 (b): 209.
22. *Weevils*, pp. 155–56. *Slave*, 19: 207–08.
23. Gandhi, *Non-violent Resistance*, pp. 117, 169. Burnham, "Loopholes," p. 60. Lynd, *Nonviolence*, p. 392. *Slave II*, 9: 3871, 3879, 4: 1163. Fisk, p. 159.
24. McDonald, *Woman's Civil War*, pp. 82–84.
25. Fisk, p. 156. UVSC, letter dated 29 May 1859, McCue Family Papers.
26. Burnham, "Loopholes," p. 59. *Weevils*, p. 166.
27. Lynd, *Nonviolence*, p. 465. VHS, letter dated 4 July 1813, David Ross Letterbook. UVSC, letter dated 5 January 1856, William W. Davis Iron Manufacturing Company Papers. Veney, *Narrative*, p. 13. UVSC, letter dated 16 April 1856, Mathews-Dundore Papers.
28. DPL, letters dated 11 November 1857, 29 March 1830, 27 November 1854, William Weaver Papers. Olmsted, *Seaboard*, p. 100.
29. Gandhi, *Non-violent Resistance*, pp. 175, 116. Scott, *Weapons*, p. 24. Lynd, *Nonviolence*, p. 467. *Slave*, 7 (a): 346.
30. UVSC, letter dated 23 November 1835, Wise Family Papers. VS, documents dated 4 November 1850, 13 March 1854, 11 December 1859, 9 January 1860, Slaves Condemned, Executed and Transported. Buckingham, *Slave States*, vol. 2, pp. 209–10. *Staunton Spectator*, 2 December 1857. *Pendleton Messenger*, 3 August 1831. Lynd, *Nonviolence*, p. 467. *Slave*, 16 (b): 67. UVSC, James Marshall Legal Notes, 1803–19, Charles J. Affleck Papers.
31. *Slave II*, 6: 2280. *Slave*, 13: 79, 7: 142, 8 (a): 104. *Weevils*, p. 157. Fisk, pp. 145, 4. *Huntsville Democrat*, 5 September 1849.

32. *Slave II*, 9: 3640. *Slave*, 12: 311, 16: 21. Illustration 10.2, website.
33. Inscoe, *Mountain Masters*, p. 100. For examples of repeated truants who were not deterred by whippings, see Lambert, *Undying Past*, p. 118. Weld, *American Slavery*, p. 88. NA, undated entry at end of 1805 file, Records of the Cherokee Indian Agency. UVSC, letter dated 31 May 1847, Socrates Maupin Papers. *Slave*, 11 (a): 47, 12: 238–39. *Slave II*, 5: 1562, 9: 3642. DPL, letters dated 22 May 1862, 21 September 1862, Alfred W. Bell Papers. *Slave*, 12: 309–10.
34. *Slave*, 16: 44. UVSC, letter dated 26 March 1857, McCue Family Papers.
35. For other examples of laying out in slave narratives, see *Slave*, 4 (b): 77, 7: 141, 16: 79. *Slave I*, 3: 101–02. *Slave II*, 5: 1560–61, 10: 4274. *Weevils*, p. 265. *Slave*, 1: 58. *Weevils*, pp. 265, 166. *Slave I*, 12: 327–29. SHC, letter dated 2 April 1850, Hoke Papers.
36. Lewis, *Coal*, p. 165. Gutman, *Black Family*, pp. 80–82n. *Ferry Hill*, pp. 25–26. *Slave II*, 6: 2284. DPL, letter dated 26 October 1860, William Weaver Papers. UVSC, letter dated 22 November 1818, Trist, Burke, and Randolph Papers. *Genius of Universal Emancipation*, 29 March 1829, p. 584. Embree, *The Emancipator*, 30 April 1820.
37. Court convictions were determined by analyzing two sets of courts records: AL, Alabama Pardons, Paroles, and Clemency Files, 1821–53 and VS, Virginia Slaves Condemned, Executed and Transported, 1783–1865.
38. Aptheker, *Negro Slave Revolts*, pp. 50, 368. UVSC, letter dated 28 December 1808, Thomas Jefferson Papers. WV, letter dated 1816, Felix G. Hansford Papers. SHC, letters dated 26 September 1821, 27 December 1835, Lenoir Family Papers. UVSC, letters dated 28 August and 3 October 1831, Breckinridge Family Papers. Dunn, *An Abolitionist*, p. 85.
39. *Clarksville Jeffersonian*, 3 December 1856. UVSC, Louisa H. A. Minor Diary, December 1856 and August 1857. UVSC, letter dated 29 December 1856, Perry, Martin, and McCue Family Papers. UT, William R. Caswell Diary, p. 22. *The Liberator*, 23 January 1857.
40. Grant, *Way It Was*, p. 51. *Athens Southern Banner*, 1 November 1860. Jordan, *Black Confederates*, pp. 3, 179–80.
41. SHC, letter dated 26 October 1860, James Gwyn Papers. UVSC, letter dated 6 May 1861, Wilson, Whitehead, and Houston Family Papers. UVSC, Diary of J. H. Davis, 1861 entries, Preston-Davis Family Papers. Dew, *Bond of Iron*, pp. 293–95.
42. Fisk, p. 9. *Slave*, 16: 15–16, 1: 162. DPL, letters dated 30 January and 8 February 1862, Alfred W. Bell Papers.
43. Dew, *Bond of Iron*, pp. 256–67. Lewis, *Coal*, p. 152. VHS, letter dated 3 June 1813, David Ross Letterbook. DPL, letter dated 2 April 1860, William Weaver Papers. Coleman, *Slavery Times*, pp. 177–78. *Slave I*, 5 (b): 32–33.
44. Franklin and Schweninger, *Runaway Slaves*, p. 58. *Richmond Enquirer*, 19 May 1807, 4 October 1808. VS, Petition of Lindsay Calamine to Virginia General Assembly, 8 December 1834, Legislative Papers. *Yadkin and Catawba Journal*, 22 April 1833.
45. HPL, letter dated 27 April 1855, Allen Family Papers. Buck, *Sad Earth*, pp. 190–92, 238. *Huntsville Democrat*, 20 August 1850.

46. UVSC, letter dated 21 December 1808, Wilson Cary Nicholas Papers. Weld, *American Slavery*, p. 179. *Abingdon Democrat*, 21 February 1857. *Weevils*, pp. 346–47.
47. *Slave*, 16: 32, 13: 80. *Slave I*, 12: 325–26.
48. Fox-Genovese, "Antebellum Households," p. 249. *Weevils*, p. 157. *Slave*, 14 (a): 101. Fountain, "Historian," p. 75. Singleton, "Archaeology," p. 126. Gruber, "Archaeology," p. 7. Kelso, "Archaeology," p. 14.
49. Stevenson, *Life*, pp. 254–55, 252. Gutman, *Black Family*, p. 219. King, "'Rais your children,'" pp. 143–62. Fisk, pp. 9–10, 12, 15. *Slave*, 10 (a): 44, 6 (a): 280, 12: 312. *Weevils*, p. 265.
50. Fisk, pp. 216–17. *Weevils*, pp. 266–67. *Slave II*, 9: 3875. Illustration 10.4, website.
51. *Slave I*, 11: 42–43. *Weevils*, p. 344. Fisk, pp. 216, 113, 4. Furman, *Slavery*, p. 26.
52. *Alexandria Daily Advertiser*, 11 May 1804. *Winchester Virginian*, 8 August 1837.
53. Naragon, "Communities," p. 71. Twenty-eight permanent escapes of Appalachian slaves are reported in Still, *Underground Railroad*; twelve were planned to avoid sale of family members. UK, letter dated 11 November 1840, Joseph and Archibald Logan Papers. For other slave runaways after sales or hires, see *Carolina Watchman*, 2 February 1833, 17 September 1836. *Staunton Spectator*, 3 January 1839. *Lexington Observer and Reporter*, 1 January 1840. UVSC, letters dated 6 October and 27 October 1848, Buck Family Papers. UVSC, letter dated 19 March 1813, Kelly-Norris Papers. *Knoxville Register*, 3 February 1824. *Raleigh Register*, 18 August 1808. *Slave II*, 6: 6. *Slave*, 16: 12. *Richmond Enquirer*, 19 May and 21 July 1807.
54. Dew, *Bond of Iron*, pp. 43, 44, 70, 75, 82, 134–35, 160–63, 253–56, 279–80. DPL, letter dated 24 November 1830, William Weaver Papers. VHS, letter dated January 1813, David Ross Letterbook. DPL, letter dated 15 December 1845, Hatchett Papers. *Richmond Enquirer*, 20 February 1838. *Lexington-Observer and Reporter*, 28 September 1838.
55. Regarding the absence of males from Appalachian slave households, see Tables 7.2 and 7.3, website.
56. VS, letters dated 30 March 1804, 3 February 1819, 19 October 1827, 2 September 1809, Letters Received, Virginia Executive Papers. Betts, *Jefferson's Farm Book*, p. 45. *Records of the Moravians*, vol. 6, p. 2799. *Slave*, 16: 46, 7: 161. *Slave I*, 5 (b): 301. Fisk, p. 144. Montell, *Saga*, p. 54. Illustration 10.3, website.
57. *Slave*, 4 (a): 303, 16: 58–59. Fisk, pp. 116–17. *Weevils*, p. 285. *Southern Agriculturalist* 7 (July 1834), p. 368.
58. *Weevils*, p. 36. *Slave I*, 9: 1424, 10: 2175, 1: 150. *Slave*, 12: 348, 4 (b): 37. Davis, *Blues*, p. 21. Still, *Underground Railroad*, p. 121. Fisk, p. 118.
59. *Slave*, 7: 160, 16: 42, 66–67.
60. Annual hires were termed "men on the road" by Appalachian slaves; see *Weevils*, p. 276. Rape convictions calculated from Alabama Pardons, Paroles and Clemency Files, 1821–25, 1837–41, 1845–47, 1849–53; from 158 death penalties in Johnston, *Race Relations*, pp. 257–59, Appendix; and from slave condemnations in VS, Letters Received, 1750–1835, Virginia Executive

Papers. Regarding Appalachian slave exports, see Tables 5.1 to 5.5, website.

CHAPTER 7

1. Opening quote is from Ambler, *Life and Diary*, p. 159. Patterson, *Slavery*, p. 5. Washington, *Future*, p. 25. Willie, *Family Life*, p. 12. Frazier, *Negro Family*, pp. 23–24. Gutman, *Black Family*, pp. 19–21. Jones, *Labor of Love*, p. 237. Holt, "Symbol," p. 195. *Slave*, 7: 161, 16: 12. *Slave I*, 5: 299. This phenomenon has also been described for immigrant males who are torn between real and past families; see Boss, "Experience," pp. 365–78. Regarding the frequency of family breakups and forced labor migrations, see Tables 5.4, 5.13, 7.1, website, and Dunaway, *African-American Family*, Ch. 3.
2. *Slave I*, 14: 79, 1: 149. Dill, "Fictive Kin," pp. 150–55. Wilk, *Household Ecology*, pp. 217–44. For the notion of child fostering after labor migrations, see Nagasaka, "Kinship Networks," pp. 67–81. *Slave*, 10 (a): 100, 12: 274. *Slave II*, 6: 2273. *CWVQ*, p. 1232.
3. Family details from Appalachian slave narratives were checked against county tax lists and Census manuscripts for 1840, 1850, 1860, and 1870 (NA). Of the 253 narratives that supply family details, I could not document two narratives in public records. In one instance, I suspect the inaccuracy of the antebellum censuses: the 1870 census manuscripts (NA) list several black families with the same surname living in the county where an ex-slave with the same surname claims to have lived.
4. *Slave*, 10 (a): 286, 289–90. Since she claimed to have been born in 1848, I checked Sarah Patterson's details against the 1850 and 1860 census manuscripts and slave schedules and against the 1870 census manuscripts for Bartow County, Georgia.
5. Blackburn, *Making*, pp. 315–25. Karras and McNeill, *Atlantic Slave Societies*, pp. 54, 63–64, 253. Kolchin, *American Slavery*, pp. 5–9. Wallerstein, *Modern World-System I*, pp. 89–94, 100n. Braudel, *Civilization and Capitalism*, vol. 3, pp. 392–99. Appalachian estimates were derived from analysis of slave narratives; U.S. estimates from Fogel, Galantine, and Manning, *Without Consent*, pp. 351–52.
6. *Slave I*, 1: 68, 8 (b): 262, 12: 293. *Slave*, 16: 43, 8 (a): 326, 13: 127.
7. Fisk, p. 199. The presence of such part-Spanish offspring in the Cherokee Nation is documented in the *American State Papers*, 2: 461. *Slave I*, 9: 1419. NA, letters dated 20 July 1818, 7 September 1819, Records of Cherokee Indian Agency. *Slave*, 6: 43–44, 7 (a): 344–47, 19 (a): 188.
8. Perdue, *Slavery and Evolution*, pp. 24–69. After 1828, the Cherokee Nation outlawed intermarriage with slaves and passed regulations making it difficult for free blacks to reside in the Nations; see *Cherokee Phoenix*, 13 April 1828. Perdue, "Cherokee Planters," p. 127n. Hill, *Weaving*, pp. 94, 154. *Slave*, 6: 234–35, 13: 130. Olmsted, *Back Country*, p. 174. DPL, Day Book, 1852–54, Fort Montgomery, William Holland Thomas Papers. *Slave I*, 9: 1424. Catterall, *Judicial Cases*, vol. 1, pp. 116, 126–27.
9. *Slave I*, 12: 381–82, 138.
10. Morgan, *Slave Counterpoint*, pp. 456, 483–84. *Slave I*, 9: 1415–24.

11. *Slave I*, 9: 1415–24, 12: 381–82, 138–39. *Slave*, 7 (a): 344–47.
12. Brown, *Narrative*, p. 51. *Slave*, 4 (a): 290. Gomez, *Exchanging*, pp. 131, 150.
13. *Slave*, 17: 336, 7: 24–25. Gomez, *Exchanging*, pp. 199–209.
14. Gomez, *Exchanging*, p. 150. *Slave I*, 9: 1416–18. Stuckey, *Slave Culture*, pp. 174–77.
15. Stuckey, *Slave Culture*, pp. 10, 14, 77. *Slave*, 7: 383–84, 16: 12, 8 (a): 326. *Slave II*, 4: 1101. *Slave I*, 5 (b): 32–33, 3: 479. Illustration 11.2, website.
16. *Slave*, 2 (a): 71, 15 (b): 129, 16 (b): 14, 17: 230. *Slave I*, 3: 272, 479, 11: 18. *Slave I*, 12: 335, 5 (b): 295. Fox-Genovese, *Plantation Household*, p. 184. Gutman, *Black Family*, pp. 97–118. Berlin, *Many Thousands Gone*, pp. 256–324.
17. *Slave II*, 3: 789. *Slave*, 12: 142.
18. Blassingame, *Slave Community*, p. 106. Only seven of the Appalachian slave narratives included reports that social gatherings were forbidden. *Slave I*, 3: 94, 1: 151, 8: 1218. *Slave*, 16: 21, 12: 138. Fisk, pp. 8, 216.
19. Of the Appalachian slave narratives, 187 describe such social gatherings, constituting two-thirds of the sample. Blassingame, *Slave Community*, pp. 106–18. Abrahams, *Singing*, pp. 83–107, 203–28. Berlin, *Many Thousands Gone*, pp. 256–89. Valentine, "Deficit," pp. 156–57. *Slave*, 1: 55–56, 4 (b): 37, 12 (a): 311, 6 (a): 280. Fisk, pp. 99–100. *Slave II*, 9: 3873–74. *Slavery Time*, p. 101. SHC, letter dated 11 December 1852, Hamilton Brown Papers. Washington, *Autobiography*, 1: 159. *Slave I*, 1: 293. Bouwman, *Traveler's Rest*, p. 225. Brewer, "History of Coosa," p. 197.
20. Spratte, "Wyoming County Folklore," p. 26. Janney and Janney, *Janney's Virginia*, p. 87–88. Washington, *Autobiography*, vol. 1, p. 395. *Slave*, 13: 81. Tucker, *Valley*, vol. 2, pp. 116–18. *Slave I*, 7: 696. Abrahams, *Singing*, pp. 278–80, 283–93. *Slave II*, 9: 3873–74. Bouwman, *Traveler's Rest*, p. 225. Illustration 11.3, website.
21. Tucker, *Valley*, vol. 2, p. 118. *Slave*, 12: 350, 311, 16: 24. *Slave I*, 1: 293, 7: 696. SHC, James Gwyn Diary, 18 September 1853, James Gwyn Papers. Fisk, p. 10. *Slave II*, 6: 2282.
22. Faulkner and Buckles, *Glimpses*, p. 35. Fisk, p. 106. Bouwman, *Traveler's Rest*, p. 225. *Slave*, 12: 312, 350, 13: 128, 16: 67. Washington, *Autobiography*, vol. 1, p. 159.
23. Hartman, *Scenes*, p. 60. *Slave I*, 5 (b): 298–99, 12: 325, 3: 480–81. *Slave*, 12: 311, 350, 13: 80, 128, 16 (a): 89, 3–4, 4 (b): 76, 37, 6: 155, 4 (a): 274. *Slave II*, 5: 1561–62, 9: 3873–74, 3: 499. Fisk, pp. 99–100, 106–107, 8–9.
24. *Booker T. Washington Papers*, vol. 1, p. 418. *Slave*, 6 (a): 155, 16 (a): 3–4, 89, 12: 350, 311, 8 (a): 325. *Slave I*, 5 (b): 323. SHC, James Hervey Greenlee Diary, 25 December 1850. HUL, Brainerd Journal, 25 December 1818. *Slave II*, 6: 2287, 228, 5: 1562. Fisk, p. 132. *Weevils*, p. 82. SHC, James Gwyn Diary, 31 December 1858, James Gwyn Papers.
25. *Slave*, 4 (b): 90, 12: 350, 13: 80. Breen, *Tobacco Culture*, p. 48. SHC, James Hervey Greenlee Diary, 1 January 1851. *Slavery Time*, p. 101. Regarding mountain slave malnutrition, see Dunaway, *African-American Family*, Ch. 2.
26. UVSC, letter dated 21 November, Bell Family Papers. *Slave*, 6 (a): 155, 280, 12 (b): 85, 16: 24, 45. *Slave I*, 7: 696, 1: 293, 3: 98. *Slave II*, 5: 1794, 1560,

9: 3873–74. *Slavery Time*, p. 101. Hartman, *Scenes*, p. 51. Illustration 11.4, website.

27. *Slave I*, 3: 272–73, 5 (b): 317, 8: 914, 13: 78–79. *Slave*, 6: 155, 279, 16 (a): 3, 32, 13: 78, 2 (b): 8, 51, 12: 311. Fisk, pp. 12, 53. *Slave II*, 3: 790. Raboteau, *Slave Religion*, pp. 31–32, 231.
28. Abrahams, *Singing*, pp. 112–22. Hartman, *Scenes*, p. 50. Oakley, *Devil's Music*, pp. 36–46. Davis, *Blues*, pp. 24–28. Janney and Janney, *Janney's Virginia*, p. 88. Berlin, Favreau, and Miller, *Remembering Slavery*, pp. 199–200. The song about patrollers was recorded in upland South Carolina by Bryant, *Letters*, p. 85 and in western North Carolina by Rumple, *History*, p. 172. Brown, *Narrative*, p. 51. *Slave II*, 5: 1794.
29. Hartman, *Scenes*, p. 78. *Slave*, 12: 143. *Slave II*, 9: 3875. Abrahams, *Singing*, pp. 269–70. Berlin, Favreau, and Miller, *Remembering Slavery*, p. 199.
30. Davis, *Blues*, pp. 7, 29. Ramsey, *Been Here*, p. 36. *Slave I*, 7: 697. Janson, *Stranger*, p. 406. Allen, *Slave Songs*, pp. 9, 37. Epstein, *Sinful Tunes*, pp. 193–215. Conway, *African Banjo*, pp. 3–4. Pryor, *My Day*, pp. 54–57. Perkins, "Negro Spirituals," p. 229. *Slave*, 14: 190, 4 (a): 201, 5 (b): 198.
31. Collins, *Black Feminist Thought*, p. 213. Epstein, *Sinful Tunes*, pp. 83, 125–60. Stuckey, *Slave Culture*, p. 88. Blassingame, *Slave Community*, pp. 39–40, 126. Jefferson, *Notes*, p. 257. Contemporary scholars support Jefferson's claim; see Epstein, *Sinful Tunes*, p. 38, 58–62. Fisk, p. 131. *Slave I*, 9: 1417–18. *Slave II*, 6: 2280–81. *Slave*, 6 (a): 280. Regarding use of the banjo by mountain slaves, see *Slave*, 16: 47; *Slave I*, 1: 293, 3: 273, 9: 1417; *Slave II*, 1: 355, 6: 2280–82. *Weevils*, pp. 82, 243, 265. Fisk, pp. 131, 218.
32. *Slave I*, 9: 1417–18, 1: 293, 3: 273. *Weevils*, pp. 82, 265, 198. *Slave II*, 5: 1794, 6: 2282, 2242. Epstein, *Sinful Tunes*, pp. 140–51. Blassingame, *Slave Community*, pp. 38–39, 108–109, 125. Abrahams, *Singing*, pp. 91–106, 127–30. *Weevils*, pp. 198, 265, 82. *Slave*, 12: 311, 6 (a): 280. UVVS, Memoir of Alansa Rounds Sterrett, pp. 3–4. "John Brown's Journal," p. 288. An 1838 painting of a kitchen ball at White Sulphur Springs, West Virginia, appears in Epstein, *Sinful Tunes*, pp. xvii–xviii. Lanier, *Science*, pp. 186–87. Janney and Janney, *Janney's Virginia*, pp. 87–88. Epstein, *Sinful Tunes*, pp. 58–62. Illustration 11.5, website.
33. Scott, "Resistance without Protest," p. 422. Rawick, *From Sundown*, pp. 107–09. *Slave*, 16: 33, 7 (a): 345. Regarding punishment for passing information between plantations, see *Slave I*, 7: 694, 12: 340. Fisk, p. 9. Webber, *Deep like the Rivers*, p. 296n35.
34. Details about Appalachian runaways calculated using descriptions of 506 escapes by Appalachian slaves that appear in slaveholder manuscripts, in Still, *Underground Railroad* and in newspaper advertisements for runaways, including 297 cases in Meaders, *Advertisements* and Parker, *Stealing*. Campbell, *Colonial Caroline*, pp. 71–72. Morgan, *Slave Counterpoint*, p. 465. Dunaway, "Southern Fur Trade," p. 235.
35. *Slave*, 16: 33, 1: 58, 101, 7: 141. *Slave II*, 9: 3641–42. Naragon, "Communities," pp. 67–81. *Macon Telegraph*, 27 November 1838. Betts, *Jefferson's Farm Book*, p. 46. Olmsted, *Back Country*, p. 55.

36. *Slave II*, 6: 2278, 9: 3642. *Slave I*, 12: 330. *Weevils*, p. 265. Fisk, p. 13. Regarding family breakups, see Table 7.1, website, and Dunaway, *African-American Family*, Ch. 3.
37. WV, Legislative Petitions of Citizens of Loudoun and Fauquier Counties, 10 December 1847, Legislative Papers. Betts, *Jefferson's Farm Book*, pp. 21–35, 46. For other examples of laying out in slaveholder manuscripts, see UVSC, letters dated 22 July and 13, 19, 31 January, 18 March, 14 April 1852, John Buford Papers. Sellers, *Slavery*, p. 287. UVSC, letter dated 19 March 1813, Kelly-Norris Papers.
38. *Slave*, 16: 32, 13, 78, 12: 310, 2 (b): 50, 3 (a): 14. Fisk, pp. 129, 105–06. Rankin, *Letters*, p. 23. Cade, "Out of Mouths," p. 318. *Cherokee Phoenix*, 17 March 1832. Russell, *Free Negro*, p. 141n. Janney and Janney, *Janney's Virginia*, p. 56.
39. Escape methods were calculated using descriptions of 506 escapes by Appalachian slaves that appear in slaveholder manuscripts, in Still, *Underground Railroad* and in newspaper advertisements for runaways, including 297 cases in Meaders, *Advertisements*, and Parker, *Stealing*. According to Franklin and Schweninger, *Runaway Slaves*, p. 230, about 7 percent of all U.S. runaways used forged documents. *Knoxville Gazette*, 4 June 1800. *Weevils*, pp. 166–67. Dunaway, *First American Frontier*, pp. 260, 292–94, 321.
40. American Board of Commissioners of Foreign Missions, *Annual Reports*, pp. 36, 93, 287. *Slave*, 7 (a): 21, 6: 269, 13 (a): 270, 16: 17. Drew, *North-side View*, p. 45. *Weevils*, p. 285.
41. *Slave II*, 3: 800–01. Graham, "Thomas Jefferson," p. 97. Fisk, pp. 57–58. *Slave I*, 8: 914, 1241–42. Fisk, pp. 57–58. *Slave*, 2 (b): 50, 12: 274.
42. UVSC, E. G. Chapman Farm Journal, 24 June 1843. *Slave II*, 9: 3875. *Weevils*, p. 156. UVSC, letter dated 18 May 1849, Southside Virginia Family Papers. *Slave*, 16: 21, 29. VHS, Mason Ellzey, "The Cause We Lost and the Land We Love," p. 6, Ellzey Family Papers.
43. Fisk, pp. 4, 131. UVSC, letter dated 30 November 1804, Thomas Jefferson Papers. VS, *Commonwealth v. Aaron*, Kanawha County, 28 October 1818, Virginia Executive Papers. VS, Legislative Petitions, Loudoun County, 11 January 1840; Rockbridge County, 12 January 1856. Petition of David M. Erwin et.al., Greenbrier County, to Virginia General Assembly, Legislative Papers. *Staunton Spectator*, 20 May 1857. Franklin and Schweninger, *Runaway Slaves*, p. 192.
44. Boggs, *Gramsci's Marxism*, p. 39. Billings, "Cultural Hegemony," p. 40. Petras, "Cultural Imperialism," p. 2070. Blassingame, *Slave Community*, p. 91. Drake, *Quakers*, p. 18. Analysis of Appalachian slave narratives. This pattern parallels that found by Fogel, Galantine, and Manning, *Without Consent*, p. 362. In the South as a whole, there was one church for every 541 inhabitants. Estimates were calculated using county totals in U.S. Census Office, *Statistics of the U.S. in 1860*, and U.S. Census Office, *Population of the U.S. in 1860*. Harrison, *Gospel*, pp. 194–95. Campbell, *Georgia Baptists*, pp. 286–88. McLoughlin, *Cherokees and Missionaries*, pp. 118–21.
45. I perused the manuscript records for VS, Mountain Plain Baptist Church; UVSC, Broad Run Baptist Church; UVSC, Goose Creek Baptist Church;

VS, Bethel Baptist Church; UVSC, New Hope Baptist Church; HPL, Market Street United Methodist Church; UVSC, Christ Episcopal Church; VHS, Zion Hill Baptist Church; UVSC, Chestnut Grove Baptist Church; UVSC, Mount Ed Baptist Church. *Slave II*, 3: 672, 802, 4: 110, 1433, 5: 1559. *Slave*, 11 (b): 207–208, 6 (a): 279, 12 (a): 349, 197, 195, 13: 128, 16 (b): 3. *Slave I*, 7: 692. Hamilton, "Minutes," p. 47. Fisk, p. 57.

46. SHC, Martha Ann Hancock Wheat Diary, 1850–66. *Slave II*, 9: 3871–72, 5: 1559–60. *Slave*, 7: 26, 6: 154–55. For example, UVSC, letters dated 26 January 1854, 8 July 1859, Preston-Davis Family Papers. Regarding slave catechisms, see Jones, *Catechism* and *Southern Episcopalian* 6 (1859): 369–75. *Southern Presbyterian Review* 8 (1855): 1–17.

47. SHC, James Hervey Greenlee Diary, 30 January 1847, 2 January 1848, 31 December 1848, 4 March 1849, 15 September 1850, 16 February 1851. *Slave*, 10 (a): 182, 11 (b): 207–08, 11 (a): 231. Fisk, pp. 98, 148. *Slave II*, 3: 555–56.

48. Blassingame, *Slave Community*, pp. 91–92. *Southwestern Baptist*, 24 July 1856, 25 April 1861. Holcombe, *History*, pp. 110–11. VS, Roanoke District Baptist Association Records, 17 March 1851. Fisk, p. 54. *Slave*, 16: 111. *Slave I*, 3: 272. Cohen, *Kanawha County Images*, pp. 46–47. Franklin, *Free Negro*, p. 176. Morgan, *Emancipation*, pp. 47–48. Jackson, *Free Negro Labor*, p. 162. Reed and Matheson, *Narrative*, vol. 1, pp. 217–22. Jordan, *Black Confederates*, p. 113. VS, folder of research notes on John Chavis, William Henry Ruffner Papers.

49. *Slave*, 4 (a): 274. 13: 84–85, 16: 89, 111, 32, 4 (b): 75–76. Fisk, pp. 217, 239, 54, 214. *Slave II*, 5: 1791.

50. Bruner, *An Abstract*, pp. 58–60. Abercrombie and Turner, "Dominant Ideology," p. 157. Church statistics derived from Tables 3, 10, 13, 16 in Blassingame, *Slave Community*, pp. 346–60. Appalachian estimates derived by using county population statistics from the 1860 Census of Population. Jordan, *Black Confederates*, p. 106.

51. *Slave*, 12: 350. Fisk, p. 106. *Weevils*, p. 287. Brainerd Journal, 2 June 1820. Lyerly, "Religion," pp. 202–26. Veney, *Narrative*, pp. 16–17.

52. Myers, *Children of Pride*, pp. 482–83. *Slave*, 16: 32, 13: 78, 80, 91–92, 10 (a): 182, 12: 349. Fisk, p. 57. SHC, James Hervey Greenlee Diary, 5 June 1849. *Slave II*, 5: 1559–60, 6: 2279, 3: 802–03.

53. Fisk, p. 100. *Slave*, 4 (a): 274. *Slave I*, 8: 914. *Slave II*, 3: 801. Pennington, *Fugitive Blacksmith*, pp. 66–68.

54. Smith, *Autobiography*, pp. 164–65. *Weevils*, p. 276. *Slave I*, 5 (b): 446, 7: 692, 1: 432. *Slave*, 7: 173, 26, 12: 138, 13: 80, 1: 55, 16: 31, 67. Dew, *Bond of Iron*, p. 179. Fisk, pp. 53, 106, 146–47, 118, 149, 98.

55. *Slave*, 4 (a): 274, 12 (a): 197–98. *Slave I*, 8: 914. Smith, *Autobiography*, p. 163. Fisk, pp. 4, 106. *Weevils*, p. 157. *Slave II*, 4: 1433, 6: 2258.

56. Gomez, *Exchanging*, pp. 213, 256, 263, 284–87, 39–58. Gramsci, *Prison Notebooks*, p. 333. Blassingame, *Slave Community*, p. 134. Davenport, *Primitive Traits*, pp. 66–79. Rawick, *From Sundown*, pp. 38–49. Raboteau, *Slave Religion*, pp 57–73. *Slave*, 10 (a): 182, 16 (b): 35. *Slave I*, 1: 20, 7:

697, 8: 1219–20, 12: 332–34. *Slave II*, 3: 673–74. *Weevils*, pp. 155–56. Dunaway, "Southern Fur Trade," pp. 227–29. Wolf, *Europe and People*, pp. 185, 197, 277.

57. Olmsted, *Seaboard*, pp. 114, 124–25. Du Bois, *Souls*, p. 338. Smith, *Autobiography*, pp. 163–64.
58. The origin and function of the iron pot practice is unclear; see Raboteau, *Slave Religion*, pp. 215–16. Rawick, *From Sundown*, pp. 39–45. Fisk, pp. 45, 118, 12, 53, 98, 117–18, 148–49. *Slave*, 1: 55–56, 16: 38, 67. *Weevils*, p. 198. *Slave I*, 1: 432–33. Illustration 11.6, website.
59. Ambler, *Life and Diary*, p. 159. Harris, *Plain Folk*, p. 51. *Carolina Centinel*, 10 May 1828. *Alexandria Daily Advertiser*, 10 July 1813. See, for example, *Slave* 16: 111; *Slave II*, 3: 801.
60. For a notion of cultural terrorism, see Petras, "Cultural Imperialism," p. 2071. *Alexandria Daily Advertiser*, 31 December 1805. *Weevils*, pp. 210, 214–15. *Abbeville Banner*, 22 June 1850, 7 July 1850, 16 August 1850, 14 September 1850. Fisk, p. 4. Hughes, *Thirty Years*, p. 54. Blassingame, *Slave Community*, p. 133.
61. *Slave*, 17: 142, 16: 89.

CONCLUSION

1. Berlin, *Many Thousands Gone*, pp. 8–10.
2. Tables 5.1 to 5.3, website, and Dunaway, *African-American Family*, Ch. 1.
3. Fogel, *Without Consent*, p. 193.
4. Genovese, *Roll*, p. 7.
5. Berlin, *Many Thousands Gone*, p. 107.
6. For more information about treatment of slaves by mountain masters, see Dunaway, *African-American Family*, Chs. 2, 3, 4.
7. Lynd, *Nonviolence*, pp. 516, 495. Gandhi, *Non-violent Resistance*.
8. Regarding higher incidence of punishment for noneconomic infractions, see Fogel and Engerman, *Without Consent*, vol. 2, p. 543. Thompson, "Folklore," pp. 254–55.
9. Fox-Genovese, "Antebellum Households," p. 249.
10. Regarding slave trading and migration, see Table 5.13, website, and Dunaway, *African-American Family*, Ch. 1.
11. The Upper South states were responsible for a higher proportion of slave executions after 1830, even though the slave population was being reconcentrated in the Lower South. See Aguirre and Baker, "Slave Executions," pp. 7–8, 11–12. One researcher has found a similar pattern in postbellum lynchings (i.e., that lynchings increased in Mississippi as the number of blacks in the population declined); see McMillen, *Dark Journey*, pp. 117–33. Regarding slave treatment by mountain masters, see Dunaway, *African-American Family*, Chs. 2, 3.
12. Quinney, *Class*, pp. 54–59. Gandhi, *Non-violent Resistance*, pp. 175, 116.
13. Tucker, "Everyday Forms," pp. 25–44. Aptheker, *Negro Slave Revolts*, pp. 50, 368. Woodson, *Negro in Our History*, p. 177. Woodson, *Education*,

pp. 85, 227–28. Woodson, *Negro Church*, pp. 38–62. Scott, *Weapons*, p. xvi.
14. Scott, *Domination*, pp. 3, 65, 92, 148. Bellah, Madsen, Sullivan, Swidler, and Tipton, *Habits of the Heart*, pp. 153–54. MacIntyre, *After Virtue*, p. 208. Couto, "Narrative," p. 61.
15. Dubnow, "Diaspora," 2: 128. Smith, *Ethnic Revival*, p. viii. Wallerstein, *End of the World*, p. 29.
16. Patterson, *Rituals*, p. 29; he cites Kolchin, "Reevaluating," p. 581 and Parish, *Slavery*, p. 76. Kolchin, *American Slavery*, pp. 137–38. Berlin and Morgan, *Cultivation*, pp. 76–79.
17. Fogel, *Without Consent*, p. 187. *Families and Freedom*, pp. 7–9. For the WPA collection as a whole, 51 percent of the ex-slaves reported family breakups; see Crawford, "Slave Family," p. 333. Berlin and Morgan, *Slaves' Economy*, pp. 1–21.
18. Fogel, *Without Consent*, pp. 169, 185–86. Rawick, *From Sundown*, p. 96. Fox-Genovese, "Antebellum Households," p. 248. Illustration 11.1, website.
19. Regarding Appalachian slave trading and disruption of slave families, see Dunaway, *African-American Family*, Chs. 1, 3.
20. Valentine, "Deficit," pp. 156–57. Gutman, *Black Family*, pp. 87, 222–23.
21. Blassingame, *Slave Community*, p. 106.
22. Boggs, *Gramsci's Marxism*, p. 39. Billings, "Cultural Hegemony," p. 40. Petras, "Cultural Imperialism," p. 2070. Blassingame, *Slave Community*, p. 91. Abercrombie and Turner, "Dominant Ideology," p. 153. Lockwood, *Solidarity*, pp. 332, 328–29. *Slave*, 17: 142.
23. Fogel, *Without Consent*, p. 169.
24. Gomez, *Exchanging*, pp. 213, 256, 263, 284–87, 39–58. Gramsci, *Prison Notebooks*, p. 333. Blassingame, *Slave Community*, p. 134. Davenport, *Primitive Traits*, pp. 66–79. Rawick, *From Sundown*, pp. 38–49.
25. Raboteau, *Slave Religion*, pp 57–73. *Slave*, 10 (a): 182, 16 (b): 35. *Slave I*, 1: 20, 7: 697, 8: 1219–20, 12: 332–34. *Slave II*, 3: 673–74. *Weevils*, pp. 155–56. In Southern Appalachia, it is unclear whether "praying on the beads" was a derivative from African Muslim customs or from the Cherokees. Cherokees acquired blue and white trade beads during the international fur trade, at the same time that these items were introduced by the Dutch as part of the slave trade in Africa. See Dunaway, "Southern Fur Trade," pp. 227–29, and Wolf, *Europe and People*, pp. 185, 197, 277.
26. Blassingame, *Slave Community*, pp. 181–82. Fogel and Engerman, *Time*, vol. 1, pp. 23–24.
27. Gomez, *Exchanging*, pp. 239, 218.
28. For discussion of the trickster in slave tales, see Joyner, *Riverside*, pp. 174–95. Thomas, *Slave Trade*, pp. 379–80, 393, 406–08. Braudel, *Civilization and Capitalism*, vol. 3, p. 435. Gomez, *Exchanging*, pp 207–08.
29. Stuckey, *Slave Culture*, pp. 4–5, 360n. Gomez, *Exchanging*, pp. 212–14.
30. Gramsci, *Cultural Writings*, p. 142. Thompson, *Making of English Working Class*, pp. 12–13. Wallerstein, "Construction of Peoplehood," pp. 77–78, 85.
31. Spivak, "Can the Subaltern Speak?" p. 127. Hershatter, "Subaltern Talks Back," p. 109. Guha, *Elementary Aspects*, pp. 129–32.

Bibliography

ARCHIVAL COLLECTIONS

AL: ALABAMA DEPARTMENT OF ARCHIVES AND HISTORY, MONTGOMERY, ALABAMA

George Brewer, "History of Coosa, Alabama," Typescript
Montevallo Coal Mining Company Records
Pardons, Paroles, and Clemency Files, 1821–53
B. Smith Letter, 15 August 1844

CWM: COLLEGE OF WILLIAM AND MARY LIBRARY, WILLIAMSBURG, VIRGINIA

Brown, Coalter, and Tucker Family Papers

DDC: DIGITIZED COLLECTIONS, DUKE UNIVERSITY, DURHAM, NORTH CAROLINA

Alice Williamson Diary, http://Scriptorium.lib.duke.edu

DPL: WILLIAM L. PERKINS LIBRARY, DUKE UNIVERSITY MANUSCRIPTS, DURHAM, NORTH CAROLINA

Thomas Adams Account Books, 1768–1808
Joseph Allred Papers
Francis Thomas Anderson Papers
John L. Bailey Collection
Daniel Baker Papers
Bedinger-Dandridge Letters
Alfred W. Bell Papers
N. L. Blakemore Papers
James Blanton Papers
William Bolling Papers
Bryarly, Samuel, Richard, and Rowland Papers
Campbell Family Papers
Clement Claiborne Clay Papers

Samuel Smith Downey Papers
Charles Ellis and George Wythe Munford Papers
Mary D. Fraser Papers and Account Books
Tyre Glen Papers
William H. Hatchett Papers
John Warfield Johnston Collection
Michael Kidwiler Papers
Henry Clay Krebs Papers
William LaPrade Account Books, 1839–60
William Law Papers
Thomas Lenoir Papers
Joseph Long Papers
Henry Kent McCay Papers
James McDowell Papers
Mary Singleton McDuffie Papers
Hugh Minor Notebooks
Battaile Muse Papers
John Quincy Adams Nadenbousch Papers
John M. Orr Papers
Green W. Penn Papers
Benjamin Pennybacker Daybook
Poor Relief Records, Augusta County, Virginia, 1791–1822
H. I. Rhodes Memorandum Book
John Rutherford Papers and Letter Books
Richard W. Sanders and John W. Greene Papers and Notebooks
Samuel P. Sherrill Account Book
Staunton, Virginia, Poor Records, 1770–1872
Vincent Tapp Papers
Augustin Louis Taveau Papers
Cabell Tavenner and Alexander Scott Withers Papers
William Holland Thomas Papers
John W. Timberlake Papers
Michael H. Turrentine Papers
William Weaver Papers
F. L. Whitehead and N. Lofftus Accounts of Slave Trading
Philip J. Winn Collection

ET: EAST TENNESSEE HISTORICAL SOCIETY, KNOXVILLE, TENNESSEE

Knoxville Industrial Association, "Facts and Figures, 1869," trade pamphlet

FC: FILSON CLUB, LOUISVILLE, KENTUCKY

Willis and Lafayette Green Papers, 1818–60
Edward Harris Letter, 1797
Willard R. Jillson, "A History of the Coal Industry in Kentucky." Paper read before the Filson Club, 7 November 1921, Typescript

Mason County, Kentucky Account Book, 1797–99
Frank B. Russell Papers, 1849–60
Peyton Skipwith Papers
John Wallace Journal
Warrick-Miller Papers

FHC: FAMILY HISTORY CENTER, CHURCH OF JESUS CHRIST OF THE LATTER DAY SAINTS, SALT LAKE CITY, UTAH

Bradley County, Tennessee Poor Commission Records
County Tax Lists for North Carolina, Virginia and West Virginia
Claiborne County, Tennessee, Livestock Brands, 1853–79
Claiborne County, Tennessee, Stage Coach Book

FUA: FISK UNIVERSITY ARCHIVES, NASHVILLE, TENNESSEE

Ophelia Egypt, H. Masuoka, and C. S. Johnson, comp. "Unwritten History of Slavery: Autobiographical Account of Negro Ex-slaves," Social Science Document No. 1 (1945), Mimeographed Typescript

HPL: HANDLEY PUBLIC LIBRARY, WINCHESTER, VIRGINIA

Ellen Afto Manuscript
L. Allan Letter
Allen Family Papers
Rebecca Ebert, "A Window on the Valley," Typescript
Market Street United Methodist Church Records, 1842–60

HSP: HISTORICAL SOCIETY OF PENNSYLVANIA, PHILADELPHIA, PENNSYLVANIA

Elihu Embree Papers

HUL: HARVARD UNIVERSITY LIBRARY, CAMBRIDGE, MASSACHUSETTS

Brainerd Journal, American Board of Commissioners for Foreign Missions Papers

LC: LIBRARY OF CONGRESS, WASHINGTON, DC

American Colonization Society Papers

MC: MCCORMICK COLLECTION, STATE HISTORICAL SOCIETY OF WISCONSIN, MADISON, WISCONSIN

Jordan and Davis Papers

MSA: MARYLAND STATE ARCHIVES, ANNAPOLIS, MARYLAND

Frederick County, Maryland, Livestock Brand Registry, 1851–53, County Land Records

NA: NATIONAL ARCHIVES, WASHINGTON, DC

Assistant Superintendents Records, Records of the Assistant Commissioner for the State of Virginia, Bureau of Refugees, Freedmen, and Abandoned Lands, 1865–68, Record Group 105, M784, M1246

Census Roll, 1835, of the Cherokee Indians East of the Mississippi

Federal Writers Project, "Slave Narratives, A Folk History of Slavery in the United States from Interviews with Former Slaves." Typewritten Records, 1941

Freedmen Labor Contracts, Records of the Assistant Commissioner for the State of Tennessee, Bureau of Refugees, Freedmen, and Abandoned Lands, 1865–68, Record Group 105, M999, Roll 20

Records of the Cherokee Indian Agency in Tennessee, 1801–35

Records of the Education Division, Bureau of Refugees, Freedmen, and Abandoned Lands, 1865–68, Record Group 105, Pub. No. 803, Roll 16

Records Relating to Court Cases Involving Freedmen, Records of the Assistant Commissioner for the State of Virginia, Bureau of Refugees, Freedmen, and Abandoned Lands, 1865–68, Record Group 105, M1048, Reel 59

Records Relating to Murders and Outrages, Bureau of Refugees, Freedmen, and Abandoned Lands, 1865–68, Record Group 105, M798, Roll 32; M843, Rolls 31–33, 39; M869, Roll 34; M999, Roll 34; M1048, Reel 59

U.S. Census Office, Census Enumerator Manuscripts for Appalachian Counties were utilized for these censuses:

Census of Agriculture, 1860
Census of Agriculture, 1870
Census of Population, 1860
Census of Population, 1870
Census of Manufacturing, 1860
Slave Schedules, 1840–60

U.S. Congress, Report No. 39, Twenty-Second Congress, First Session

NC: NORTH CAROLINA DEPARTMENT OF ARCHIVES AND HISTORY, RALEIGH, NORTH CAROLINA

Walter Clark Papers
David L. Swain Papers

SHC: SOUTHERN HISTORICAL COLLECTION, UNIVERSITY OF NORTH CAROLINA, CHAPEL HILL, NORTH CAROLINA

Walter Alves Papers
John McPherson Berrien Papers

John Houston Bills Papers
John Luther Bridges Papers
Hamilton Brown Papers
Farish Carter Papers
Calvin J. Cowles Papers
William G. Dickson Papers
H. B. Eiler Letter Book
George Phifer Erwin Papers
Peachy R. Grattan Papers
James Hervey Greenlee Diary, 1848–53
James Gwyn Papers
Peter Wilson Hairston Papers
Stephen B. Heard Papers
Hoke Papers
Nathaniel Hunt and Company Papers
Gen. Edmund Jones Papers
Jones and Patterson Family Papers
Lenoir Family Papers
James Lee Love Papers
Lucilla Gamble McCorkle Diary, William McCorkle Papers
Silas McDowell Papers
Peter Mallett Papers
James Mallory Diary
Theodore Morrison Papers
Pettigrew Family Papers
George Wesley Race Diary
Jacob Siler Papers
Thomas George Walton Papers
Plowden C. J. Weston, "Plantation Instructions"
Martha Ann Hancock Wheat Diary, 1850–66
Willis R. Williams Papers
Benjamin Cudworth Yancey Papers

TROY: TROY STATE UNIVERSITY LIBRARY, TROY, ALABAMA

John Horry Dent Farm Journals and Account Books, 1840–92

TS: TENNESSEE STATE LIBRARY AND ARCHIVES, NASHVILLE, TENNESSEE

Knox County Road Commissioners Minutebook, 1808–19
Chris D. Livesay Papers

UH: DIGITIZED COLLECTIONS, UNIVERSITY OF HOUSTON, HOUSTON, TEXAS

Mintz, Steven, ed. "Excerpts from Slave Narratives," http://vi.uh.edu/pages/mintz/primary.htm

UK: UNIVERSITY OF KENTUCKY SPECIAL COLLECTIONS, LEXINGTON, KENTUCKY

Buckner Family Papers
William Calk Papers
Diary of Judge Cabell Chenault, Chenault-Bowmar Family Papers
J. Winston Coleman Papers on Slavery, Typescripts
Forsythe Family Papers
Francis M. Goddard Diary, 1834–50
Graham Account Book
John Halley, "Journal of Trips to New Orleans"
Halley Family Papers
Hilton Family Diaries
Hunt-Morgan Family Papers
Kentucky House Journal (1838–39)
Joseph and Archibald Logan Papers
Means-Seaton Papers
National Society of the Colonial Dames, "Old Furnaces of Kentucky," Typescript
Scott Family Papers
Cyrenius Wait Papers
Wickliffe-Preston Papers

UT: UNIVERSITY OF TENNESSEE SPECIAL COLLECTIONS, KNOXVILLE, TENNESSEE

Caldwell Papers
"Diary of William R. Caswell, 1856," Typescript
John Sevier Papers
O. P. Temple Papers

UVSC: SPECIAL COLLECTIONS DEPARTMENT, ALDERMAN LIBRARY, UNIVERSITY OF VIRGINIA, CHARLOTTESVILLE, VIRGINIA

Charles J. Affleck Papers
Edmund Bacon Memoranda Book
Barbour Family Papers
Barringer Family Papers
Baumgardner Family Papers
Bell Family Papers
Berkeley Family Papers
Blackwell Family Papers
James Breckenridge Papers
Breckinridge Family Papers
Broad Run Baptist Church Minutes, 1762–1859
Austin Brockenbrough Papers
Bruce Family Papers

Buck Family Papers
John Buford Papers
Byers Family Papers
William D. Cabell Papers
Calender of Thomas Jefferson Papers
Carr Family Papers
E. G. Chapman Farm Journal
Chestnut Grove Baptist Minute Books, 1773–1860
Christ Episcopal Church, Parish Register, 1830–65
William W. Davis Iron Manufacturing Company Papers
Nancy Emerson Diary, Emerson Family Papers
Etna Furnace Papers
Folly Farms Papers
Richard Foster Papers
Goose Creek Baptist Church Records, 1775–1853
William T. Gordon Diary, Gordon Family Papers
Graham Family Papers
Grinnan Family Papers
Holland Family Papers
John Hook and Bowker Preston Papers
Hubard Family Papers
Phoebe Jackson Account Book
James River and Kanawha Canal Company Papers
Thomas Jefferson Papers
Keith Family Papers
Kelly-Norris Papers
Kohler Papers
Gen. Joel Leftwich Papers
Lewis, Anderson, and Marks Family Papers
McCue Family Papers
McDowell Family Papers
Massie Family Papers
Mathews-Dundore Papers
Socrates Maupin Papers
Callohill Mennis Papers
Louisa H. A. Minor Diary, 1855–66
Mount Ed Baptist Church Minute Book
Nelson County Business Ledgers
New Hope Baptist Church Minute Book, Thomas S. Bobcock Papers
Wilson Cary Nicholas Papers
Page-Walker Family Papers
Perry, Martin, and McCue Family Papers
Preston-Davis Family Papers
Randolph Family Papers
Register of Free Blacks, Washington County
Rives Family Papers
Rust Family Papers

Southside Virginia Family Papers
Alexander H. H. Stuart Letters
George Thrift Papers, 1844–58
Trist, Burke, and Randolph Family Papers
Nathaniel Beverly Tucker Papers
Virginia Letters Collection
Walker Family Papers
Wallace Family Papers
Watson Family Papers
Weaver-Brady Iron Works and Grist Mill Papers
Weaver-Brady Records
White Family Papers
Floyd L. Whitehead Papers
Wilson, Whitehead, and Houston Family Papers
Wise Family Papers
Wright Family Papers

UVVS: VALLEY OF THE SHADOW, ELECTRONIC TEXTS, INSTITUTE FOR ADVANCED TECHNOLOGY IN THE HUMANITIES, UNIVERSITY OF VIRGINIA, CHARLOTTESVILLE, VIRGINIA

http://jefferson.village.virginia.edu/vshadow2
B. S. Brooke Letter, 14 November 1859
Mary M. Burton Will
Mary G. Calhoun Will
Robert Christian Will
Henry Kenneday Will
Memoir of Alansa Rounds Sterrett

VHS: VIRGINIA HISTORICAL SOCIETY, RICHMOND, VIRGINIA

Campbell-Preston Papers
Caperton Family Papers
John Dawson Letters
Ellzey Family Papers
John E. Fletcher Papers
Holburn Letterbook, Taylor Papers
James Lawrence Hooff Diary
James River and Kanawha Company Papers
David Ross Letterbook, 1812–13
William Macon Waller Papers

VP: VIRGINIA POLYTECHNIC INSTITUTE AND STATE UNIVERSITY LIBRARY, BLACKSBURG, VIRGINIA

Virginia and Tennessee Railroad Minutes, Virginia and Tennessee Railroad Collection

VS: VIRGINIA STATE LIBRARY AND ARCHIVES, RICHMOND, VIRGINIA

Bethel Baptist Church Character Certificates, Garnett Ryland Collection
Legislative Papers, a Collection of 25,000 Petitions Sent to the Legislature of Virginia, 1775–1860
Lewis Medical Account Book
Loudoun County Court Records
Cyrus H. McCormick Letter, 2 December 1854
Mountain Plain Baptist Church Minute Book, 1833–69
Registers of Death, 1853–60
Roanoke District Baptist Association Records
William Henry Ruffner Papers
Slaves Condemned, Executed and Transported, 1783–1865, Records Group 48, Auditor of Public Accounts
Tredegar Letterbook, Tredegar Company Records
Virginia Board of Public Works Reports, Legislative Documents
Virginia Executive Papers, Letters Received, 1750–1835
Zion Hill Baptist Church Records

WL: WASHINGTON AND LEE UNIVERSITY LIBRARY, LEXINGTON, VIRGINIA

Etna Furnace Company Account Book, 1854–57

WV: WEST VIRGINIA COLLECTION, WEST VIRGINIA UNIVERSITY LIBRARY, MORGANTOWN, WEST VIRGINIA

Baltimore and Ohio Railroad Records
Barbour County Manuscripts and Articles
Barbour County, Miscellany Papers # 1115
Barbour County Typescript
John Bassel Papers
Alfred Beckley Papers
Louis Bennett Papers
Daniel Boardman Papers
Arthur I. Boreman Papers
Brooke County Archives
James M. Burnside Papers
Andrew Nelson Campbell Papers
Charles L. Campbell Typescripts
Chapin Family Papers
John P. Clarke Papers
Coal River and Kanawha Mining and Manufacturing Company Account Books
Justus Collins Papers
Courtney Family Papers
James M. Crump Typescript
Ruth Woods Dayton Papers
Deakins Family Papers
Marmaduke Dent Papers

J. Q. Dickinson and Company Papers
Donnally and Steele Kanawha Salt Works Records, 1813–15
William Henry Edwards Papers
Stephen B. Elkins Papers
William Ewin Papers
Ralph Fairfax Records
Fairmont General Store Records
Fleming Family Papers
L. J. Forman Papers
Free Negro Register, Monroe County Archives
Freeman Family Papers
M. J. Garrison and Company Records
A. C. L. Gatewood Papers
David Goff Papers
Great Kanawha Coal, Oil and Metallurgic Company Papers
Jacob Guseman Records
Harrison Hagans Papers
William Hall Papers
Felix G. Hansford Papers
Harper's Ferry Typescript
Harrison County Tax Book, 1831–32
R. H. Hendershot Shipping Bills
Henderson-Tomlinson Families Papers
Adolphus P. Howard Papers
Alfred Hughes Stock Certificates
Ice's Ferry Typescripts
Iron Furnaces Typescript
George W. Johnson Papers
Kanawha County Archives
Kanawha County Court Records
John Pendleton Kennedy Papers
Ku Klux Klan, Monongalia County Manuscripts
Peter T. Laisley Papers
Frederick B. Lambert Papers
Legislative Petitions of Kanawha County
Eugene Levassor Papers
Lewis Family Papers
Lightburn Family Papers
John R. Lynch Papers
John McClaugherty Papers
McCoy Family Papers
Isaac McNeel Papers
McNeill Family Papers
John Williamson Marshall Papers
Marshall County Archives
John D. Martin Papers
Mason County Court Records

Lewis Maxwell Papers
Maysville, Kentucky, Papers
Edward E. Meredith Papers
H. E. Metheny Papers
Henry O. Middleton Correspondence
Charles C. Miller Farm Records
William D. Mintz Papers
R. Emmett Mockler Papers
Monogalia County Land and Legal Papers, 1783–1859
Monroe County Archives
Monroe County Road Records, 1812–62
James Rogers Moreland Papers
Henri Jean Mugler Diary
William P. L. Neale Manuscript
Fred T. Newbaugh Papers
Bradford Noyes Recollections
Lawrence William Nuttall Papers
Ohio County, West Virginia, Brand Registration, 1772–1935
Parkersburg Town Council Journals, 1855–62
Carleton Custer Pierce Papers
George McCandless Porter Papers
Preston County Papers, 1775–1918
William Price Papers
Raleigh County Archives
Rathbone Family Papers
Thomas P. Ray Diary, 1829–52
C. R. Rector Typescript
John Rogers Papers
Ruffner-Donally and Company Records
Salt Sulphur Springs Records
James B. Shahan Letter
Samuel W. Shingleton Records
"Salt Manufactuing in Mason County, West Virginia," Typescript
Sloan Brothers Papers
George W. Smith Papers
William Sommerville Papers
Stover College Records
George Cookman Sturgiss Papers
George W. and Lewis Summers Papers
Summers County Archives
Sweet Springs Records
Talbott-Tolbert Family Papers
Taverns Typescript
Roy Thistle Papers
Samuel D. Thorn Ledger
William Tompkins Papers, Roy Bird Collection
White Sulphur Springs Company Records

Luke Willcox Diary, 1853–54
Nathaniel V. Wilson Correspondence
Wilson-Lewis Family Papers
Wilson-Stribling Families Papers
Winifrede Mining and Manufacturing Company Documents
Woodbridge-Blennerhassett Papers
William Gordon Worley Papers

PUBLISHED PRIMARY SOURCES

Adair's History of the American Indians, 1775, edited by Samuel Williams. Johnson City, TN: Watauga Press, 1930.

"Address of James Barbour," *American Farmer* 7 (December 1825): 287–92.

Allen, William F., ed. *Slave Songs of the United States*. New York: A. Simpson, 1867.

Ambler, Charles H., ed. *The Life and Diary of John Floyd*. Richmond, VA: Richmond Press, 1918.

American Board of Commissioners of Foreign Missions. *First Ten Annual Reports with Other Documents of the Board*. Boston: T. R. Marrin, 1834.

American State Papers, 38 vols. Washington, DC: Gales and Seaton, 1831–60.

Appalachian Regional Commission. *Appalachia: A Reference Book*. Washington, DC: Government Printing Office, 1979.

Ashe, Thomas. *Travels in America in 1806*. London: E. M. Blount, 1808.

Ball, Charles. *Slavery in the United States: A Narrative of the Life and Adventures of Charles Ball, A Black Man*. 1837. Reprint. New York: Negro Universities Press, 1969.

Betts, Edwin M., ed. *Thomas Jefferson's Garden Book, 1766–1824 With Relevant Extracts from His Other Writings*. Philadelphia: American Philosophical Society, 1944.

ed. *Thomas Jefferson's Farm Book with Commentary and Relevant Extracts from Other Writings*. Princeton, NJ: American Philosophical Society, 1953.

Blassingame, John W., ed. *Slave Testimony: Two Centuries of Letters, Speeches, Interviews and Autobiographies*. Baton Rouge: Louisiana State University Press, 1977.

Bontemps, Arna, ed. *Great Slave Narratives*. Boston: Beacon Press, 1969.

Bremer, Frederika. *The Homes of the New World*, 2 vols. New York: G. B. Putnam, 1853.

Brewer, William M. "The Gold Regions of Georgia and Alabama." *American Institute of Mining Engineers Transactions* 25 (1895): 569–87.

Brown, John. *Slave Life in Georgia*. 1855. Reprint. Savannah, GA: Beehive Press, 1972.

Brown, William W. *Narrative of William Wells Brown, A Fugitive Slave*. Boston: Antislavery Office, 1847.

Brownlow, William G. *A Sermon on Slavery*. Knoxville, TN: By Author, 1857.

Bruner, Clarence. *An Abstract of the Religious Instruction of the Slaves in the Antebellum South*. Nashville, TN: Peabody College for Teachers, 1933.

Bryant, William Cullen. *Letters of a Traveller*. New York: G. P. Putnam, 1850.

Picturesque America, 2 vols. New York: D. Appleton and Co., 1872–74.

Buck, William P., ed. *Sad Earth, Sweet Heaven: The Diary of Lucy Rebecca Buck during the War between the States*. Birmingham, AL: Cornerstone.

Buckingham, James S. *The Slave States of America*, 2 vols. London: Fisher, 1842.

Bushman, Katherine G., ed. *The Registers of Free Blacks, 1810–1864: Augusta County, Virginia and Staunton, Virginia*. Verona, VA: Midvalley Press, 1989.

Campbell, Jesse H. *Georgia Baptists: Historical and Biographical*. Macon, GA: J. W. Burke, 1874.

Cannel Coal Company. *Report of the Board of Directors of the Cannel Coal Company of Coal River, Virginia*. New York, 1855.

The Carolina Chronicles of Dr. Francis LeJau, 1707–1717, edited by Frank J. Klingberg. Berkeley: University of California Press, 1956.

Carpenter, Charles, ed. "Henry Dana Ward: Early Diary Keeper of the Kanawha Valley." *West Virginia History* 37 (1976): 34–48.

Catterall, Helen T., ed. *Judicial Cases Concerning American Slavery and the Negro*, 4 vols. Washington, DC: Carnegie Institution, 1926–37.

Charter of the Coal River and Kanawha Mining and Manufacturing Company, Virginia, Together with the Report of Joseph Gill, Esq., State Engineer. New York: By Company, 1855.

The Code of the State of Georgia, edited by R. H. Clark, T. R. R. Cobb, and D. Irwin. Atlanta: State of Georgia, 1861.

Coffey, David W., ed. "'Into the Valley of Virginia': The 1852 Travel Account of Curran Swain." *Virginia Cavalcade* 39 (Spring 1990): 14–27.

Colyer, Vincent. *Brief Report of the Services Rendered by the Freedpeople to the U.S. Army in North Carolina in the Spring of 1862 after the Battle of Newbern*. New York: By Author, 1864.

Creekmore, Pollyanna. "Early East Tennessee Tax Lists." *East Tennessee Historical Society Publications* 23–32 (1959–60).

Criswell, Robert. *Uncle Tom's Cabin Contrasted with Buckingham Hall, the Planter's Home*. New York: Charles Scribner's Sons, 1852.

DeBrahm's Report of the General Survey in the Southern District of North America, edited by Louis DeVorsey. Columbia: University of South Carolina Press, 1971.

Douglass, Frederick. *Narrative of the Life of Frederick Douglass, an American Slave*. 1845. Reprint. New York: Dover Publications, 1995.

Drew, Benjamin. *A North-side View of Slavery*. Boston: John P. Jewett, 1856.

Dunn, Durwood, ed. *An Abolitionist in the Appalachian South: Ezekiel Birdseye on Slavery, Capitalism, and Separate Statehood in East Tennessee, 1841–1846*. Knoxville: University of Tennessee Press, 1997.

Embree, Elihu. *The Emancipator*. 1820. Reprint. Nashville: B. H. Murphy, 1932.

Families and Freedom: A Documentary History of African-American Kinship in the Civil War Era, edited by Ira Berlin and Leslie S. Rowland. New York: New Press, 1997.

Featherstonhough G. W. *Excursion through the Slave States, From Washington on the Potomac to the Frontier of Mexico, With Sketches of Popular Manners and Geological Notices*, 2 vols. 1844. Reprint. New York: Negro Universities, 1968.

A Canoe Voyage Up the Minnay Sotor. London: Richard Bentley, 1847.

Fedric, Francis. *Slave Life in Virginia and Kentucky*. London: Wertheim, Macintosh, & Hunt, 1863.

Ferry Hill Plantation Journal: Life on the Potomac River and Chesapeake and Ohio Canal: 4 January 1838–15 January 1839, edited by Fletcher M. Green, Thomas F. Hahn, and Nathalie W. Hahn. Shepherdstown, WV: American Canal and Transportation Center, 1975.

Ford, Paul L. *The Writings of Thomas Jefferson*. New York: Putnam and Sons, 1892–99.

Fox, Dixon R. *Harper's Atlas of American History*. New York: Harper and Brothers, 1920.

Furman, Jan, ed. *Slavery in the Clover Bottoms: John McCline's Narrative of His Life during Slavery and the Civil War*. Knoxville: University of Tennessee Press, 1998.

"General Slade's Journal of a Trip to Tennessee." *Historical Society of Trinity College Papers* 6 (1906): 37–56.

Grund, Francis J. *The Americans in Their Moral, Social and Political Relations*. Boston: Marsh, Capen and Lyon, 1837.

Hall, James. *Notes on the Western States*. Philadelphia: Harrison Hall, 1838.

Hamilton, Kenneth G., ed. "Minutes of the Mission Conference Held in Spring Place." *Atlanta Historical Bulletin* 14 (Winter 1970): 42–69.

Harrison, William P. *The Gospel among the Slaves*. Nashville: M. E. Church Publishing House, 1893.

Helper, Hinton R. *The Impending Crisis of the South: How to Meet It*. 1851. Reprint. Cambridge, MA: Harvard University Press, 1986.

Holcombe, Hosea. *A History of the Rise and Progress of the Baptists in Alabama*. Philadelphia: Ring, 1840.

Howe, Henry, ed. *Historical Collections of Virginia*. Charleston, SC: Babcock, 1845.

Hughes, Louis. *Thirty Years a Slave: From Bondage to Freedom*. 1897. Reprint. New York: Negro Universities Press, 1969.

Janney, Werner, and Asa M. Janney, eds. *John Jay Janney's Virginia: An American Farm Lad's Life in the Early 19th Century*. McLean, VA: EPM Publications, 1978.

Janson, Charles W. *The Stranger in America, 1793–1806*. 1807. Reprint. New York: Press of the Pioneers, 1935.

Jefferson, Thomas. *Notes on the State of Virginia*, edited by William Peden. 1787. Reprint. New York: W. W. Norton, 1982.

"John Brown's Journal of Travel in Western North Carolina in 1795," edited by A. R. Newsome. *North Carolina Historical Review* 11 (1934): 284–313.

Jones, Charles C. *Catechism of Scripture, Doctrine and Practice for Families and Sabbath Schools, Designed also for the Oral Instruction of Colored Persons*. Savannah, GA: T. Purse and Co., 1837.

"Journal of John Sevier," *Tennessee Historical Magazine* 5–6 (1919–20): 156–94, 232–64, 18–68.

Journals of the Continental Congress, 1774–1789. Washington, DC: Government Printing Office, 1904–37.

Kemble, Frances A. *Journal of a Residence on a Georgian Plantation in 1838–1839*. 1864. Reprint. Athens: University of Georgia Press, 1984.

Killion, Ronald, and Charles Waller, comp. *Slavery Time When I Was Chillun Down on Marster's Plantation*. Savannah, GA: Beehive Press, 1973.

Lanier, Sidney. *The Science of English Verse*. New York: J. P. Putnam, 1880.

Lanman, Charles. *Letters from the Allegheny Mountains*. New York: G. B. Putnam, 1849.

Laws of the Cherokee Nation Adopted by the Council at Various Periods. Tahlequah, OK: Cherokee Advocate Officer, 1852.

"Letters to Jefferson from Archibald Cary and Robert Gamble." *William and Mary Quarterly* 6 (1926): 122–32.

"The Lonaconing Journals: The Founding of a Coal and Iron Community, 1837–1840," edited by Katherine A. Harvey. *Transactions of the American Philosophical Society* 67 (2) (1977).

Lord, William G. *Blue Ridge Parkway Guide*. Washington, DC: Eastern Acorn Press, 1990.

Lynd, Staughton, ed. *Nonviolence in America: A Documentary History*. Indianapolis, IN: Bobbs-Merrill, 1966.

McDonald, Cornelia P. *A Woman's Civil War: A Diary with Reminiscences of the War, from March 1862*, edited by Minrose C. Gwin. Madison: University of Wisconsin Press, 1992.

McKivigan, John R., ed. *The Roving Editor or Talks with Slaves in the Southern States, by James Redpath*. University Park: Pennsylvania State University Press, 1996.

Malet, William W. *An Errand to the South in the Summer of 1862*. London: R. Bentley, 1862.

Martin, Joseph. *A New and Comprehensive Gazetteer of Virginia and the District of Columbia*. Charlottesville, VA: W. H. Brockenbrough, 1835–36.

Mason, Frances N. *John Norton and Sons, Merchants of London and Virginia, being the Papers from Their Counting House for the Years 1750 to 1795*. Richmond, VA: Dietz Press, 1937.

Mathew, William M., ed. *Agriculture, Geology and Society in Antebellum South Carolina: The Private Diary of Edmund Ruffin, 1843*. Athens: University of Georgia Press, 1992.

Meaders, Daniel, ed. *Advertisements for Runaway Slaves in Virginia, 1801–1820*. New York: Garland Publishing, 1997.

Melish, John. *The Traveler's Directory through the United States, containing a Description of all the Principal Roads*. Philadelphia: By Author, 1822.

The Traveler's Directory through the United States, containing a Description of all the Principal Roads. Philadelphia: By Author, 1849.

Mississippi Provincial Archives, 1729–1740, edited by Dunbar Rowland and A. G. Sanders. Jackson, MS: Dept. of Archives and History, 1927–32.

Mooney, James. "Myths of the Cherokee." *Bureau of American Ethnology Annual Report* 19 (1900).

Moore, Glover. *A Calhoun County, Alabama Boy in the 1860s*. Jackson: University Press of Mississippi, 1978.

Moorman, John J. *The Virginia Springs: Comprising an Account of all the Principal Mineral Springs of Virginia*. Richmond: J. W. Randolph, 1854.

Myers, Robert M., ed. *The Children of Pride: A True Story of Georgia and the Civil War*. New Haven, CT: Yale University Press, 1972.

Nitze, H. B., and M. Wilkens. "The Present Condition of Gold Mining in the Souhern Mountain States." *American Institute of Mining Engineers Transactions* 25 (1895): 678–87.

Olmsted, Frederick L. *Journey in the Seaboard Slave States with Remarks on Their Economy*. New York: Dix and Edwards, 1856.

A Journey in the Back Country, 1853–1854. New York: Mason Brothers, 1860.

One Hundred Years of Progress of the United States. Hartford, CT: L. Stebbins, 1870.

The Papers of John C. Calhoun, edited by Clyde N. Wilson. Columbia: University of South Carolina Press, 1958.

The Papers of Zebulon Baird Vance, edited by Frontis W. Johnston. Raleigh, NC: State Department of Archives, 1963.

Parker, Freddie L., ed. *Stealing a Little Freedom: Advertisements for Slave Runaways in North Carolina, 1791–1840*. New York: Garland Publishing, 1994.

Pennington, James W. C. *The Fugitive Blacksmith, or Events in the History of James W. C. Pennington, Formerly a Slave*. London: C. Gilpin, 1849.

Perdue, Charles L., T. E. Barden, and R. K. Phillips, eds. *Weevils in the Wheat: Interviews with Virginia Ex-slaves*. Charlottesville: University Press of Virginia, 1976.

Peterson, Frank P., and Frank H. Flynn. "The Walhalla District, S.C." *Engineering and Mining Journal* 101 (February 1916): 379–86.

Playfair, Robert. *Recollections of a Visit to the United States and British Provinces of North America in the Years 1847, 1848 and 1849*. Edinburgh: T. Constable, 1856.

Pryor, Sara R. *My Day: Reminiscences of a Long Life*. New York: Macmillan, 1909.

Ramsey, Frederic. *Been Here and Gone*. New Brunswick, NJ: Rutgers University Press, 1960.

Rankin, John. *Letters on American Slavery Addressed to Mr. Thomas Rankin, Merchant at Middlebrook, Augusta County, Virginia*. 1837. Reprint. Westport, CT: Negro Universities Press, 1970.

Rawick, George P., comp. *The American Slave: A Composite Autobiography*, 19 vols. Westport, CT: Greenwood Press, 1972.

The American Slave: A Composite Autobiography, Supplement I, 12 vols. Westport, CT: Greenwood Publishing, 1977.

The American Slave: A Composite Autobiography, Supplement II, 10 vols. Westport, CT: Greenwood Publishing, 1979.

Records in the British Public Record Office Relating to South Carolina, 1663–1684, edited by A. S. Salley, 5 vols. Columbia: Historical Commission of South Carolina, 1928–47.

Records of the Moravians in North Carolina, edited by Adelaide L. Fries. Raleigh, NC: Edwards and Broughton, 1922–30.

Reed, Andrew, and James Matheson. *A Narrative of the Visit to the American Churches*. London: Jackson and Walford, 1835.

Reid, Joseph D. "Antebellum Southern Rental Contracts." *Explorations in Economic History* 13 (1976), 69–87.

Report of the Commissioner of Patents for the Year 1851: Agriculture. Washington, DC: U.S. House of Representatives, 1852.

Riordan, John L., ed. "Albermarle in 1815: Notes of Christopher Daniel Ebeling." *Papers of the Albermarle County Historical Society* 12 (1951–52).

Rogers, William B. *Report of the Geological Reconnaissance of the State of Virginia.* Philadelphia: DeSilver, Thomas and Co., 1836.

Roughley, T. *The Jamaica Planter's Guide.* London: Longman, Hurst, Rees, Orme, and Brown, 1823.

Royall, Anne. *Southern Tour, or Second Series of the Black Book,* 2 vols. Washington, DC: By Author, 1830–31.

Ruffin, Edmund. *Slavery and Free Labor Described and Compared: Address to the People of West Virginia.* 1847. Reprint. Bridgewater, VA: Green Bookman, 1933.

St. Abdy, Edward. *Journal of a Residence and Tour in the United States of America, from April, 1833 to October, 1834.* London: John Murray, 1835.

Shepard, E. Lee, ed. "Trip to the Virginia Springs: An Extract from the Diary of Blair Bollings, 1838." *Virginia Magazine of History and Biography* 96 (2) (1988): 193–212.

Siler, Tom. *Tennessee Towns: From Adams to Yorkville.* Knoxville: East Tennessee Historical Society, 1985.

Silliman, Benjamin. "Remarks on Some of the Gold Mines and on Parts of the Gold Region of Virginia, Founded on Personal Observations, Made in the Months of August and September, 1836." *American Journal of Science* 32 (1837): 98–130.

Smith, J. Gray. *A Brief Historical, Statistical and Descriptive Review of East Tennessee, United States of America: Developing Its Immense Agricultural, Mining and Manufacturing Advantages, with Remarks to Emigrants.* London: J. Leath, 1842.

Smith, James L. *Autobiography including Reminiscences of Slave Life.* Norwich, CT: Press of the Bulletin, 1881.

Smyth, John F. D. *A Tour of the U.S.A., Containing an Account of the Present Situation of that Country.* London: G. Robinson, 1784.

The South: A Collection from Harper's Magazine. New York: Gallery Books, 1990.

Spratte, Carol. "Wyoming County Folklore." *AFFword* 3 (1973): 26.

Still, William. *The Underground Railroad: A Record of Facts, Authentic Narratives and Letters.* Philadelphia: Porter and Coates, 1872.

Stroud, George M. *A Sketch of the Laws Relating to Slavery in the Several States of the United States of America.* Philadelphia: H. Longstreth, 1856.

Stuart, James. *Three Years in North America,* 2 vols. Edinburgh: Robert Cadell, 1833.

The Tennessee Civil War Veterans Questionnaires, compiled by Gustavus W. Dyer and John T. Moore. Easley, SC: Southern Historical Press, 1985.

Tennessee Historical Markers. Nashville: Tennessee Historical Commission, 1980.

"Thomas Lenoir's Journey to Tennessee in 1806," edited by James W. Patton. *Tennessee Historical Quarterly* 17 (1958): 156–66.

Thwaites, Reuben G. *Travels West of the Alleghanies, III.* Cleveland: Arthur H. Clark Co, 1904.

Tilley, Nannie M., ed. "Journal of the Surry County Agricultural Society." *North Carolina Historical Review* 24 (1947): 494–531.

Townsend, Joseph. "Dissertation on the Poor Laws by a Well-wisher to Mankind." In *A Select Collection of Scarce and Valuable Economical Tracts*, pp. 403–19. London: n.p., 1859.

Truman, Benjamin. *History of the World's Fair*. Chicago: n.p., 1893.

Tucker, George. *The Valley of the Shenandoah, or Memoirs of the Graysons*. New York: C. Wiley, 1824.

United States Census Office. *Population of the United States in 1860*. Washington, DC: Government Printing Office, 1864.

Special Reports: Mines and Quarries, 1902. Washington, DC: Government Printing Office, 1905.

Statistics of the United States, Including Mortality and Property in 1860. Washington, DC: Government Printing Office, 1866.

United States Commissioner of Education Report, 1899–1900. Washington, DC: Government Printing Office, 1900.

Veney, Bethany. *The Narrative of Bethany Veney: A Slave Woman*. Worcester, MA: A. P. Bicknell, 1890.

Vigne, Godfrey T. *Six Months in America*, 2 vols. London: Whitaker, Treacher and Co., 1832.

Washington, Booker T. *The Future of the American Negro*. Boston: Small and Maynard, 1899.

An Autobiography: The Story of My Life. Naperville, IL: J. L. Nichols, 1901.

Booker T. Washington Papers, edited by Louis R. Harlan, 10 vols. Urbana: University of Illinois Press, 1972.

Weld, Isaac. *Travels through the States of North America, and the Provinces of Upper and Lower Canada During the Years 1795, 1796 and 1797*. London: John Stockdale, 1800.

Weld, Theodore D. *American Slavery as It Is: Testimony of a Thousand Witnesses*. 1839. Reprint. New York: Arno Press, 1968.

Wiggington, Eliot, ed. *Foxfire 2*. Garden City, NY: Anchor Books, 1973.

Foxfire 3. Garden City, NY: Anchor Books, 1975.

Williams, Samuel C., ed. *Early Travels in the Tennessee Country, 1540–1800*. Johnson City, TN: Watauga Press, 1928.

Wilson, Clyde N., ed. *The Papers of John C. Calhoun*. Columbia: University of South Carolina Press, 1979.

The WPA Guide to Tennessee. 1939. Reprint. Knoxville: University of Tennessee Press, 1986.

SECONDARY SOURCES

Abercrombie, Nicholas, and Bryan S. Turner. "The Dominant Ideology Thesis." *British Journal of Sociology* 29 (1978): 149–70.

Abrahams, Roger D. *Singing the Master: The Emergence of African American Culture in the Plantation South*. New York: Penguin Books, 1992.

Aguirre, Adalberto, and David V. Baker. "Slave Executions in the United States: A Descriptive Analysis of Social and Historical Factors." *Social Science Journal* 36 (1) (1999): 1–28.

Ahern, L. R., and R. F. Hunt. "The Boatyard Store, 1814–1825." *Tennessee Historical Quarterly* 14 (1955): 257–77.

Allen, Turner W. "The Turnpike System in Kentucky: A Review of State Road Policy in the 19th Century." *Filson Club History Quarterly* 28 (1954): 239–59.

Allman, John M. "Yeoman Regions in the Antebellum Deep South: Settlement and Economy in Northern Alabama, 1815–1860." Ph.D. diss., University of Maryland, 1979.

Ambler, Charles H. *A History of Transportation in the Ohio Valley*. Glendale, CA: Arthur H. Clark, 1932.

A History of West Virginia. New York: Prentice-Hall, 1933.

Sectionalism in Virginia from 1776 to 1861. New York: Russell and Russell, 1964.

Amin, Samir. *Accumulation on a World Scale: A Critique of the Theory of Underdevelopment*. New York: Monthly Review Press, 1974.

Anderson, Eric. *Race and Politics in North Carolina, 1872–1901: The Black Second.* Baton Rouge: Louisiana State University Press, 1981.

Andrews, Susan C., and Amy L. Young. "Plantations on the Periphery of the Old South: Modeling a New Approach." *Tennessee Anthropologist* 17 (1) (1992): 1–12.

Aptheker, Herbert. *American Negro Slave Revolts*. New York: International Publishers, 1974.

Ash, Stephen V. *Past Times: A Daybook of Knoxville History*. Knoxville, TN: Knoxville News Sentinel, 1991.

Ashe, Samuel A. *History of North Carolina*. Raleigh, NC: Edward and Broughton, 1925.

Atack, Jeremy. "The Agricultural Ladder Revisited: A New Look at an Old Question with Some Data for 1860." *Agricultural History* 63 (1989): 1–25.

Bailyn, Bernard. *The Peopling of North America: An Introduction*. New York: Alfred A. Knopf, 1986.

Baine, Rodney M. "Indian Slaves in Colonial Georgia." *Georgia Historical Quarterly* 79 (2): 418–39.

Banks, Alan J. "Emergence of a Capitalistic Labor Market in Eastern Kentucky." *Appalachian Journal* 7 (1980): 188–99.

Banta, R. E. *The Ohio*. New York: Rinehart and Co., 1949.

Battalio, Raymond C., and John Kagel. "The Structure of Antebellum Agriculture: South Carolina, A Case Study." In *The Structure of the Cotton Economy of the Antebellum South*, edited by William N. Parker, pp. 25–43. Washington, DC: Agricultural History Society, 1970.

Bellah, Robert N., Richard Madsen, William Sullivan, Ann Swidler, and Steven Tipton. *Habits of the Heart: Individualism and Commitment in American Life*. Berkeley: University of California Press, 1985.

Berdan, Marshall S. "The Spa Life: Taking the Cure in Antebellum Bath County." *Virginia Cavalcade* 40 (3) (1991): 110–19.

Berlin, Ira. *Many Thousands Gone: The First Two Centuries of Slavery in North America*. Cambridge, MA: Harvard University Press, 1998.

and Philip D. Morgan, eds. *Cultivation and Culture: Labor and the Shaping of Salve Life in the Americas*. Charlottesville: University of Virginia Press, 1993.

and Philip D. Morgan, eds. *The Slaves' Economy: Independent Production by Slaves in the Americas.* London: Frank Cass, 1991.

Marc Favreau, and Steven F. Miller, eds. *Remembering Slavery: African Americans Talk about Their Personal Experiences of Slavery and Emancipation.* New York: New Press, 1998.

Billings, Dorothy K. "Cultural Hegemony and Applied Anthropology." *Canberra Anthropology* 15 (1992): 35–57.

Billings, Dwight, and Kathleen Blee. "Agriculture and Poverty in the Kentucky Mountains: Beech Creek, 1850–1910." In *Appalachian in the Making: The Mountain South in the Making*, edited by Mary B. Pudup, Dwight Billings, and Altina Wallers, pp. 233–69. Chapel Hill: University of North Carolina Press, 1996.

Bishir, Catherine W. "Black Builders in Antebellum North Carolina." *North Carolina Historical Review* 61 (1984): 423–61.

Bissell, Richard. *The Monongahela.* New York: Rinehart and Co., 1949.

Blackburn, Robin. *The Making of New World Slavery: From the Baroque to the Modern, 1492–1800.* London: Verso, 1997.

Blassingame, John. The *Slave Community: Plantation Life in the Antebellum South.* New York: Oxford University Press, 1972.

Boggs, Carl. *Gramsci's Marxism.* London: Pluto Press, 1976.

Booker, Robert J. *Two Hundred Years of Black Culture: Knoxville, Tennessee, 1791–1991.* Virginia Beach, VA: Donning Co., 1993.

Bordieu, Pierre. *Outline of a Theory of Practice.* Cambridge: Cambridge University Press, 1977.

Boss, Pauline G. "The Experience of Immigration for the Mother Left Behind: The Use of Qualitative Feminist Strategies to Analyze Letters from My Swiss Grandmother." *Marriage and Family Review* 19 (3/4) (1993): 365–78.

Botkin, B.A., ed. *Lay My Burden Down: A Folk History of Slavery.* Chicago: University of Chicago Press, 1945.

Boughter, Isaac F. "Internal Improvements in Northwestern Virginia: A Study of State Policy Prior to the Civil War." Ph.D. diss., University of Pittsburgh, 1931.

Bouwman, Robert E. *Traveler's Rest and the Tugaloo Crossroads.* State of Georgia: Department of Natural Resources, 1980.

Boydston, Jeanne. "To Earn Her Daily Bread: Housework and Antebellum Working-Class Subsistence." *Radical History Review* 35 (1986), 19–38.

Brackett, Jeffrey R. *The Negro in Maryland: A Study of the Institution of Slavery.* Freeport, NY: Books for Libraries Press, 1889.

Bradford, Sydney. "The Negro Ironworker in Antebellum Virginia." *Journal of Southern History* 25 (1959): 194–206.

Braudel, Fernand. *Civilization and Capitalism, 15th–18th Century*, translated by Sian Reynolds, 3 vols. New York: Harper and Row, 1981.

Breen, T. H. *Tobacco Culture: The Mentality of the Great Tidewater Planters on the Eve of Revolution.* Princeton, NJ: Princeton University Press, 1985.

Brewster, Lawrence F. "The Summer Migrations and Resorts of South Carolina Low-Country Planters." Ph.D. diss., Duke University, 1942.

Brooks, Robert P. *The Agrarian Revolution in Georgia, 1865–1912*. Madison: University of Wisconsin Press, 1914.

Brown, Cecil K. *A State Movement in Railroad Development: The Story of North Carolina's First Effort to Establish an East and West Trunk Line Railroad*. Chapel Hill, NC: University of North Carolina Press, 1928.

Bruce, Kathleen. *Virginia Iron Manufacture in the Slave Era*. New York: Century Co., 1939.

Burford, Herschel W. "Steam Packets on the Kanawha River." *West Virginia History* 27 (1966): 111–35.

Burnett, Edmund C. "Hog Raising and Hog Driving in the Region of the French Broad River." *Agricultural History* 20 (1946), 95–110.

Burnham, Michelle. "Loopholes of Resistance: Harriet Jacobs' Slave Narrative and the Critique of Agency in Foucault." *Arizona Quarterly* 49 (2) (1993): 53–73.

Burt, Jesse. "The Nashville and Chattanooga Railroad, 1854–1872: Era of Transition." *East Tennessee Historical Society Publications* 23 (1951): 58–76.

Cade, John B. "Out of the Mouths of Ex-Slaves." *Journal of Negro History* 20 (1) (1935): 294–337.

Callahan, James M. *Semi-Centennial History of West Virginia*. Charleston: Semi-centennial Commission of West Virginia, 1913.

Campbell, John C. *The Southern Highlander and His Homeland*. New York: Russell Sage Foundation, 1921.

Campbell, T. E. *Colonial Caroline: A History of Caroline County, Virginia*. Richmond, VA: Dietz Press, 1964.

Campbell, T. J. *The Upper Tennessee*. Chattanooga, TN: By Author, 1932.

Carson, W. Wallace. "Transportation and Traffic on the Ohio and the Mississippi before the Steamboat." *Mississippi Valley Historical Review* 7 (1920): 26–38.

Censer, Jane T. *North Carolina Planters and Their Children*. Baton Rouge: Louisiana State University Press, 1984.

Chase-Dunn, Christopher. *Global Formation: Structures of the World-Economy*. London: Basil Blackwell, 1989.

Clark, Christopher. *The Roots of Rural Capitalism: Western Massachusetts, 1780–1860*. Ithaca, NY: Cornell University Press, 1990.

Clark, Thomas D. "Trade between Kentucky and the Cotton Kingdom in Livestock, Hemp and Slaves from 1840 to 1860." M.A. thesis, University of Kentucky, 1929.

"Early Lumbering Activities in Kentucky." *Northern Logger* 13 (1965), 17–38.

The Kentucky. Lexington, KY: Henry Clay Press, 1969.

Clarkson, Roy B. *Tumult on the Mountains: Lumbering in West Virginia, 1770–1920*. Parsons, WV: McClain Printing Co., 1964.

Cohen, Stan. *Kanawha County Images: A Bicentennial History, 1788–1988*. Charleston, WV: Pictorial Histories Publishing, 1987.

Coleman, Elizabeth D., and W. Edwin Hemphill. "Boats Beyond the Blue Ridge." *Virginia Cavalcade* 3 (4) (1954): 8–13.

Coleman, J. Winston. *Slavery Times in Kentucky*. Chapel Hill: University of North Carolina Press, 1940.

"Kentucky River Steamboats." *Register of the Kentucky Historical Society* 63 (1965): 299–322.

Coleman, Kenneth, ed. *A History of Georgia*. Athens: University of Georgia Press, 1991.

Collins, Patricia H. *Black Feminist Thought: Knowledge, Consciousness and the Politics of Empowerment*. Boston: Unwin Hyman, 1990.

Conway, Cecilia. *African Banjo Echoes in Appalachia: A Study of Folk Traditions*. Knoxville, TN: University of Tennessee Press, 1995.

Corkran, David. *The Cherokee Frontier: Conflict and Survival, 1740–1762*. Norman, OK: University of Oklahoma Press, 1954.

Couto, Richard A. "Narrative, Free Space, and Political Leadership in Social Movements." *Journal of Politics* 55 (1) (1993): 57–79.

Crane, Verner. "The Tennessee River as the Road to Carolina: The Beginnings of Exploration and Trade." *Mississippi Valley Historical Review* 3 (1916): 3–18.

Craven, Avery O. "Poor Whites and Negroes in the Antebellum South," *Journal of Negro History* 15 (1930): 14–25.

Craven, Paul, and Douglas Hay. "The Criminalization of 'Free' Labour: Master and Servant in Comparative Perspective." *Slavery and Abolition* 15 (2) (1994): 71–101.

Crawford, Stephen. "Quantified Memory: A Study of the WPA and Fisk University Slave Narrative Collections. Ph.D. diss., University of Chicago, 1980.

"The Slave Family: A View from the Slave Narratives." In *Strategic Factors in Nineteenth Century American Economic History*, edited by Claudia Goldin and Hugh Rockoff, pp. 331–50. Chicago: University of Chicago Press, 1992.

Crowther, M. A. *The Workhouse System, 1834–1929*. Athens, GA: University of Georgia Press, 1981.

Darst, H. Jackson. "Benjamin Darst, Sr., Architect-Builder of Lexington." *Proceedings of the Rockbridge Historical Society* 8 (1979): 61–76.

Davenport, Frederick M. *Primitive Traits in Religious Revivals*. New York: Macmillan, 1905.

Davidson, Donald. *The Tennessee: The Old River, Frontier to Secession*. Knoxville, TN: University of Tennessee Press, 1946.

Davis, Angela. *Blues, Legacies and Black Feminism*. New York: Pantheon Books, 1998.

Davis, Julia. *The Shenandoah*. New York: Farrar and Rinehart, 1945.

Day, Marie, and W. Calvin Dickinson. "The Netherland Inn." *East Tennessee Historical Society Publications* 60 (1988): 67–77.

Delfino, Susanna. "Antebellum East Tennessee Elites and Industrialization: The Examples of the Iron Industry and Internal Improvements." *East Tennessee Historical Society Publications* 56–57 (1984–85): 102–19.

Depew, Chauncey M. *One Hundred Years of American Commerce, 1795–1895*. New York: D. O. Haynes, 1895.

Dew, Charles B. *Bond of Iron: Master and Slave at Buffalo Forge*. New York: W. W. Norton, 1994.

Dill, Bonnie Thornton. "Fictive Kin, Paper Sons and Compadrazgo: Women of Color and the Struggle for Family Survival." In *Women of Color in U.S. Society*, edited by Maxine B. Zinn and B. T. Dill, pp. 149–70. Philadelphia: Temple University Press, 1994.

Dolan, J. R. *The Yankee Peddlers of Early America*. New York: Clarkson and Potter, 1964.

Donnelly, Ralph W. "The Bartow County Confederate Saltpeter Works." *Georgia Historical Quarterly* 54 (1970): 305–19.

Douglas, Byrd. *Steamboatin' on the Cumberland*. Nashville: Tennessee Book Co., 1961.

Doyton, Roy R., and Thomas W. Hodler. "Secessionist Sentiment and Slavery: A Geographical Analysis." *Georgia Historical Quarterly* 73 (2) (1989): 323–48.

Drake, Thomas E. *Quakers in Slavery in America*. New Haven, CT: Yale University Press, 1950.

Druyvesteyn, Kent. "The James River and Kanawha Canal." *Virginia Cavalcade* 21 (3) (1972): 22–45.

Dubnow, Simon. "Diaspora." In *Encyclopedia of the Social Sciences*, edited by Edwin R. Anderson, 15 vols., 2: 126–30. New York: Macmillan, 1931.

Du Bois, W. E. B. *The Souls of Black Folk*. New York: Signet Books, 1969.

Dunaway, Wayland F. "History of the James River and Kanawha Company." *Columbia: University Studies in History, Economics and Public Law* 104 (2) (1922).

Dunaway, Wilma A. "The Incorporation of Southern Appalachia into the Capitalist World-Economy, 1700–1860." Ph.D. diss., University of Tennessee, 1994.

"The Southern Fur Trade and the Incorporation of Southern Appalachia into the World-Economy, 1690–1763." *Review of the Fernand Braudel Center* 17 (2) (1994): 215–42.

"The 'Disremembered' of the Antebellum South: A New Look at the Invisible Labor of Poor Women." *Critical Sociology* 21 (3) (1995): 89–106.

The First American Frontier: Transition to Capitalism in Southern Appalachia, 1700–1860. Chapel Hill: University of North Carolina Press, 1995.

"Rethinking Cherokee Acculturation: Women's Resistance to Agrarian Capitalism and Cultural Change, 1800–1838." *American Indian Culture and Research Journal* 21 (1997): 155–92.

The African-American Family in Slavery and Emancipation. Cambridge: Cambridge University Press, Forthcoming.

Dupre, Daniel. "Ambivalent Capitalists on the Cotton Frontier: Settlement and Development in the Tennessee Valley of Alabama." *Journal of Southern History* 57 (1990): 215–40.

Transforming the Cotton Frontier: Madison County, Alabama, 1800–1840. Baton Rouge: Louisiana State University Press, 1997.

Durrenberger, Joseph A. *Turnpikes: A Study of the Toll Road Movement in the Middle Atlantic States and Maryland.* Cos Cob, CT: J. E. Edwards, 1931.

Dykeman, Wilma. *The French Broad*. New York: Holt, Rinehart and Winston, 1955.

"Appalachia in Context." In *An Appalachian Symposium: Essays Written in Honor of Cratis D. Williams*, edited by J. W. Williamson, pp. 28–42. Boone, NC: Appalachian Consortium Press, 1977.

Ebert, Rebecca A. "A Window on the Valley: A Study of the Free Black Community of Winchester and Frederick County, Virginia, 1785–1860." M.A. thesis, University of Virginia, 1986.

Eisterhold, John A. "Lumber and Trade in the Lower Mississippi Valley and New Orleans, 1800–1860." *Louisiana History* 13 (1972): 71–91.

"Charleston: Lumber and Trade in a Declining Southern Port." *South Carolina Historical Magazine* 74 (1973): 61–73.

"Savannah: Lumber Center of the South Atlantic." *Georgia Historical Quarterly* 57 (1973): 526–45.

Eller, Ronald D. *Miners, Millhands and Mountaineers: Industrialization of the Appalachian South, 1880–1930*. Knoxville: University of Tennessee Press, 1982.

Epstein, Dena J. *Sinful Tunes and Spirituals: Black Folk Music to the Civil War*. Urbana: University of Illinois Press, 1977.

Eslinger, Ellen. "Antebellum Liquor Reform in Lexington, Virginia." *Virginia Magazine of History and Biography* 99 (2): 163–86.

Faulkner, Charles C., and Carol K. Buckles, eds. *Glimpses of Southern Appalachian Folk Culture*. Knoxville: Tennessee Anthropological Association, 1978.

Fischer, Charles E. "Internal Improvement Issues in Maryland, 1816–1826." M.A. thesis, University of Maryland, 1972.

Flanders, Ralph B. "The Free Negro in Antebellum Georgia." *North Carolina Historical Review* 9 (1932): 250–72.

Plantation Slavery in Georgia. Chapel Hill: University of North Carolina Press, 1933.

Fletcher, Arthur L. *Ashe County, a History*. Jefferson, NC: Ashe County Research Associates, 1963.

Fogel, Robert W. *Without Consent or Contract: The Rise and Fall of American Slavery*. New York: W. W. Norton, 1989.

and Stanley L. Engerman. *Time on the Cross: The Economics of American Negro Slavery*, 2 vols. Boston: Little, Brown and Co., 1974.

and Stanley L. Engerman, eds. *Without Consent or Contract: The Rise and Fall of American Slavery*. Vol. 2. *Technical Papers: Conditions of Slave Life and the Transition to Freedom*. New York: W. W. Norton, 1992.

Ralph A. Galantine, and Richard L. Manning, eds. *Without Consent or Contract: The Rise and Fall of American Slavery*. Vol. 3. *Evidence and Methods*. New York: W. W. Norton, 1992.

Folmsbee, Stanley J. "The Turnpike Phase of Tennessee's Internal Improvement System of 1836–1838." *Journal of Southern History* 3 (1937): 453–77.

Sectionalism and Internal Improvements in Tennessee, 1796–1845. Knoxville: East Tennessee Historical Society, 1939.

Fountain, Daniel L. "Historian and Historical Archaeology: Slave Sites." *Journal of Interdisciplinary History* 28 (3): 67–77.

Fox-Genovese, Elizabeth. "Antebellum Southern Households: A New Perspective on a Familiar Question." *Review of the Fernand Braudel Center* 7 (1983): 215–54.

Within the Plantation Household: Black and White Women of the Old South. Chapel Hill: University of North Carolina Press, 1988.

Franklin, John H. *The Free Negro in North Carolina, 1790–1860*. Chapel Hill: University of North Carolina Press, 1943.

and Loren Schweninger. *Runaway Slaves: Rebels on the Plantation*. New York: Oxford University Press, 1999.

Frazier, E. Franklin. *The Negro Family in the United States*. Chicago: University of Chicago Press, 1939.

"Furnaces and Forges." *Tennessee Historical Magazine* 9 (1925–26): 190–92.

Gaines, William H., Jr. "Going Underground in Virginia: Caverns of the Shenandoah Valley." *Virginia Cavalcade* 3 (4) (1954): 23–29.

Gamble, J. Mack. "Steamboats in West Virginia." *West Virginia History* 15 (1954): 124–38.

Gandhi, M. K. *Non-violent Resistance*, edited by Bharatan Kumarappa. New York: Schocken Books, 1951.

Gauding, Harry H. "History of Water Transportation in East Tennessee Prior to the Civil War." M.A. thesis, University of Tennessee, 1933.

Gawalt, Gerard W. " James Monroe. Presidential Planter." *Virginia Magazine of History and Biography* 101 (2) (April 1993): 251–72.

Genovese, Eugene D. *In Red and Black: Marxian Explorations in Southern and African-American History*. New York: Pantheon Books, 1971.

Roll, Jordan, Roll: The World the Slaves Made. New York: Random House, 1974.

Gilchrist, Dorothy. "The Virginia Springs: A Mirror of Antebellum Society." M.A. thesis, University of Virginia, 1943.

Gilliam, Catherine M. "Jordan's Point – Lexington, Virginia: A Site History." *Proceedings of the Rockbridge Historical Society* 9 (1982): 109–38.

Glickstein, Jonathan A. *Concepts of Free Labor in Antebellum America*. New Haven, CT: Yale University Press, 1991.

Gomez, Michael A. *Exchanging Our Country Marks: The Transformation of African Identities in the Colonial and Antebellum Period*. Chapel Hill: University of North Carolina Press, 1998.

Goodall, Elizabeth J. "The Manufacture of Salt – Kanawha's First Commercial Enterprise." *West Virginia History* 26 (1965): 234–50.

Goodspeed's History of Tennessee. Nashville, TN: Goodspeed Publishing, 1887.

Graham, Pearl M. "Thomas Jefferson and Sally Hemings." *Journal of Negro History* 46 (1961): 89–103.

Gramsci, Antonio. *Selections from Cultural Writings*. Cambridge, MA: Harvard University Press, 1985.

Selections from the Prison Notebooks, translated and edited by Q. Hoare and G. N. Smith. London: Lawrence and Wishart, 1971.

Grant, Donald L. *The Way It Was in the South: The Black Experience in Georgia*. New York: Carol Publishing Group, 1993.

Gray, Lewis C. *History of Agriculture in the Southern United States to 1860*, 2 vols. Gloucester, MA: Peter Smith, 1958.

Green, Fletcher M. "Georgia's Forgotten Industry: Gold Mining." *Georgia Historical Quarterly* 19 (1935): 93–111, 210–28.

"Gold Mining: A Forgotten Industry of Antebellum North Carolina." *North Carolina Historical Review* 14 (1937): 1–19, 135–55.

"Gold Mining in Antebellum Virginia." *Virginia Magazine of History and Biography* 45 (1937): 227–35, 357–66.

Gruber, Anna. "The Archaeology of Slave Life at Thomas Jefferson's Monticello: Mulberry Row Quarters r, s, t." *Archaeological Society of Virginia Quarterly Bulletin* 46 (1) (1990): 2–9.

Guha, Ranajit. *Elementary Aspects of Peasant Insurgency in India*. Delhi: Oxford University Press, 1983.

Gutheim, Frederick. *The Potomac*. New York: Rinehart and Co., 1949.

Gutman, Herbert. *The Black Family in Slavery and Freedom, 1750–1925*. New York: Pantheon Books, 1976.

Haites, Erik F., and James Mak. "Ohio and Mississippi River Transportation, 1810–1860." *Explorations in Economic History* 8 (1970): 153–80.

and James Mak. "Social Savings Due to Western River Steamboats." *Research in Economic History* 3 (1978): 263–304.

James Mak, and Gary M. Walton. *Western River Transportation*. Baltimore: Johns Hopkins University Press, 1975.

Hamer, Philip M. ed. *Tennessee, A History*. 1673–1932. New York: American Historical Society, 1933.

Harlow, Alvin F. *Old Towpaths: The Story of the American Canal Era*. 1926. Reprint. Port Washington, NY: Kennikat Press, 1954.

Harris, J. William. *Plain Folk and Gentry in a Slave Society: White Liberty and Black Slavery in Augusta's Hinterlands*. Middletown, CT: Wesleyan University Press, 1985.

Hartman, Saidya. *Scenes of Subjection: Terror, Slavery, and Self-Making in Nineteenth-Century America*. New York: Oxford University Press, 1997.

Harvey, Katherine A. *The Best-Dressed Miners: Life and Labor in the Maryland Coal Region, 1835–1910*. Ithaca, NY: Cornell University Press, 1969.

Head, Sylvia, and Elizabeth W. Etheridge. *The Neighborhood Mint: Dahlonega in the Age of Jackson*. Macon, GA: Mercer University Press, 1986.

Heath, Milton S. *Constructive Liberalism: The Role of the State in Economic Development in Georgia to 1860*. Cambridge, MA: Harvard University Press, 1954.

Hecht, Arthur. "Lead Production in Virginia During the Seventeenth and Eighteenth Centuries." *West Virginia History* 25 (1964): 173–83.

Henlein, Paul C. *Cattle Kingdom in the Ohio Valley, 1783–1860*. Lexington: University of Kentucky Press, 1959.

Henretta, James A. "Families and Farms: Mentalite in Pre-Industrial America." *William and Mary Quarterly* 35 (1978): 3–32.

Henry, H. M. "The Slave Laws of Tennessee." *Tennessee Historical Magazine* 2 (1916): 175–203.

Hershatter, Gail. "The Subaltern Talks Back: Reflections on Subaltern Theory and Chinese History." *Positions* 1 (1) (1993): 103–30.

Herskovits, Melville J. *The Myth of the Negro Past*. Boston: Beacon Press, 1958.

Hill, Carol A., and Duane DePaepe. "Saltpeter Mining in Kentucky Caves." *Register of the Kentucky Historical Society*, 77 (1979): 247–62.

Hill, Sarah H. *Weaving New Worlds: Southeastern Cherokee Women and Their Basketry*. Chapel Hill: University of North Carolina, 1997.

Hilliard, Sam B. *Hog Meat and Hoecake: Food Supply in the Old South, 1840–1860*. Carbondale: Southern Illinois University Press, 1972.

A History of Etowah County, Alabama. Birmingham, AL: Etowah County Centennial Committee, 1968.

Hofstra, Warren R. "Land Policy and Settlement in the Northern Shenandoah Valley." In *Appalachian Frontiers: Settlement, Society, and Development in the Preindustrial Era*, edited by Robert D. Mitchell, pp. 105–26. Lexington: University Press of Kentucky, 1991.

Holcombe, Hosea A. *A History of the Rise and Progress of the Baptists in Alabama*. Philadelphia: Ring Brothers, 1840.

Holland, James W. "A History of Railroad Enterprise in East Tennessee, 1836–1860." M.A. thesis, University of Tennessee, 1930.

Holmes, Tony. "The Last Eight Ferry Boats in Tennessee." *Tennessee Historical Quarterly* 46 (1987): 65–78, 129–40.

Holt, Sharon A. "Symbol, Memory and Service: Resistance and Family Formation in Nineteenth-Century African America." In *Working Toward Freedom: Slave Society and Domestic Economy in the American South*, edited by Larry E. Hudson, pp. 192–210. Rochester, NY: University of Rochester Press, 1994.

Hopkins, James F. *Hemp Industry in Kentucky*. Lexington: University of Kentucky Press, 1951.

Hoskins, Katherine B. *Anderson County*. Memphis, TN: Memphis State University Press, 1979.

Hsiung, David C. *Two Worlds in the Tennessee Mountains: Exploring the Origins of Appalachian Stereotypes*. Lexington: University Press of Kentucky, 1997.

Hudson, Charles. *The Juan Pardo Expeditions: Exploration of the Carolinas and Tennessee, 1566–1568*. Washington, DC: Smithsonian Institution Press, 1990.

and C. C. Tesser, eds. *The Forgotten Centuries: Indians and Europeans in the American South, 1521–1704*. Athens: University of Georgia Press, 1994.

Hulbert, Archer B. *Historic Highways of America*, 12 vols. Cleveland, OH: Arthur H. Clark Co., 1901–11.

Hunter, Louis C. "Studies in the Economic History of the Ohio Valley." *Smith College Studies in History* 19 (1–2) (1934).

Steamboats on the Western Rivers. Cambridge, MA: Harvard University Press, 1949.

Hunter, Robert F. "The Turnpike Movement in Virginia, 1815–1860." Ph.D. diss., Columbia University, 1957.

"Turnpike Construction in Antebellum Virginia." *Technology and Culture* 4 (1963): 177–200.

Ierley, Merritt. *Traveling the National Road: Across the Centuries on America's First Highway*. Woodstock, NY: Overlook Press, 1990.

Innes, Stephen, ed. *Work and Labor in Early America*. Chapel Hill: University of North Carolina Press, 1988.

Inscoe, John C. *Mountain Masters, Slavery, and the Sectional Crisis in Western North Carolina*. Knoxville: University of Tennessee, 1989.

"Mountain Masters as Confederate Opportunists: The Profitability of Slavery in Western North Carolina, 1861–1865." *Slavery and Abolition* 16 (1995): 84–100.

Irwin, John Rice. *Alex Stewart: Portrait of a Pioneer*. West Chester, PA: Schiffer Publishing, 1985.

Irwin, Marjorie F. "The Negro in Charlottesville and Albermarle County." *University of Virginia Phelps-Stokes Fellowship Papers* 9 (1929).

Isaac, Rhys. *The Transformation of Virginia, 1740–1790.* Chapel Hill: University of North Carolina Press, 1982.

Jackson, Luther P. *Free Negro Labor and Property Holding in Virginia, 1830–1860.* New York: D. Appleton-Century Co., 1942.

Jackson, Olin, ed. *A North Georgia Journal of History*. Woodstock, GA: Legacy Communications, 1989.

Jeffrey, Thomas E. "Internal Improvements and Political Parties in Antebellum North Carolina, 1836–1860." *North Carolina Historical Review* 55 (1978): 111–56.

Jenkins, Gary C. "The Mining of Alum Cave." *East Tennessee Historical Society Publications* 60 (1988): 78–87.

Johnson, Guion. "Recreational and Cultural Activities in the Antebellum Town of North Carolina." *North Carolina Historical Review* 6 (1929): 17–37.

Antebellum North Carolina: A Social History. Chapel Hill: University of North Carolina Press, 1937.

Johnston, James H. *Race Relations in Virginia and Miscegenation in the South, 1776–1860.* Amherst, MA: University of Massachusetts Press, 1970.

Jones, Jacqueline. *Soldiers of Light and Love: Northern Teachers and Georgia Blacks, 1865–1873.* Chapel Hill: University of North Carolina Press, 1980.

Labor of Love, Labor of Sorrow: Black Women, Work, and the Family from Slavery to the Present. New York: Vintage Books, 1985.

Jones, Norrece T. *Born a Child of Freedom, Yet a Slave: Mechanisms of Control and Strategies of Resistance in Antebellum South Carolina.* Hanover, NH: University Press of New England, 1990.

Jones, Richard E. "A Study of the Economic Influence of the Chesapeake and Ohio Canal on Washington County." M.Ed. thesis, Shippenburg State College, 1964.

Jordan, Ervin L. *Black Confederates and Afro-Yankees in Civil War Virginia.* Charlottesville: University Press of Virginia, 1995.

Joyner, Charles. *Down by the Riverside: A South Carolina Slave Community.* Urbana: University of Illinois Press, 1984.

Karras, Alan L., and J. R. McNeill, eds. *Atlantic Slave Societies from Columbus to Abolition, 1491–1888.* London: Routledge, 1992.

Kelso, William M. "The Archaeology of Slave Life at Thomas Jefferson's Monticello: 'A Wolf by the Ears.'" *Journal of New World Archaeology* 6 (4) (1986): 5–20.

Kincaid, Robert L. "The Wilderness Road in Tennessee." *East Tennessee Historical Society Publications* 20 (1948): 37–48.

King, Wilma. "'Rais your children up rite': Parental Guidance and Child Rearing Practices among Slaves in the Nineteenth-Century South." In *Working Toward Freedom: Slave Society and Domestic Economy in the American South*, edited by Larry E. Hudson, pp. 143–62. Rochester, NY: University of Rochester Press, 1994.

Kirby, David. "Canalization of New River." *West Virginia History* 15 (1954): 112–27.

Kivisto, Peter. *Americans All: Race and Ethnic Relations in Historical, Structural and Comparative Perspectives.* Belmont, CA: Wadsworth Publishers, 1995.

Klebaner, Benjamin. "Public Poor Relief in America, 1790–1860." Ph.D. diss., Columbia University, 1952.

Klein, Rachel N. "Ordering the Backcountry: The South Carolina Regulation." *William and Mary Quarterly* 38 (1981): 611–80.

Knapp, John W. "Trade and Transportation in Rockbridge: The First Hundred Years." *Proceedings of the Rockbridge Historical Society* 9 (1982): 211–31.

Kolchin, Peter. *American Slavery, 1619–1877*. New York: Hill and Wang, 1993.

Koning, Hans. *The Conquest of America: How the Indian Nations Lost Their Continent*. New York: Monthly Review Press, 1993.

Lacy, Eric R. *Vanquished Volunteers: East Tennessee Sectionalism from Statehood to Secession*. Johnson City: East Tennessee State University Press, 1965.

Lambert, Darwin. "The Oconaluftee Valley, 1800–1860: A Study of the Sources for Mountain History." *North Carolina Historical Review* 35 (1958): 415–26.

The Undying Past of Shenandoah National Park. Boulder, CO: Roberts-Rinehart, 1989.

Lander, Ernest M. "Slave Labor in South Carolina Cotton Mills." *Journal of Negro History* 38 (2) (1953): 161–73.

Lauber, A. W. "Indian Slavery in Colonial Times within the Present Limits of the United States." *Columbia University Studies in History, Economics and Public Law* 54 (1913).

Leavitt, Charles T. "The Meat and Dairy Livestock Industry, 1819–1860." Ph.D. diss., University of Chicago, 1931.

Lee, Susan P. "The Westward Movement of the Cotton Economy, 1840–1860." Ph.D. diss., Columbia University, 1975.

Levine, Bruce. *Half Slave and Half Free: The Roots of Civil War*. New York: Hill and Wang, 1992.

Lewis, Eulalie M. "The Valley of the Conasauga." *Georgia Historical Quarterly* 42 (3) (1958): 313–22.

Lewis, Ronald L. *Coal, Iron and Slaves: Industrial Slavery in Maryland and Virginia, 1715–1865*. Westport, CT: Greenwood Press, 1979.

Littlefield, Douglas R. "Maryland Sectionalism and the Development of the Potomac Route to the West." *Maryland Historian* 14 (1983): 31–52.

Livingood, James W. "The Chattanooga Country in 1860." *Tennessee Historical Quarterly* 20 (1961): 159–66.

Lockwood, David. *Solidarity and Schism: The Problem of Disorder in Durkheimian and Marxist Sociology*. New York: Oxford University Press, 1992.

Low, W. A. "Merchant and Planter Relations in Post-Revolutionary Virginia, 1783–1789." *Virginia Magazine of History and Biography* 61 (1953): 308–18.

Lyerly, Cynthia L. "Religion, Gender, and Identity: Black Methodist Women in a Slave Society, 1779–1810." In *Discovering the Women in Slavery: Emancipating Perspectives on the American Past*, edited by Patricia Morton, pp. 202–26. Athens, GA: University of Georgia Press, 1996.

McCurry, Stephanie. *Masters of Small Worlds: Yeoman Households, Gender Relations, and the Political Culture of the Antebellum South Carolina Low Country*. New York: Oxford University Press, 1995.

McDougle, Ivan E. "Slavery in Kentucky." *Journal of Negro History* 3 (3) (1918): 211–332.

MacIntyre, Alasdair. *After Virtue: A Study in Moral Theory*. Notre Dame, IN: University of Notre Dame Press, 1981.

McKenzie, Robert T. "From Old South to New South in the Volunteer State: The Economy and Society of Rural Tennessee, 1850–1880." Ph.D. diss., Vanderbilt University, 1988.

McKinney, Gordon B. *Southern Mountain Republicans, 1865–1900*. Chapel Hill: University of North Carolina Press, 1978.

McLoughlin, William G. *Cherokees and Missionaries, 1789–1839*. New Haven, CT: Yale University Press, 1984.

McMillen, Neil R. *Dark Journey: Black Mississippians in the Age of Jim Crow*. Urbana: University of Illinois Press, 1989.

Mak, James, and Gary M. Walton. "Steamboats and the Great Productivity Surge in River Transportation." *Journal of Economic History* 32 (1972): 619–40.

Malone, Henry T. *Cherokees of the Old South: A People in Transition*. Athens: University of Georgia Press, 1956.

Malone, Miles S. "Falmouth and the Shenandoah: Trade before the Revolution." *American Historical Review* 40 (1935): 693–703.

Marlin, Lloyd G. *The History of Cherokee County, Georgia*. Atlanta: Walter W. Brown Publishing, 1932.

Martin, William E. "Internal Improvements in Alabama." *Johns Hopkins Studies in Historical and Political Science* 20 (4) (1902).

Meillassoux, C., ed. *The Development of Indigenous Trade and Markets in West Africa*. London: Oxford University Press, 1971.

Milling, Chapman J. *Red Carolinians*. Chapel Hill: University of North Carolina Press, 1940.

Montell, William L. *The Saga of Coe Ridge: A Study in Oral History*. New York: Harper and Row, 1972.

Moore, Tyrel G. "The Role of Ferry Crossings in the Development of the Transportation Network in East Tennessee, 1790–1974." M.A. thesis, University of Tennessee, 1975.

"An Historical Geography of Economic Development in Appalachian Kentucky, 1800–1930." Ph.D. diss., University of Tennessee, 1984.

Moore, Warren. *Mountain Voices: A Legacy of the Blue Ridge and Smokies*. Chester, CT: Globe Pequot Press, 1988.

Morgan, Lynda J. *Emancipation in Virginia's Tobacco Belt, 1850–1870*. Athens: University of Georgia Press, 1992.

Morgan, Philip D. "Task and Gang Systems: The Organization of Labor on New World Plantations." In *Work and Labor in Early America*, edited by Stephen Innes, pp. 189–220. Chapel Hill: University of North Carolina Press, 1988.

Slave Counterpoint: Black Culture in the Eighteenth-Century Chesapeake and Lowcountry. Chapel Hill: University of North Carolina Press, 1998.

Morris, Richard B. *Government and Labor in Early America*. New York: Columbia University Press, 1946.

Mosby, Maryida W. "Salt Industry in the Kanawha Valley." M.A. thesis, University of Kentucky, 1950.

Murphy, James B. "Slavery and Freedom in Appalachia: Kentucky as a Demographic Case Study." *Register of the Kentucky Historical Society* 80 (1982): 151–69.

Murphy, James M. "Transportation on the Little Kanawha River in Gilmer County." M.A. thesis, West Virginia University, 1950.

Nagasaka, Itara. "Kinship Networks and Child Fostering in Labor Migration." *Asian and Pacific Migration Journal* 7 (1) (1998): 67–92.

Naragon, Michael D. "Communities in Motion: Drapetomani, Work and the Development of African-American Cultures." *Slavery and Abolition* 15 (3) (1994): 63–87.

Newby, Howard. "The Deferential Dialectic." *Comparative Studies in Society and History* 17 (2) (1975): 139–64.

Niemi, Albert W. "A Further Look at Interregional Canals and Economic Specialization, 1820–1840." *Explorations in Economic History* 7 (1970): 499–520.

Niles, Blair. *The James: From Iron Gate to the Sea*. New York: Rinehart and Co., 1939.

Noe, Kenneth W. *Southwest Virginia's Railroad: Modernization and the Sectional Crisis*. Urbana: University of Illinois Press, 1994.

Norris, E. J. *History of the Lower Shenandoah Valley Counties of Frederick, Berkeley, Jefferson and Clarke*. Chicago: A. Warner and Co., 1890.

Oakley, Giles. *The Devil's Music: A History of the Blues*. New York: Harcourt Brace Jovanovich, 1976.

Orser, Charles E. *The Material Basis of the Postbellum Tenant Plantation: Historical Archaeology of the South Carolina Piedmont*. Athens: University of Georgia Press, 1988.

Parkhurst, Jessie W. "The Role of the Negro Mammy in the Plantation Household." *Journal of Negro History* 23 (3): 349–69.

Parrillo, Vincent N. *Strangers to These Shores: Race and Ethnic Relations in the United States*. Boston: Allyn and Bacon, 1997.

Patterson, Orlando. *Rituals of Blood: Consequences of Slavery in Two American Centuries*. New York: Basic Civitas, 1999.

Patterson, Orlando. *Slavery and Social Death: A Comparative Study*. Cambridge, MA: Harvard University Press, 1982.

Patton, Sadie S. *The Story of Henderson County*. Asheville, NC: Miller Printing Co., 1947.

Pawlett, Nathaniel M. *A Brief History of the Roads of Virginia, 1607–1840*. Charlottesville, VA: Virginia Highway and Transportation Research Council, 1977.

Pearre, Nancy C. "Mining for Copper and Related Minerals in Maryland." *Maryland Historical Magazine* 59 (1964): 15–33.

Pease, Louise M. "The Great Kanawha in the Old South, 1671–1861." Ph.D. diss., West Virginia University, 1959.

Pentecost, Percy M. "A Corporate History of Knoxville, Tennessee before 1860." M.A. thesis, University of Tennessee, 1946.

Perdue, Theda. "Cherokee Planters: The Development of Plantation Slavery before Removal." In *The Cherokee Nation: A Troubled History*, edited by Duane King, pp. 110–28. Knoxville: University of Tennessee Press, 1979.

Slavery and the Evolution of Cherokee Society, 1540–1866. Knoxville: University of Tennessee Press, 1979.

Perkins, A. E. "Negro Spirituals from the Far South." *Journal of American Folklore* 25 (1922): 216–32.

Petras, James. "Cultural Imperialism in Late 20th Century." *Economic and Political Weekly* 29 (32) (6 August 1994): 2070–73.

Phifer, Edward W. "Slavery in Microcosm: Burke County, North Carolina." *Journal of Southern History* 28 (2) (1962): 137–65.

"Champagne at Brindletown: The Story of the Burke County Gold Rush, 1829–1833." *North Carolina Historical Review* 40 (1963): 489–500.

Burke: The History of a North Carolina County, 1777–1920, with a Glimpse Beyond. Morganton, NC: By Author, 1977.

Phillips, Peter D. "Incorporation of the Caribbean, 1650–1700." *Review of the Fernand Braudel Center* 10 (1987): 781–804.

Phillips, Ulrich B. *A History of Transportation in the Eastern Cotton Belt to 1860.* 1908. Reprint. New York: Octagon Books, 1968.

Pinchbeck, Raymond B. "The Virginia Negro Artisan and Tradesman." *Publications of the University of Virginia* 7 (1926): 1–146.

Plater, David D. "Building the North Wales Mill of William Allason." *Virginia Magazine of History and Biography* 85 (1977): 45–50.

Pudup, Mary B. "Social Class and Economic Development in Southeastern Kentucky, 1820–1880." In *Appalachian Frontiers: Settlement, Society, and Development in the Preindustrial Era*, edited by Robert D. Mitchell, pp. 235–60. Lexington: University Press of Kentucky, 1991.

Quinney, Richard. *Class, State and Crime.* New York: Longman, 1977.

Raboteau, Albert J. *Slave Religion: The "Invisible Institution" in the Antebellum South.* New York: Oxford University Press, 1980.

Rawick, George P. *From Sundown to Sunup: The Making of the Black Community.* Westport, CT: Greenwood Publishing Co., 1972.

Reed-Danahay, Deborah. "Talking about Resistance: Ethnography and Theory in Rural France." *Anthropological Quarterly* 66 (4) (1993): 221–31.

Reniers, Perceval. *The Springs of Virginia: Life, Love and Death at the Waters, 1775–1900.* Chapel Hill: University of North Carolina Press, 1941.

Reynolds, Hughes. *The Coosa River Valley.* Cynthiana, KY: Hobson Book Press, 1944.

Rice, Philip M. "Internal Improvements in Virginia, 1775–1860." Ph.D. diss., University of North Carolina, 1948.

Robert, Joseph C. *The Tobacco Kingdom: Plantation, Market, and Factory in Virginia and North Carolina, 1800–1860.* 1938. Reprint. Gloucester: Peter Smith, 1965.

Roberts, Nancy. *The Gold Seekers: Gold, Ghosts and Legends from Carolina to California.* Columbia: University of South Carolina Press, 1989.

Rohrbough, Malcolm J. *The Trans-Appalachian Frontier: People, Societies, and Institutions, 1775–1850.* New York: Oxford University Press, 1978.

Rollins, Leonard H. "The Tennessee River as a Trade Route and Its Relation to the Economic Development of East Tennessee." M.S. thesis, University of Tennessee, 1928.

Rouse, Parke. *The Great Wagon Road from Philadelphia to the South.* New York: McGraw-Hill, 1973.

Rumple, Jethro. *The History of Presbyterianism in North Carolina*. Richmond, VA: Union Theological Seminary, 1966.

Russell, John H. *The Free Negro in Virginia, 1619–1865*. 1913. Reprint. New York: Negro Universities Press, 1969.

Salmon, John S. *The Washington Iron Works of Franklin County, Virginia*. Richmond: Virginia State Library, 1986.

Sanderlin, Walter S. *The Great National Project: A History of the Chesapeake and Ohio Canal*. Baltimore: Johns Hopkins University Press, 1946.

Scharf, J. Thomas. *History of Western Maryland*. Philadelphia: Louis H. Everts, 1882.

Schlotterbeck, John T. "The Internal Economy of Slavery in Rural Piedmont Virginia." In *The Slaves' Economy: Independent Production by Slaves in the Americas*, edited by Ira Berlin and P. D. Morgan, pp. 150–71. London: Frank Cass, 1991.

Schwarzkopf, S. Kent. *A History of Mt. Mitchell and the Black Mountains: Exploration, Development, and Preservation*. Raleigh, NC: Department of Archives and History, 1985.

Scott, James C. *Weapons of the Weak: Everyday Forms of Peasant Resistance*. New Haven, CT: Yale University Press, 1985.

"Resistance without Protest and without Organization: Peasant Opposition to the Islamic Zakat and the Christian Tithe." *Comparative Studies in Society and History* 29 (3) (1987): 417–52.

Domination and the Arts of Resistance: Hidden Transcripts. New Haven, CT: Yale University Press, 1990.

Searight, Thomas B. *The Old Pike*. Uniontown, PA: By Author, 1894.

Sellers, James B. *Slavery in Alabama*. University: University of Alabama Press, 1950.

Sellers, Leila. *Charleston Business on the Eve of the American Revolution*. Chapel Hill: University of North Carolina Press, 1934.

Semes, Robert L. "200 Years at Rockbridge Alum Springs." *Proceedings of the Rockbridge Historical Society* 7 (1966–69): 46–54.

Shadburn, Don L. *Cherokee Planters in Georgia, 1832–1838*. Roswell, GA: W. H. Wolfe Associates, 1989.

Simms, L. Moody. "John Jordan: Builder and Entrepreneur." *Virginia Cavalcade* 23 (1) (1973): 19–29.

Singleton, Theresa A. "The Archaeology of Slavery in North America." *Annual Review of Anthropology* 24 (1) (1995): 119–40.

Slaughter, Thomas P. *The Whiskey Rebellion: Frontier Epilogue to the American Revolution*. New York: Oxford University Press, 1988.

Smith, Anthony D. *The Ethnic Revival*. New York: Cambridge University Press, 1981.

Smith, James L. "Historical Geography of the Southern Charcoal Iron Industry, 1800–1860." Ph.D. diss., University of Tennessee, 1982.

Smith, Ross. "The Building of the East Tennessee and Virginia Railroad." *East Tennessee Roots* 5 (2) (1988): 53–56.

Snell, William R. "Indian Slavery in Colonial South Carolina, 1671–1795." Ph.D. diss., University of Alabama, 1972.

Soltow, Lee. *Men and Wealth in the United States, 1850–1870*. New Haven, CT: Yale University Press, 1975.

"Land Inequality on the Frontier: The Distribution of Land in East Tennessee at the Beginning of the 19th Century." *Social Science History* 5 (1981): 275–91.

Spencer, Esther A. "Transportation in the Kanawha Valley, 1784–1890." M.A. thesis, Marshall College, 1941.

Spivak, Gayatri C. "Can the Subaltern Speak? Speculations on Widow-Sacrifice." *Wedge* 7 (1985): 120–30.

Stampp, Kenneth. *The Peculiar Institution: Slavery in the Antebellum South*. New York: Alfred A. Knopf, 1956.

Starling, R. B. "The Plank Road Movement in North Carolina." *North Carolina Historical Review* 16 (1939): 13–36.

Starobin, Robert S. *Industrial Slavery in the Old South*. New York: Oxford University Press, 1970.

Stealey, John E. "The Salt Industry of the Great Kanawha Valley of Virginia: A Study in Antebellum Internal Commerce." Ph.D. diss., West Virginia University, 1970.

"Slavery and the Western Virginia Salt Industry." *Journal of Negro History* 59 (1974): 105–31.

Stevens, William O. *The Shenandoah and Its Byways*. New York: Dodd, Mead and Co., 1941.

Stevenson, Brenda E. *Life in Black and White: Family and Community in the Slave South*. New York: Oxford University Press, 1996.

Stokely, Jim, and Jeff D. Johnson, eds. *An Encyclopedia of East Tennessee*. Oak Ridge, TN: Children's Museum, 1981.

Stuckey, Sterling. *Slave Culture: Nationalist Theory and the Foundations of Black America*. New York: Oxford University Press, 1987.

Tadman, Michael. *Speculators and Slaves: Masters, Traders, and Slaves in the Old South*. Madison: University of Wisconsin Press, 1989.

Tarkington, Terry W. "Saltpeter Mining in the Tennessee Valley." *Tennessee Valley Historical Review* 2 (1973): 17–25.

Taylor, Rosser H. "The Free Negro in North Carolina." *James Sprunt Historical Publications* 17 (1) (1932): 5–26.

Antebellum South Carolina: A Social and Cultural History. Chapel Hill: University of North Carolina Press, 1942.

Templin, Eleanor. "Making a Road through the Wilderness." *Franklin County Historical Review* 6 (2) (1975): 80–87.

Tennessee Valley Authority. *A History of Navigation on the Tennessee River System*. Washington, DC: Government Printing Office, 1937.

ter Braake, Alex L. "Postal History of the James River and Kanawha Turnpike." *West Virginia History* 33 (1971): 27–54.

Terrell, Bruce G. "The James River Bateau." *Virginia Cavalcade* 38 (4) (1989): 180–91.

Teuton, Frank L. "Steamboating on the Upper Tennessee." *Tennessee Valley Perspective* 7 (1976): 11–16.

Thomas, Hugh. *The Slave Trade: The Story of the Atlantic Slave Trade: 1440–1870*. New York: Simon and Schuster, 1997.

Thompson, E. P. "Folklore, Anthropology and Social History." *Indian Historical Review* 3 (2) (1977): 247–66.

The Making of the English Working Class. London: Victor Gollanz, 1963.

Thornton, Russell. *The Cherokees: A Population History*. Lincoln: University of Nebraska Press, 1990.

Toothman, Fred R. *Great Coal Leaders of West Virginia*. Huntington, WV: Vandalia Book Co., 1988.

Trouillot, Michel-Rolph. *Silencing the Past: Power and the Production of History*. Boston: Beacon Press, 1995.

Trout, W. E. "The Goose Creek and Little River Navigation." *Virginia Cavalcade* 16 (3) (1967): 38–41.

Tucker, James. "Everyday Forms of Employee Resistance." *Sociological Forum* 8 (1) (1993): 25–44.

Valentine, Charles A. "Deficit, Difference, and Bicultural Models of Afro-American Behavior." *Harvard Educational Review* 41 (2) (1971): 137–57.

Van Benthuysen, Robert N. "The Sequent Occupance of Tellico Plains, Tennessee." M.A. thesis, University of Tennessee, 1951.

Verhoeff, Mary. *The Kentucky Mountains: Transportation and Commerce, 1750 to 1911*. Louisville, KY: Filson Club Publication No. 26, 1911.

The Kentucky River Navigation. Louisville, KY: Filson Club Publication No. 28, 1917.

Virginia Writers Project. *Roanoke: Story of County and City*. Roanoke, VA: Work Projects Administration, 1942.

Wade, Richard C. *Slavery in the Cities: The South, 1820–1860*. New York: Oxford University Press, 1967.

Wahl, Jenny B. "American Slavery and the Path of the Law." *Social Science History* 20 (2) (1996): 281–316.

Walker, Juliet E. "The Legal Status of Free Blacks in Early Kentucky, 1792–1825." *Filson Club History Quarterly* 57 (1983): 382–95.

Wallace, David D. *South Carolina: A Short History, 1520–1948*. Chapel Hill: University of North Carolina Press, 1961.

Wallerstein, Immanuel. *The Modern World-System I: Capitalist Agriculture and the Origins of the European World-Economy in the Sixteenth Century*. New York: Academic Press, 1974.

The Modern World-System II: Mercantilism and the Consolidation of the European World-Economy, 1600–1750. New York: Academic Press, 1980.

Historical Capitalism. London: Verso Editions, 1983.

The Modern World-System III: The Second Era of Great Expansion of the Capitalist World-Economy, 1730–1840s. New York: Academic Press, 1989.

"The Construction of Peoplehood: Racism, Nationalism, Ethnicity." In *Race, Nation, Class: Ambiguous Identities*, edited by Etienne Balibar and I. Wallerstein, pp. 71–85. London: Verso Press, 1991.

The End of the World as We Know It: Social Science for the Twenty-First Century. Minneapolis, MN: University of Minnesota Press, 1999.

Walls, David S. "On the Naming of Appalachia." In *An Appalachian Symposium: Essays Written in Honor of Cratis D. Williams*, edited by J. W. Williamson, pp. 56–76. Boone, NC: Appalachian State University Press, 1977.

Walvin, James. "Slaves, Free Time and the Question of Leisure." *Slavery and Abolition* 16 (1) (1995): 1–13.

Watson, Alan D. "The Ferry in Colonial North Carolina: A Vital Link in Transportation." *North Carolina Historical Review* 51 (1974): 247–60.

Wayland, John W. *A History of Shenandoah County, Virginia*. Strasburg, VA: Shenandoah Publishing House, 1927.

Twenty-Five Chapters on the Shenandoah Valley. Strasburg, VA: Shenandoah Publishing House, 1957.

The Valley Turnpike: Winchester to Staunton. Winchester, VA: Winchester-Frederick County Historical Society, 1967.

Weaver, C. C. "Internal Improvements in North Carolina Previous to 1860." *Johns Hopkins University Studies in Historical and Political Science* 21 (3–4) (1903).

Webber, Thomas L. *Deep like the Rivers: Education in the Slave Quarter Community, 1831–1865*. New York: W. W. Norton, 1978.

West, Don. "Freedom in the Mountains." In *Appalachia: Social Context Past and Present*, edited by B. Ergood and B. E. Kuhre, pp. 19–21. Dubuque, IA: Kendall-Hunt, 1983.

"West Virginia River Ferries." *West Virginia Review* 13 (1935): 172–73.

Westfall, Eugenia. "The Internal Improvements of the Great Kanawha River." M.A. thesis, West Virginia University, 1943.

Whisnant, David E. *All That Is Native and Fine: The Politics of Culture in an American Region*. Chapel Hill: University of North Carolina Press, 1983.

White, Roy R. "The Salt Industry of Clay County." *Register of the Kentucky Historical Society* 50 (172) (1952): 237–48.

Wiley, Richard T. *Monongahela, The River and Its Region*. Butler, PA: Ziegler Co., 1937.

Wilk, Richard R. *Household Ecology: Economic Change and Domestic Life among the Kekchi Maya in Belize*. Tucson: University of Arizona Press, 1991.

Williams, David. "Georgia's Forgotten Miners: African-Americans and the Georgia Gold Rush," *Georgia Historical Quarterly* 75 (1991): 76–89.

Williams, Michael. *Americans and Their Forests: A Historical Geography*. Cambridge, UK: Cambridge University Press, 1989.

Williams, Thomas J. C. *A History of Washington County, Maryland from the Earliest Settlement to the Present Time, Including a History of Hagerstown*. Hagerstown, MD: By Author, 1906.

"Washington County, Maryland." *Maryland Historical Magazine* 2 (1907): 345–58.

and Folger McKinsey. *History of Frederick County, Maryland*. Baltimore: L. R. Titsworth and Co., 1910.

Willie, Charles V. *The Family Life of Black People*. Columbus, OH: Merrill, 1970.

Wilms, Douglas C. "Cherokee Indian Land Use in Georgia, 1800–1838." Ph.D. diss., University of Georgia, 1974.

Wilson, Charles R., and William Ferris, eds. *Encyclopedia of Southern Culture*. Chapel Hill: University of North Carolina Press, 1989.

Wiltse, Charles M. *John C. Calhoun*. Indianapolis, IN: Bobbs-Merrill, 1944.

Winston, Sanford. "Indian Slavery in the Carolina Region." *Journal of Negro History* 19 (4): 431–40.

Wolf, Eric R. *Europe and the People without History*. Berkeley: University of California Press, 1982.

Womack, Walter. *McMinnville at a Milestone, 1810–1860*. McMinnville, TN: Standard Publishing Co., 1960.

Wood, Peter. "Slave Resistance in Colonial South Carolina." In *Atlantic American Societies from Columbus through Abolition, 1492–1888*, edited by Alan L. Karras and J. R. McNeill, pp. 144–73. London: Routledge, 1992.

Woodlief, Ann. *In River Time: The Way of the James*. Chapel Hill, NC: Algonquin Books, 1985.

Woodson, Carter G. *The Education of the Negro Prior to 1861*. Washington, DC: Associated Publishers, 1919.

"Freedom and Slavery in Appalachian America." *Journal of Negro History* 1 (2) (1916): 132–50.

The History of the Negro Church. Washington, DC: Associated Publishers, 1921.

The Negro in Our History. Washington, DC: Associated Publishers, 1922.

Woodward, C. Vann. "History from Slave Sources: A Review Article." *American Historical Review* 79 (2) (1974): 470–81.

Wooster, Ralph A. *Politicians, Planters and Plain Folk: Courthouse and Statehouse in the Upper South, 1850–60*. Knoxville: University of Tennessee Press, 1975.

The Secession Conventions of the South. Princeton, NJ: Princeton University Press, 1962.

Worsley, Peter. *The Three Worlds: Culture and World Development*. Chicago: University of Chicago Press, 1984.

Wright, Gavin. *The Political Economy of the Cotton South: Households, Markets and Wealth in the Nineteenth Century*. New York: W. W. Norton, 1978.

Wright, James M. *The Free Negro in Maryland, 1634–1860*. New York: Columbia University Press, 1921.

Yetman, Norman R. "The Background of the Slave Narrative Collection." *American Quarterly* 19 (3) (1967): 534–53.

Young, Otis E. "Origins of the American Copper Industry." *Journal of the Early Republic* 3 (1983): 117–38.

Index

To expedite genealogical searching, names have been grouped under the headings "Cherokee slaveholder," "Free black," "Poor white," "Slave," "Slave trader," and "Slaveholder."